josh
FLYINGKIWI!

Andy McGechan

HarperSports
An imprint of HarperCollins*Publishers*

National Library of New Zealand Cataloguing-in-Publication Data
McGechan, Andy, 1961-
Josh : flying Kiwi! / Andy McGechan.
ISBN 978-1-86950-620-9
1. Coppins, Josh, 1977- 2. Townley, Ben, 1984- 3. Motocross.
4. Motorcyclists—New Zealand—Biography. I. Title.
796.7560922—dc 22

HarperSports
An imprint of HarperCollinsPublishers

First published 2008
HarperCollinsPublishers (New Zealand) Limited
P.O. Box 1, Auckland

ISBN 978 1 86950 620 9

Cover design by Gra Murdoch, Aqualuna Design
Photographs courtesy of Andy McGechan, BikesportNZ.com;
Glenn and Robyn Bayly; Josh Coppins' family; Tom Jacobs; Yamaha
Typeset by Springfield West
Printed by Griffin Press, Australia, on 79gsm Bulky Paperback

79gsm Bulky Paperback used by HarperCollinsPublishers is a natural, recyclable product made from wood grown in a combination of sustainable plantation and regrowth forests. It also contains up to a 20% portion of recycled fibre. The manufacturing processes conform to the environmental regulations in Tasmania, the place of manufacture.

Acknowledgements

THANKS, FIRST AND foremost, go to my wife, Sara, and children, Connor, Bridget and Lexie, for their understanding and patience while I locked myself away in my office for long periods of time. Thanks to Viv and Ted Coppins, also Josh's sisters, and Glenn and Robyn Bayly; Murray Thorn for his candid comments; Blair Selfe; GP riders Stefan Everts and Ben Townley, Ben for his insight into life behind the scenes with Josh; Russell Burling for sponsoring me to Europe in 2005; Neil Ritchie for his incredible memory; Paul Pavletich and the staff at Motorcycling New Zealand; the crew at www.BikesportNZ.com; Pete McPhee at *Kiwi Rider* magazine for his endless support; top-notch international photographers Red Eye (Gary Freeman), Geoff Meyer, Tom Jacobs, Stefan Geukens and Ray Archer for their advice and help; Josh's press agent Glen Dempsey; Suzuki factory team boss Sylvain Geboers for taking the time to talk to me during a busy GP weekend at Namur; CAS Honda team chief Harry Ainsworth; Rinaldi Yamaha Team boss Carlo Rinaldi; GP press officers Pascal Haudiquert and Daniele Rizzi for easing the way and opening doors for me in Europe; Simon Meade and Tom Peck at Suzuki New Zealand; Peter Payne at Yamaha New Zealand; Lorain Day and Eva Chan at HarperCollins Publishers in Auckland, for their patience and tireless work; and, of course, Josh Coppins himself.

About the author

ANDY MCGECHAN IS a Qantas award-winning newspaper and magazine journalist, photographer, sub-editor and editor with more than 29 years' experience.

Andy used to race motocross in his early twenties and finished a career-high third in the New Zealand TT Championships and won a provincial motocross title in 1985. He still rides socially in a couple of major cross-country endurance races each year, thanks to support from Kawasaki, Yamaha and Suzuki in New Zealand who supply bikes, support and free entry, and uses these rides as a rich source of material for the regular columns he writes for magazines in New Zealand and Australia.

Recently retired from the newspaper and magazine journalism scene, Andy now dedicates himself exclusively to the motorcycle industry. He is a frequent traveller, and has photographed and written about his visits to world championship motocross events in Australia, the Netherlands, Belgium, England, Ireland and the United States, although he mostly contents himself with covering domestic events throughout New Zealand.

He has also covered world championship road-racing and enduro events. He is the media liaison officer for the sport's governing body in New Zealand, Motorcycling New Zealand, and frequently assists several of the country's major motorcycle importers with their media needs.

Andy is a regular columnist for motorcycling magazines in Australia and New Zealand and is the motocross editor for this country's largest-circulation motorcycle publication, *Kiwi Rider*. The magazine is New Zealand's leading and longest-serving bike magazine, established in 1984.

Andy also operates his own website, www.bikesportnz.com, as well as the official website for Motorcycling New Zealand.

Andy and his wife Sara have three children.

Contents

Introduction

THERE WOULDN'T BE many Kiwi sportsmen who could pluck a glossy magazine off the shelf of any bookstore in Germany, Britain, France or Belgium and see his own face grinning back at him from the cover. Josh Coppins is one New Zealander who would fit the bill. The man from Motueka, a small South Island town of about 12,000 people, is currently one of the fastest motocross men on the planet. He was runner-up in the 2002 and 2005 world championships, and would have been the undisputed 2007 world champion if it hadn't been for a disastrous accident.

In 2002 he was beaten to the top spot by his Suzuki team-mate, Frenchman Mickael Pichon, and in 2005 he finished behind the legendary Stefan Everts, a man who was the Belgian Sportsman of the Year time and time again in that motocross-mad little country, and a record ten times motocross world champion before the end of 2006 when he finally hung up his helmet and boots.

Finishing second to Pichon or Everts was never going to be good enough for Josh — he has always wanted to be number one, and nothing less will do. He's been known for a long time as 'Mr Consistent' and it's a tag he would be happy to wear if consistency meant win after win after win, but it has only been in recent years that Josh has become a regular on the world championship podium. In fact, it didn't happen until 2004, his ninth season in Europe, when he won his first Grand Prix.

It takes an extraordinary amount of patience and determination to get to the pinnacle of world championship level in any sport, let alone

9

one that demands that you put your body on the line every time you race. It has been a long and bumpy road for Josh, who has persisted in the face of adversity, injury, setbacks and plenty of spine-tingling scares along the way.

As a fresh-faced 17-year-old in 1995, Josh finished 41st at the end of his world championship debut season. Over the years he continued to chip away at the rankings, coming 23rd the following season, 17th in 1997, 13th in 1998 and seventh in 1999, when even though only a support rider he had consistently outperformed the highly paid Suzuki factory riders. Not surprisingly, he was brought into the factory enclosure for the first time in 2000 and rewarded the faith shown in him by his new Suzuki bosses when he gave them the number four ranking — without winning a single race.

A difficult season in 2001 saw him slump to sixth, the first time he'd slipped backwards since arriving in Europe, but a change of team for 2002 had Josh moving forwards again. Riding for the Italian-based Vismara Honda team, Josh finished the 2002 season with the world number two ranking.

His 2003 season was over before it had even begun after a supercross smash in Phoenix left him in hospital, written off by the medical experts and all but his most hardened fans. He proved them wrong and defied the odds to be back on the podium by the end of the season, salvaging a world ranking of number 12 from the debris.

Josh also made history that year — with the big 450cc four-stroke bikes now the most popular weapon of choice in the elite MX1 class, Josh's podium finishes as the season wound down were the last achieved in the class by a rider on a 250cc two-stroke motorcycle.

The 2004 season that followed was a year of firsts. He raced the hefty 450cc four-stroke bike in MX1 for the first time, and the New Zealand national anthem was played for the first time as Josh savoured his first Grand Prix win at the Isle of Wight in May, on his way to the world number three ranking.

The following year Josh endured a season-long battle with Everts and Kiwi compatriot Ben Townley to take the number two spot, then teamed up with Townley and Cody Cooper, a youngster from Opotiki, to create a formidable New Zealand team for the year-ending Motocross des Nations in Ernee, France. Josh had also been a key component of the New Zealand teams that finished third at the 1998, 2001 and 2006 Motocross des Nations, an event regarded as the Olympic Games of motocross.

The 2005 world teams championship was a mixed bag for the Kiwis, with Townley and Coppins proving to be the second- and third-best individuals overall, behind all-conquering American champion Ricky Carmichael. With Honda rider Cooper (an 11th-hour draftee to the squad to replace injured Hawera Suzuki rider Daryl Hurley) battling for mid-pack finishes, the Kiwi team wound up fourth overall, missing the podium by just one frustrating point.

Nevertheless, that fourth placing was a remarkable achievement. The Motocross des Nations event is huge — you can't swing a trophy around the pits without hitting a current or former world champion. For three young guys from New Zealand to take on the cream of the world's motocross riders and finish fourth was extraordinary. It can come as quite a surprise to those who don't follow the sport to find out just how immense it is worldwide. Even without the Motocross des Nations, a once-a-year event, the clamouring crowds on the Grand Prix circuit leave nobody in doubt that motocross is hugely popular. It is followed with passion in both Europe and the United States, where riders such as Stefan Everts command the same sort of hero worship that we in New Zealand generally reserve for All Black rugby captains.

Motocross is woven into the culture of the European continent, and regularly attracts thousands of bellowing, die-hard, face-painting, banner-waving, air-horn-tooting fans to its hillside circuits. All of this could be extremely daunting for a young man from a tranquil small town in New Zealand, but to Josh the Belgian town of Hulsen is now his second home, and he has his own dedicated army of fans who follow him on the circuit.

The 2006 series marked Josh's 12th season in Europe and he held a coveted spot as a factory rider for the mighty Honda team, racing under the British CAS Honda team banner. While a pre-season accident meant his 2006 season didn't get off the ground until the year was halfway over, he didn't give up — it's just not in the man — and he showed the same steely determination towards the back end of the 2007 season, battling severe pain and a crippling injury whilst defending his dwindling lead in the world championship standings.

The sport of motocross is intense, both mentally and physically, and a good deal of courage is required just to survive a race, let alone win, yet Josh has been doing both with almost clockwork consistency over the past decade. This is no mean feat, as motocross is one of the most physically demanding sports around — the ultimate hybrid of athleticism and motorsport, in which a rider makes up 85 per cent of the human-machine equation.

It is perhaps the only form of motorsport where an individual can purchase a race-ready machine off a showroom floor in almost any town in almost any country — a motorcycle that, with minimal tweaking and the right rider, can be raced to the front of a world championship event. By comparison, imagine racing in the World Rally Championship or Formula One with the family car!

In motocross, this is virtually what happens, with young men buying bikes off the showroom floor, tuning the engine, changing the tyres, tweaking the suspension and then heading off to a Grand Prix. However, for this to work, the guys have to be super-human, like Everts or Coppins — chiselled athletes with nerves of steel.

Josh's achievements over the years have been remarkable, but perhaps what's even more amazing in his case is that he comes from a country where motocross — or dirt bike racing as it's known — is very much a minority pursuit. Even so, New Zealand continues to box above its weight in world motocross. New Plymouth's Shayne King was the first Kiwi to win the 500cc motocross world championship in 1996, remarkably just three seasons after he first arrived on the continent. His elder brother, Darryll King, was twice vice-champion — in 1997 and 1998 — in the same category. Taupo's Ben Townley was MX2 world champion in 2004, running away with the new classification that combined 125cc two-stroke bikes with 250cc four-strokes to replace the old 125GP class.

The King brothers have since retired from racing in Europe, and Townley has left for a racing career in the United States, leaving Josh Coppins to wave the silver fern in Europe. And what a job he's been doing! This is his story.

Andy McGechan

A history lesson

NOTHING GETS A competitor's heart pounding more than the start of a motocross race, when the rider approaches a 90-degree, funnel-like corner at near-highway speeds, with 20 bikes to the left and 20 bikes to the right. Each rider has the same thing in mind: to make it to the corner first — known as 'getting the holeshot' — and to do it without too much personal carnage. You don't give way and you can't afford to back off.

There are many different elements that make a motocross racer, including strength, endurance and concentration. Then there's courage, lots of it, and the skill to synchronise your body with your bike's multitude of moving parts — handlebars, levers and footpegs — and be able to do it instinctively, reacting in a split second to changing forces and conditions without losing control of a beast that unleashes 50 or 60 horsepower at the rear wheel.

A motocross racer must have all of these attributes. A physically strong rider with no endurance will have a blazing-fast first couple of laps then tire and fall to the back of the pack. A rider with endurance but no strength will have a tough time getting out of tricky situations, when the bike flicks from side to side, hits a deep rut or rock and threatens to spit him off. If a rider can't concentrate, he'll make mistakes, and these errors quickly compound into huge, high-speed accidents. And it hurts.

Most importantly of all, a rider must have enormous courage, or he won't be willing to do what it takes to win the race.

If you have ever ridden a few laps on a motocross bike, you will know why motocross is such a physically demanding sport. A lot of people think that all that is required is to climb on and twist the throttle. Not true. You're responsible for a snarling lump of steel, pitching forward and sideways at heart-stoppingly scary speeds. There is no comparison between the power-to-weight ratio of a motocross bike and a Formula One car — the motocross equation is much more impressive. It takes a lot of energy to ride a motocross bike.

People race in different classes based on skill levels: from minis (riders as young as four or five), juniors (aged anywhere between eight and 16) and then the senior classes, intermediate and pro. The classes are also broken into age groupings, such as veteran (over 35 or over 40, for example) and are also split into engine size, such as 50cc, 85cc, 125cc, 250cc or open class.

A race is usually split into two heats, first place gaining the most points and last place the least, but points are typically only rewarded down to 20th position. Below that and it may just seem like a lot of energy wasted, although even the slowest rider generally enjoys the experience. The rider with the most combined points wins the class. The track usually has a number of obstacles, like double jumps, triple jumps, whoops (corrugations), drop-offs, hills, banked corners, or flat corners, and all of it constructed on different types of soil, be it clay or sand, virgin grass or mud.

Let's look at the reasons why motocross is a physically demanding sport. It's all about cardio fitness. During an average race, a rider's heart rate will spike to 200 beats per minute, then remain at 190 for the duration of the race — and that could be for anything from 20 to 30 or, in the case of GP (Grand Prix) racing, 35 to 40 minutes.

It's an extreme sport, hard on both man and machine, and with all the bright colours, the rich smell of burning fuel, the harsh noise of straining engine exhausts and, of course, the high risks involved, it's not hard to see why young people head for local motocross events in droves. GP motocross is the ultimate thrill.

But before we dig into the achievements of New Zealand motocross star Josh Coppins and his peers in recent years, it's probably a good idea to look back at the roots of the sport and understand where it all began and how it developed into a sport that would capture the imagination of this young champion from our corner of the South Pacific.

The first motorcycle was built just over 120 years ago, and it was not long before brave men began to race them. Spawned from the imagination of German gunsmith and engineer Gottlieb Daimler, who later made a name for himself by designing upmarket cars, the first bike was a frail wooden-framed contraption with not even the barest hint of the fantastic machines that would follow.

Powered by a half-horsepower engine, Daimler's first motorbike made its maiden run in 1885 at Bad Cannstatt, near the city of Stuttgart, on 10 November. Remarkably, it was less than 40 years later that the sport of motocross — defined then, as it is now, as racing motorcycles across natural terrain — was spawned.

From wooden frame and solid rubber in the late 1800s to carbon fibre and titanium in 2007, the rapid upward spiral of motorcycling technology takes your breath away, but the beginnings were very humble indeed. The sport of motocross traces its roots to 1924, when a group of motorcycling friends in England got together in Camberley, Surrey, to stage their own version of Yorkshire's famous Scott Trial.

An annual event still held to this day, the Scott Trial takes place on some of the bleakest terrain imaginable within the Yorkshire dales. Essentially it is a long-distance trials event and, as such, challenges not only the competitors' riding skills, but also their stamina and navigation.

No huge leap of imagination is required to picture what would happen if a traditional trials event such as this were to have its conventions and rules ignored — the most basic rule being that riders must not touch their feet on the ground, with speed the priority. Without the constraints of the no-feet-down rule trials riding would become a mad frenzy as riders threw caution and finesse out the window and attacked the track at full throttle — starting to sound a bit like motocross?

Because there were no observed sections, the Auto Cycle Union, the sport's governing body, was unable to grant the event trials status, and one of the 80 starters remarked at the time that this would be 'a fair old scramble'.

With the riders in Surrey taking the Scott Trial concept and giving it their own special interpretation — dropping the observed sections where points could be lost for 'dabbing' feet and other crimes — the new sport of motocross, or scrambling, was born.

The first race took place at Frimley, in Surrey, won by a rider called Arthur Sparkes. More than half the entrants were forced to retire due to the severity of the course and machine failure, but it was still considered a huge success.

Prior to the Second World War, the sport was primarily a British pursuit, but it soon caught on across the English Channel in Belgium, France, Germany and the Netherlands. The bikes used weren't much more than road bikes with all-weather tyres, similar to the ones that army courier and dispatch riders would later use during the war.

Early motocross machines were incredibly primitive by today's standards. They were heavy, underpowered, and equipped with rudimentary suspension systems that did little to smooth out the rough terrain. But motocross had two undeniable elements that promised the sport's future success: it provided an affordable but highly challenging sport for participants, and offered incredible, up-close action for spectators.

Following the war, in 1947 the world's governing body, the Federation Internationale Motorcycliste (FIM), created the Motocross des Nations, an annual event to determine the world team motocross champion. The first motocross championships were held in 1952 — the 500cc European championships — and in 1957 FIM created the 250cc class. A few New Zealanders during this time may have watched and listened to these European antics from afar, but the sport in New Zealand was, in those days, virtually non-existent.

Then, in the 1960s, a young man called Tim Gibbes arrived from Australia to settle in the Manawatu in the central North Island. He was a former GP motocross rider and was determined to see the sport he cherished flourishing in his adopted country. Gibbes was the driving force behind the now-legendary annual Woodville Motocross, just a few kilometres up the road from Palmerston North.

From a fairy-tale beginning in the 1960s, the event has since flourished and matured and, remarkably, it lists current and former (and perhaps future) world champions among its lists of winners. Woodville, a small farming service town between Manawatu and Hawke's Bay, has hosted some of the world's biggest names in motocross, providing a ring-side seat to GP-quality racing and a valuable learning tool for avid Kiwi racers. Held at the same grassy farmland venue every year since 1961, the New Zealand Motocross Grand Prix at Woodville has grown to become the country's largest and most popular off-road motorcycle event.

When Gibbes arrived in the Manawatu to make a home with his wife, local woman Joan Cleghorn, he was near the end of an eight-year professional career, racing in 250cc and 500cc motocross world championship events all over Europe and in the United States. Gibbes had done it all, first climbing aboard a motorcycle on a farm on the York Peninsula in South Australia, where he spent many hours rounding up stock, and chasing kangaroos and foxes for fun.

In 1955, at 22 years of age, he had sailed to England to become a tester and works rider on English-made Matchless, AJS, Greeves, DOT and Ariel bikes. Sharing travel expenses with his brother-in-law-to-be, fellow racer Ken Cleghorn, Gibbes competed with success at high-profile international events and world championship GPs from 1955 to

1963. During the European winter, Gibbes would travel to the United States and race there. 'It was tough back then,' he recalls. 'It took about three years to get anywhere better than living in vans or sleeping on the ground.'

Gibbes' motorcycling experiences were as diverse as they were thrilling. In 1962, a Hollywood film crew arrived in southern Germany to begin filming the Second World War movie classic *The Great Escape*. The marathon two-hour 48-minute movie has only about five minutes of motorcycle action in it, but what great action it is. Gibbes was friendly with one of the American stuntmen, Bud Ekins, and was hired as a stand-in for filming that involved a young actor called Steve McQueen.

The film required McQueen's character, a hard-case habitual POW escaper, to steal a motorcycle and race it across country, chased by steel-helmeted Nazis on similar bikes, before attempting to leap his bike over a tall barbed-wire fence. A motocross GP rider at that time, Gibbes helped out with several sequences by acting as a stuntman, where he met McQueen. 'He was a typical young American Hollywood star — brash and a bit of a show-off. But I did meet him again a few years later, by which time he'd mellowed. He'd become a much more genuine person.'

Back home in New Zealand between the European motocross events, jet-setting riding buddies and brothers-in-law Gibbes and Cleghorn found it difficult to settle. In New Zealand, motocross — or scrambling as it was then known — was little more than a bunch of leather-jacketed riders on street bikes, with little or no public profile. Never content to sit still for long, the pair hatched a plan to stage an international-style motocross event, modelled along the lines of the big European GP events they'd enjoyed so much. Gibbes even offered one of the flashier trophies he'd won in America to be used as the winner's trophy.

Staged on the Woodville farmland owned by Cleghorn's Uncle Arthur, Gibbes and Cleghorn fought handlebar to handlebar in December

1961 at the inaugural event, Cleghorn eventually taking away Gibbes' silverware. Gibbes took his revenge and won it back the next month, in January 1962. Then in 1963, a group of 53 riders entertained a crowd of around 3000, Taranaki's Malcolm Campbell winning the day, and in 1964 Gibbes was able to reclaim his trophy again.

The Woodville honour roll over the years reads like a who's who of leading New Zealand motocross talent, and also features some of the best riders of the day from Switzerland, Germany, Austria, Sweden, England, Wales, Australia and the United States. Even legendary British two-time former world champions Jeff Smith and Dave Bickers raced at Woodville. Smith, the 500cc motocross world champion in 1964 and '65, beat Bickers, the 250cc world champion in 1960 and '61, to the Woodville trophy in 1970. The pair tied for the Gold Leaf series trophy, of which the Woodville event was one round, and proceeded to cut the enormous silver cup in half at the prizegiving.

To date, only eight riders have won more than once at Woodville, including Shayne King, Taranaki's 1996 500cc world champion, his elder brother Darryll, and Josh Coppins.

A lot has changed since the 1960s and '70s. Thanks to cellphone technology, satellite link television, cheaper air travel, emails and the ever-expanding Internet, the world has become a lot smaller, and New Zealand is no longer so far behind the rest of the motocross world.

It was during the late 1970s and early '80s that Kiwis first ventured overseas with dreams of international glory, typically packing engine parts in their carry-on suitcases. Young men such as Ivan Miller, Chris Maindonald, Bryan Patterson and Craig Coleman tried Europe, while others, such as Graeme Allan, Leon Andrew and, in more recent times, Mark Penny, Cody Cooper, Luke Burkhart and Michael Phillips, gave our trans-Tasman cousins a try. It's probably fair to say that the King brothers from Taranaki — Darryll, Shayne and Damien — have contributed more than most in putting New Zealand on the motocross map. Thanks to them, Tokoroa's Darryl Atkins and, in recent years, Josh Coppins, Ben Townley and Stefan Merriman, the Kiwi name is now well respected internationally.

European and even American eyes have increasingly looked to this part of the world for fresh talent and, at the same time, New Zealand fans have been treated to a variety of very exciting international riders, something that's also helped Kiwi racers to develop and learn. Most surprisingly, some of the sport's international 'stars' who have made their way to New Zealand over the past 20 years include a few who, rather than use New Zealand as a twilight trip or swansong stopover, came here when they were at the height of their powers. When Japan's Akira Watanabe came to New Zealand in the early 1980s, he was a recent world champion (the 1978 125cc class champion). Australian Jeff Leisk popped over in 1983, Englishman Perry Leask visited in 1984 and 1985, and Aussie Craig Dack arrived in 1986, each when they were either on the rise or at the top of their game — a rare privilege for local fans.

And while all this was happening, New Zealand was developing its own home-grown talent, including a young Josh Coppins, growing up in Motueka and just beginning to experience the joys of dirt bike racing. Inspired by all the activity with magazine pin-up riders Leisk, Leask and Dack racing at different spots throughout New Zealand, Josh immersed himself in the sport. Incredibly, it was barely seven years from the day Josh first raced in an official motocross event in 1988, as an 11-year-old, before he was heading to Europe to seek fame and fortune on the world championship scene.

Another Kiwi who would, in later years, become Josh's close friend, house-mate and sometimes rival, Taupo's Ben Townley also began to develop during this time. When Townley won the national 8–11 years 80cc title in April 1996, who would have believed he would be a 125cc GP winner in Europe just six years later?

It was also in 1996 that Kiwi hotshots Shaun Fredricksen and Ben

Gage-Brown finished first and second respectively in the junior national supercross championships. And the man they beat? None other than Aussie Chad Reed, now considered one of the sport's superstars in the United States.

Here are some of the famous riders who came to New Zealand during those formative, developmental and growth years of motocross, the 1980s and early '90s, who lit sparks in the eyes of young men such as Josh Coppins and Ben Townley and set them on the path to international glory:

JAPAN:

1978 125cc world champion Akira Watanabe

AUSTRALIA:

Jeff Leisk, Stephen Gall, Ray Vandenberg, Dave Armstrong, Craig Dack, James Deakin, Grant Covus, Vaughan Style, Glen Bell, Mark Kirkman, Greg Scott, Dale Britton, Ben Perese, Dean Burt, Geoff Ballard, Kim Ashkenazi, Steven Andrew, Anthony Gobert (before he went road-racing), Paul Grant, Joel Elliott, Brent Landman, Matthew McKenna, Steven Powell, Peter Melton, Brett and Shane Metcalfe, Craig Anderson, Danny Ham, Chad Reed, Andrew McFarlane, Lee Hogan, Mitch Hoad, Jay Marmont, Matt Kadel, Ian and Jamie Cunningham, Paul Broomfield, Wade Thompson, Mick McDermid, Cameron Taylor

---

SWITZERLAND:

Pius Beeler, Kurt Theomet, Franz Muff, Gaudenz Gisler (and loved New Zealand so much he made it his home) and Christian Chanton

---

SWEDEN:

Espin Blikstad and Alexander Elgh

ENGLAND:

Jeff Smith, Dave Bickers, Tony McNeice, Howard Lucas, Steve Harrison, Peter Mathia, Jonathan Wright, Perry Leask, Greg Hanson, Julian Clarke, Chris Benford and James Marsh

SCOTLAND:

Barry Morris (another who has since made New Zealand his home), John Morton, and brothers Neil and Stuart Flockhart

UNITED STATES:

Frankie Brundage, Gary Semics (the first AMA supercross champion, crowned in 1974, and later the trainer of supercross legend Jeremy McGrath), 'Flash' Gordon Ward, Willie Simons, Eddie Warren, 'Wild' Willie Surratt, Mercedes Gonzalez, Bob Ashleigh, Keith Johnson, Kelly Smith, Andy Harrington and Jason Thomas

In this same 20-year period we have seen the crowning of several Kiwis, young men who have either won world championships or come very close to it, winning some very respectable GP trophies along the way:

KIWI WORLD CHAMPIONS:

Shayne King (1996 500cc MX)
Stefan Merriman (2004 E1, 2003 250cc two-stroke enduro, 2001 400cc four-stroke enduro, 2000 400cc four-stroke enduro)
Ben Townley (2004 MX2)

KIWI WORLD CHAMPIONSHIP RUNNERS-UP:

Darryll King (1997 and 1998 500cc MX)
Josh Coppins (2002 250cc MX, 2005 MX1)

Motocross has developed at a remarkable pace over the past 30–40 years, primarily in the realms of technology, including engine improvements and suspension refinements, but also in terms of riding technique and competition format. Perhaps the most obvious change has been power-plant preferences and the engines used. A battle raged through the 1950s and '60s between riders who thought they could go faster with a lighter and easier-to-handle bike, instead of having to fight the hefty four-stroke beasts popular at the time. The four-strokes were reliable and powerful but heavy to manoeuvre, while the two-strokes offered good handling but fragile reliability.

The power-to-weight argument gradually won the day and, as two-stroke engines became more reliable and the major Japanese manufacturers began pouring huge resources into the technology, the 'crackle and ping' of big, single-cylinder two-strokes became the norm at motocross events worldwide. Two-strokes took over for the next 25 years.

In 1993 the winds of change really started to blow at the 125cc world championship round near Perth, Australia — not that anyone realised the significance of what was happening in the 500cc class at that time. True, the two-strokes were to remain dominant for a while in the smaller engine classes but, half a world away, a Belgian called Jacky Martens was making history and winning open class races on a four-stroke bike, something that hadn't happened since the 1960s. Four-stroke powered bikes had been the weapons of choice from the beginning, and so it stayed through the 1950s and '60s, with big-bore two-strokes ruling the ruts from the 1970s. But when Martens won the 500cc crown on a four-stroke Husqvarna in 1993, the big Japanese bike manufacturers started to think about embracing four-stroke power again. Within a few short years, the 500cc two-strokes were fading away, dinosaurs from a past age, and four-strokes took over. When New Zealand's Shayne King won the 500cc world title in 1996, it was the end of an era, his KTM 360 the last two-stroke bike to win the open class crown.

None of this had much bearing on the first nine years of Josh Coppins' GP career. He raced primarily in the 250cc class at the world championship level and only raced four-stroke bikes from the end of 2003, when a combination of mechanical advancements and changes to the GP racing format began to have a profound effect on the direction of the sport.

By 2003 and 2004, the impact of developments in four-stroke technology was certainly beginning to be felt. While still a fan of the 250cc two-stroke bikes with which he was very familiar, Josh opted to stick with the Honda CR250 in 2003, the first year the FIM brought 450cc four-strokes and 250cc two-strokes together on the start line, the world championships being renamed MXGP. In hindsight, that may have been a mistake; riders on the big four-strokes dominated, and Josh finished 12th that year.

He's now a convert to the big four-stroke and will probably finish his career racing one, with the 500cc two-stroke virtually extinct, and 250cc and 125cc two-stroke bikes becoming rarer by the day.

In just over a decade, Josh went from a fresh-faced schoolboy on a 125cc two-stroke, making his senior debut at the big annual Woodville motocross, to become one of the world's elite on the world championship scene, giving nothing away as he wrestled a fire-breathing 450cc four-stroke alongside some of the toughest men on the planet.

Family matters

THE BIRTH NOTICE in the local newspaper may well have read something like this: Joshua William Coppins, born in Motueka, 11 March 1977, son of Ted and Vivienne Coppins, a little brother for Tina and Leila, and grandson for Nana and Pop Whelan and Chas Coppins.

Josh grew up on the family farm in a country town called Ngatimoti where he went to Ngatimoti Primary School and then Motueka High School, not that schooling was something he ever considered to be important. The family had two farms: one the home farm, called Louisville, on the corner of State Highway 61 and the other a hill block about one kilometre up a side road. His grandparents, Nana and Pop Whelan, had another farm called Marybank, which was on the corner of State Highway 61 and Green Hill Road. The Coppins family property surrounded the Ngatimoti Primary School, which had been built in the early 1950s after the land was sold to the Education Department by Viv's father.

Josh's first bike was a brand-new 50cc Suzuki, which he was given in 1981 for his fourth birthday. At the time, he wasn't able to touch the ground on both sides of the bike because his legs were too short. Josh was an early riser and would ride his motorbike to Nana and Pop's house for breakfast every morning, come rain, hail or shine. At that time, they had to start the bike for the return trip because Josh wasn't big enough to kick-start it. As he got older, Viv remembers him riding it until he came to a hill, then jumping off and running beside it to the top before jumping back on — it didn't have enough power to take him up the hill.

His father, Ted, recalls that Josh was a very happy, easy-going kid who loved everyone and everyone loved him. As a young country boy, Josh Coppins did all the things farm kids do — eeling and swimming in the river across the road from the family home, docking lambs, helping in the shearing shed, hay making, and working on the family farm, growing and cultivating tobacco. But, above all, he loved driving tractors and, by the age of four, he was riding motorbikes, both on and off the road.

As a boy, he had three motorbikes: the Suzuki JR50, then a Suzuki DS80, followed by a Suzuki RM80. Josh still owns his original bike, which in the meantime has also been used by his cousins, the son of close family friend and mentor, Murray Thorn, and in later years by his nieces and nephews. When it came time to go to school, Josh would ride his little motorbike up to the fence, jump over it and go to class, although this had to stop when he started giving motorbike demonstrations to his mates during breaks between lessons.

Like most small boys growing up in the country, Josh had his fair share of accidents. One day, when he was five, his mother was recovering at home after abdominal surgery, while his father was busy in the shed, building a horse truck. Josh asked if he could drive one of the tractors around the orchard paddock, which was beside the shed where Ted was working. This particular tractor could do about 30 mph in top gear, but was so high-geared in top that the driver had to slip the clutch to avoid stalling the motor. Ted gave his permission, but told Josh not to put it into top gear.

Soon Josh was weaving slowly around the trees, but eventually temptation got the better of him, and he slipped the tractor into top gear — and for the first time ever it didn't stall. Ted takes up the story: 'The tractor takes off, flat-out, and I'm worried he'll go through the fence and drop on to the road — about a five-metre drop. I'm running behind the tractor, trying to catch him, but I run out of puff, so I start screaming to him to turn the key off.'

Instead of looking where he was going, Josh looked back at his father and drove straight into an apple tree, putting the fan through the radiator and hitting his head on the steering wheel, knocking himself out. He was fine, but it quietened him down for a while. By the time he was six though, Josh was a competent tractor operator, able to plough and cultivate a paddock.

Ted recalls that his son was a tough little character. When Josh was about six years old, he was playing with a friend, Michael Holdiway, at the Ngatimoti Hall, where they were sliding down the bank next to the hall; Josh caught his shin on a jagged rock and cut it badly. His father was amazed — Josh didn't cry once, not even when the doctor put in over 60 stitches.

Josh's first brush with the law was as a six-year-old. All his mates — the Rose boys, the Smart boys and the Dalton boys — had motocross bikes, which they rode up the forest fire breaks. These kids all lived in the neighbouring valley, and to get there Josh would ride his Suzuki RM80 on the road. One evening, his father saw Josh shoot up the side road, into the farm and home through the paddocks. In the meantime, the local policeman flew past up the side road, looking for Josh. For the next few days, he parked up the valley, waiting for the six-year-old on his motorbike, but failed to catch him.

There were further accidents. When Josh was aged seven, he rang his father at work one day. 'This time he was crying and I knew this one was pretty serious,' Ted recalls. One of Josh's after-school jobs was to put the horses' covers on. 'He would never walk up the paddock to do this, always taking the motorbike or the Ferguson tractor,' Ted says. 'He pretty much learned to drive on this tractor and loved getting it bogged in the creek paddock. On this particular day, he had already covered up his horse, Johnny, with the others, so instead of walking, he rides bareback.' Unfortunately, while galloping, Josh fell off and broke his wrist. This required surgery and put him out of action for several weeks.

When he was eight, Josh had his second brush with the law. Ted recalls: 'I was driving my tractor up the river to a friend's place to borrow his plough, and Josh followed me on his motorbike. I was too slow, Josh reckoned, so he passed me and carried on up the road. I get up the road to where a foot swingbridge crosses the river, only to see the policeman standing at the end, watching Josh roar off.' It was to be the first of many escapes.

After school, Josh used to spend hours riding the track up the creek paddock. At the time, the neighbouring property was owned by a Danish couple, the Pontopedons, who used to visit New Zealand each summer. Mr Pontopedon was an ardent trout fisherman, and Mrs Pontopedon an artist. One particular day, Ted was working under Viv's car when Josh told him Mr Pontopedon wanted to talk to him. Ted stayed under the car and asked his son what Mr Pontopedon wanted.

Josh replied: 'He says I'm not allowed to ride the creek paddock.'

Ted shot out from under the car, ready to tell Mr Pontopedon to take a hike. But his neighbour had an interesting proposition. 'We will pay Josh $1000 each summer if he only rides the creek when we put the flag on the fence . . . but the flag will be there for at least two hours a day.' Agreement was quickly reached, and the arrangement continued until the farm was sold.

As a child, Josh had a natural connection with animals, as he did with people — he loved them and they loved him. His first dog was a black labrador called Kerry; the two were inseparable, going everywhere together and, according to Ted, 'doing some things we knew about and a lot we didn't'.

Horses played a big part in the life of the Coppins family. Both of

Josh's sisters rode from the age of five or six and, within a few years, they were competing all over the top half of the South Island. Of course, little brother Josh came along to watch. 'We had a fabulous pony called Johnny that the girls outgrew, and we were faced with having to find a good home for him,' says Viv. Out of the blue, Josh asked if he could ride Johnny, providing a great solution for the family, who didn't want the pony to have to go to a new home.

Josh took to horse riding like a duck to water, and was soon a crowd favourite because he was so small. According to his father, Josh could get Johnny to do anything he wanted. 'Some things met the approval of the pony club and some were frowned upon,' Ted laughs. The one thing Josh didn't like doing was grooming the pony, and Viv suspects that he didn't do a good job on purpose so that his sisters would do it for him — they couldn't bear to see him riding a dirty pony.

Even though he was small, Josh was expected to help look after the horses, but because he was so small he was unable to do a lot of the things that needed to be done. By this time the family had between four and six horses, and while he couldn't reach up to put their covers on, he could manage to take them off. His mother remembers that his favourite job was to take them off in the morning, because he was able to do it with the tractor and tray. 'He had to go up to the horse paddock, take the covers off and bring them back to the house to hang them up for the day.' More often than not, according to Viv, the covers had bounced off the tray by the time he got back because he was going too fast.

The Springston Trophy is the largest pony club event in the Southern Hemisphere and is held in the South Island every spring over three days. It is an event for teams of six riders (two juniors, two intermediates and two seniors) and provides ordinary riders from pony club branches — those who may never attend a championship — the opportunity to compete. 'We used to go every year. It was our annual holiday,' recalls Viv. 'Over the years, Ted built us a number of horse trucks in which we could live and travel to the events. For two years running, Josh was the youngest rider on the oldest pony at the event.

At one event, held in Kaikoura, Josh was helping a friend shift horses into paddocks. After they had taken the horses off the float, he was helping put the ramp of the horse float up, but the ramp shut quicker than he expected and his fingers were crushed. 'He hardly made a noise. It wasn't until some time later that we realised how bad it was and took him to the emergency department of Kaikoura Hospital,' remembers Viv. 'Josh had done the dressage and cross-country stages of the competition before all of this happened, so there was only the last day left to ride. We've got some great video footage of Josh doing his show jumping with his finger very prominent, sticking up, in a very big white bandage.'

Young Josh was to see the inside of accident and emergency departments many times in years to come, although Viv says that from a very early age, her son was always a very sensible child. 'He didn't seem to do the stupid things most kids do. Of course, he made his fair share of mistakes, as they all do, but he always seemed to think about things before he did them. I suppose he was a child with an older person's head on his shoulders. He also didn't have too much to think about because he had two big sisters who looked after him pretty well.'

His sister Justina — known as Tina — is six years older, and Leila — known as Lib — is four years older than Josh. 'He was very good at letting people do things for him if they wanted to,' Viv says. 'His attitude was that there was no point in doing something if you could get others to do it for you.'

When Josh was 11 and still attending Ngatimoti Primary School, Ted was working at Talley's Fisheries and Viv was working at Westpac, both in Motueka, which was about 20 km away. Both his sisters were at Motueka High School and didn't get home until about 4.00 p.m. One day after school, Josh decided to ride another pony called Hyland Rebel, who had a lot more get up and go than Johnny. On this particular day he decided to ride him bareback up to the paddock, but Rebel shot away and Josh fell off, breaking his wrist again.

'Because he was at home on his own, Josh had to make his way back to the house and phone for help,' remembers Viv. 'I didn't know it then, but by the time he phoned me he'd already phoned Ted, who was already on his way home. Josh didn't tell me this, so I took off home as well. Imagine my surprise to see Ted coming at a great rate of knots in the other direction, having gone home and picked Josh up, and on the way to take him to the hospital.'

But life was shortly about to change for the Coppins family, with tobacco farming becoming less viable due to the marked decline in the popularity of smoking and government policy which kept prices for cigarettes high through taxation as a disincentive to smoking. As tobacco farming was gradually phased out, Ted found extra work driving trucks for Talley's Fisheries during the week and stock farming on the weekends, a move that would later have a beneficial impact on Josh's ability to compete around the South Island. The family eventually moved closer in to town.

When Josh's interest began to turn towards motocross, surprisingly it was Ted who said no while Viv was all in favour. 'Josh was an unbelievable horse rider and I felt he had the capability to go a long way with horses,' explains Ted. The interest was sparked in 1988 when Josh was just 11. Ted had taken him to his first motocross, a Nelson club event held at Eves Valley. 'I relented a little and said he could ride motocross when there were no horse events,' Ted says. Soon they were going to motocross on a regular basis, although only to local events.

Josh remembers it well: 'My first race was a club day in Mapua on my friend's farm and all the 80cc bikes were together. I don't know where I finished, but when I was 11, I won my second race, the 8–11 years' 80cc class. I still have the trophy. It was in 1988, in the Equestrian series. It was sponsored by a hotel and was South Island-wide. I remember showing off to my mates and flipping the bike over backwards. Dad was pissed off because I broke off the rear guard.'

Not long after moving into town, Viv decided apple growing was the thing to do, so the family bought an orchard, where Ted's first priority was to build a motocross track. Soon afterwards, tragedy struck when Josh's horse Johnny fell into a hole. He was stuck fast, became distressed and had to be put down. 'After all the injuries and pain I have seen Josh go through, I have never seen him cry like he did when Johnny died,' his father says.

After Johnny was buried, Josh never rode on that track again.

Some serious wheels

TED COPPINS WAS into speedway riding, and used to ride as 'swinger' in a side-chair for champion rider Graham Biggs, and Josh still remembers his father taking his side-chair down south in the horse float. 'I loved to ride my bike on the farm, then my dad took me to a race and I was hooked straight away. Dad and Graham won the South Island champs, so I think they weren't too bad.

'I used to love going to the speedway with him. I'd walk around the pits, checking everything out. I used to love the smell of methanol. All the other kids my age weren't allowed in the pits and I got to stay up late. Often Dad would go to the speedway clubrooms after racing for a beer. I thought I was the cat's pyjamas, being part of that.'

As Josh graduated to bigger bikes, his sisters were keen to try them out, but he wasn't having any of it. The bike was his — definitely a girl-free zone.

Once his sisters tried hard to persuade him to let them have a ride, but he refused and stayed on the bike all day. Finally Viv got him inside and into the bath — always a challenge with any boy — but no sooner was he in the bath than Leila started the bike up and Tina jumped on the back. Josh leapt out of the bath and shot outside to stop them. He was completely naked but didn't give a damn. Stunned by the sight, Leila stalled the bike, spoiling their planned getaway and creating a family story for years to come.

Viv still laughs about the day he ran out of petrol during a race and made his dad push his Suzuki back to the pits. 'That was no easy feat, as there were some very steep hills.'

Josh and Ted began to attend the DB motocross series meetings, where they met people such as Robin Ridden and Kev Pahi. Initially, Pahi was to have a huge influence on Josh, with Ted freely admitting that he was completely green to this sport and didn't know what he was getting into.

By this stage the old RM80 was dead on its feet and Josh started to pester his father for a new bike, in particular a Kawasaki KX80, much to Ted's disgust. The old RM had given such good service that he was reluctant to change, but change they did. 'By this time I had been conned into Josh competing in a round of the DB series and more events after that.'

A night before one of the DB series meetings, Josh's new KX80 was stolen. 'Some people by the name of Holland heard about the theft and loaned Josh a Honda CR80 to ride on the second day of the South Island champs. The next event was in Canterbury the following weekend, at Glentunnel, so during the week we tried to revive the old RM80.'

They took it to the local Suzuki man, a bloke called Murray Thorn, someone Ted had only known casually up to that point. Thorn looked at the bike, laughed, and said, 'This thing's dead on its feet. Why don't you buy a new one?' When Ted said he couldn't afford it, Thorn suggested he take a new bike and pay him later. Initially dubious, Ted took the bike and Josh began to race on it.

After a while Josh came back to Ted and told him the bike needed a new ring. Ted was incredulous, as the bike had only done about 40 hours, so Josh decided to change the ring himself. To separate the barrel from the crankcase, Josh drove a screwdriver between the two to break the seal and put a huge indentation in the crankcase. At the time, a mechanic up in Auckland was supposed to be the best for 'hotting up' motors, so the Coppinses sent the motor up to him.

When it came back, the bike went like a scalded cat and Josh raced it at the North Island championships at Pataetonga in the Waikato. At one point he was lying in about second place when he came in from a race and told his father the bike had no power. 'It can't be the bike, we've spent all this money,' Ted replied. 'Just get out there and race.' Josh did his best, but with the bike performing poorly, he could only manage to finish fifth.

When they arrived back home, they found a message waiting for them from the police — they'd recovered the stolen Kawasaki. Despite the good news, Josh was still unhappy as the Suzuki wasn't performing, and Ted was unhappy about how much all of this was costing the family. Despite his concerns, he put new rings in the bikes and the following weekend took Josh and both bikes to Kaikoura, just south of Blenheim, for the South Island championships. But once again, after the practice race, Josh complained that the Suzuki had no power. Ted told him to ride the Kawasaki instead, and that night he rang Murray Thorn.

Thorn arrived in Kaikoura the next day and asked to see the problem for himself. As soon as he saw the bike he wanted to know who had been working on it. When Ted, not wanting to look foolish, told him it was Josh, Thorn suggested Ted should drop the bike off at his shop the next day.

When Ted dropped the bike in, Thorn took him to one side. He was keen on following a bit of motocross, and he could see that Josh had potential, so he was prepared to make Ted an offer. He would fix the bike free of charge on the condition that he did all future work on it. It was the beginning of a very powerful and supportive friendship that has now been going strong for more than 18 years. Ted became the pit boy and Thorn the mechanic and manager of Team Coppins, and the two men became good drinking buddies.

'Murray Thorn was my coach, but I think he quickly became out of his depth, because it wasn't long before I was much faster than him,' Josh recalls, a mischievous glint in his eyes as he enjoys firing a cheeky broadside at his former mentor, who is still a close personal friend. 'Murray took me everywhere, and wasn't too shy to tell me when I was shit. I guess I needed that. I thought he was too tough sometimes, but he had my best interests at heart. Murray always wanted the best for me — he took so much time away from his family and business. Dad had a busy job, so Murray took me to the events and Dad worked and paid for it. Murray also made sure my bikes were good, and helped build a strong relationship with Suzuki that still exists today.'

Like many kids at the time, Josh's bedroom was littered with motorbike magazines; he was an avid reader of anything relating to GP motocross. 'I looked at a lot of magazines, but I didn't admire any one rider,' Josh recalls. 'At first I looked up to the top local riders, and then, as my experience grew, I respected the top riders South Island-wide, then New Zealand-wide, and then Australia. From there, I came to respect a lot of riders in Europe and the United States. I liked South African Greg Albertyn [a former world champion] a lot. When I met him in later years, he was very good to me and I was impressed because he won in Europe and the United States. Not many riders do both. He was a really genuine bloke — no bullshit.'

On one memorable occasion they were competing in the DB motocross series at Waipara in north Canterbury, travelling down from Nelson in the Talley's truck, with Murray, Josh and Ted in the front and five bikes on the back. Murray had decided to compete himself, and Josh's friend Matt Wratten joined the pit crew. Both boys gave Murray hell, telling him he had to win 'or else'. His reputation was at stake.

After the first race Murray came in totally knackered, with sweat pouring off him. As he sat down to wipe away the sweat, another rider came up and asked him if he had a front brake lever for sale. Murray said he did and duly handed the guy the lever. Unfortunately the rider only had change in his pocket and paid for the lever in five-cent and ten-cent pieces. In disgust, Murray threw the money in his briefcase and went out for the next race.

On the very last lap he was thrown over the handlebars, and was not a happy man. Even Josh and Matt Wratten had enough sense not to say anything when he came in from the race with a face like thunder. Then the rider who had bought the brake lever came up, saying he no longer needed it and could he have his money back. Murray took great delight in telling him where to go and what to do with the lever, and Ted and the boys nearly died laughing.

Eventually Thorn would tell Ted that Josh had reached his limit in the South Island. He needed tougher competition and, to progress, he would have to travel to events in the North Island. 'This was when the fun and travelling really took off,' says Ted. 'We had a lot of great times.'

Not surprisingly, Viv Coppins had a different view of this development, and admits she used to worry about the boys all getting back safely in one piece. 'Josh had a big sign on the front of his van that said: "Get in, sit down, hold on and shut up".'

The long distances hauling the bikes around the country took their toll on Josh, who had suffered from car-sickness since babyhood — he even got car-sick on the short trip from Ngatimoti to Motueka. As he got older, he could make it to Motueka, but not as far as Nelson, before throwing up. Viv tried dosing him with car-sickness pills, but they didn't seem to do much good, and Murray thought they would affect his motocross performance.

Viv has vivid memories of Josh being sick out the window of the ute on the way to Christchurch, but they weren't able to stop because they were running late. 'I don't ever remember Josh complaining. To him it was just something he had to put up with if he wanted to compete. It can't have been much fun racing all day after being sick most of the way to a meeting.' The car-sickness would continue to be a problem, improving only when Ted moved to Talley's and was able to borrow a truck from work.

In the early days, the motocross scene was like one big family. The truck would set off to the meeting with as many as six or eight bikes jammed on the back, and all the families — the Urquharts, Thomases, Baigents, Crawfords, Myttons, Coppinses and Wrattens — would follow behind in their cars; few of them had vans in those days. When the event was in Christchurch, they would all stay with the Pahi family.

Kev Pahi was involved with running motocross, and his son, Kahu, was riding at that time. Kev was an inspiration to a lot of kids, including Josh, and the Nelson contingent used to have a huge amount of fun staying at the Pahis', where the kids were always playing jokes, not only on each other, but on the adults as well, and in particular Mike Baigent, father of rider Tim Baigent.

Josh and his friend Matt Wratten were travelling with Murray, returning home from a meeting in Christchurch one winter's afternoon, when Josh started singing the Beatles' song, 'Yellow Submarine'. The singing went on and on, and Murray was starting to seethe, telling the boys to knock it off or he'd kick them out and make them walk. They ignored him and carried on with the annoying singing. Finally, Murray reached breaking point and stopped the vehicle. Even though it was cold, wet and snowing, he kicked the boys out, drove off and left the two 12-year-olds on the side of the road.

Continuing on for about 100 kilometres, Murray stopped for a meal at a place called Springs Junction. As his meal was delivered, he looked out the window to see Josh and Matt jump out of a transport truck — they had managed to hitch a ride with the driver, and were only a few minutes behind.

The song wasn't heard again until quite a few months later, when the families attended a supercross meeting held in Shed 5 on the Wellington waterfront, which coincided with the V8 street car races. 'It was a night event and finished about 11.00 p.m.,' remembers Ted. 'We still had the Talley's van which was loaded with a heap of bikes and people and, as we left, Murray decided to do a few laps of the Wellington street race circuit. After about the fourth lap, a security car started to chase us, so Murray shot off the track and headed for our motel, which was in Adelaide Road in Newtown. We checked into the motel, put the boys to bed and started having a few drinks.'

Josh was in the bedroom with Matt Wratten, Cameron Holland, Darcy Lutton and Kahu Pahi, and all the boys started singing 'Yellow Submarine' over and over. This time the kids thought they'd been smart — they'd barricaded the door shut — but Murray Thorn grabbed the dry powder fire extinguishers, forced a gap in the doorway and let them off. All went quiet. Unbeknown to the adults, the boys had bailed out the window because they couldn't breathe, the dry powder extinguishers taking all the oxygen out of the room.

The next morning, they were due to catch the Cook Strait ferry, and when the adults woke the boys they found white powder and stolen road signs everywhere. When the boys had made their temporary escape the night before, they'd found some road works, and when they were able to climb back into their room, they'd taken all the road signs with them.

When the group arrived at the ferry, Matt Wratten realised he'd lost his wallet. After telling him it served him right, Murray decided to ring the motel and confess about the messy room, which the motel owner had already discovered. The owner also told Murray they'd found Matt's wallet, with $400, which they quickly agreed would cover the cleaning bill.

After shifting to town, Josh took up a paper run to help fund things. From delivering newspapers on his BMX bike in small-town New Zealand to standing on the podium at the world championships in Europe just a few years later was to be a huge leap. But, then again, big leaps are what Josh is best at. As a youngster, the best Josh could hope for was to be speedy on a bicycle and get airborne off curbs as he delivered the local newspapers.

He soon worked out that he could make more from tips than the actual paper route. 'The older people always wanted to stop me and have a chat about the war,' Josh says. 'I knew nothing about it, of course, but I'd listen for ages and I think they liked that, because I always got a few tips at Christmas time. I never really made any money from the route itself. I got $7 a week, but I couldn't do it on a Saturday because I was racing, so I'd get a mate of mine, Robert Wells, to do it for me and I'd have to pay him $5 for one day. I didn't really care though, because I got to ride my BMX bike and I loved the movie *BMX Bandits* as a kid — I considered myself one of them.'

Josh was also playing rugby around this time, as second five-eighth or centre, and he made the schoolboy rep team. A few girlfriends popped onto the scene at this time too, but, even with the distractions of rugby and the opposite sex, Josh remained focused on his motocross dream.

Tragedy struck one night when his beloved pet labrador, Kerry, was run over. Kerry's place was taken in turn by a German shepherd called Kooge and the pair quickly became inseparable. 'Each summer you'd swear Kooge could sense when Josh was coming home from Europe,' Viv says.

According to Josh, Kooge was an awesome dog. 'He went everywhere I went and loved to go in the van with me. If the door was open, he was in, waiting just in case I'd go somewhere. He was a great running partner as well. He knew my route and always wanted to lead. As we got nearer to home, I'd increase the jogging pace and pass him, then he'd pass me — we'd race all the way home. As soon as I got home from Europe for the summer break he'd stick by my side, almost as if he was scared I was going to leave again.'

Sadly, Kooge died in 2004.

All revved up

As a teenager, Josh developed a serious hay fever problem, with dramatic effects that Viv remembers vividly. 'My dad was a hay-baling contractor and he used to come and bale our hay. One particular evening, Ted and the children went up the paddock to help pick up bales. I stayed at the house to prepare the evening meal. Before very long, Josh came back home. I couldn't believe somebody's appearance could change so quickly! He was a mess — his face was all swollen, eyes running and so on. That was the first time it happened, and he has suffered a lot since.'

Life moved on, with Josh stopping his paper run and working part-time for orchardist Barry Wratten for a short period, before he started working with his dad, at Talley's Fisheries, where he drove forklifts, repaired wooden pallets and washed trucks. When he was 14, Josh went to work for Murray Thorn after school and on Saturday mornings. This involved pushing bikes in and out of the workshop, sweeping floors, some small mechanical work and, of course, riding motocross on the weekends.

'My parents weren't into motocross very much; Dad could never watch me, and Mum just wanted me to have a normal boy's upbringing,' Josh says. 'The best way they helped was by supporting and not pressuring me. My dad would always tell me my riding looked fine, even when I knew I wasn't going that well. He had a good way of getting me to relax. I know they spent a lot of money on me — I wouldn't be where I am today without their help.'

As the racing became more competitive and the rivalry more intense, people started buying their own vans and travelling independently. The Coppinses followed suit, using a diesel van from Talley's for about two years until Josh blew up the motor one night coming home from Christchurch.

Josh and Murray always sat in the front, with Ted relegated to a chair at the back of the van and, according to Ted, they spent the entire journey taking the mickey out of each other. Josh and Murray had a fetish for Kentucky Fried Chicken. 'We stopped at every damn Kentucky Fried Chicken shop in New Zealand,' Ted says.

For manager Murray Thorn, second-best was not good enough. His mottos were 'Do it once, do it right' and 'Second is the first loser'. Ted Coppins shared his philosophies and admired the way in which Thorn won the confidence of riders. 'If he told Josh he could jump that triple at half-throttle in third gear and clear it easily, he would be right,' Ted says. 'This built a tremendous relationship which is as strong today as when we first started.'

Murray Thorn is an excellent rider in his own right, and has excelled on a road bike, trials bike and in motocross and enduro riding. He also knows the dangers and the pain that top riders have to endure if they want to get to the top.

While riding an enduro event in the Motueka Forest one year, he had a near-fatal accident when flags were turned mid-race and Murray and another rider collided head-on. He spent six months recovering n Lower Hutt Hospital, and underwent plastic surgery for some considerable time after that to replace his nose and cheek bones.

Undeterred, one Saturday he called Ted and said, 'Let's go for a ride.' Thorn loaned Ted a Suzuki DR650, while he rode an 1100 Suzuki. The two riders left Motueka and went up the valley to Lake Rotoiti, then back through Golden Downs to Nelson and home to Motueka. Ted thought he was doing pretty well, sitting on 140 to 150 kph, when Murray went past him as if he was standing still. By the time Ted made it home, Murray had made a cup of coffee and was watching television.

Ted was parked outside the house when the kids came out to talk to him — the bike was still running and the clutch was in. Still talking, Ted had his left foot on the ground in front of the foot peg, and without thinking he let the clutch out. The bike shot forward, rolling his ankle under the foot peg and breaking it. Josh drove his father over to the A&E department, to be greeted by a doctor with, 'Hi Josh, what have you broken now?'

Josh took great delight in being able to say, 'Not me this time, it's my dad.'

The doctor laughed and told Josh to save them all time and fill out the forms while they fixed his dad up. 'You've been here so many times, you know what to do.'

By now Josh was very well known at A&E departments all over the South Island. Somehow he always seemed to suffer bad luck when racing in Marlborough. While riding in a supercross event at the Blenheim speedway circuit, he tore the anterior cruciate ligament in his knee, when he was caught mid-air by a freak gust of wind. Next morning it was off to Nelson Public Hospital, where the doctor proceeded to give Viv a huge dressing-down about how her son shouldn't be allowed near motorbikes. By the time Viv had finished answering him, the doctor probably wished he hadn't said anything at all. In due course, Josh arrived home in plaster right up to his thigh.

On another occasion, Josh was riding in and winning the 80cc section of the Marlborough champs at Blenheim when a trackside peg hit and broke his arm. They took him to the trackside ambulance for treatment, but there was still one race to go, so Josh asked the St John crew to wrap it tight so he could ride the last race. All hell broke loose. The ambulance crew didn't see the funny side and, once again, Josh arrived home in plaster. At that point in his early career, Josh had broken his wrist, had a full knee reconstruction and broken his arm.

By this stage the old Talley's van was just about dead on its feet. On one occasion, when they were leaving Mohaka and driving up the long hill, there was so much black smoke billowing out the back of the van that other drivers were too scared to overtake. When they finally did get past, they would shake their fists and toot their horns, with Josh ducking down to hide with embarrassment.

Ted describes another memorable trip, on the way to the supercross at Gore. 'We were on the Killmog Road, heading into Dunedin. Murray was driving flat out to pick up speed for the next hill. There were two stock trucks with a heap of traffic stuck behind, so Murray pulled out and passed the whole line of traffic down the hill. Then we hit a very steep uphill section, and the old van slowed as it gradually lost power. We were down to a crawl, black smoke pouring out the back like hell. Before we reached the top of the rise, all the cars, including the stock trucks, had passed us. Murray was pretty grumpy.'

Eventually Murray put it to Ted that the team had to become more professional. He suggested it was time to buy a van and, coincidentally, his own 1984 Toyota Hiace was on the market. 'That van was bought and sold between us at least four times as our financial situation dictated,' says Ted, who still has it to this day, with the number plate LIZID. According to Thorn, the origin of Josh's now famous nickname came from simple beginnings. 'He was always very quick, darting around the place like a lizard. He was very quick for his age and good at rugby too. He'd zip all over the paddock . . . very energetic. That's why I came up with this nickname for him, Lizid, or sometimes just Liz, to tease him, because it's a girl's name.'

At that time, Suzuki didn't have a big-wheel 80cc bike, so Murray set about building one for Josh, who was riding two classes, 80cc and 125cc. The bike proved to be extremely successful and several were built for other kids. 'Even to this day I don't believe Josh has ridden any faster than he did on those big-wheel 80s that Murray built,' Ted says. 'But this caused other problems, because everyone thought Josh's bikes were hotted up and tricked up with good gear, giving him an unfair advantage. This was so far from the truth, it's not funny. The only time one of Josh's motors was altered was when we sent his first competition motor up to Auckland, a mistake I never repeated.'

Murray firmly believed that the only time you ever considered altering the motor was when — and only when — the boy riding it was extracting everything possible out of a standard bike. Ted is equally convinced that Murray has a skill in tuning a standard motor that no one else can match in this country. 'He's able to listen to a bike on the circuit and say whether it's too rich or too lean, or whether it has too much power mid-range and not enough down low. He has the same ability with regards to suspension.

'There's no question that, together, Josh and Murray were a class act. Josh most certainly wouldn't be where he is today without Murray.'

Josh's continuing success led to some of his competitors spending fortunes hotting up their motors. This in turn often made them less reliable and too peaky, which in turn produced worse results, frustrating them even further. It became personal from time to time, with some fairly harsh things said to Josh and Murray, and this, to some extent, had an effect on Josh. In the entire time he raced Suzukis, Josh never lost a race due to gear failure, and Suzuki New Zealand — and, in particular, Suzuki boss Tom Peck — were hugely important to his early career. Josh still has an immense respect for Tom, holding him in very high regard — it's a strong emotional link that persists to this day.

By 1988 Josh was excelling at major events in both the North and South Islands of New Zealand, and an opportunity arose to travel to Australia and compete in the Australian motocross champs in a town called Broadford, west of Melbourne.

Ted is the first to confess that they were totally green when it came to competing overseas. 'There was no one to help us so we made a lot of mistakes, but we learned a huge amount too.' With Ted unable to travel to Australia at the time, Murray went with Josh. The bike was partially stripped and crated so that they could take it as luggage. They had to organise customs clearance for the bike and pay goods and services tax on the value of the bike and on the freight charges, with the GST recoverable on the bike returning to New Zealand, an exercise Ted describes as a pain in the backside.

A rental van was arranged and, en route to Broadford, Murray noticed a car following him. As usual, he accelerated. The other car stuck with him, so Murray accelerated some more, but still the car stuck with him. By this stage Murray was up to 160 kph and enjoying the race, with the old van stretched to the max, until he noticed the red and blue flashing lights in the grill of the car giving chase. Realising it was an unmarked police vehicle, Murray pulled over, telling Josh to keep quiet, while he showed him how to handle the situation.

The policeman walked up to the driver's window and told Murray and Josh to get out and put their hands on the side of the van, so angry with them that he could barely speak. He left them standing there in silence for five minutes. Eventually, he came back and issued them with a ticket and a warning, and Josh went on to compete, finishing second in the 80cc class. When the pair made it back to New Zealand, the ticket was waiting for Murray — $1500 Australian.

The next trip was to Australia for the 1992 Motocross des Nations, near Perth. Josh was riding the 80cc support class on the RM80 big-wheel special, where he finally made his breakthrough and was recognised for his ability on the track. Friendships were made with the big-name

Australian riders — Troy Doran, Kim Ashkenazi and Craig Dack — along with Suzuki Australia team manager Jay Foreman and others who were to be helpful in years to come, providing bikes and accommodation. This assistance made crossing the Tasman a comparative breeze, and the generosity was returned here in New Zealand when the Australians competed in the Trades Fair Supercross in Wellington, the waterfront Shed 5 supercross events, and the Addington Showgrounds and Ruapuna supercross meetings in Christchurch, cementing friendships that exist to this day.

On another memorable occasion, Murray and Josh arrived in Perth for a big race, but Murray was too impatient to clear customs with the motorbike and persuaded an official to speed things through. As a result, the entry papers weren't properly signed off. This was fine until they were ready to come home, when the next set of customs officers told Murray he couldn't take the bike home to New Zealand as it hadn't officially entered Australia. A red-faced Murray realised he couldn't argue with the logic, and a valuable lesson was learned.

By now, Josh was riding most major supercross events in Australia in the 80cc class, travelling the Tasman on a regular basis, and in the years to come he would be selected to represent New Zealand in the annual Oceania series, travelling and competing in Australia, Japan, the United States and India. Between them, Josh and Murray successfully paved the way for future New Zealand riders to travel and compete overseas.

Ted and Viv freely admit that, during Josh's teenage years, Murray probably saw more of their son then they did, and both agree that Josh has a lot to thank him for, although Viv admits there are many stories of their journeys around New Zealand and overseas that she hasn't heard, and is quite grateful for the fact. 'The ones I know about are bad enough. Once Murray took Josh to Australia and asked me if he could take him to a strip club. This was very unusual, because Murray didn't usually ask my permission for anything. Anyway, I said it was OK, as long as Josh didn't come home with any terrible disease!'

With his mother's permission, Murray took Josh and another young rider to the red light district of Kings Cross to visit a strip club, where they saw a woman with a large snake. Murray told the boys not to move if she came over to them, and sure enough, over she came. Josh and Murray sat dead still and, as expected, she put the snake on the other rider, who promptly freaked out and fled the strip joint.

In between competing overseas, Josh was still competing at home in New Zealand and was racing almost every weekend. The New Zealand motocross championships were being held that year at Pataetonga, about 50 kilometres south of Auckland. 'Once again, we had a van full of bikes and kids,' Ted says. 'We could squeeze five bikes and six people into the Toyota Hiace. As you can probably imagine, the van was slow as all hell with a load like that on board.

'While in Auckland we stayed with my sister, Maree, and her husband, Lewis, and did a bit of sight-seeing. There was a log-jam of vehicles at the traffic lights, so Murray gave us his trademark "Watch this folks" and scooted up onto the footpath. He zipped along inside all the traffic, right up to the lights. As we arrived at the lights, they turned green, so he tried to pull back into the line of traffic. Not one of the cars would let him in. Needless to say, Murray got hell from all of us in the van.'

During the 1990s, the Coppins family had a bach at Parapara Beach in Golden Bay, about one-and-a-half-hours' drive from Motueka. Josh developed a love of watersports then which has never left him, and he would spend hours fooling around with a jet boat and a small dinghy that converted into a sailboat. All the family loved the bach, and took the tractor with them to help launch the jet boat. It was also used for sack rides up and down the beach, towing three or four kids at a time. The sacks used to wear out very quickly, so one day Josh suggested using a car bonnet. A suitable bonnet was found at the local tip, attached behind the tractor with a rope and away they went.

'After a couple of minutes, Josh is screaming for me to stop,' laughs Ted. 'I stopped and went back to see what was wrong, and he was complaining about a sore bum. Friction had heated the bonnet so much that it had burnt his backside.' Not to be beaten, Josh suggested putting a bar out to one side so that the bonnet rode just in the water. This seemed to work and everything was fine, until Ted turned too sharply and the bonnet took off and tried to overtake the tractor, before it finally dug into the mud. 'All I could see were arms and legs flying through the air,' Ted laughs. 'Thinking about it afterwards, we realised that if the bonnet had hit the kids, serious injury could have occurred.' That was the end of the tractor rides.

Matt Davidson, Josh's best mate, loaned Josh a jet-ski and every morning, at the crack of dawn, Josh would be out on this jet-ski. One particular morning, Ted was standing at the kitchen sink, having an early morning coffee and watching Josh out the window. 'Next thing we know, he crashes the jet-ski and I see Josh swimming like fury, trying to catch the jet-ski, which is now heading to Farewell Spit.' Fortunately, a neighbour from up the road saw it as well and went and rescued Josh. 'It turns out he hadn't hooked up the kill switch,' Ted says. 'He was lucky — that jet-ski would have kept on going, right over the horizon until it ran out of fuel.'

Josh and his mates had a lot of fun riding their motorbikes up and down the beach, until one day when there was a knock on the door of the bach. It was the local policeman, saying he was going to book the kids for riding on the beach. It was all sorted out — the kids stopped riding on the beach and the cop left, after having been told in no uncertain terms that his parents weren't married and he had an extremely low IQ.

School and beyond

As a teenager, Josh Coppins was a typical Kiwi boy. Any excuse to goof off and avoid the rigours of schoolwork was welcomed. Josh also had a willing partner in crime — his pal Matt Davidson. 'Matt was my best mate through high school and still is,' says Josh. 'We often skipped class together and would go and help Kenny Traineer, the school caretaker. We'd drive his tractor around school, making sure we passed our classroom windows, giving our mates a wave as we went by.'

Another mate was Shannon McSherry, who also raced motocross at the weekends. When Josh wasn't working at Talley's Fisheries or Murray Thorn's shop, he would often stay with him, describing him as a good racer — a real hard bugger who never gave up. He is still a best mate. While Josh always knew that Matt didn't really like motocross, he always supported what Josh wanted to do, while Shannon was and remains very protective of his racing. 'He wants me to win as much as I do,' Josh says.

Matt and Josh got up to a lot of trouble at school — nothing bad, just boys' stuff, but the pair always took it to the limit. Both struggled with classwork, and Josh remembers teachers warning them they'd never make it in real life. 'Funny thing is, Matt's got a great business head on him, and is doing really well for himself these days. We always joke that a lot of the brainy sparks at school never achieved the great things that were expected of them, yet we've done OK.'

One day Matt and Josh arrived late for a typing exam. In order not to disturb the rest of the class, the teacher put the pair in a small room, which separated her class from the next one along, with a window in the connecting door that looked through into the next classroom. 'We started off giving the lads in the next class rude gestures through the window,' Josh recalls. 'We soon got bored with that, then realised there was a false ceiling in the room.

'I had a plaster cast on my whole leg from a knee injury and was on crutches. Nevertheless, I climbed up on a desk to get access to the ceiling. Matt was pushing me with the crutch, trying to poke me up through the hole in the ceiling. I was halfway in when he stopped prodding. I yelled at him to keep pushing, but I hadn't realised the teacher had come in from the other room. The other kids had dobbed us in for the gestures — and she wasn't happy. Our plan had been to hide in the roof so that when the teacher came to let us out of the locked room she'd think we'd vanished. It seemed to be a great idea at the time.'

Josh was growing up fast. Along with Matt Wratten and Matt Davidson, the boys pooled their money to buy a ute, called 'The Pig', from a local mechanic who worked for Murray Thorn. At that stage none of them had a car licence, but somehow they managed to buy the vehicle and drive it to Matt's uncle's farm, where they decided to repaint it. When the paint had dried, they decided to drive it up to the fire breaks in the nearby forest, where they roared around and managed to roll the ute. Somehow they got it back on its wheels, with the help of Uncle Barry's tractor, then carried on roaring around until late afternoon, when someone had the bright idea of blowing it up.

They filled it with petrol and drove to a paddock, where they parked it then spread some armchairs around. They put a fuse into the petrol tank, lit it, and sat back and waited for it to blow up. It didn't — the petrol tank was so full of fuel it wouldn't explode. Instead, the boys sat there, happily warming themselves as they watched their ute burn to the ground.

By this stage, Josh was starting to ride two classes: the 125cc and 250cc bikes. The transition to the bigger bikes was seamless. On one particular occasion, Murray, Ted and Josh travelled to a meeting at Orewa, north of Auckland, and towards the end of the meeting Josh, riding the 125cc, was winning his class.

Unbeknownst to the men, Viv had arranged for Josh to fly home on the Saturday evening so he could attend his high school ball. Just before the last race, Josh's cousin Paul arrived to collect him. When Murray and Ted asked what was going on, Josh told them he was off home and, after peeling his riding gear off, away he went with his cousin, leaving the two friends to drive home to Motueka without him.

Viv recalls the incident with a smile, adding that Josh never did most of the things other boys his age did on weekends. 'He was always travelling around the country to attend motocross meetings. I always thought he might regret this later in life. Josh was always a year younger than the others in his class, which meant that when his friends turned 15 and were getting their drivers' licences, he was turning 14 and had to wait another year. When he reached the fifth form, which was no mean feat because Josh and Murray didn't think school was at all necessary, I was determined that he was going to make it to his high school ball.'

Without discussing it with Ted and Murray, Viv organised the hire suit, booked a flight from Auckland to Nelson, and enlisted the aid of cousin Paul, who lived in Auckland, to get him to the airport straight after the meeting. Unfortunately, the meeting was running late and Josh missed the last race.

Clearly school held little interest for Josh, who much preferred to do his own thing. By the age of 15, he had his driver's licence and was working as a trainee car salesman for Murray Thorn's dealership. 'I'd passed my fifth form exams, so I said to Dad I was off to university to cruise for a bit, but he said, "Oh no, you're not! I've got you a job . . . you start tomorrow." I went to work full time at Murray's motorbike shop, and that's probably where I'd still be if I hadn't turned professional.' Ted and Viv were philosophical about the decision. 'School wasn't doing much for him and he wasn't doing much for the school,' Ted says.

By this stage, motocross was occupying every weekend, and Ted, Murray and Josh were travelling from as far as Invercargill to Auckland. As his manager, Murray Thorn knew that for Josh to develop and improve they would have to travel.

Fortunately, Ted's boss at the time, Peter Talley, was an avid petrolhead, keen on all forms of racing. Taking an interest in Josh's results, he soon became a major sponsor and remains an inspiration to Josh to this day, playing a large part in his eventual success.

Ted is convinced there is an ulterior motive. 'When Josh is home from Europe, Peter Talley is always taking him to car racing events. He wants to get him into a race car — he's even sent him to the Ruapuna driver training school [in Christchurch], driving in both Formula Ford and V8s and, to this day, is always asking when Josh will give up the bikes and swap to cars.'

It is a rare thing for Grand Prix motocross to venture outside of Europe, so in 1993, when Australia was granted a round of the 125cc world championships — at a place called Manjimup, near Perth — it was an opportunity too good to miss for a 15-year-old, who had to obtain an age exemption to race.

This was arguably the biggest step in Josh's career so far, but in his typically matter-of-fact manner, he talks down an event that was undoubtedly a turning point. 'It was in Australia, so it was what the Europeans would regard as an overseas GP, rather than just another GP in Europe, and a lot of the field weren't there — only the top 10 or 20 riders attended. It was too far for a lot of them to travel, so while it wasn't really a true reflection of the event, it was a true test against the faster guys. It was also a good opportunity for me to see if I liked the GPs, so it was quite good from that point of view.'

The track was sand — something new for Josh — the bikes 'awesome', and the Europeans' gear very different from what he was used to seeing in the American motocross magazines. Instead of Fox and No Fear, they were using UFO and Axo, with sponsors he'd never heard of before, like Chesterfield. 'I saw one guy with an open-face helmet, and I thought that was pretty unusual.'

A three-race-per-GP format operated that year, and Italian Andrea Bartolini won the day's first two races, with Dutch rider Davey Strijbos winning the third. Interestingly, a man who seven years later would become Josh's factory Suzuki team-mate, Frenchman Mickael Pichon, also raced that day, finishing third, fifth and DNF (did not finish), and winding up fifth in the 125cc championship by season's end.

Josh was rapt, soaking up the atmosphere and filing away the sights, sounds and smells. 'I remember the last race of the day. I almost made the holeshot from way out wide. That was pretty cool. I also saw the GP guys jump and how far they'd go, and see them trying for a hot lap for qualifying — that totally blew me away.'

Murray, Ted and Josh were now travelling north regularly and getting to know the roads and people quite well. One such event, a supercross held inside a large sheep shed at the Masterton Showgrounds, finished around 11.00 p.m. After the prizegiving they were ready to go to the motel when Josh suddenly said, 'Let's go.' When Ted agreed, saying the motel was just up the road, Josh said, 'No, let's go home.' They drove to Wellington and caught the 2.00 a.m. inter-island Cook Strait ferry home — it was a sleepless night. The following morning, Ted realised his son was a home boy at heart who didn't like staying away any longer than necessary. Home-sickness had quite an impact when Josh went to Europe and, to this day, he still misses home.

Josh was away travelling so much that his job as a car salesman wasn't working, so he joined the evening shift in the cool store at Talley's Fisheries, which gave him time during the day for training and his weekends free for riding. By the time he was 16 he was riding in both the 125cc and 250cc classes regularly and, after the Oceania series, competed in most Australian supercross events. It was time to branch out.

The recognition he had gained at home and in Australia led to an invitation to compete professionally in Indonesia. It was his first big break and the first time he'd been paid money to ride. Other riders that lined up alongside Josh in Jakarta included Kim Ashkenazi, Troy Dorron, Steven Andrews, Lee Hogan and Chad Reed. Soon Murray and Josh were travelling to Indonesia once a month and Australia in between, as well as competing in New Zealand.

With the help of Tom Peck and Suzuki New Zealand, bikes and gear were supplied, and life got a little easier for Team Coppins. At the time, Suzuki New Zealand were supplying up to six new bikes annually, plus a parts budget. 'I had worked a year, and I could train and work on my bikes and really make it happen,' Josh says. 'However, I was crashing a lot because I was tired all the time. There were only two options really — go to work and back off the racing, or become a professional racer. I was already racing in Indonesia quite a lot and was making a few dollars doing that, so I thought I'd give the professional life a go.'

With all the major New Zealand events being held in the North Island — the New Zealand motocross championships, the New Zealand supercross championships and the Shell Darbi series — travel became a significant part of Josh's life. To save on expenses, Josh lived with Pete Crowley and his family in New Plymouth; Pete's son, Blair, was a fellow competitor.

The Crowley family were incredibly supportive, and their hospitality meant a lot to Josh, who would have his van, bikes and gear at their place for months on end. Murray and Ted would fly over to Wellington from Nelson on a Friday night, pick up a car that Ted had left at Wellington airport, and drive to New Plymouth. Early Saturday morning they would drive to wherever that weekend's event was being held, then on Sunday night drive back to Wellington airport to catch the Monday morning 5 o'clock mail plane to Nelson. From Nelson airport they would drive home to Motueka, where Ted would start work at 8.00 a.m.

'If any major work had to be done on the bike, we would go north on the Thursday night and work on the bikes on Friday,' Ted says. 'The car I had at the time was a blue AU model Ford Falcon with a five-speed manual gearbox, capable of 200 kph, but with a bad habit of breaking down.' One weekend, the Falcon died just as they were leaving Wellington. As it was a relatively new vehicle, a Ford dealership in Wellington arranged for a rental car, a Nissan Maxima. Already three hours behind schedule, Murray was in a foul mood.

'We took off, flat out. Somewhere between Wanganui and Patea major roadworks were underway and, to slow the traffic down, the road workers had built a speed bump out of shingle,' Ted says. 'I was asleep in the passenger seat and Murray was driving. The next minute, all hell breaks loose as Murray hits this speed bump at full speed. The Maxima flies into the air and lands sideways-on — we went into a huge gravel slide.'

Fortunately Murray's driving skills were able to control the skid and they carried on unscathed. The next morning they set off from the Crowleys', heading to Pukekohe. Once again Murray was driving, with Pete Crowley following in his van with Taranaki man Henry Plowright and one other as passengers.

'We were in front, so going down the hill into Te Kuiti I suggested to Murray that at the bottom of the hill we should shoot behind the gas station and I'd jump out and fill a bag with water. While we were doing this, Pete drove past. Just north of Te Kuiti there is a straight which goes past the airport. Murray pulled alongside Pete and I motioned to him to wind his window down. With that, I threw the plastic bag of water through their window. It worked perfectly, hitting the inside of their windscreen and bursting, showering Pete, Henry and the other guy with water.'

Starting out in Europe

T WO YEARS LATER, in 1995, Glenn Bayly (now a Mt Maunganui bike dealer) and his wife, Robyn, were in Europe to help Daniel Marshall, another New Zealander with high ambitions. Danny Marshall was a very fast rider and was riding with the Johnson Bieffe factory Suzuki team, run by Belgian Sylvain Geboers. To get a position in a works team, a rider had to either be very good or have excellent contacts. Rotorua bike dealer Don Perry was a personal friend of Sylvain's and was able to arrange a works ride for Danny, with Glenn Bayly as his mechanic.

Very early in the deal, disaster struck when Danny crashed and blew the ligaments in his knee. Josh was able to step into the now-vacant position, and Glenn Bayly agreed to remain in Europe as his mechanic. Danny's mobile camper and workshop were also vacant, and Josh was offered the lease. 'There was considerable discussion on whether to accept or not,' says Ted Coppins. 'This decision was to have the most profound effect on our lives.'

Though he gives most of the credit to his father for giving his racing career a financial kick-start, Josh says that initially there were a lot of misconceptions about just what his father contributed. 'My dad is the manager at Talley's Fisheries, not the owner. We aren't a rich family, but he works hard and he spent his life savings getting me into Europe. It was a big risk. He never put any pressure on me, but I still felt I owed it to him to work hard and not disappoint him. I put all the pressure on myself — I didn't want to let him down. He always said that if I didn't make it, he would just write the money off, but I was still worried.

'After a year or two as a factory rider, I'd already recouped the money he'd put in. While I offered to pay him back, he advised me to invest it to secure my future and then we'd talk about paying him back. As long as I'm not wasting the money, he's in no hurry.'

Whilst Ted worked to provide the money for Josh to race and Murray Thorn acted as driver/manager, it was Viv who was the brains behind the team — she worked out all the flights and did the detailed planning. 'It was really just those three people behind me, right through until I left for Europe, and even for the first few years while I was in Europe,' Josh says. 'Murray was good at getting me organised and Dad always believed in me, even if I was doing badly.'

Josh was only 17 years of age, so Murray agreed to accompany Josh to Europe and make the introductions. Money was extremely tight, and the work schedule and travelling involved were mind blowing. Not only was Glenn Bayly needed as a mechanic, but he also drove the team all over Europe, from event to event, from their Belgian base at Sylvain's workshop. 'There was no flat or house, so things like washing and cooking meals were arduous to say the least, particularly during the cold European winter,' Ted says. 'How poor Robyn coped with all of this is beyond me. Glenn did extremely well, and we'll always be in their debt for the effort they put in to supporting Josh.'

While the buy-in contract was enough for Josh to get his foot in the door in Europe, he knew he still had a long way to go. He soon discovered that while he had a dozen or so New Zealand and a couple of Australian titles to his credit, it didn't mean a thing on the European circuit. The factory teams weren't looking for riders from overseas. They had talent enough in Europe and, besides, a European sponsor would rather have a European rider to front his company. It made financial sense — a European rider would be much easier to sell to the fans than somebody from a tiny country on the other side of the globe. Unfortunately, New Zealand companies weren't keen on supporting New Zealand riders in Europe either — why would they, when they wouldn't be able to benefit from any coverage of that rider competing on the other side of the world?

'So I had two choices: go it alone, or lease material from Suzuki whilst in Europe,' Josh says. 'I chose the second option, and slowly worked my way up. Suzuki New Zealand was able to help me in that respect, because it was even difficult just to get the chance to lease the bikes.'

With a small foothold in the European scene, and a long way from most of his friends and family, the 17-year-old was ready to tackle one of the toughest sports around, and at an elite level. Glenn Bayly, unflustered by the change in circumstances, says that it was a simple thing to change his focus from helping Danny Marshall to helping Josh Coppins.

'I had been marketing manager for Suzuki New Zealand, and I'd already helped a lot of riders in New Zealand, including Josh,' says Bayly. 'Josh was an up-and coming junior at that time in my career, and had progressed to senior by the time I'd left Suzuki to work for BMW. By the time Danny Marshall was making moves to go to Europe, I was about 28 and looking at doing something different.'

When the opportunity to work with Danny Marshall came along, it seemed like a good opportunity for Glenn and Robyn Bayly to take a year off, help a young Kiwi and see a bit of the world. Bayly had been involved in trying to get Stacey Oldeman, another talented Kiwi rider, to Europe. Stacey had been one of Suzuki's better senior riders in New Zealand at the same time that Josh had been a junior rider. Stacey had achieved a few rides in Europe, but couldn't get the money together to continue.

'I have to admire people like Darryl Atkins, Darryll King, Shayne King . . . they took the privateer route and did it the hard way,' Bayly says. 'They went over there with nothing — they were basically riding for food. It wasn't until I got to Europe that I could see how much respect those guys had earned.' It certainly hadn't been easy — sometimes they'd been forced to ride under a made-up Belgian name because, at the time, you had to be a local to ride in the Belgian championships. It was the only way to win prize money and put food on the table or petrol in the tank for the next event.

'I'd gone to Europe because I wanted to help Danny Marshall — I'd known him for years,' Bayly adds. 'Don Perry and I had stitched the deal together for him to ride in Europe with one-year-old factory machinery, the top gear the factory guys had raced the season before.' Though now past their best and superseded by fresher factory models, the bikes were still better than anything that could be purchased publicly or privately, and a gifted rider such as Danny Marshall or Josh Coppins would be able to make the most of them.

'We had full parts support and technical support from the Suzuki factory team, but we still had to find our own mechanic. That's where I stepped in. Technically speaking, I'm not a mechanic, but I knew enough of the basics. I'd known Scott and Alison Marshall [Danny's parents] for years through my association with Suzuki. They were looking for a couple to go over there and be stand-in mother and father to their son. My wife and I had just got married, and the idea was for us to go to Europe for a year.'

The deal involved Marshall buying a contract to race for Suzuki, for which a substantial fee was paid. According to Bayly, such a contract on the other side of the world — 'where you don't know anything about where to go and find things' — was invaluable. 'That support from the factory team extended beyond the provision of bikes and gear to telling us where to buy the special fuel and helping us find oil sponsorship. It was worth a lot, because there is so much more to it than just turning up at a GP and riding. The factory gave us somewhere to live to start with, and pointed us in the right direction at the supermarkets — they made sure we bought beef and not horse. These were things the privateers like Atkins and King would have learned the hard way.'

Danny Marshall had already picked up the motorcycles and a motor-home from the Kawasaki team, a Mercedes camper that used to belong to Stefan Everts, by the time the Baylys arrived. Tragically for Marshall he suffered a devastating knee injury in his very first test session in Europe. Just seven days after leaving Auckland airport, his factory career was over.

There was some thought of Danny having an operation and having the contract delayed for a year, but in the end, after discussions that carried on through February and March, the decision was made for the Coppins family to buy out the Marshall contract, with Josh taking over where Danny had left off.

'We'd known Josh from before, but there'd been an expectation of what Robyn and I would do with our particular capabilities. Now we had to sell ourselves to the Coppins family and Josh's great mentor, Murray Thorn,' remembers Glenn Bayly. 'We had to convince Murray that we could fix the motorbike if it broke down and drive Josh around Europe.'

Initially Murray Thorn joined the Baylys in Europe, and the Kiwi team became a group of four. Their first trip was to Spain, 2400 kilometres from the workshop in Belgium, to the season's first GP at Talavera. Many people back home in New Zealand would struggle to appreciate the driving distances involved, which on top of the racing and the mechanical work meant their workload was staggering. 'From the moment Josh arrived until the end of the season, it was just full-on,' Bayly recalls. 'We weren't being paid, but Robyn and I were happy with that and it all added to the fun. There were a lot of things Josh had to learn and a lot of things I had to learn.'

Each GP weekend road trip was fraught with difficulties, not least being the time needed to travel the vast distances across Europe. The foreign languages, border crossings, customs, money and food issues all had to be sorted. Fortunately the Kiwi adventurers had plenty of laughs to break the tedium and soothe the stresses.

'On our first trip to Spain, I remember Murray was driving. He'd only been in Europe about four days, but he was going on like he knew it all,' Bayly says. 'Murray was stubborn. An argument developed about which way they needed to go to exit Paris and he shot off down an exit that wasn't suited for a tall motor-home.' The entrance barrier before an underground tunnel ripped the top off the camper, and tent poles that had been lashed to the roof were scattered down the road behind them; they also lost the skylights off the top of the truck.

'Fortunately there was an escape route out the side before we had to commit ourselves to the tunnel, otherwise I don't know how we would have got out. There was traffic everywhere — an unbelievable amount of traffic. I don't think the downtown traffic jams in Motueka were anything like the ones that Murray had to deal with in Paris. We duct-taped everything back together and rolled onward to the motocross. Murray was a bit quiet for a while after that.'

The first impression the Kiwis had at Talavera was just how fast the European riders went into the first corner. Unlike the other riders, Josh was jumping very high while all the European stars kept their bikes low over the jumps. Josh looked spectacular, but compared with the others he was wasting time going up in the air instead of going forward. Eventually someone came in to the pits and commented that Josh must have come close to the overhead wire across the track. Bayly checked Josh's helmet and, sure enough, there was a big black mark up the back of his helmet where he'd touched the wire each time he'd jumped. 'We realised then that the New Zealand style of racing was just so different,' Bayly says.

It wasn't so much that the different style of jumping was an issue; it was also that the Europeans' corner speed was so much faster, and this was quickly identified as an aspect of his riding that Josh needed to improve. While he had all the basic skills, he needed to work on his corner speed, and for his first year that is exactly what he did.

Expectations of Josh weren't high, as each week the aim was simply to qualify, an achievement in itself and, once again, very different from his New Zealand experience, where with a smaller pool of riders, simply being in the top 40 meant that you would race. As Josh quickly discovered, pre-race qualifying was important — the fastest qualifiers got the best choices for a starting position on the gate. Only one good lap was needed during the timed session, so riders would save up their strength, wait for the track to clear in front of them, then explode into a frenzy of speed for one hot lap, hoping to trip the electronic lapping computer with a favourable time. Josh's steep learning curve had begun.

He had to learn how to do a fast lap. There were riders on the European circuit who were ultra-fast qualifiers, good for one hot lap, but who couldn't race to save themselves, so the team worked hard each weekend just so Josh could achieve that one fast lap. Luck also played a big part in the racing, with fickle weather enough to throw the whole equation out the window. Often they would have a dry start to a session, but then it would start raining before Josh had found clear space in the traffic to try for his hot lap. The art of qualification and the ability to do a hot lap under pressure were important lessons he had to learn — and learn fast.

Josh, Glenn, Robyn and Murray made a point of parking as closely as they could to the official factory Suzuki team tent and truck, hoping for crumbs of support to fall their way, including tips with suspension settings or words of advice from the 'factory stars', with Belgians Marnicq Bervoets and Werner de Wit the riders under the factory awning.

'We'd park as close to them as we could, but they had factory privileges,' recalls Bayly. 'Their tyre deal meant that their tyres were changed first. If I was lucky, I'd be the last sets of tyres changed before the next track session, or I'd just change them myself. It was the same with parking in the paddock — we had to park off to the side. While our truck wasn't decorated the same as theirs, we used to run in the same sponsors' colours, with Josh riding in the same shirts as Bervoets and de Wit.'

While Josh may have appeared to be part of the factory line-up, only the bikes and clothes bore any resemblance to the lifestyle of the factory stars. Week in and week out, Josh, Murray, Glenn and Robyn would battle to hold everything together, get organised and prepare for the next GP, with more long trips on the autobahns, autostradas and motorways.

'We were always looking for the next McDonald's for Murray, the only thing that would keep him happy,' Glenn laughs. 'He'd drive for miles to get to a McDonald's — we'd be scanning the skyline for the big golden M signs whenever we'd go into a town or city. I remember one time when we arrived in Paris in the middle of the night. We didn't know where we were. We had a shower before going to bed, forgetting that the waste water just ran out of the truck. When we opened the door the next morning, there were thousands of people walking past — we'd parked right in the middle of the city.

'Murray was keen to see a few of the sights in Paris. He wanted to see the Eiffel Tower, and kept asking people where the Leaning Tower of Pisa was — in Paris! But, generally, there was no time to do the tourist thing. We might take a day here or a day there occasionally, but to do that we'd have to drive all through the night to get to a place for the day. Normally, we'd spend the Monday driving as we had to be back in the workshop by the Tuesday morning after a GP, otherwise we wouldn't have enough time to get the bikes rebuilt and ready for the next event.'

Fortunately, while GP life had its moments of stress, it also had its moments of relief. 'Everyone was good to us,' Bayly remembers. 'People knew how hard Josh was trying. They could see how his results were improving day by day, and he won himself a few fans. I think there was an incredible amount of admiration for how hard Josh and everyone around him was working.

'Robyn and I had bought a little Volkswagen Golf for about NZ$1000 and Josh would grab that whenever he needed to go somewhere, like the gym, otherwise he'd have to push-bike around the place. Getting around wasn't that easy because the workshop was out of town — we lived wherever the truck was.'

New Zealand motocross riders Mike Cotter and Craig Brown went to Europe for a couple of months that season, presenting Josh with an opportunity to let off steam and go out nightclubbing with his mates. By now he was 18, and about to be initiated into the famous Dockside Café in Hasselt, Belgium, where plenty of weird and wonderful things went on and girls were available in abundance. He was growing up, but he also knew what he had to do professionally, and his social life never got out of hand. While he occasionally got involved with girls, drinking and nightclubs, he still trained hard every day.

By now Josh was riding in the GP circuit events, often competing against his childhood heroes — men he'd previously read about back home in bike magazines imported from overseas — and it could have been overwhelming. He was up against the men he'd admired for most of his life, and was impressed by just how phenomenally fast they were. Nevertheless, Josh was fast enough to race in the big prize-money events between the GPs, where he was up against local riders or regional champions instead of all the other GP riders, and was able to make a living for himself.

He now had two local managers, Renee and Angela Lichens, who specialised in working for private riders. They'd worked for Darryll King and other Kiwi riders in the past, and were able to organise paid rides for Josh, as well as making sure all his papers were right for each GP in the different countries. The French races were particularly lucrative, and sometimes he could earn as much as US$5000 just for showing up on the start line, with the opportunity to compete for prize money on top of that. As a GP rider, he was a drawcard for the event promoters, who could then advertise a Kiwi on the programme. Because of the groundwork done by Daryl Atkins, Darryll and Shayne King, and Craig Coleman and Ivan Miller before them, Kiwis had a reputation as riders who could race, and there was a great deal of respect for them in Europe.

While Bayly now thinks that Josh probably wasn't quite ready for it all, it was a good way to learn. Dropped in at the deep end, the learning process had to be speedy, with wrong turns on motorways, lost or damaged gear and mistakes with paperwork all costing the low-budget team. In addition, they had to contend with the natural wear and tear generated by racing at the optimum level, exacerbated by the fact that Josh's riding technique was still developing.

'It was always new clutch, new clutch, new clutch . . . I lost count of how many times we'd have to replace the clutch on Josh's bikes,' says Bayly. Because of his riding style, they were wearing out a new one at every GP. He had learned to ride aggressively, and it was the clutch that bore the brunt of his aggression. As that first season wore on, he gradually learned to go easier on the clutch as he realised that to get points he had to finish races. It was all part of the learning curve.

Josh also realised that he had to ride harder to keep up. Fortunately the factory contract meant the replacement gear was at no cost to the team. In basic terms, the contract provided a race bike and a practice bike. The race bike would always stay in mint condition for the GPs and, after each event, would be stripped down completely, right back to the frames. The paint would be touched up and it would be rebuilt from the ground up. The expectation from the Suzuki factory was that Josh's bike always raced looking as fresh as a new bike — just like the full factory bikes of Bervoets and de Wit.

'We'd pretty much get the gearbox out of Bervoets' bike after one race, so it was still fairly new,' Bayly says. 'Then we'd do one race with it before throwing it out in the trash. We'd have new a piston and rings, and the suspension would be completely redone every weekend.' The prevailing attitude was that Josh was flying the flag for Suzuki just as much as the full factory contract riders, and the company didn't want one of their bikes on the track that didn't look pristine.

Despite everything, every race was a challenge, including just getting to the start line. Sometimes they'd arrive at an event that was considered to have an easier track and expect to be on fire, but would struggle in practice and it would turn out to be a disappointment. At other events, on tracks that looked really challenging, Josh and the bike would both perform really well.

Their lifestyle was fairly haphazard. Living and competing on the GP circuit was to live like a motley band of gypsies, with a wagon train of trucks and motor-homes travelling in convoy across Europe.

On one Italian trip they arrived at Asti for the weekend, and teamed up with some of the other team trucks to park up in a supermarket car park. Eventually they were there for a week, expecting each day to be asked to move on. They kept themselves busy painting frames and rebuilding engines, and had crowds of locals standing around and staring, but nobody seemed worried, and the supermarket proprietor never approached them. The motocross tracks in Italy were fantastic, particularly at Maggiora, which had massive hills that were just phenomenal, with big jumps from top to bottom.

Bayly recalls that one of the hardest trips during 1995 was driving back from the double-header Scandinavian GPs in Finland and Sweden, back-to-back on consecutive weekends. 'We had to be at the ferry at 6.00 a.m. to catch the boat from Stockholm to Helsinki. We'd already driven about 2500 kilometres non-stop, and because I was the only one who had a truck licence, I was doing all the driving.' They made good time and had about three hours up their sleeves to get to the ferry. While the other teams had told them how far it was and how long the journey would take, they all had multiple drivers to spell one another. The Kiwis were trying to do it with just one.

'I'd probably been on the go for about 24 hours without stopping, and then it started snowing. I was absolutely wrecked — unbelievably tired. I'd been rebuilding the bikes before we left, so I hadn't had any sleep since before the race. In the end, I got to the point where I had to wake Josh. It was about 5.00 a.m. and I knew I'd burnt myself out and we weren't going to make it. Snow was coming in hard and fast, and when I looked down at the speedo I saw we were only doing about 35 kph. I wasn't falling asleep at the wheel, but I remember thinking, "Oh, no, I'm driving this thing backwards." I was hallucinating, I think — my mind was playing games on me. So here was 18-year-old Josh, with no truck licence, driving in the snow to get us to the ferry.'

There would be many times like that, where the team had to push themselves to the limit.

Josh, Glenn and Robyn lived almost full time in the motor-home until June, when they found a flat for themselves in Belgium. 'With the motor-home, we'd often get woken up in the middle of the night by the police and be asked to move on. We had to be careful where we parked and what we did with the waste and so forth,' Glenn Bayly says. Dealing with the waste was Josh's job — one of those jobs that nobody wanted to do. He wore a special pair of motocross gloves and a pair of overalls, and balancing the bucket of waste precariously on the scooter he'd take it over to the bike wash bay where he'd use the steam cleaner.

They were all relieved when they were finally able to take a small two-bedroom flat. 'It was great, except it had absolutely no furniture. We had to use the plastic chairs out of the truck. There was no dining table, nothing. We'd eat sitting on the floor, but it was just so good to have a place to come back to and unload. It wasn't until we went to the British GP that we could go into a supermarket and buy brands of food we were familiar with. That was exciting.' The trio had been eating all sorts of things in Belgium without actually knowing what they were.

'It was a tough existence,' Bayly laughs, 'but Tom Peck [back at Suzuki in New Zealand] made sure that we never went without. We never got much money from anyone, but Tom was brilliant. I'm certain that's why Josh still feels a certain loyalty to Suzuki to this day.'

Occasionally the tight budget would have an unexpected boost, like the time they found a phone box in Poland where you could ring anywhere in the world for no charge — a very good score in those days, before mobile phones became common. 'Robyn and Josh were on the phone the whole time, calling home to New Zealand and all over the show — and it cost nothing. It was quite remarkable really. We never had the luxury of calling home very often because our budget was so tight, so this was a nice surprise.'

Josh was steadily learning and improving, and starting to achieve the sort of results that would earn him money. As he wasn't a Belgian rider, he had trouble getting sponsors, and at the time not many thought he would ever win a championship and be a contender for the position of number one in the world. While he was known as a hard worker, the X-factor wasn't yet apparent. Few people realised just how determined and stubborn this Kiwi rider was learning to be as he continued to battle seemingly impossible odds on his long journey towards a motocross world championship title.

As his debut season in Europe wound down, that possibility seemed a long way off. While factory Suzuki star Bervoets had the number four on his bike and de Wit was number six, Josh started the season with number 77 on his lease bikes. The only significance was that it was the year of his birth. It wasn't until following years that the numbers began to plot his steady upward progress, with the number he wore at the beginning of the racing year reflecting where he had finished the previous season. By the end of his debut 1995 season, Josh had earned the right to paste the number 41 on his bike.

'Actually, it can get confusing,' Bayly says. 'We had different race numbers at every meeting for a while there in that 1995 season. He had 77 for the GPs but, at midweek or non-GP international events, he'd have whatever number he was given. I think Josh was happy with 41st. He'd got through that first year in a hell of a hurry, still in one piece, and learned an awful lot along the way. I think he would have liked to have finished quite a lot higher up, and there were times when his race results could have been better. But, mostly, the placings weren't Josh's fault. There were times, of course, when Josh made some mistakes — after all, it was a year for learning. I don't think everyone would be pleased with 41st, but, on the other hand, considering how the season had a disrupted start, I think it was a fabulous result.'

Ted Coppins has no illusions. 'In Josh's first year, we were happy just to qualify. Sometimes he did, sometimes he didn't. For him to be lining up alongside name riders — guys such as Joel Smets, Sebastien Tortelli and Marnicq Bervoets — was overwhelming. Josh improved over time and I can well remember when he rang home one night, delighted that he was 17th in one race and had scored his first GP points.'

As the end of the season rolled around, the Baylys announced that it was time to break away from their transient life as GP mechanic, driver and assistant and put down their roots again. 'At the time Josh wasn't sure he was going to come back [to Europe] and was hoping he would have earned himself some sort of paid ride with the Suzuki team,' Glenn Bayly says. 'While the set-up costs from the first year weren't going to be there, he still had to find some money for the bikes, so it was a time of doubt.

'He wanted to return to Europe, but it was a matter of what was available to him. He was quite keen to stay with Suzuki — after all, his whole career up to that point had been with Suzuki, and he was comfortable with the brand. Robyn and I got to September and we didn't know what Josh was going to do for the following year. I'd been offered the position as marketing manager at Suzuki Australia a month or so earlier. I wasn't all that serious about the job, to be honest, so we waited to see what Josh was going to do. It got to the point where Robyn and I decided we had to do what was best for us, so we accepted the Australian job offer.'

Josh was going to need a new mechanic for 1996, and another uncertain and disrupted start to the season looked to be in store for the rising Kiwi star.

1996–1999: Hard yards

At the beginning of 1996 a young man from Waikanae, Glenn Woodman, arrived in Europe. He was keen to see the world and work his passage as a GP mechanic. A young Kiwi mechanic and a teenage Kiwi rider, both in the early stages of their professional careers — it was an ideal union. Josh left New Zealand that summer with the Woodville motocross crown packed safely away, having wrestled the glittering prize away from the King brothers — Darryll and Shayne — who had, between them, owned the Woodville event for the previous six seasons.

It was a positive and encouraging start, but tough times were ahead of Josh in Europe, with the Spanish GP in March starting off the 250cc world championship season. In 24-degree temperatures, Josh struggled to 19th and 17th in the day's two 45-minute races. Defending world champion Stefan Everts, riding for the British-based RWJ Honda team, won both races to establish a 12-point advantage over American rival Tallon Vohland, who was riding for Kawasaki. Josh scored nothing for his day's work, with points at that time only allocated to the top 15 finishers.

It set the tone for the year: Everts typically on the podium and Josh, on the leased ex-factory Suzuki bikes, struggling to turn solid performances into anything significant. But it was encouraging, at least, that Josh had qualified a surprising sixth-fastest in Spain. His speed was good, he declared, with just his starts letting him down in both outings. 'It was hard to come from behind. I gave it 110 per cent, but it meant fatigue got the better of me by the second race. I was going well, up to 13th at one stage, but slipped back. I had no more left to give.'

Things then went from bad to worse. In the five-day break between rounds one and two, Josh crashed during a practice session and broke his collarbone. Metal pins were inserted into the shoulder, but he would be out of action for at least three weeks.

While Josh was dealing with his injury problems, things were even worse for fellow Kiwis Craig Brown and Mike Cotter, also in Europe to take a crack at the GP scene. Brown, originally from Morrinsville, crashed while practising on his Honda, badly breaking his left arm. He landed awkwardly from a jump and was spat off the bike, breaking the same arm he'd broken in Europe the season before. Forced to spend three days in hospital, he decided after consulting medical staff not to race again that season. Cambridge man Cotter had finished fourth in the New Zealand championships just prior to arriving in Europe, but despite his speed and status on the domestic scene, he was unable to qualify at GP level, at least for those early events.

The broken collarbone put a significant dent in Josh's campaign, and he was unable to return until round five, the Italian GP, where he qualified a creditable 11th in his group. The comeback was short-lived as his racing took another painful turn. 'I had a bad start in the first race, and was pushing hard to get through the traffic when I crashed again and landed on my sore shoulder. The collarbone break area was fine, but it pushed the pin in my shoulder deeper into the bone.' Despite the intense pain, he managed to finish 16th out of the 40 starters in the next race, but still had no points to show for his efforts.

Finally, at round ten in the Italian GP at San Marino, Josh broke the drought and scored his first world championship points of the year. 'The track was absolutely rock hard and it was nearly cancelled when it rained. It was like riding on ice,' Josh says. He finished 12th in the GP's second race and locked away his first points of the year.

A week later, in the first week of August, at the French GP at Iffendic, Josh went even better. He finished a career-best ninth in the day's second race, one spot behind the then world series leader, Belgian Marnicq Bervoets, the full factory Suzuki rider with whom Josh shared the pits. When Bervoets was later disqualified for receiving outside assistance from spectators to get back on the track after a crash, Josh was promoted to eighth.

Now with 12 points to his credit, Josh found himself elevated from obscurity to 25th overall in the championship standings, equal on points with well-known American Honda rider Bader Manneh. By season's end, Everts was world champion again, following a protest-riddled battle with Bervoets, and Josh had moved up from 41st to 23rd place in the world standings.

While injury had forced him out of three GPs and he'd opted to skip the Brazilian GP (round nine) because of the expense of travelling there, he had scored a total of 17 points from three of the 13 events (rounds ten, 11 and 12) and there was something to celebrate. His points came from a 12th in the second race at San Marino (worth four points); a ninth (later elevated to eighth after Bervoets was disqualified) in the second race in France (worth eight points); and an 11th in the second race at the Belgian GP at Kester (worth five points).

At several big, cash, non-championship events that year, Josh also impressed by beating fellow Kiwis Darryll and Shayne King, the Kiwi number one and number two riders at that time, who were focusing their careers on the separate 500cc class. Fewer than 50 riders from 15 different countries scored world championship points in the premier 250cc class that season, and Josh was one of only four riders not from the motocross stronghold of Europe or the United States. He also finished as the year's fourth-best Suzuki rider on the table.

With a solid season under his belt, Josh now looked ahead to the 1997 season. He would still be leasing the factory bikes that had been used the previous season, but he'd have a new right-hand man to help him.

Oamaru's Blair Selfe replaced Glenn Woodman as Josh's mechanic in Europe when Glenn moved on to work for Joel Smets at the KTM factory. Selfe stayed with Josh for the following five years and throughout that time they formed a close bond, Selfe remaining as Josh's mechanic even when Josh was finally welcomed into the Suzuki factory stable as a full works rider in 2000.

Josh still returned home at the end of each season to spend a short time on a working holiday, racing New Zealand events over the summer and making the most of the pleasant riding conditions while much of Europe was under ice and snow. Whilst there, he would come up against the King brothers — Darryll, Shayne and now Damien — and he enjoyed the battles he had with these riders, also home from their GP expeditions. Josh didn't often cross paths with the King brothers, as they were racing a different division in Europe, campaigning in the 500cc class. 'The best help I got from the King brothers was to race against them,' Josh says. 'They were at the top of the 500cc class at the time in Europe, but I'd mostly beat them in New Zealand, which gave me confidence when it was time to go back to Europe.

'Those first few years in Europe — 1995, 1996 and 1997 — I just didn't do well and didn't really excel because, financially, they were really tough years. I had some sponsorship from Talley's Fisheries and a few small companies, and Suzuki New Zealand helped a lot, but it was mostly my dad who paid the bills. Financially it was very hard because it cost about $100,000 to lease the previous year's factory bikes direct from the factory stable. We looked hard at it — there were so many different ways that we could do it.'

At that time there were really no overseas riders from outside Europe being offered a place in a factory team — even Shayne and Darryll King were on small privateer 500cc teams rather than official factory teams. 'For me to go over there, I had only a few choices. I could try to rent facilities and buy bikes and parts, but I didn't know where to start. I didn't know where to obtain all of that. We sat down and did all the numbers, and to do it properly and race for the year, if I had to pay retail for everything, it was going to cost me the same amount of money anyway. By doing it the way we did, we were able to get ex-factory parts and to ride with the best riders, like Marnicq [Bervoets] and Werner [de Wit], which really helped me. But, in hindsight, it was really tough.'

With that sort of figure hanging over his head, Josh felt the pressure on him. At the back of his mind was the constant fear that he would disappoint or fail his father, his sponsors and all those others who had sacrificed so much to get him there. Should he take risks to achieve a result and risk wrecking the bike that had cost so much? Should he risk injury, and put himself in the impossible position of not being able to ride at all? Could he afford to race conservatively? Surely he'd never succeed with that attitude. These were the thoughts that went through his mind every time he lined up to race.

'The real problem for me was that I had nobody to guide me at a time in my career when I most needed a mentor. If I'd had someone like Murray Thorn there to take care of everything and take the burden off me, I could have concentrated on my riding. But because I had so much going on around me and I was so worried about general everyday details, I never really excelled as a rider for those three years. Until I matured enough to withstand that burden, I was like a V8 stuck in the mud and going nowhere. They were pretty tough years. I had a lot of help from Murray Thorn, who did what he could from New Zealand, but it wasn't the same.'

By 1996 Josh had been racing in Europe for three years and began to doubt that he was doing the right thing. 'I was starting to ask myself if this was really going to work. By that stage I had been over there for three years and was pretty much on my own. But it wasn't that so much — it was more that I was a shy guy, which didn't help. I'm not that outgoing, which made it quite hard to go out and meet people.'

Fortunately, Josh had some experienced team-mates in Bervoets and de Wit to learn from, even if it meant learning some lessons the hard way. 'I wasn't on the big money, and Werner de Wit was the factory rider. We were heading off to a race in the south of France; both my mechanic and his mechanic had already left to go and get everything set up early. Werner picked me up in his new Mercedes and was driving us to the airport. I couldn't help looking at my watch and thinking we were going to be late. He was just cruising along with no apparent urgency. We finally got to the airport check-in and our flight was closed. I was desperate to get down there — it wasn't a GP race, just an international race with good prize money, and I needed the money.

'Werner was quite happy just to turn around and go back home, but I wanted to get another flight. We managed to book another flight, but I had to sleep on a chair at the Paris airport and listen out for a connection to Toulouse. Werner could have come too, but he told me to tell Renee [their race manager] that he couldn't get on the flight. So I went off on my own and he drove home. Werner didn't really need the money at that time, but a few years later, the roles were reversed. Werner was still part of the Suzuki team, but he'd been injured a few times and wasn't riding any more. Sylvain was kind enough to give him a job at the factory headquarters. It's funny how things turned around.'

Like soldiers in wartime, there is often a 'brothers in arms' relationship that grows between motocross team-mates. Though they are rivals on the track and fighting one another for GP points, they also live in close proximity, share the team's trials and tribulations, and suffer the same stresses and strains.

Josh's friendship with Belgian rider Marnicq Bervoets, who shared the same Suzuki awning between 1995 and 1998, was one that gained strength with every season. A smile creeps across Josh's face when the name Marnicq Bervoets comes into the conversation, the friendship between the two conjuring up some warm memories. 'I'm still good friends with Marnicq,' Josh says. 'I see him riding a lot sometimes and we still cycle together. He is a very quiet guy, and while I used to kid around and do things like hide his car, he never played a trick on me. He really struggles to get out of bed in the mornings. I used to drive to his house and train with him, otherwise he just wouldn't get up. He's a strong guy though, and he was really fit.

'He now races the amateur league in Belgium. I saw him training a while ago and I told him I was coming to watch. He said I needn't bother because he's shit now and there is nothing to see. We laughed, but he's a cool guy — he never changes.'

Life as a GP battler offered plenty of ups and downs, with one particular incident standing out. 'In 1996, I was at a French international south of Paris with Glenn Woodman. As we were driving the truck through Paris, the compressor broke. We kept going as it is hard to stop in the middle of Paris, but the brakes started to come on and smell as we ran out of air. We slept at the gas station and had a mechanic look at it the next day.'

After $1500 and a whole day, the mechanic still couldn't fix it and Josh was out of money, with his credit card maxed out. 'A friendly Belgian guy who was interested in motocross suggested we wind in some bolts on the brakes and it would release them. One of my Belgian sponsors was an ice-cream company, and they had Mercedes trucks and a workshop. They said they would fix the truck for free, so we drove it home with no brakes at all — and I mean none. At the toll booths, I'd jump out and run ahead, pay and get them to put the barrier up. If we had to stop, we would stall the engine and dump the clutch. Once the traffic thinned, we drove all the way home. We were only able to touch the brakes lightly about three times, all the way from Paris to Hulsen. We were going pretty slow. We left at midnight and drove until 4.00 a.m., so there wasn't much traffic. It was scary, but I had no choice.'

In 1997 Josh began to spread his wings and feel more confident about where his career was going. At Nismes for a round of the Belgian championships he found himself racing alongside Frédéric Bolley, the Frenchman who became 250cc world champion in 1999 and 2000. 'In those days, Stefan Everts [the then three-times 250cc world champion] used to cruise around in the Belgian championships and I would race with him. That was when I started to believe in myself. I've always been learning a little at a time — physically, mentally, and knowing what to do with the bike. I worked hard on all those things, and I learnt about the importance of training.'

But it wasn't until Josh's fourth year in Europe in 1998 — as a privateer Suzuki rider — that things really started to happen for the young Kiwi. It turned out to be his breakthrough year as he began to finish in the top ten on the GP circuit, and Suzuki began providing more support, this time for free. 'As soon as that financial burden was off my shoulders, I was able to excel as a rider because I didn't have to worry so much about the day-to-day things. Also, by that time, I was a much more mature rider, which helped.'

Josh's boss, the manager of the factory Suzuki team, was Sylvain Geboers, a former GP star in his own right and the elder statesman of a family that stands above all others in the sport of motocross. Not much has happened in motocross over the past 30 years without the five Geboers brothers being at the forefront.

While all the Geboers siblings have been heavily engaged in the sport, only Sylvain, who is the eldest brother, and Eric, 19 years his junior, have remained involved in the new millennium. Eric Geboers was the sport's original 'Mister 875', the first man to claim world motocross titles in the three capacity classes, 125cc, 250cc and 500cc. He achieved that status when he wrapped up the first of his two 500cc titles in 1988. It would be 13 years before anyone else could match him, with Stefan Everts claiming the 'Mister 875' name tag in 2001.

The Geboers family name is interwoven with the rich tapestry of the sport in Europe, and fans who followed the sport through the 1980s will smile at a mention of names like Lackey, Carlqvist, Thorpe, Jobe, Malherbe . . . and Geboers. When Kiwis such as Ivan Miller, Bryan Patterson and Craig Coleman headed to Europe, or Australians Jeff Leisk and Craig Dack made the trip, hundreds of young Kiwis waited with interest for news to filter back about how the men from Down Under had fared against the sport's living legends. Geboers was one of those legends.

Leisk, the freckle-faced teenager who ran away with the New Zealand 500cc title in 1983 (ahead of Rotorua's Patterston), was the Honda team-mate of Dave Thorpe and Eric Geboers when he finished world vice-champion in 1989 (Leisk finishing behind Thorpe but ahead of Geboers). It could well have been that achievement by Leisk — seen racing at Pukekohe, Paraparaumu and Christchurch just six years earlier — that lit the wick for the young men in Australia and New Zealand, when Leisk showed the Anzacs they could succeed on the world stage.

It was just a few years later that the Kiwi King brothers, Josh Coppins and Ben Townley would arrive in Europe and give their hosts a bit of a shake-up. While Shayne King won the 500cc world title in 1996, just three years after arriving in Europe, the 1980s belonged to Eric Geboers and his European rivals.

The small-framed Geboers, dubbed 'The Kid' by many of his followers, won the 125cc title in 1982 and '83, the 250cc title in 1987, and the 500cc crown twice, in 1988 and '90. Stefan Everts was 125cc champion in 1991, 250cc champion for three consecutive years, in 1995, '96 and '97, and, after two seasons spoiled by injury, finally put that behind him with his 500cc class victory in 2001.

It is worth noting that, in the early 1980s, Geboers' chief rival was none other than Everts' father, Harry, himself a motocross icon with four world titles (250cc in 1975 and 125cc in 1979, '80 and '81) to his credit.

Now that the sport is restricted to just MX2 and MX1, that 'Mister 875' title is no longer an option for today's stars. But, whether it was winning races, collecting world titles, organising factory GP teams, staging world championship meetings, or building world-beating bikes, there was no one to better the Geboers brothers of Belgium.

Sylvain Geboers can be credited as the first man in the GP paddock to recognise the spark of talent in Josh Coppins, who then fanned it over the following years until the Kiwi battler became a burning star in his own right.

'Every talent is welcome in my team,' Geboers says. 'It is not about nationality. We were very pleased when we had Josh Coppins in our team, and pleased to see Ben Townley come over here to Europe. We understand how difficult it is for these guys to come so far and leave everything behind them and start a new life over here. We see young talent in Belgium, but they have been treated differently. The New Zealand guys who come here work much harder than our European stars, who have it all so easy. I think Kiwis are winners.'

It was a huge risk on Geboers' part to bring Josh under his wing. With a limited budget and very few sponsorship spin-offs from hiring a non-European rider, Josh was a long-shot bet for the Suzuki team boss. While Geboers owned the team, he had no official status within the Suzuki company. 'It is an independently owned Suzuki team,' he explains. 'We have contact with the factory of course, and it comes from a long relationship I have with Suzuki, first as a rider, then mechanic and now manager. The team is run under my terms and conditions, but accepted by the factory. Everything has to be approved by Suzuki.

'I have been very passionately involved with Suzuki from my very first visit to Japan. I was tainted yellow from an early stage. I was so impressed by the way they support motocross and by their technology. From year to year I am always looking forwards to the new technology they bring to the races. They are always striving to improve and develop.'

Sylvain Geboers has a passion for everything concerning motocross, most critically with its structure and future direction. With such a long involvement in the sport, he has witnessed a lot of changes — not all of which he agrees with. He sees much that is right with the sport, but also a few areas he'd like to change. 'We must work hard to keep motocross where it is. We should try to improve, because all other sports are competing for attention these days. When I was a young motocross rider in Belgium we had soccer, we had cycling and we had motocross. That was all. And now, people can follow so many kinds of sports every weekend — that's the big difference from my day.'

His advice to the FIM is to sit down with all the organisers and managers in the sport and try to find a way to finance a world championship that includes more than just Europe. 'We should also have rounds going in Asia and Africa, the United States, New Zealand and Australia — everywhere. After all, it's supposed to be a world championship.' He concedes that, despite New Zealand and Australia having so many good riders, the world championships are staged a long way from home for these individuals, and despite what Josh Coppins and Ben Townley have achieved, the sport might be seen by young Kiwis as 'mission impossible'.

Geboers disagrees with many of his colleagues who believe motocross is a European sport. 'We cannot deny the rest of the world outside Europe the chance to compete and host such events. There must be a way to spread the costs equally among all the host venues, so that Australia and New Zealand promoters do not have to pay any more than their counterparts in Europe. A race in Japan, or a race in Belgium, or a race in South America, or wherever, should not cost differently for the organisers.'

In recent years, travel has become less of an issue, with teams travelling the globe in search of better climates and surfaces during the pre-season testing when northern Europe is snow- and ice-bound. While

Geboers thinks Europe will always remain the centre of the sport, that doesn't mean the world championships should stay in Europe. 'We must travel so that the sport can be seen and so that the manufacturers can sell more motorcycles worldwide.'

Josh showed his gratitude for Geboers' support with hard work and a Kiwi can-do attitude, knowing he was extremely lucky to be on the fringes of the factory team. The 1999 season was a turning point for Josh, and the decision to branch out and form his own privateer team, with Dutchman Leon Giesbers and Danish rider Brian Jorgensen as team-mates, was a bold move. He still raced a Suzuki RM250 two-stroke but was now receiving a small income from the Suzuki factory.

'The 1999 season was awesome because I was a privateer. I ran my own team, I made good money and it was all my own doing. It was exciting. Here I was, a young guy, beating the best Suzuki guys who were all on factory equipment, and I was using the previous year's stuff. I had my first podium finish, which made it an awesome year for me. My mechanic at the time was [fellow Kiwi] Blair Selfe; his wife travelled with us, and we all got on together really well.'

Geboers was impressed. Here was a rider from a lesser team, using his second-hand parts to beat the best riders on the Suzuki team, and who ended the year as the top Suzuki finisher. While some might have thought Geboers erred in not taking Josh into the team a year earlier, the Kiwi himself is pragmatic about the decision. 'To be fair to Sylvain, there's a huge leap between 13th and seventh position. I never expected to get a factory ride in 1999. I was happy with what I was doing and to be making some money for once.'

Josh's performance in 1999 set a few tongues wagging, and the powers-that-be at Suzuki began to consider looking a little more seriously at the young man from New Zealand. Josh was pumped and primed for 2000, and ready to accept the factory offer when it came.

2000: Simply awesome

IT MUST HAVE been Josh's favourite word, because he said 'awesome' a great deal throughout the 2000 season, despite there being an unpleasant sting in the tail. 'Yes, it was an awesome year for me — my first full factory year. I finally sold the Mercedes camper and bought my own car; I even bought a place to live [in Balen, Belgium]. The Suzuki factory team paid for Blair [Josh's mechanic] and provided someone to drive to the events and do the cleaning and fetching. At last there was enough money to buy groceries.

'It was also the last time I was able to return to New Zealand and ride at the Woodville motocross and do the New Zealand supercross championships before heading offshore again. Being my first year as a factory rider, it was my first big contract, and it seemed huge to me at the time.' He was also finally able to recoup some losses, with his first year as a factory rider basically repaying him what it had cost to lease the bikes for the two previous years. 'After 2000, I broke even with the cost of my career in Europe, paying for all the years leading up to it.'

Josh had also made good money in 1999 by organising his own clothing sponsors. As the third rider in the team he was allowed to do this, unlike his team-mates, Dutchman Leon Giesbers and Danish rider Brian Jorgensen, who had to wear the team's sponsored apparel. For Josh it was like having his cake and eating it too. He could ride some of the best machinery, be paid a salary by Suzuki, and negotiate his own contracts for 'contingency' items like helmets and apparel, boots and gloves — an exclusive, separate deal where he kept the money from whatever terms he arrived at with the accessory companies.

It was all looking good, but once the season got underway in March, things didn't go quite to plan. Josh finished fifth in the opening moto (race) at round one in Talavera, Spain, but crashed out of the points and came home 16th in the second leg, leaving him a disappointed 12th overall. 'I had a better start in the second race — maybe fifth or sixth position, which I was reasonably happy with. It gave me something to work on. Then I made a small mistake and crashed. The bike was bent and things were hanging off it. I thought it was rideable, but it was scary over the jumps,' Josh says.

He bounced back with fifth and sixth placings at round two in Portugal a week later, and was elevated to seventh in the standings, equal to the world ranking digit on the number boards of his bike. 'I got good drive off the start of the first race in Portugal; I was up there at the corner, but then world champion Fred Bolley forced me wide and several guys came under me to put me about seventh,' he says. 'I was completely alone in fifth place but I was focusing on Michael Maschio in front. At first I was up with him, then I lost my rhythm and he pulled away, so I just couldn't close the gap. It's a very difficult track to ride so I was happy with my position.'

Josh had a battle on his hands during the opening laps of the second moto, sandwiched between several riders. 'I got the drop out of the start, but got held up on the opening lap. I kept going, but I was riding very tense. I lost fourth position to British rider Paul Cooper, who was right with me, and then in the closing laps I made another mistake, drifted off the track and picked up marker tape in my rear brake. I eventually slipped back to sixth, but was glad to be coming away with good points.'

After two rounds, the New Zealand champion was 38 points behind the series leader, Mickael Pichon, his new factory Suzuki team-mate. Frenchman Pichon had joined Josh in the factory Suzuki squad near the end of the 1999 season, a late call-up to bolster the Suzuki assault after Josh's original team-mates, Giesbers and Jorgensen, had failed to impress. Right from the start Pichon proved far more worthy, finishing on the podium throughout the first half of the season. He also bagged a couple of third placings in Spain and two convincing wins in Portugal, and was looking like a real contender for the world title.

At round three in the Netherlands, the Dutch GP at Valkenswaard — which was also the first of the new triple-headers being given a trial that season — Josh was starting to fire. He took his Suzuki RM250 to seventh and fifth in the two races, lifting himself another placing to sixth in the series standings. 'I was happy with my ride at Valkenswaard,' Josh says. 'Sand is not my speciality, but I had two consistent rides, and I'd moved up in the championship after my mistake in Spain, so I was happy to come away with good points again.'

In the first race, Josh ran off the track while trying to put seventh-placed British rider Justin Morris, riding a Yamaha, under pressure. 'I knew I could pressure him into a mistake, but he didn't want to give his position up so easily. I ran wide and went through the plastic marker tape. I was getting a little frustrated being stuck behind him. I was lucky the tape didn't get in the rear brake and cause it to fade,' he says. 'I tried a few aggressive moves, but he held on, and then I made a pass stick and managed to get away from him and focus on Yves Demaria, the French Yamaha rider, who was in front of me. Yves was looking tired. I could see by his riding that he was desperately hanging on.' Josh tried several times to get by Demaria, but ran out of time and finished in seventh place, just behind him.

Race two at the Dutch GP saw yet another good start from Josh. After a battle with defending champion Bolley on the opening lap, he settled into sixth spot, but soon wore down Dutch Kawasaki rider Remy van Rees with 15 minutes to go. 'I had a small problem with my arms, which caused me to fade towards the end of the race,' he says. 'Claudio

Federici, the Italian Yamaha rider, caught and passed me, which I was disappointed about, but still, fifth was a good result. During the off-season, I had worked too much on strengthening my arms and not enough on endurance. I was paying for that.'

Josh had scored top-ten finishes in five of the season's first six races, which included three GP events, and was only two points behind the rider who was fifth in the standings, Irishman Gordon Crockard, who was riding for the CAS Honda team. Pichon was the man to beat during this early part of the season. The 24-year-old from Ruille-en-Champagne had a world ranking of 15th, despite contesting only the five final GPs in 1999, but after the first three GPs of 2000, Pichon was holding the number one position.

Pichon stamped his authority on the season by finishing third and first at the Dutch GP, putting himself 33 points ahead of Bolley and 34 points ahead of German Pit Beirer (riding for Winfield Kawasaki). At this early stage, Josh was 53 points adrift of Pichon. He worked solidly through the middle stages of the championship and pocketed good points by scoring consistent third, fourth and fifth placings. With two-thirds of the season complete, Josh was up to fourth overall in the points standings and closing in on Beirer.

Round 12 of the series in Grobbendonk, Belgium, was to be a fateful GP for several riders that season. It could be said the world title was decided at Grobbendonk as series leader Pichon won the first race, but crashed hard in the day's second race and sustained a shoulder injury, something which was to seriously hamper his progress. The crash also caused Pichon a few off-track problems when his father became involved in a heated scuffle with paramedics, putting his son in danger of disqualification. Only days later, though still in pain, Pichon decided to continue his campaign at the next GP, in Namur, but slipped down the field, losing his grip on the championship lead.

Josh finished second in both races at Grobbendonk, although it was only good enough for the second step on the podium as Crockard finished third and first, and took the top spot as the champagne corks popped on the dais. Even so, it was a high point in Josh's career and added enough points to the Kiwi's season tally to push him up to just seven points behind Beirer.

Two GPs later and Josh had leapt past Beirer, thanks to the German having a miserable time at the Luxembourg GP at Folkendange where he finished an unaccustomed 12th in the first race and then recorded a rare zero in the next outing. With just two GPs remaining, it would come down to the wire between Josh and Beirer as to who would take the number three spot in 2000.

Roggenburg, Switzerland, was the site of the final GP of the season, and Josh went there with a handy nine-point margin over Beirer. With Pichon already settling for second place and missing the final round to undergo a shoulder operation, all eyes in the Suzuki camp were on Josh.

The track, however, was dreadful. Rain had lashed down prior to the event, and during the Saturday qualifier Josh crashed at high speed in the extremely muddy conditions, leaving him with heavy bruising to his neck and chest. The bad luck continued in the first race on Sunday when Josh was taken down in the first turn. 'I lost a whole load of places and had to fight hard to get back into contention. I managed to get back up to tenth by the end of the opening lap, and as the track dried out I managed to pull up to seventh. The track was hard to pass on, with a single race line and, although I managed to get by American Ryan Hughes, I slipped up and he passed me to leave me with seventh place at the flag.'

Heavy rain fell again in the break before the second race, and the track was badly cut up from the 500 GP race, but Josh again managed a good start and was in sixth place when he was again taken down in a multi-rider pile-up. 'I had to remove my right glove because it was covered in mud and very slippery. I got going again, but my goggles got filled in and I had to throw them away. After that I was practically riding blind and just kept on crashing. In the end, the bike got completely bogged and filled in, and I knew the game was up.' He didn't finish the second race, but while he felt frustrated at the weekend's events, he still ended up with number four on his Suzuki for the following year, an improvement on the number seven with which he had started the year, while Bolley benefited from Pichon's late-season demise to retain the 250cc world title.

'Despite that sting in the tail at the end of the season — when I had to settle for fourth instead of third — 2000 was a satisfying year,' Josh says. 'It was a frustrating way to finish the year. I had qualified second [at the season-ending GP] which was awesome, but I thought I could have qualified fastest, pushed myself and just rode over my head a bit. It was a sign of immaturity really.'

From that season onward, Josh would become a much more important ingredient in the factory Suzuki campaign, although, looking back on those days, he recalls it was still a difficult time. He can now see how much of the problem came from his own shyness and lack of experience, but at the time he didn't enjoy riding for Sylvain Geboers, finding him hard to talk to; it left him with the impression that Geboers didn't care too much about his riders.

'Sylvain himself was a great racer and a smart businessman, but I always felt he could have helped me more in my early days. His lack of warmth made me think he didn't believe in me. I was shy and this didn't help my cause . . . it's only now, years later, that I realise what a top bloke he really is. I admire his team and work ethic. He's from a different generation, and I think he struggles to gel with the new generation. But, in a way, I feel he changed when I left the team. I think he realised he had made some mistakes and could have done more.

'I guess a lot of the problem came from my side, for all the hard times I went through financially while I rode for him. But now, looking back on it, it made me who I am today. I'm about to line up against his top riders and I know I'm more of a fighter than his boys because of the hard times I went through in those early days.'

2001: Seeing red

WITH A WORLD ranking of number four to start the 2001 season, Josh Coppins believed he was now truly ready to successfully challenge for the world crown. Unfortunately, it was to be another year of frustration. In addition to being one of the world's top five riders and one of the 'target' men for talented young riders on their way up, Josh also had to adapt to a range of fresh demands.

It was his second year on the Corona Suzuki factory team and, as one of just a handful of full factory stars on the circuit, he knew he must perform or lose his highly paid job. Once again he found himself sharing space under the yellow and blue awning with Frenchman Mickael Pichon.

The racing itself had a whole new look for 2001, with the two-race format gone. Instead, each GP would consist of just one 45-minute race. The points calculation was different too, the race winner scoring 25 points instead of 20 and the runner-up taking 20, followed by 17, 15, 13, 11, 10, 9, 8 and so forth, down to one point for a 15th placing. The attention of the media, spectators and sponsors was now split, with each of the 14 GPs being triple-header affairs for the first time, and the pit paddock shared with the 500cc and 125cc GP stars.

Josh thought he was up to the task. 'I really thought the number one spot was where I was heading. It was certainly where I was aiming. I could no longer say that I would have been happy with settling for anything less — to be content with second or third would have been stupid.'

His career path to that stage had plotted a steady upward slope. As an 18-year-old, Josh had finished 41st on his world championship debut season in 1995 and steadily chipped away at the rankings for each year that followed. He was 23rd the next season, then 17th in 1997, 13th in 1998, seventh in 1999 and in 2001 he was the proud holder of the number four plate. 'It was very frustrating not to actually win a race in 2000, but really, that's not the most important thing. You can win the world title without winning a single race.' But with fewer than half as many races, that feat would now be doubly difficult to achieve. There were 14 GPs in 2001 and this meant only 14 races, instead of the 30 (two at each of the 15 GPs) raced the year before.

'That meant I had to make things happen — I had to put my neck out a little bit more. I couldn't bide my time and wait for an opportunity to present itself. I had to make the openings for myself, and if that meant getting physical and banging handlebars with the other riders, then so be it. The season was going to be just as long and tiring as it ever was, but now I couldn't afford even one dud race.'

He rated all his fellow top-ten riders as potential champions and threats to his own aspirations, but there was one man, above all others, that Josh really wanted to beat. While all the riders had to be respected, he desperately wanted to beat Pit Beirer, the German rider who had pinched the number three spot from him in the final stages of 2000. 'Beirer was an amazing rider. He had more heart than anyone in Europe. He was always riding on the very edge and looked likely to lose it at any moment. I was very surprised he didn't crash more often. When I was following him, I could usually see both side panels of his bike,' Josh says, his hands gesturing the violent side-to-side movement of Beirer's bike kicking left and right. The trick, Josh learnt, was not to line up next to him at the start gate.

'To tell the truth, when I first came to Europe, I never really thought that one day I would be in the position that I was at in 2001. I come from small-town New Zealand and looked up in awe to riders such as Beirer. Now I was right up there with guys like that.' Although now a glossy magazine pin-up boy in Europe, Josh was honest enough to admit his own strengths and weaknesses. 'I put a lot of time into my training but, if I did have one particular weakness at that time, it was that I was a slow starter. I simply wasn't going fast enough in the first ten minutes and the others got away from me. I'd take time to settle into a rhythm before I'd start charging.' That was a tactic that had to change — he couldn't afford to sit back and think of saving energy for the second race. This season there wasn't going to be a second race.

Another difference was that this year he had been assured that he and Pichon would be treated equally by the team, with the same equipment. Unlike the year before, he wouldn't be expected to pull over and let Pichon pass to take the points. In 2001 it would be every man for himself.

Instead it proved to be the year of lost opportunities. While he had expected his brilliant year in 2000 to roll over into 2001 and to reach a whole new level, the reality proved to be a bitter disappointment. In stark contrast, while Josh suffered a frustrating year, everything his team-mate touched seemed to turn to gold, and after the first three GPs, Pichon was unbeaten.

Round three that year was at Broadford, just outside Melbourne, and this presented an ideal opportunity for race fans from Josh's part of the world to take the short hop across the Tasman to see their hero in GP action. The battle that day between Josh and Australian rival Chad Reed, riding a Kawasaki, had the 32,000 crowd at Broadford screaming themselves hoarse, but it was also an omen of how the year would pan out for the Kiwi.

Pichon shot away at the start, with Josh close behind. As Reed entered the first turn, he hit a mud hole and almost sailed over the handlebars of his bike, popping out of the first turn in 25th position. But the partisan crowd was soon roaring in appreciation as the 19-year-old Reed progressively picked off rider after rider in a powerfully impressive surge through the field. By the second lap, Reed had moved up an incredible four places and passed one rider on each of the following three laps. By halfway through the race, Reed had powered to an astonishing eighth place and was now dicing with Beirer.

Josh, meanwhile, had had an excellent start, but within just a few laps, his bike mysteriously began misfiring. First Englishman Paul Cooper, then Irishman Gordon Crockard and reigning world champion Frenchman Frédéric Bolley had slipped past. Josh was going backwards. Before long, Reed was hounding Josh, and the crowd was going ballistic.

With the air horns of Australian fans blaring his progress, Reed passed Josh and disappeared off into the distance, then hunted down and passed Cooper, Briton Justin Morris and Belgian Danny Theybers. But while Josh may have been down, he wasn't out. Miraculously, his sputtering carburettor cleared, and the factory Suzuki man looked as if he'd been born again. Josh gritted his teeth and set off after Reed, finally hauling him in and nailing him with just three laps to go. For good measure, and a few more points, Josh also dealt to Theybers and finished fifth, less than two seconds behind Crockard.

The Coppins-Reed dust-up was the talking point of the race. In the end, Reed had made up 20 places to finish a tremendous race in sixth place, and he moved up from 12th to tenth place overall in the championship. 'There was one corner where I thought I could hear Coppins' bike. I worked it out that he was having problems,' Reed said afterwards. 'Then, when he caught me up again, I worried too much about him instead of just keeping my charge going. It's a bit of a shame. Once he got back beside me, I just tried to hang on to him. To hear everyone screaming and yahooing was just great.'

For Josh, the day brought mixed feelings. 'I was happy, but sad also. I got points, but should have had more. About the second lap, something started going wrong with the bike. It was running really rich. On the uphill I had no power and everyone was just driving past me — it was the electrics or fuel playing up. It was maybe like that for five laps and

Josh Coppins, aged four, on his first motorcycle, a Suzuki JR50.

A fresh-faced 16-year-old Josh Coppins, pictured in 1994, during his last season of domestic racing before heading to Europe for the first time.

Here's Josh (on bike number 77, Josh's birthday year), racing at his first 250cc GP, at Talavera in Spain, in March 1995.

Ted Coppins (left) and Glenn Bayly, busy at work on Josh's bike in a car park in Asti, Italy, in April 1995.

This was a good day for team Suzuki with the team finishing first and second at the Finnish GP in Helsinki in May 1995. The riders are (from left) Werner De Wit (runner-up), Marnicq Bervoets (GP winner) and then Kawasaki rider Stefan Everts (right), who took third on the podium. Everts had the last laugh, though, winning the title that season.

Factory Suzuki rider Werner De Wit shows his sense of humour with pants pulled up high, as he has a little fun in Reiserberg, Germany, in August 1995.

Injuries are all an occupational hazard for a top motocross rider. Josh returned home after surviving his debut season in Europe and then hurt himself racing at Taupo in October 1995.

Josh in full flight at the final round of the New Zealand Motocross Championships in Wanganui in March 1996. He finished the two-round series third overall in the 250cc class, behind brothers Darryll and Shayne King, then immediately headed straight back to Europe.

Josh Coppins with Glenn Woodman, his new mechanic for the 1996 season in Europe.

It's March 1997, the New Zealand Motocross Championships final round at Nelson, and Ted Coppins is on flag marshal duties.

It's the annual Woodville Motocross in 1998 and Josh Coppins (bike number 111) is caught in traffic as Palmerston North's former national champion Leon Andrew (bike 40) gets the jump at the start. Josh went on to win the Roddy Shirriffs Memorial Trophy at Woodville that day, the prize for the top rider aged under 21, while rival Shayne King (bike 01) won the main prize, the overall Woodville crown. Josh went on to win the national 125cc and 250cc titles six weeks later — giving Suzuki their first motocross title wins in New Zealand since 1989 — before he headed back to Belgium.

Josh Coppins (bike number 1) blasts from the start gate at the Woodville Motocross in 1999. Josh scored the double at Woodville that year, again winning the Roddy Shirriffs Memorial Trophy as well as winning the event outright.

Manawatu's Blair Meyer (Yamaha number 31) gets the jump on the field at a very muddy Woodville Motocross in 1999, leading Auckland's Nigel Smith (bike 27) and eventual winner Josh Coppins (bike 1).

Oamaru's Blair Selfe, Josh Coppins' mechanic and right-hand man throughout the years from 1997 until 2001.

Two men who would have a huge influence on the racing career of Josh Coppins, Murray Thorn (left) and Shayne King, deep in discussion at the New Zealand Motocross Championships round at Nelson in 1997.

The author's son, Connor McGechan (then aged six), enjoys a little one-on-one time with his hero, Josh Coppins, at the Woodville Motocross in 2001.

Victoria, Australia, in 2001 was the scene for round four of the 2001 Motocross World Championships and Josh Coppins was having all sorts of problems that day.

Mechanic Blair Selfe (left) assists his rider, Josh Coppins, by pointing out a few lines he's observed at the Australian Motocross GP in 2001.

The 2001 season was fraught with problems for Josh Coppins but he continued to smile for his fans.

Josh Coppins had a new mechanic to take care of his bike from 2002, Italian Fabio Santoni.

Josh Coppins (Honda number 5), flanked by fellow Kiwi Ben Townley (KTM number 30) and Belgian rider Marvin van Daele (Honda number 75), launches from the start gate at the Belgian GP at Namur in 2005.

It is wet and slippery under the wheels but Josh Coppins (Honda number 5) still finds plenty of traction as he races his old foe and former team-mate, Frenchman Mickael Pichon (Honda number 2), towards turn one at the Belgian GP at Namur in 2005.

It is a relaxed Josh Coppins in the CAS Honda enclave in the pits at the Belgian GP at Namur in 2005.

Against a spectacular backdrop of ancient Roman fortifications, Josh Coppins flies around the hill-top castle known as the Citadelle, at Namur, in 2005.

With the track set among the battlements of this fairytale-like castle, high above the city of Namur, the Belgian GP here is perhaps the most famous of all.

CAS Honda team boss Harry Ainsworth (left) chats with his number one rider, Josh Coppins, during a break between races at the Belgian GP in 2005.

Three amigos . . . these Kiwi buddies (from left), Josh Coppins, Ben Townley and mechanic Craig Behl, enjoy a little light-hearted horseplay at the Belgian GP in 2005.

Taupo's Ben Townley, Josh Coppins' best mate in Europe for several seasons until Townley left to chase fame and fortune in the United States at the end of the 2005 GP season.

Having a bit of fun during a photo shoot in Belgium, Josh Coppins was quite happy to pose with this child's bike.

Respected rivals Stefan Everts (left) and Josh Coppins share a few words just before the start at the Motocross of Nations in England in 2006. Everts went on to win both races and Coppins — with Kiwi team-mates Ben Townley and Cody Cooper — took the third step on the podium.

Josh Coppins attacks a berm during the 2006 Motocross of Nations in England. The three-rider New Zealand team finished on the podium behind the United States and Belgium.

Belgian motocross legend Stefan Everts surveys the scene at the Belgian GP at Namur in 2005. Everts won an incredible ten world titles before finally hanging up his helmet after the 2006 Motocross of Nations in England (where he was the top individual, helping his team to finish runner-up) and a brief tour of New Zealand in November that year.

The greatest name in GP motocross, Stefan Everts, who signed off his racing career at Taupo in 2006. However, he was beaten that day in the Taupo world championships by rival Josh Coppins.

Josh Coppins (Honda number 2) blasts through the sawdust section of the track at Taupo in 2006.

Josh Coppins gets it all wrong and his bike pitches him over the handlebars at Taupo in 2006. Josh picked up the bike and charged back through the field to finish third in this race, enough for him to beat Stefan Everts and win the day overall.

When ten-time world champion Stefan Everts showed up at Taupo in November 2006 for the last big ride of his career, New Zealand motocross fans responded by turning up in their droves. More than 10,000 Kiwis showed up at Taupo just to see Everts race . . . and to see Josh Coppins beat him.

Josh Coppins (bike number 6), in a drag race with Belgian Steve Ramon (bike 11) and American Mike Brown (bike 4) at the Bulgarian GP at Sevlievo in June 2007. Ramon would eventually win the world title when injury forced series leader Coppins to the sideline.

Josh Coppins grits his teeth as he rides through the pain of a broken shoulder at the British GP at Donington Park in August 2007.

With his shoulder shattered, Josh Coppins is barely able to ride at the British GP at Donington Park in August 2007. He withdraws after just a few laps and ultimately sees his MX1 world title hopes shrivel up.

I was trying to compensate on the downhills and the turns.

'Everyone has a problem at some stage through the year, so I have to say I was happy to score points. But I should have been second. If the bike hadn't broken, I'd have been second in the championship standings.'

In contrast, a trouble-free Pichon won the day and stretched his championship lead.

In August, similar wretched luck again cost Josh valuable points at round nine in the Belgian GP at Namur, a spectacular circuit that weaves around the stone battlements of the Citadelle de Namur, an ancient castle perched atop a steep rock overlooking the city. It was certainly not the sort of track you'd appreciate something like misfiring spark plugs, dirty fuel or a blocked carburettor. It was the third time in nine races that mechanical trouble left Josh struggling to stay with the leaders, and again he limped home in fifth place.

'It was the same problem as I had in Australia,' he says. 'The bike started cutting out on the very first lap — it just wouldn't pull cleanly.' There are some huge climbs around Namur, where the track comes up from the bottom of the citadel, and several times Josh thought he wasn't going to make it. 'Coming to the big downward jumps, I was terrified. If the thing had cut out as I launched, I was history.'

He survived, grateful to lock away a handful of points, but it was more frustration in a miserable campaign that he could see slipping from his grasp. To add insult to injury, Pichon again enjoyed a flawless run to notch up his seventh win in nine GPs that saw him open up a virtually unassailable lead in the 250cc world title chase, which he went on to wrap up two GPs later in Germany. The season simply sparkled for Pichon. He won easily at the German GP at Gaildorf and took the 250cc world title with three rounds still left to run.

Unlike 2000, the season simply didn't roll for Josh. 'I went from being the rider who was happy with everything to being the rider who now wanted everything. I was the number two rider in the team, and I was now standing up for myself and starting to demand things.'

While Pichon was regarded as the Suzuki team's number one man, even on a good day, Josh found Pichon a difficult character to get along with. Such was the abrasive nature of the Frenchman that people within the Suzuki enclosure were constantly walking on eggshells so as not to rile the Gallic star. On occasions he would refuse to speak to media who had arrangements to interview him and was widely regarded by journalists as a tough interview, with his manner completely at odds with the more relaxed and by now more socially adept Coppins.

'Pichon was the team's pretty boy and it just wasn't working for me. My relationship with my girlfriend at the time wasn't going so well — it was a year where nothing really went right. Even though I finished sixth, it was very disappointing. I had a lot of mechanical problems in 2001, electrical problems at Broadford [the Australian GP], Namur [one of three Belgian GPs that season] and Teutschenthal [one of two German GPs] and, in the year of the one-race-per-GP system, that was fatal for my campaign.'

With only 14 races that season, a bad run meant that the chances of Josh taking a top ranking were slight. A rider couldn't afford to have a single DNF ('did not finish' the race), but Josh had three. The 2001 season was also the year Josh was joined in Europe by another Kiwi keen to do well on the international stage, a young man from Taupo who in November 2000 finished runner-up in the New Zealand 125cc championships.

Ben Townley was only 16 years old when he made the big career decision to head to Europe, a risky move for a teenager who had only just finished his fifth-form year at high school and had never been away from home.

But Ben was different from most Kiwi teens, and within no time at all he had formed an unbreakable bond with Josh, a man more than seven years his senior. It was a partnership made in heaven, the two New Zealanders bouncing off one another, sharing the tough moments and learning from one another as they both strived to achieve greatness on the far side of the globe.

It was tough in the beginning, with the two riders chasing titles in different categories, and although they were soon sharing accommodation in Belgium, they often headed in different directions as Ben chased 125cc class glory and Josh pursued honours in the premier 250cc class.

While his results weren't what he wanted in 2001, Josh was quick to explain he attached no blame to the Suzuki team. It is exactly this attitude — Josh's determination not to burn any bridges — that sees the Kiwi still command respect and enjoy a friendship with his former Suzuki boss. 'Suzuki is a class outfit,' he explains. 'It has to be — it won the world championship the year I left them. I have no hard feelings from my Suzuki days, and nothing but respect for the product.

'While I had a few disappointments that year, I knew that the lead rider of the team [Pichon] was always going to get the best support — and that's normal, but it was a bit difficult for me to accept. In saying that though, I can understand it from the team management's point of view. If you compare the two of us I'm much more relaxed about things — I'm a Kiwi — and can take care of myself.

'I'd been on target for a good season in 2001, with a podium at the second round, and I went to Australia to win and stamp my authority on the championship.' But after the problems in Australia, it proved to be a roller-coaster season of ups and down, as Josh began to feel distant from the team and frustrated at the points he was losing. 'In the last three GPs I started making stupid mistakes, and by that time I didn't even want to be at the start line. For the first time in my life I was finding it really hard to get motivated. Of course I had some bad races where I got taken down in the start, but that's racing. I honestly feel I was well prepared and there to do a good job, until three GPs from the end, when my heart was broken and I'd had enough.'

Even through this stressful time, Josh still found time to help Ben Townley who was still feeling his way into the GP culture with a fledgling privateer Suzuki team, Phase Suzuki. Townley, who just four seasons later — in 2004 — became a factory rider for the Austrian KTM factory and won the MX2 world championship, is quick to recognise Josh's contribution. 'Josh is a great person,' Townley says. 'I know we never, ever had an argument during the time I shared a house with him. He is so easy going — he'd do anything for me. He was like a big brother for me while I was in Europe. He never babied me, but he was always there to make sure things would be going right. I appreciate all that he did for me. He's been in Belgium now for so long and he's got a great following over there.'

When Townley first went to Europe in 2001, it was to ride an RM125 for the German-funded satellite Suzuki team, while Josh was one of the 'glamour' boys in an elite team, riding the 250cc championships for the Suzuki factory. From his privileged position, Josh did all he could to help his young mate, something Townley says he will always appreciate. Even when Townley graduated to the elite factory ranks with a rival bike brand, Josh still supported his mate. 'There were a lot of situations where he and I were the only ones who could talk about stuff. Obviously it was an amazing relationship. We were flat-mates and friends off the track, but rivals on it [when Townley jumped to the MX1 class in 2005]. He was always there to talk to or bounce ideas off.'

Townley agrees that it was pretty special. 'The only thing I think I helped him with was learning to ride a trials bike properly, or ride BMX. It was just a great relationship, and we definitely have some good stories to tell.

'Josh has maybe only a few more years left in Europe. The way the scene is in Australia now there's a good chance for him to go back to that part of the world and race from home. You can't ask for much more than that — to be out riding motorcycles and be paid to do it, and live at home. I think he'll probably be looking to do that, just like the King brothers and Daryl Hurley are doing now.'

Josh also has kind words for his mate Townley. 'Ben is a little bit special. He came in and just blasted his way to a title in his first few seasons. I don't have the same freakish natural ability that Ben has. My success has been down to hard work.'

Aside from season-ending glory at the Motocross des Nations in Namur, Belgium, where Josh led the New Zealand team to third place on the podium, the 2001 world championship season had been a frustrating one, and eventually the 24-year-old saw red. For the first time since he had embarked upon a GP career in Europe in 1995, he had failed to improve on his ranking, slipping instead from number four to number six, and he made the shock announcement in November 2001 that he was leaving Suzuki. He would now ride for Berni Honda Racing of Italy, a fully factory-backed Honda team, with the bikes supplied by Honda Europe.

'Sylvain was angry when I told him I was leaving, but my manager told him of my decision to leave at the Swiss GP, to give him time to look for another rider,' Josh says. 'Suzuki New Zealand wished me well. It was so hard for me to tell them I was leaving the company. They are great people, who are trying to help the sport in New Zealand. It was a very tough decision for me, but the way I was feeling, I knew I was going to move — I think I'd really made up my mind by the season's halfway point.'

Disagreements between Josh and the team were the catalyst for change. 'I thought the problem with my Suzuki in Broadford and at Namur was electrical, while the team thought I had water in my kill-switch that shorted out the system, until it dried out and then the bike would start running well. But, on both occasions, it was only after 20 minutes and the bike never stopped completely — it was like it was starved of fuel.' In Germany and Lierop he used a factory gear selector, which was longer than standard and therefore gave a smoother gear change, but its teeth broke off on lap one while Josh was taking the holeshot. 'I continued with no second gear, and had trouble shifting gear until four laps from the end, when the cases broke due to the gear selector teeth breaking off and grinding up.'

Josh's mechanic had the same access to parts as Pichon's, but their bikes were not the same, although close. 'Pichon had his training bike set up the same as his race bike, but I didn't and it was frustrating for me to do all my training on a different set-up to the one on which I'd race. Often Blair was left to do everything on his own, because the rest of the team were busy working on Pichon's bikes.'

At the end of 2001, Blair Selfe returned to New Zealand after a long and happy partnership with Josh. Although Josh said it was sad to see his old mate go, he was at the stage where he was ready to make a change himself and step up in his career. He believed Vismara Honda was the team to help him do it. It was as the 2001 season wound down that Josh also met the man who would become his new right-hand man, Italian mechanic Fabio Santoni, who would be behind the scenes of his career from that point onwards.

'In 2001, just before the Swiss GP, I went down to the Vismara workshop in Bologna in Italy. There were four riders in the team at that time and I think Alessio Chiodi [the Italian three-time 125cc world champion] was in the team. I saw Chiodi's mechanic and got chatting with him — it was Fabio Santoni — and straight away I knew I wanted him. He was very passionate about what he was doing. He worked very hard and gave off good vibes.

'I asked him about bikes and what would he do with a new bike — when they are new, for instance, the frames are very stiff and some riders don't like them. He told me that, with Chiodi's bike, he'd put the new frame in the practice bike and let him practise on that for a few days until it became more flexible, and then take that frame out and put it into the race bike. You're talking about the mechanic having to do an extra day's work — and some mechanics would wave you away and tell you just to use the new frame — but Fabio wanted the best for his rider. He was happy to go the extra mile. That was what I wanted.'

2002: Busted

A CHANGE OF team and bike brand brought a bright, fresh new outlook for Josh. 'That 2002 season was a fantastic one for me,' he recalls. 'I was quite nervous because I had never ridden for the Italians before. The Vismara Honda team, owned by Fabrizio Berni, was based in Bologna, where the Yamaha team was the year before. But the workshop had been moved to be near their team manager, Corrado Maddii, in Florence.'

Honda is the largest motorcycle manufacturer in the world. The company produced six million motorcycles in 2000, 2.5 million cars and 3.6 million power products. Honda employs 10,000 staff members dedicated to research and development, with about 2000 of those in motorcycling.

'The bikes were from HRC [Honda Racing Corporation] and you can't get better than that. Fabrizio Berni had been given the responsibility of running the official HRC team in the world champs,' Josh says. 'I loved my new Honda. I had plans to ride the first four rounds of the West Coast 125 supercross series in the United States. After that, I was to go to Italy for six weeks' training and testing of the 250.'

He would then return to Europe, after a visit home to New Zealand, in time for the GP kick-off in Spain on 17 March, facing a new-look 250cc class that now welcomed 125cc champion James Dobb, former 125cc champion Alessio Chiodi, defending champion Mickael Pichon (Josh's former team-mate at Suzuki) and world number three Gordon Crockard, now on a KTM. He would also face Australian Andrew McFarlane, now on a 250cc Kawasaki instead of the open class Yamaha, Japanese GP newcomer Yoshitaka Atsuta (Honda) and, of course, GP veterans Fred Bolley and Claudio Federici, the pair now team-mates at Yamaha.

In an interesting twist of fate, Josh's arch foe from 2001 was now his team-mate. German Pit Beirer, the man who for two consecutive seasons had snatched away higher honours from Josh was to now share space with his old enemy in the factory Honda enclosure. That alone made for some interesting dynamics. 'I got on pretty well with Pit, considering we always seemed to be battling in the championship. He was a normal, no bullshit kind of guy. I had certainly had much more difficult team-mates than him in the past.'

The sponsor, Vismara, was an Italian delicatessen company. Team boss Berni had been president of Socalbe Spa, a large food distribution company, manager of the group Nestlé and sales and marketing manager of the Berni Spa, so Josh had a good manager behind him, one with plenty of experience at the sport's top level. Race team manager Corrado Maddii had been the 125cc world motocross number two in 1982 and again in 1984, and had a team of ten men to deal with everything from tuning and prepping the bikes and driving the giant team truck to handling media and hospitality functions. The professional set-up impressed Josh, and he soon felt at home with the Italians.

'This was a breakthrough year for me, as far as my riding went. I improved no end, and Corrado and Fabio taught me the work ethic it takes to be a champion. I went to America at the start of the year with Fabio and rode some 125cc supercross events. We lived out of a motorhome and it was great because we began to form a bond. I then went down to Italy and stayed with Corrado. I really admire him. He's a former world championship motocross rider and knows his stuff. He had great facilities, and working together with him and Fabio was a fantastic experience. It brought me on in leaps and bounds. They showed so much commitment that I knew I couldn't let them down — it spurred me on. Suddenly I had pressure on me again, but it was good pressure.'

Josh's move to the red bike was a dramatic switch after years of being aligned to the yellow Suzuki brand, but after five years as a privateer in the world championship, then two years on the official works Suzuki team, Josh knew what he was seeking. When he was approached by Berni's Freetime team, the outfit that had run Yamaha machines with Skittles sponsorship the previous season, it was a very easy decision.

'I was aware of several top guys who would have loved to be on this bike and I was very grateful to Fabrizio Berni for making it happen for me. It was a very professional set-up and I believed at the time that the team fitted perfectly with my approach to winning the world championship. Berni's support was amazing — they asked me how I wanted things set up and what back-up I needed, and that was even before the race season had begun. It was the first team to have its own separate hospitality unit at the GPs, just like at the road races.'

Josh had had discussions with Honda earlier in 2001, after the company approached him to introduce its new four-stroke 450 machine in the 500 class. 'We talked a long way down the track, but I found it difficult to abandon my dream of winning the 250 title — it had been my life for seven years at that point. That's a long time to devote to something, and it was impossible for me just to walk away.' The Berni-operated Vismara Honda team had instead signed experienced Italian star Andrea Bartolini to ride the new CRF450R machine in the open class. The team was based at Reggio Emilia in northern Italy, near the Ferrari factory at Maranello, although Josh was to spend most of his Italian visits further south, at Levane, near Arezzo, where team manager Maddii was based.

'To most of the Italians I met, I was a bit of a curiosity,' Josh says. 'They associated Kiwis mostly with America's Cup yachting and a little bit with rugby, but that was about it. I began brushing up my Italian, which is such a lovely language, and I didn't need any introduction to pasta.'

Josh was also keen to sample a bit of his mum's home cooking over the Christmas and New Year period, but kept a low profile while at home. As he was still under contract with Suzuki until 31 December, he was unable to race in New Zealand over that time.

While he already had his Honda bikes, they were only to be used for training, and in order to do everything he could to prepare himself for the 2002 season ahead, he built his own supercross track in his parents' backyard in Motueka. It was a replica of the one at Anaheim, in California, and he was out riding whenever it wasn't raining, aware that his riding style still needed fine-tuning. In particular he wanted to be smoother on the bike and more aggressive with his opponents, and also knew he needed to increase his level of confidence on the new bikes. As part of his plans to toughen up, Josh arranged to fly to the United States and race several events in the 125cc west supercross series.

'I had always wanted to race in the States at some time. I'd had an opportunity to go there in 2001 for two outdoor meetings, but Suzuki wouldn't let me.' He'd considered some options to race in the United States in 2002, but his heart was still with the GPs, although he still had reservations about the direction the GP scene was taking. 'Personally, I hated the one-race-per-GP format, but it was the same for everyone, so I just had to knuckle down and get better at it.'

As it turned out, Josh had a very good crack at the world title. 'I won a lot that year and challenged Pichon for the title. Corrado took me in like a son. He was a really cool guy. He worked 24/7 for motocross and his attitude was similar to that of a Kiwi — he was laid back, but when it came to the job, he was in there giving it 100 per cent. He had a knack of making you feel like you were welcome, and he trusted you. Unfortunately the team ran out of money during the season.'

Even though Corrado wasn't being paid, he spent his own money to get the team to the races. While Fabio wasn't getting paid either, neither man put that burden on Josh. 'We started racing a lot of international races outside of the GP world championship circuit, events with decent prize money. We'd make between NZ$5000 and $10,000 a weekend and I'd split the money with Fabio and keep us alive in the world championships. I could have just taken the money and run, but I respected these guys so much that we just carried on and paid the bills as best we could from my prize money.'

It proved to be a tough year in many ways, as even though Josh finished second in the world championships — his best-ever position — behind arch rival and former Suzuki team-mate Mickael Pichon, he banked nothing. 'I got really close to Pichon in 2002 and challenged him hard. I never won a GP, but came really close in Russia. I had achieved some pole positions in qualifying, for the first time ever, and had been on the podium for eight out of the 12 GPs.' But because the team had run out of money, all he was paid was the bonus money for finishing second in the world championships, worth NZ$200,000, because that came from Honda Europe.

He had been promised a salary of 240,000 euros, at that time about NZ$480,000, which would have been his biggest payday, but ended the year with just the bonus money. 'Sure, I was bitter about it, but at the same time I was excited about how my racing was going. When I reflect on it now, the money would have helped me so much for the future, but you live and learn. Touch wood, that's the only time I've ever had problems like that. Any professional athlete or businessman has a year where things don't pan out financially — mistakes are made, or things don't go the way you want them to — but that's life.'

His philosophical demeanour belies the searing blowtorch of pressure that had been applied to him in a turbulent season full of trials and tribulations. Even though fully occupied in challenging Pichon for the world title while, in the background, his Vismara team was scrambling to stay afloat financially, in June 2002 Josh was also forced to deal with another major off-track distraction.

The world came tumbling down around his ears when he was slammed with a doping charge after routine tests following the Austrian 250cc GP at Kärntenring on 9 June, the sixth of 12 rounds in the 2002 world series. It was a charge that derailed his 2002 campaign and threatened to end his career, just as it was beginning to gather a full head of steam.

Josh had finished third that day, behind Pichon and Irishman Gordon Crockard, but any celebrations he might have been planning soon began to unravel. Anti-doping controls were carried out at Kärntenring, and Josh's sample tested six times over the limit for the stimulant pseudoephedrine.

According to the official FIM release from the sport's governing body:

> Among the urine samples taken, one was found not in accordance with the rules of the FIM Anti-Doping Code. This sample comes from New Zealand rider Joshua Coppins, who competes in the 250cc class. The sample of Mr Coppins contains a concentration of 157 micrograms/ml of pseudoephedrine (cut-off level: 25 micrograms/ml) and a concentration of 7.4 micrograms/ml of cathine (cut-off level: 5 micrograms/ml). Both products are sanctioned by the FIM Anti-Doping Code, article 10.3, Prohibited Classes of Substances. Mr Coppins renounced to ask for a counter-test with the B sample.

Josh faced a suspension of up to six months if he was found guilty. It would spell the end of his career in Europe, with the punishment enough to cripple his 2002 campaign, and the stigma of drug abuse a lingering blight on his name — something any sportsman would find difficult to shake. All of the other samples taken and tested that day showed the absence of any banned substances.

Josh responded swiftly to the charges: 'This is a minor issue, and a very simple one. It involves a hay fever tablet. I have nothing to hide. I am confident the matter will be cleared up when I meet with the FIM. It is unfortunate that publicity besmirches my name in the meantime. I have a long and impeccable record in motocross and I would never do anything to jeopardise it, especially not anything involving banned substances.'

It was such a simple mistake. Josh had gone to a chemist shop in an Italian town, showed the girl behind the counter the prescription he had been taking for hay fever. He also explained he couldn't take banned substances and the chemist gave him the medicine for the hay fever. Unbeknown to Josh, the medicine contained pseudoephedrine, a banned substance.

Soon afterwards, the International Disciplinary Court convened at the FIM headquarters in Switzerland for a public hearing, where the court handed down the following ruling:

- Mr Coppins is excluded from the results of the Austrian Grand Prix held in Kärntenring on June 9, 2002.
- The FIM championship points, prizes, medals and trophies are withdrawn.
- Mr Coppins is suspended for a period of three months from all activities under FIM control. This suspension is conditionally deferred for a period of one year.
- Mr Coppins must pay a fine of US$5000.
- The costs of the hearing are to be borne by Mr Coppins.

The world motocross championship standings were amended to read: 1. Mickael Pichon (FRA-Suzuki), 213; 2. Pit Beirer (GER-Honda), 161; 3. Joshua Coppins (NZL-Honda), 160; 4. Frédéric Bolley (FRA-Yamaha), 126; 5. James Dobb (GBR-KTM), 126; 6. Kenneth Gundersen (NOR-Kawasaki), 122; 7. Gordon Crockard (IRL-KTM), 119; 8. Johnny Aubert

(FRA-Yamaha), 100; 9. Andrew McFarlane (AUS-Kawasaki), 95; 10. Alessio Chiodi (ITA-Yamaha), 79.

Josh had been dropped from second to third in the series standings. The chief beneficiary of Josh's punishment was his own team-mate, Pit Beirer, promoted from fourth on the day to a podium spot at the Austrian GP and elevated past Josh in the championship standings, from third to the number two position overall.

At home in New Zealand, the reaction to Josh's drug controversy from the mainstream media was disappointing. That night the state-owned television news channel had Josh's 'fall from grace' as one of its lead items. New Zealand motocross fans were annoyed when Television New Zealand dug out some old film clips and splashed a 30-second item on the news. Until that point in the season (seven rounds had been raced before the drug news broke on 25 June) Josh was running second in the world series, yet had enjoyed barely a mention on the television news, despite being on the world championship podium five times in the last few months. Instead TVNZ showed dated footage of Josh racing a Suzuki (instead of the Honda he'd been riding all season) and reported the drugs charge. Two months later, in August, when Josh had a fair hearing and was cleared by the International Disciplinary Court, television viewers in New Zealand heard and saw nothing.

There is a huge difference between taking an over-the-counter hay fever medication and snorting lines of white powder, and the drugs he had taken were hay fever tablets to stop him sneezing inside his helmet. Pseudoephedrine increases the heart rate, not something a motocross racer wants or needs to do, and does nothing to build strength or stamina, so can hardly be described as performance enhancing. He was docked the 20 points he had earned for placing third at the Austrian GP and received a three-month suspension, deferred for a period of one year.

But Josh Coppins is no cheat, and there is no room in the slick, fast world of motocross for anything that impairs your judgement. There is no pill that will make you race faster. The disappointment for motocross fans in New Zealand was seeing that the only time motocross could bump rugby off the television screens was when something shocking happened.

During the months that followed the charge, Josh had no alternative but to knuckle down and concentrate on his racing while the controversy swirled around him. He knew that if he kept himself out of trouble, the entire incident would likely blow away. If not, he had alternatives to consider, perhaps even a career racing in the United States.

The next event was the Swedish GP at Uddevalla and, once again, as was becoming typical for the season, Josh finished runner-up to his old foe, Pichon. While Josh was grateful to bank the points, he still had the drugs cloud hanging over him and, with a one-month break in the GP season before the Belgian GP in August, he took a trip to the United States.

He showed up at round eight of the United States national championships at Unadilla, northwest of New York, scoring sixth and eighth in the 250cc class, impressing many as he outrode noted American riders Ezra Lusk, Steve Lamson, Kyle Lewis and John Dowd. He then returned to his European base, the GP season and the waiting FIM courtroom hearing.

He was philosophical as he considered his fate. 'Things were really out of my hands at that point, but I knew I had ten other offers for the following year, both in Europe and in the United States. I hadn't inked anything and I didn't plan to until my court case was decided. I didn't take drugs then, and I never will. I had proof from the pharmacy that they'd made a mistake and sold me the wrong medication. I had proof that I suffer badly from hay fever. I had proof I took it for medical reasons and I hoped, with a good lawyer, that it would hold up in court.

'But the truth was there was an illegal substance inside me at the Austrian GP, whether I was aware of it or not. There had to be some kind of punishment. I could handle that, but if the FIM were planning to screw me to the wall and treat me unfairly, I planned to go straight back to the United States and abandon my dream of being world champion.'

Instead he rode in the next GP, on 4 August, at Genk, in Belgium, where once again he finished runner-up to Pichon. Soon afterwards, two months after the drugs charges had been laid, he was informed that they had been dismissed and he was absolved of any guilt.

It was perhaps the most difficult and stressful period of Josh's life and he had survived, but the whole affair had cost him dearly. In addition to the price of an expensive legal battle, his competition points were never reinstated. 'It was pretty tough because it cost me money to defend myself, and that was money I didn't have — I wasn't getting paid while the Vismara team struggled without financial backing.'

Though declared innocent, there were still plenty of people who would choose to believe Josh had crossed the line. His relationship with other riders, particularly his team-mate, also left a sour taste in Josh's mouth. 'It's always very hard to get along with your team-mate when you're close in a championship. When I moved to Berni's Vismara Honda team, Pit Beirer had already been there for a year. He was their golden boy. The workshop had moved to near Corrado Maddii's home in Italy. Pit was living there in Corrado's old house and I was in an apartment with the mechanics. I loved it because we always had fun. Pit was really nice away from the track, and I got along well with him.

'But once the championship hit the halfway stage, things changed. I was in second place in the championship and Pit was third, the team had run out of money, and Pit wasn't the best-performed rider in the team any more. I still got along OK with him off the track, but on the track he was a changed man. When he put his helmet on, he was 100 per cent on the attack. I passed him on the last lap in the Italian GP [the team's home GP]. I had come from 16th and was on fire. He couldn't do anything to stop me, and each lap I reeled him in. I finally caught and passed him, but on the next corner he tried a lame take-out move on me, but crashed himself. I wasn't too bothered, but our relationship worsened after that. I was now Honda's golden boy, which I think was hard for Pit to accept.

'When the drug thing kicked off I was in Austria. By the next GP I had lost my job from the team. Pit was still very close to the owner, but the bikes were Honda's and they wanted it to play out in court and support me until there was a verdict. Corrado Maddii had another team of his own, as well as running the Berni Vismara Honda outfit. He was really cool and liked my fighting spirit. I liked his passion for the sport. He moved me into his truck and I carried on as normal.'

It proved to be a hellish time for Josh who managed to keep racing, although it wasn't easy. He was unable to concentrate on his riding or training, his mind constantly wandering back to the drugs cloud that hung over him. 'I knew I hadn't deliberately cheated, and if anything, all I was guilty of was negligence, but nothing more.'

The next GP was three weeks later in Sweden, and Josh heard that Pit Beirer, Mickael Pichon and (British rider) Jamie Dobb were talking about refusing to race if he was allowed on to the start line. Their attitude didn't surprise him — after all, together they were the top four in the championships at the time and he was a threat to them all. 'I went to the head of the FIM, Wolfgang Srb, and he said to me, "Don't worry, but if they all strike, I will have no choice but to pull you out." On one hand he says don't worry, and then he says he'll bow to this pressure and not support me.

'I was scheduled for the FIM court a fortnight later and I thought it would be sorted there and then. I didn't want it to be sorted by a rider boycott outside of the court. I just wanted to race. I didn't care that I was losing a lot of money and that my reputation and dignity were taking a hammering.'

It was hard because all the pressure was starting to show. 'I had a massive crash in training in Sweden, but luckily I was unhurt. In the actual race itself, I rode well, which surprised me. I came from around tenth at the start to finish second, right on Pichon's tail. I was riding with anger and, when I passed Pit, I made an aggressive pass. I felt like pushing him wide into the ditch, but I thought, I've got enough problems, so let's not add to them by risking a protest.'

Josh finished runner-up at the next GP in Genk, Belgium, once again a step below Pichon on the podium. 'I think this proved I could perform without any help from drugs. I think that if my results had dropped off after the Austrian GP, questions would have been asked about how much of what I'd achieved until then had been because of drugs. I was delighted to finish second in Sweden and again in Belgium.'

Immediately after the Belgian GP, Josh climbed into his lawyer's car for a long drive south to Switzerland and the hearing where he was given the thumbs up and the nightmare was finally over.

'From that moment on I didn't have much time for Pit. We worked out of the same truck at the Russian GP [the final round of the season] and we didn't speak a word, even though we changed in the same room all weekend. I was very angry at the time.' A year later Pit Beirer was paralysed in a crash. 'I sent him a "get well soon" note via his website because I'd never wish that upon anyone. It's funny — he's now high up the pecking order at the KTM factory and he called my manager in 2005 to ask about me joining the team. I turned that down. Our relationship is better, but not that good.' At one time KTM asked Josh what it would cost for him to join their team and he put a silly price on his head because he wasn't interested in joining Beirer.

'I feel sad about it all now, but in the past I used to look at a story in the newspaper and see that a cyclist or some other professional sportsman had been done for drugs, and think "Oh, he's guilty . . . he's a cheat!" but because it happened to me, I can now see it all in a different light. I was totally innocent. I now strongly believe in the adage "innocent until proven guilty". It was pseudoephedrine, a cold remedy I was using. It was my fault, but it was an honest mistake and an accident to use that drug without checking properly that it would get me into trouble.'

Even with his history of suffering from hay fever, drug taking was not something that Josh's parents could imagine him being involved in, so when charges were laid against him, it came like a bolt from the blue. Viv in particular was shocked. 'At the beginning I just thought it would go away, but it got worse and worse. When you are in New Zealand, really there is nothing you can do. I was in Belgium when he went to court and I was amazed at how he just carried on with everything going on around him. At the time his team wasn't paying him, and a lot of people he thought of as friends turned against him. He showed me how strong he is. I couldn't believe the way he just put his head down and kept going — anyone else would have buckled under that pressure.'

Ted was equally disturbed by the seriousness of the drugs incident. 'There had been a few problems over the years, apart from the enormous struggle just to make it in Europe. By this I mean lack of money, lack of accommodation and lack of food, but the worst was when the drug scare happened and the Vismara Honda team went into liquidation at the same time,' Ted says. 'The drug scandal was just so bizarre — it was laughable to anyone who knows Josh. They would know it just wasn't right. Josh learned who his real friends were — he finished the season on a borrowed bike, with his mechanic, Fabio, supporting him to the full.'

Ted and Viv spent thousands of dollars in legal fees to prove his innocence. 'Had Josh been found guilty, he would have had a three-year suspension,' Ted says.

Despite the drugs controversy, Josh finished the 2002 season as world number two, his best overall result up to that point. Pichon won the crown with 288 points, 66 more than Josh, so in the end, the 20 points he lost in Austria had no effect on the overall outcome. Beirer was third, another 17 points behind Josh.

At the final round of the season, the Russian GP, Josh announced he was switching from the Vismara Honda team, based in Italy, to ride for the CAS Honda team, based in England. 'It was a sad day when I moved on from Corrado's team,' Josh says. 'I wanted to stay, but when Berni folded, Corrado didn't have the money to run me, so Fabio and I shifted on from there to CAS Honda.'

Now in a new team, with a new world ranking of number two and with the drugs scandal now firmly behind him, Josh was ready to start afresh.

2003: The phoenix

JOSH HAD BEEN friendly with the CAS Honda team owner, Harry Ainsworth, since about 2000, just seeing him around the pits and so on. 'I wanted to stay with Honda, although I had plenty of other choices,' Josh says. 'I spoke with [Yamaha team boss] Michele Rinaldi, but I didn't want to go back into a situation where I was the second-string rider in a team. I would have been number two in the Yamaha team to Stefan Everts, just as I had been when I was teamed with Mickael Pichon at Suzuki.'

At that time, Everts was the reigning 500cc world champion, and a six-time former world champion with titles in all three (125cc, 250cc and 500cc) classes. He was also regarded as a living legend in the sport and was the Belgian Sportsman of the Year. Josh knew it was probably impossible to supplant national hero Everts as any team's leading man, and the CAS Honda deal allowed him at least to be treated equally with the other team riders.

In addition, with the motocross world championships changing format again for 2003 — combining the 250cc and 500cc categories into one 'super class' called MXGP — Josh thought it best to stay with Honda. Significantly, Josh also opted to stay with the same capacity machine with which he'd tasted so much success whilst racing in 2002, the 250cc two-stroke Honda CR250, even though, as he would later discover, this would put him at a distinct disadvantage against rivals such as Everts, who raced the meaty 450cc four-stroke bikes.

'Harry Ainsworth seemed like a good guy and we got along really well. I went to CAS because I wanted to stay with Honda, because I liked the bike and I could take Fabio with me, and that was important.'

In reality Josh found that the CAS Honda team was too big, with four riders and something like ten staff. While he found them all to be good people, passionate and honest, he felt strongly that there was too much going on for the size of the team, and was uncomfortable with their more casual approach. Josh's team-mates at CAS Honda were Ireland's Gordon Crockard, Japan's Yoshitaka Atsuta and Finland's Jussi Vehvilainen, but the season was doomed almost before it had really begun.

From the glory of standing on a podium and clutching a trophy to gripping a bedpan in a hospital bed, Josh would remember his 2003 season for all the wrong reasons. Having come out of 2002 surviving the drugs allegations and, remarkably, rocketing to a career-high world ranking of number two, Josh had been determined to step up in 2003 and finally claim the world crown. As the big teams reshuffled at the start of the year and pre-season musings began to reach a crescendo, Josh had been widely tipped to threaten the mantle of Stefan Everts.

In anticipation of, and preparation for, a great season, 26-year-old Josh rented an apartment in Los Angeles, just up the road from Disneyland, and made plans to race three or four races in the hot California climate to ensure he started his European campaign a few weeks later at the peak of his form.

Instead, before he could immerse himself in a tough training regimen, his 2003 world championship campaign suffered a major setback, one that saw him centimetres away from ending his career in a wheelchair. Josh crashed heavily while practising for his first big supercross in the United States, the Phoenix Supercross in January. As he accelerated up the first stage of a big triple jump at the 45,000-seat stadium, something failed in the engine, leaving Josh committed to the jump, but without enough power to make it. A yawning chasm appeared beneath him. Quickly realising what was happening, Josh bailed off the back of the bike, clipping the bike's back mudguard and falling awkwardly, breaking three toes and dislocating two.

As he crashed, he was unable to coil his body and roll away as he'd done a dozen times before. There was a searing pain in both feet. His left foot took the brunt of the impact and, even inside his sturdy, carbon fibre-reinforced boots, his ankle splintered. His right foot also gave way as bones snapped. He felt his back compress on impact. First, he felt winded. As he gasped for air, dirt filled his mouth, covering his goggles and, in the panicked confusion, he relied solely on sound, smell and touch.

'I had broken my right foot in three places, and dislocated it in two on my left foot. The foot had four pins in it and I was in a plaster cast for six weeks.' He had also chipped a small piece of bone off his left ankle that had to be screwed back on. That was the most serious injury because it only had an 80 per cent chance of healing and affected the stability of the ankle joint. He had also compressed and fractured two vertebrae in his back and broken a rib.

Even through the fog of pain-killers, Josh vividly recalls being wheeled into the operating theatre at Sun City Hospital. 'It was a bit of a freaky place. It was down in the bottom of the building and the operating room was huge. When I told the surgeon to do the best he could he suggested I take up car racing.'

The following day, the doctor came to Josh's bedside to report he'd broken his back and more surgery was in store. The delicate surgery that followed left him with five screws in his back and four pins and a screw in his left ankle. 'It was by far my worst injury and my first really bad break,' Josh says.

While the crash had been nothing but spectacular, the awkward way he landed had caused the damage. But, even though incapacitated, Josh still considered himself a contender for the 2003 motocross GP title despite the potentially crippling and career-ending injury he had sustained. In reality, it was wishful thinking. His body was a mess and he felt helpless, not only because he was unable to ride, but also because he was powerless to do anything to stop the onward march of his rivals, Mickael Pichon and Stefan Everts.

He would not be back in top form and attacking the GPs until many painful months later, and by then there was no chance of taking a top ranking into the following year. Even so, in March, just a few days before the world championship opener in Spain and less than two months after his smash, he remained convinced he'd be a starter for the first GP of the year. That belief wasn't the work of an overactive imagination or the delusion of someone believing he was some kind of superman. It was testimony to his faith in his extreme physical fitness and ability to heal quickly, and a pointer to his never-say-die attitude, a mindset that would stand him in good stead throughout his professional career.

'The first week after the crash was the hardest. I was flat on my back in hospital, doing nothing and feeling like I was just fading away. Everything was in place and that was one of the hardest parts of the few months I lay there injured, not being allowed to join up with the new team and being a part of life in the world championship.'

After his treatment in America, Josh went back home to New Zealand where he spent the next two months feeling dejected, bored, disappointed and very frustrated, before eventually returning to racing again five months later, at round four at Montevarchi, in Italy, on 1 June. It was his debut ride for his new CAS Honda team and he finished 15th to pocket six points. Josh accepted he was a long way off the pace, but at least he was riding again. With just one event of four under his wheels, Josh found himself a whopping 87 points behind the leader at that time, his old 250cc rival and former team-mate, Pichon.

'I had to revise my plans for the year and set new targets — one being to get into the top ten before the season wrapped up — but I was also keen to find my 2002 form again. I knew I could do it — I'd moved to a new level in 2002, and I was confident I could get there again. I'd known the CAS Honda team owner, Harry Ainsworth, for a number of years. He's a good, honest man and straight up with the way he deals with the team and its riders. For the sake of Harry and the team, I wanted to get back to racing, get a smile on my face again, and go into 2004 as a genuine title contender.'

In one way, Josh felt that the injury had made him stronger. 'I had to be realistic — I couldn't expect to go through my motocross career and not have any injuries. I put all negative thoughts aside and set about the hard work and dedication that was needed to get myself back to the top again.'

Once Josh was back in the thick of the action, the rise and rise of the Kiwi fighter through the 2003 season bordered on miraculous. Just as the fabled phoenix bird rose from the ashes of defeat, Josh rose again from his own personal disaster. He lifted himself from the surgeon's operating table in the United States in January to the podium at the final round of the motocross world championships in France, in September, just eight months later — a remarkable feat, and a miracle in anyone's language.

His parents, friends, supporters, fans and sponsors had all held their breath when Josh sustained his potentially crippling injury in Phoenix. They breathed again when he had recovered enough to rejoin the GP circus at round four in Italy, barely five months later, but even the most faithful of his followers still harboured doubts that he'd be able to regain the devastating form that won him the number two world ranking the year before.

How wrong they were. Nobody had counted on the strength of Josh's will to win. 'When I had the big accident, I was told I'd never race again, and that my racing career was over,' Josh says. 'For some reason, I knew that wasn't going to happen — I don't know why, I just knew.'

He went on to finish on the podium twice in eight of the 12 rounds he contested in 2003, and was consistently among the top ten, good enough for him to take the number 12 spot at the end of the season. In addition to missing the opening three rounds, he also dipped out of round six in Austria when his still-recovering leg became infected after overdoing the training. But his season record plotted a steady upward path: DNS (did not start), DNS, DNS, 15th, 17th, DNS, tenth, ninth, third, 12th, fourth, third.

'Things went well once I got back up to speed,' he says. 'But I have to say it was a lot harder than I expected. I thought I'd get back to speed a lot faster, but looking back on it now, I couldn't have expected it to have gone any faster really. To get back to 90 per cent is not too hard — it's the last 10 per cent that's really hard. It requires a lot of patience — you can't push it, you just have to let it come. And, of course, you get a lot of other problems too, like recurring injuries.'

His personal woes aside, a lot of other things happened in motocross in 2003. It was an evolutionary year, with the creation of the MXGP class; the rules were tinkered and formats tweaked in response to the snowballing development of four-stroke technology by the major bike manufacturers. The jury was still out on whether a 250cc two-stroke could fairly match a 450cc four-stroke, but by the end of that season, there was little doubt that the big four-strokes held the upper hand. Of the front-runners that season, Pichon's RM250 was the only two-stroke bike to feature among the top placings, the Frenchman finishing third. All the rest were 450cc four-stroke riders.

Even with only half the MXGP season under his wheels because of the supercross injury, Josh finished a remarkable 12th (on a 250cc two-stroke against the dominant 450cc four-strokes). It was tough coming back, and Josh puts much of what he did manage to achieve that season — including a podium finish — down to his 'father-figure' boss, Harry Ainsworth, a man Josh felt comfortable around and who knew how to coax out the best from his riders and staff.

'Harry and I had fun. I always took the piss out of the Poms and we always talked about stuff other than motocross — rugby, road-racing, the weather, you name it. If Harry didn't get a call from me every day, he started to worry. Harry was a good salesman — he knew how to tell someone what they wanted to hear. I was wise to H, as I referred to him, right from day one though. I think I was a little smarter than any of his previous riders, but I loved him and his passion for motocross.

'He lost his son to a motocross accident, so it still blows my mind how he is so involved in the sport after that happened to him. I mean, he spends so much money and it takes up all his and wife Vanessa's time, yet he's flat out into it.

'If H does have a problem though, it's that he can't say no. It gets him in the shit all the time. He never wants to let anyone down. To be honest, when I got to this team, it was a bit of a shambles. As soon as I achieved some good results, I started to gain some power and I dragged him aside and had a word. H knew what I was already telling him, and together we had some great years with some good results.'

It had taken him eight months, but Josh had risen from the disaster of Phoenix. He was back on the podium, among the top three, by the final round of the world championships, in France, in September.

The 2003 season-ending Motocross des Nations, at Belgium's Zolder circuit that September, was another hurdle to clear — his debut ride onboard the big four-stroke Honda CRF450R. With little strength in his legs, however, he became incredibly tired, yet managed to win his semifinal, helping to make the New Zealand team one of the favourites for a podium finish.

However, the dream started to come apart in the main race, with one of Josh's team-mates, Ben Townley on the small-engined KTM bike, going down very hard in the first turn, ending the young Kiwi star's race weekend. That left a big job for Shayne King and Josh to try and get a decent result with only two riders, before King suffered a major setback on lap one, losing his left handgrip and having to fight the deep sand of Zolder for 35 minutes with just the end of a shiny alloy bar to hang onto.

'I got a great start in the top 15,' Shayne recalls, 'and being a late substitution for the New Zealand team [due to Daryl Hurley's exclusion because of injury], I was placed at the very outside of the start gate, which meant I managed to avoid the carnage on the inside of the turn that caught Ben out. But as I went into the turn, I felt my left grip starting to move. Then it just came off completely in my hand — I couldn't believe it! It took me a good ten to 15 minutes to adjust to riding and hanging on with no grip, but then I started to move forward and started picking up a lot of the places that I had lost earlier.

'My mechanic, "Jimmy" [Glenn] Macartney, was keeping me well informed via the trusty pit board, and at one stage I saw that we had dropped to sixth place, so I turned on the afterburner and gave it everything I could. I managed to get myself up to 14th place, which was good enough, with Josh's fifth placing, to put the team in fourth.'

Ben was very disappointed — he felt he'd had a good shot at a top five placing and, talking after the race, he said, 'I was coming into the first turn and just got shunted from behind. The next thing I knew I was getting run over and bikes were everywhere. Josh and Shayne did us proud, and got a great result for New Zealand.'

Also speaking after the race, Josh said: 'I got an awesome start running with Smets and Everts. I ran with them for the first few laps and was feeling very good. Carmichael passed me, and then I was sitting comfortably in fourth place, but towards the end of the race, I made a mistake in the sand section and Gordon Crockard [Ireland] passed me and I ended up fifth. All in all, it was a great weekend for New Zealand.'

As a team, New Zealand finished fourth overall in what is known as the 'Olympic Games of Motocross' behind Belgium (their team comprising Stefan Everts, Joel Smets and Steve Ramon), the United States and Finland. Remarkably, Italy, the defending Motocross des

Nations champion country, and Australia, Spain and Sweden all failed to make the cut. Josh was the fifth-highest ranked individual — not bad for a man having his first ride on a four-stroke bike and on the comeback from horrific injuries.

Josh earned a number of plaudits for his gutsy comeback. He had often been seen limping around the pits, unable to climb over even small obstacles, just a few weeks earlier. Doctors had told him he could face life in a wheelchair with his broken back, but he was racing within three months of his spinal surgery. The surgeons also warned him he would never race again as his ankle and feet were almost beyond repair. And yet, remarkably, he had led the New Zealand team to a proud fourth in the sport's showcase event.

Just a month before the big Zolder meeting, Josh had reinjured his foot, squashing it against race fencing when he ran wide on a turn. A toenail fell off and he thought his toe was broken, but it came right in time for Zolder.

Immediately following that event, Josh went under the surgeon's knife again, this time to adjust the hardware in his shattered leg. 'The bone it was holding had not grafted properly and it had broken up, restricting the joint. I didn't have proper movement and it was pretty painful when I walked. It had been OK when I was riding, with my race boot holding everything in place, so I waited until the end of the season to allow myself plenty of time to recover.'

2004: First GP win

IT WAS CONTRACT time again as the start of the 2004 season rolled around, but thankfully, Josh had done enough near the end of the previous year to show he was still worth a punt. Each GP would now comprise two races again, the format reverting to what it had been four seasons earlier.

Harry Ainsworth was one man who was particularly satisfied to see Josh come back from his injuries and return to the top of the MX1 class. 'Josh had proven to everyone he was a fighter and that he would never back away from the heat of battle,' Ainsworth says. 'He is one of the nicest guys you could ever meet, and he is not complicated in any way. He really fitted into the environment we wanted for this team. We also had ambitions, and winning a world championship was one of them. With Josh we felt we could do this.' It was vindication for Josh. His never-say-die Kiwi can-do attitude had won him many friends and admirers, and perhaps none more important than his Honda team boss.

His race performance at Zolder, where he rode the Honda CRF450 four-stroke for the first time, was important for three reasons. Josh had shown he was back to his best, the circuit where he'd performed so well was the venue for the opening round of the world championships in 2004, and he'd also shown he was ready to take the big 450cc four-stroke into battle in the GPs. This meant that for the 2004 season he'd have horsepower to equal Stefan Everts, and be able to match Everts and the others out of the starting gate and down the big straights.

Aside from the new bike, there were other changes in the wind for Josh, as the hard decision was taken to cut the size of the team, with

Irishman Crockard the unlucky rider as the CAS Honda team was shaved to three riders — Josh, Finland's Jussi Vehvilainen and Japan's Yoshitaka Atsuta.

By the start of 2004, Josh had returned to the same form which had seen him finish second in the 250cc world championships in 2002, and after the first three rounds Josh was fourth in the championship standings, despite running out of fuel when his fuel tank was damaged in the opening race of the Portuguese GP, in round three of the series at Agueda in April. 'We were three GPs into the season and that was six races,' Josh says. 'The previous year we only did 12 races in the entire year. I have to say I love the two-race format.'

His results began to reflect this. 'The first GP — in Zolder — was plagued with rain. I liked the track as it was fun, but it was really difficult with lots of ruts. I was happy to go home safe and with a bunch of points.' The track caught out a lot of riders with unpredictable ruts, mud and jumps. 'I personally had a lot of trouble with the gusting wind — it was really scary jumping the big-finish table-top jump because you didn't know if you were going to be swept away or land safely.'

In the first race he rode really tight and stiff and only managed seventh place. 'I was pissed off with that result and wanted to improve for the second race which I did — second place — and I led for a long time, only to let [Belgian] Cedric Mellote past.' While he really wanted the win, he wasn't prepared to take any risks to win at the first GP of the season.

They took things easy between the Zolder GP and round two at Bellpuig, in Spain. Josh managed to fit in some trials riding with Ben Townley, and on the Wednesday before the Spanish GP he went riding in Durler, in southern Belgium, with Fabio, before the mechanic drove the motorhome on to Spain. 'Tom Church [England], Everts, Bervoets and half the GP paddock were on our Friday flight to Barcelona,' Josh recalls.

'Bellpuig went well for me, even though it was raining once again. The track was very one-lined, so a second and third result wasn't too bad. The best thing was that I was only four points from the championship lead and I wanted the red leader's number plate really badly.'

They had a bit of hard luck when the rental car broke down and they had to drive the motorhome back to Belgium. 'I was pretty much over the idea of driving for 14 hours after a tough GP,' Josh says. 'Ben had first shift, with Tom sound asleep. I got the graveyard shift [1.00 a.m. to 4.00 a.m.]. Man, were we buggered, but we got home safe and sound.'

After Spain, the three were off again, this time to Portugal. 'I got a little sick in the week leading up to [round three in] Portugal, so took it easy and tried to ride on the Wednesday at a track called Den Dungen in Holland. It was a cool track, but because I was not feeling too well, I took it easy and just cruised,' Josh says. On Friday he and Tom flew to Porto where they were once again welcomed by a wet track. However, this time, their luck would change as it looked as if it would dry out in time for Sunday's race. The track layout had some big jumps and Josh thought it looked pretty good.

'Race one started off well for me — I got a great start,' Josh says. 'I was second into the first corner, behind Everts.' But when Kenneth Gundersen hit him in the third turn, he went down hard and damaged the fuel tank. 'I remounted last and charged back to tenth, only to run out of fuel on the last lap — that was a bummer. In the second race, I finished third and tried to push past Everts at the 20-minute mark for second place, but he was riding well and I couldn't get by. Obviously I was disappointed to have dropped back to fourth in the points.'

The big breakthrough for Josh happened in England on 30 May 2004, when he celebrated his first outright GP win. It was a triumphant homecoming for his CAS Honda team at Arreton, Isle of Wight, the first British GP in four years.

Josh finished second and first in the two races in front of 23,000 boisterous fans, all there to lap up the sunshine on the Isle of Wight. The Arreton circuit, praised from all corners of the paddock for the technical and spectacular offering, proved to be a strong course for the 450cc as Honda took its second win of the 2004 MX1 season and its first one-two slot on the podium. Tiscali Honda team rider Mickael Pichon grabbed a first and second finish to secure second place for the day, equal on points with Josh, but taking the second step on a countback, with Josh having the superior finish in the second outing.

The racing was nothing short of sensational. In both 35-minute races, Pichon and Josh pulled away from the chasing pack consisting of factory heavyweights Steve Ramon (the KTM star finishing third in the first race) and Yamaha's Stefan Everts, who was third on the podium after posting fourth and third. Pichon held the upper hand in the first race, but showed some side-effects of a shoulder injury he sustained at Teutschenthal several weeks earlier by fading in the day's second race.

Josh could smell his first GP win and set about closing in on the rapidly tiring Frenchman. As the race progressed, Pichon made a few mistakes and gave up his lead. Josh probably should have pulled away to a comfortable margin, but Pichon rallied and closed the gap. Approaching the last two laps, the two men were wheel-to-wheel in the charge to the chequered flag, but Josh held on and took the overall champagne celebration for the event, thanks to his superiority in the second race.

He was now six points behind third-ranked Pichon in the world championship standings, but they were both a long way (76 points) adrift of series leader Stefan Everts, who admitted to having an 'off day'. Belgian Cedric Melotte was also ahead of both Pichon and Josh in the championship standings, 20 points better than Pichon, although he too was a demoralising 56 points back from Everts.

Championship mathematics were briefly forgotten by an elated Josh, who was happy to break through the barrier that had eluded him for so long. 'It has taken so long for me to win a GP. I have been close before and I have had more second placings than I can remember; I'm so happy to have finally taken first,' he said at the time. 'I didn't feel so good in the first few laps of the second race, but I concentrated on riding my own race and it brought me up to second place. I saw Mickael had some good lines, but I was riding very easily and was able to make a pass. Five laps from the end, I started to feel a little tired, so focused on making a smooth race. I made one mistake near the pits and he was able to draw close, but right near the end I managed to hold my concentration, and carried it to the flag.'

Pichon made excuses for his showing. 'I have only ridden twice in the last two weeks, so I knew today was not going to be easy. I had to rest my shoulder, and cycling and running are no substitute for actually getting on the bike,' he said after the race. 'It was a good track here, but the conditions were difficult because it was so rough. I am happy with second place because I know I tried my hardest to win. I was following Josh and could catch him again after he passed me in the second race. In the last few laps I tried to push, but he did not make a mistake, whereas I did on the last lap. I'm glad we put on a good show for the fans. Josh was going so fast and I was really surprised.'

That Pichon had conceded he was a worthy adversary was enough to make Josh smile.

He finished the season as world number three in the premier class, now renamed MX1. 'The 2004 season was good for me, finishing third,' Josh says. 'This gave me more power to have a say in the team, and I now said we had to cut it down to just two riders. And that's what happened. We were down to just me and Jussi Vehvilainen in the team for 2005 and had more staff and a better workshop. There were now more people looking after me and making things right for me. We were trying hard to keep up with the factory teams.'

A view from inside the fence

New Zealand is a very long way from the hotbed of international motocross, an arduous 24 hours by air from the South Pacific to central Europe. It stands to reason that New Zealanders feel a little remote from what's going on in Belgium, Spain, the Netherlands, France, Italy or Germany, and for many years motocross enthusiasts in New Zealand were starved of results and news from the race tracks. The pricey magazines, when they finally arrived by slow boat from Europe, were often months out of date.

While we can now soak up the information in 'real time', it is really only in recent years that motocross fans in New Zealand have enjoyed electronic access to events, with the story, results, photos and even video action arriving almost instantly thanks to zippy, high-speed broadband access. Failing that, television channels in New Zealand might, if viewers are very lucky, screen a highlights package a fortnight or so after the event. But, when all is said and done, there's truly nothing like being there. Even television or video footage doesn't do justice to the pace and atmosphere at any live sporting event.

The truth is, many Kiwi motocross fans would happily walk on broken glass to stand among the heaving throngs of spectators at a European GP event and scream themselves hoarse while the racers put their lives on the line. And true to the gladiatorial nature of this sporting spectacle, the GP event of choice would be the Belgian GP at Namur, where the racing begins and ends inside a large Roman-style arena in the grounds of an ancient fortress castle. So when I was invited to tag along on a visit to Namur, it was a dream come true. I had long since dismissed the idea that this balding but happily married father-of-three would ever get to a motocross GP in Europe.

When the phone call came, it was completely unexpected. 'Got your passport handy? How'd you like to go to Europe for a week and see a motocross GP? My treat.'

The man on the other end of the phone was a former motocross GP mechanic, and someone who in recent years has put his money where his heart is — into the sport of motocross. Auckland-based Russell Burling is managing director of Rapson Holdings, New Zealand importers of the Korean Ssangyong motor vehicle marque, a man who has also sponsored many motorcycling events in New Zealand and had obtained naming rights for Prime Television's motorsports show.

Of course, it would have been rude to decline Russell's offer. And so, from small-town New Zealand (New Plymouth to be precise) to the vast heart of motocross in central Europe, here was a chance for this die-hard fan to see at first-hand the huge impression Motueka's Josh Coppins, Taupo's Ben Townley and New Plymouth mechanic Craig Behl have made in a part of the world where motocross is king.

Ben Townley, the MX2 class world champion in 2004, had established himself as one of the international stars of the sport. Just four years after arriving in Europe, Townley went from a pimple-faced high school student in short pants to the highly paid number one rider on the factory KTM team, a glossy magazine pin-up boy and hero to thousands worldwide. For the 2005 season he stepped up to the MX1 class — the category for riders of the big bikes, the 450cc four-strokes — and came up against his new house-mate, Josh Coppins. Josh was similarly blessed with poster-boy star status in Europe, although by now he'd ditched the 'new kid' tag. The third Kiwi making waves in Europe was Craig Behl, a young Taranaki-trained mechanic whose work with spanners and screwdrivers was second to none.

My trip to Europe began with a short flight from New Plymouth to Auckland early on a Tuesday morning. After three planes, dozens of snack meals and several acrobatic scrambles across sleeping passengers to reach the toilets, Amsterdam's Schiphol airport was a welcome sight to this stubble-faced zombie.

It didn't take me long to get into the swing of European life. The food was good, the beer fantastic and almost everyone spoke what passed for

English. The average Belgian and Dutchman certainly speak better English than the average Kiwi speaks Flemish, Dutch, French or German.

A short train journey to Brussels, and the journey from New Zealand to the Belgian GP track was almost complete. The view from the train featured concrete bunkers left over from the Second World War and more graffiti than you could shake an aerosol can at — so much history right there outside the window.

That night I enjoyed a Belgian restaurant meal with Russell, Josh, Ben, Craig and assorted hangers-on before it was finally time to relax. I slept like never before and, after croissants and coffee the next morning, it was on the road for a short drive to Namur.

Six-lane highways and traffic all motoring along at 130 kph were impressive enough, but so were the frequent roadside cafés and truck stops. The café stops were interesting. Dogs, it seemed, were welcome and, during one particular stop, a little dog was perched on the table, right beside the plate from which its mistress was nibbling. Urgh!

At a stop-over to grab a quick sandwich in Balen in south-western Belgium, the proprietor insisted his visitors attempt to speak to him in French or Dutch. 'Hey, when other Kiwis come in here, they talk to me in my language,' he insisted. What other Kiwis? 'Your Josh Coppins comes in here for lunch every day and he talks a few words in our language.' A quick glance at one another and a roll of the eyes, and we chorused a reply: 'Yeah right, mate.' Moments later and who should walk in the door but Josh himself. It was one of those moments — you'd almost think the Candid Camera crew had scripted it.

A couple of hours later, after stopping off at the Suzuki headquarters and a chat with Sylvain Geboers, and dropping in on his brother, Jan Geboers, who had a vintage motocross parts store you could only dream about, Namur loomed large on the horizon.

The first-time view of the citadel, its massive stone battlements overlooking the town below, was breathtaking. Surely this was the weirdest place in the world to stage a motocross GP. More reminiscent of a fairytale scene, the remarkable wooded hillside circuit of Namur is probably the most famous motocross venue of them all, and was to be the site for round four of the 2005 season's 16-round GP series.

On the day before the GP weekend, the cobblestoned streets below the castle were bustling with an open-air market. A little shopping was in order. It was 'rue de la this' and 'rue de la that' before the car was eventually squeezed into a parking space. It was soon apparent that the language of choice in this Wallonian region of southern Belgium was French. Conversing was mostly trouble-free and a knack soon developed for prefacing each attempt at conversation with the question 'Parlez vous Anglaise?' (Do you speak English?) The inevitable answer was, 'A little . . . ' And that's exactly what English they knew — the word 'a' and the word 'little'.

Namur itself looked just like a picture postcard — tall, thin, brick buildings rammed up against one another in narrow streets. The place reeked of history, but equally pungently of the dog turds littering the streets. The Belgians sure love their mutts.

Built on the steep granite hill overlooking the town of Namur, the citadel is centrepiece to a motocross course that is spectacular in the extreme. It is the dirt bike equivalent of the F1 Grand Prix at Monte Carlo. Starting in the flat 'esplanade' arena in front of the citadel, the course then launches the riders 30 metres into the muddy forest and eventually down to the cobblestoned streets below, now carpeted with soil for the occasion. The bikes roar past the Le Chalet du Monument Café before winding up the hill again, past ancient moats and battlements and, finally, about three minutes later, heading back into the spacious arena. Boldly etched into the citadel's highest point are the words *Ludos Pro Patria*, which means 'Games for the People', and the connection between the riders and the public at Namur is close and intense.

Namur has been a regular GP venue since 1957 and only missed the GP calendar on three occasions (1965, 1984 and 2002). Most of the riders have respect for the track, even if it has always been difficult to negotiate, with its special 'enduro-like' characteristics. It is the longest track on the GP schedule, designed in the park between 100-year-old trees, and everything is more difficult than usual — watering, security, crowd control and track maintenance. The Namur event in the 2005 season was to be held in May instead of July or August — the first time the date had been changed — and that created even more problems, with spring rain drenching the already tricky circuit and making it a nightmare for riders and spectators alike.

But, problems aside, everyone talks with a reverential tone when the subject of Namur is raised, perhaps none more so than Belgian motocross legend Stefan Everts. 'I discovered Namur on my bicycle when my father was racing the GPs. It has always been like a playground for me. I raced there for the first time only in 1998, as I was involved in the 250cc class, while Namur had the 500cc GPs, and since I have competed there I have always won. I won seven GPs there — 1998, 2001, 2002, 2003 in two classes, 2004, 2005 and 2006 — and with my individual win at the Motocross des Nations in 2001 I'm the same as Roger de Coster who won seven GPs at Namur.'

A Friday afternoon walk around the course with Ben Townley and Danish rider Brian Jorgensen revealed plenty, but only on race day, when 30 bikes and riders at a time battle at full throttle, would the gnarly course give up her secrets — slippery tree roots revealed and knee-deep ruts developing to make an already dangerous track lethal.

The so-called leisurely pre-race walk was itself a physical trial. So steep were some of the muddy slopes that even former world champ Townley lost his footing and slithered to the bottom of one drop-off. Only by clutching the metal trackside fencing could Brian ('Jorgy' to his mates) lower himself safely and avoid the same fate. 'This can't be part of the track?' I wondered aloud. A grim-faced nod from Townley confirmed it was.

As it was later to turn out, my pre-race track reconnoitre couldn't have been in better company — by late on Sunday afternoon, barely 48 hours after our walk together, these riders would make up two-thirds of the final one-two-three podium celebration.

Early on race-day morning, a mad melee of motocross fans thronged through the paved pit area, the tarmac already glistening with the day's first drenching, their faces painted, and their flags and banners cracking in the damp air. Some had already been filling up at the ubiquitous Jupiler beer tents and it was only 8.00 a.m. Stefan Everts look-alikes swarmed everywhere, fans dressed as their national hero, the multiple world champion and Belgian Sportsman of the Year for the previous four consecutive years.

The value of my sit-down interview with Everts the day before the main event was realised when, turning into the pit lane on race-day Sunday, a sea of multi-coloured humanity barred the way to Everts' giant Yamaha enclosure. When racing began it was difficult to hear the engines rev over the cacophony of air horns, cheering and an excited French commentator screaming over the loudspeakers

Jorgensen won the first race, followed by Everts. Josh was sixth and Ben seventh — not a grand performance, but respectable considering the treacherous conditions. The second 40-minute race was just two hours later, so both riders and bikes were washed and refuelled, the jostling spectators also well fuelled and primed for more vocal encouragement.

Although riders disappeared into the undergrowth for three minutes each lap, a giant television screen tracked their progress for the 26,000 fans seated on the citadel's stonework. It didn't matter if one of the many cameras missed the action — the rising crescendo of gasps, horns and cow bells announced the riders' progress, and most particularly heralded the progress of Everts as he parried the thrusts of Townley, who was challenging for the race lead. The noise travelled like a wave through the forest, culminating in a roar each time the riders flew back into the esplanade.

The day's final MX1 race came down to the final two corners, Townley closing to within a bike length of the Belgian legend. But the Kiwi bobbled and nearly fell, his momentum lost, and Everts wrapped up a record 82nd GP win.

Ben Townley's seventh and second results earned him the third step on the podium, and Josh bagged a pair of sixth placings, well below his best, but remained fourth in the championship standings at that stage and still within strike range. As it transpired, by the end of the season it was Stefan Everts, Josh Coppins and Ben Townley, in that order, at the top of the series standings.

On that cool, damp day in the city of Namur, I witnessed the best that motocross has to offer, and saw them racing around the most famous circuit of them all.

Everts said afterwards that the noise from his supporters meant he'd found it difficult to hear Townley coming as the Kiwi bridged a five-second gap during the closing stages of the second race. 'I tried to stay calm and ride smart,' he said. 'I got a little excited when Mickael Pichon was behind me at the Portugal GP and I didn't want that to happen to me at Namur. I knew that catching me was one thing, but passing me was something else.'

Too true . . . catching and passing Everts on any motocross track are two very different things, and very few individuals can actually do either, particularly when this man is in his own childhood 'playground'.

It was interesting to see the television coverage on New Zealand's Sky Sports channel a fortnight after the Namur event — it was nothing like being there, and emphasised just how flat, lifeless and tame the small screen can render extreme sports. There's nothing like standing trackside as Stefan Everts, Joel Smets, Ben Townley and Josh Coppins roar past, seeing the dirt roost, feeling the ground shake, smelling the fumes, and soaking in the atmosphere.

The podium celebration was a moment for typical Kiwi derring-do. Despite the security guard warning me that I shouldn't go up the steps, as soon as his back was turned and he sauntered away, up I scampered. I was the only person among the 68-strong troupe of international photo-journalists to get shots overlooking the shoulders of Everts and Townley as the champagne sprayed.

Going to Namur . . . interesting. Watching the racing . . . exciting. Getting on the podium . . . priceless.

2005: On top of the world

IN 2005 JOSH finally achieved the kind of results of which he had long known he was capable. Perhaps inspired by his own first GP win at the Isle of Wight the previous season, Josh was now a more regular podium visitor and one of only two riders able to challenge the mighty Stefan Everts. The other rider was house-mate and fellow Kiwi Ben Townley.

Josh scored his second career MX1 victory and his first-ever double-race success at the Swedish GP at Uddevalla in July 2005, in round 10 of the series, where he out-paced Townley, Everts and former champion Joel Smets to shave 14 points off Evert's championship lead. Josh was just 45 points behind Everts, with six rounds remaining and, significantly, still 300 points to be claimed before the trophy was given out. Was this finally going to be his year?

Sunshine, patchy cloud and high temperatures greeted the 28,000 fans that packed into the Uddevalla circuit and littered the rocky hillside. The track was hard, rough and dusty. Overtaking was difficult and the crucial moment of the gate drop determined the running order in both the MX1 and MX2 competitions.

Josh, who was second fastest after timed practice on the Saturday afternoon, started brightly behind Jonathan Barragan (KTM) who had taken the holeshot. When the Spaniard crashed on lap four, Josh had a clear track and proceeded to establish a small margin over Townley.

The race almost seemed over by the halfway stage as Josh enjoyed a lead of more than five seconds and the championship picture was looking even rosier with defending number one and current series leader Everts far adrift in fourth.

Townley then started to attack in the final few laps and Josh had to work hard to defend his lines. Josh eventually sealed only his third MX1 world championship race win, by just 0.4 of a second. It was the first time Josh had won the first race of a GP.

In the second race, Josh took the holeshot and again set an example from the front. On this occasion, he raced away from Belgian former world champion Joel Smets, with Townley making ground from the low reaches of the top ten to move up to third. Everts had a nightmare start and had to push hard for the duration of the race to eventually depose fellow Belgian Steve Ramon on the last lap and score an unaccustomed fourth.

Josh made a mistake in the final few minutes that saw him fall, allowing Smets to close, but the gap was still reasonable and the New Zealander had another GP win, the first for CAS Honda since the Isle of Wight the previous August. RWJ Honda's James Noble overtook Frenchman Pascal Leuret two laps from the chequered flag to capture sixth spot and carry the same standing in the overall classification to remain as the second-best Honda rider behind Josh.

With Everts again finishing fourth in the second race of the day, Josh now trailed the Belgian hero by just 45 points on the world championship table. Josh was rapt to win both motos. 'That was the first time for me. I'd been having problems with my first lap and not making enough of an impact from the gate, but I had a good feeling in Sweden and my mechanics had prepared the bike really well. I was expecting a good result so I was happy to have proved myself. I had a headache towards the end of the second race after I had over-jumped and jarred my neck, and that didn't help my concentration — it led to the mistake. I was able to get going again quickly, and had a lead of four or five seconds over Joel, so it was not too bad. It was good to close ground on Stefan.'

The world only had to wait a fortnight for the Josh Coppins Express to deliver again. At round 11 of the world series in South Africa, Josh again finished first in both races, moving even closer to Everts at the top of the standings.

More than 18,000 fans showed up in the hot sunshine at Sun City, where the newly renovated terrain of the supercross-style track offered a technical test for the GP riders. Many fell victim to the slippery, hard-packed sections.

Josh had to push hard for the win in race one at Sun City, battling with Everts throughout. The tussle started off as a three-way battle between Josh, Everts and factory KTM rider Townley. But Townley crashed hard just before the finish line jump, rejoining the race in fourth place and leaving the battle for the win between Everts and Josh. They swapped positions several times before Josh took the lead and held it to the finish.

Second overall at Sun City went to the then eight-time world champion Everts with two second placings, although he was very upset with his final results. Everts was in control of the second moto and on his way to a second–first overall win (and 85th career victory), but during the last lap, in celebration of his imminent victory, he let go of the bars while jumping, waving out to greet the audience. Losing his balance he fell and damaged the front brake.

Josh, meanwhile was closing in and, to his disbelief, overtook Everts, turning and looking back over his shoulder three times — he couldn't believe Everts had gifted him the GP victory. Everts was furious with his error and annoyed to see his series lead now slimmed to 39 points. Factory KTM rider Steve Ramon took third overall with his two third placings finish for the day, earning the Belgian his first podium of the season.

'I was pretty lucky!' Josh said afterwards. 'Of course it's always good to win, but I never expected to win like that. It's better to win because you're the best. I was the best in the first moto, but got a lot of cramps in the second. Even though Stefan had a big lead in the title chase, we'd seen him make mistakes — more this year than ever before — and we saw this in the last lap. This was the time for me to push and make as many points as possible. At that stage it had been the best GP of my career.'

Both Josh and Ben Townley ended their 2005 MX1 campaigns with a flourish, finishing second and third respectively in the Irish GP behind Everts. For Townley, it was a bitter-sweet, emotional moment on the podium. It was his last GP in Europe where he had been campaigning for the past five seasons, culminating with his MX2 world title in 2004. For 2006, the KTM works rider would be fulfilling a childhood dream of racing in the United States in their motocross and supercross series. 'I had built up some great friendships while I had been in Europe and I was going to miss everyone,' Townley said at the time.

Josh had played a big role in bringing 16-year-old Townley to Europe in 2001, then mentoring him through the years that followed. 'I wanted to be on the podium with Ben at his last race [in Europe],' Josh says. 'Two riders on the podium from one country — especially a country as small as New Zealand — was pretty special.' It was the third time the duo shared a podium in 2005 after they went first and second in France (Townley, Josh) and Sweden (Josh, Townley). The New Zealanders could have pushed Everts harder but for early season frustrations — Townley with an unreliable bike and Josh with injury and illness.

Meanwhile, Everts had signalled he wanted to win another world title in 2006 and then hang up his helmet. That became the next challenge for Josh: to try to beat Everts while he was at the top of his game before he left the race scene.

With two GP outright wins under his belt in 2005, not to mention a second consecutive British motocross title, it seemed Josh's goal for 2006 might be a very realistic one.

The Motocross des Nations

JOSH COPPINS HAS been an integral part of New Zealand's Motocross des Nations efforts since he first went to Europe, representing his country in the three-rider world teams championship squad each time since 1995, with mixed success. New Zealand has a long and proud association with what is widely regarded as the world's most important motocross event, yet which started almost by accident, with riders from a different off-road bike code.

When New Zealand enduro riders travelled to Holland for the International Six Days Enduro in 1984, it was hastily agreed that they would form a team to enter the Motocross des Nations. In those days the event was the forerunner to what would in 1985 become the Motocross des Nations — but back in 1984 it was still three separate meetings: the Coupe des Nations for 125cc bikes, the Trophée des Nations for 250cc bikes, and the Motocross des Nations for 500cc bikes.

Aucklander Tony Cooksley was one of the Kiwi riders that year. 'We were all just enduro guys at the time, over there for the International Six Days Enduro in Holland, but we did OK to be competitive. My team-mates were Graham Oliver, Chris Maindonald, Peter Gibbes and Graeme Harris.' The team finished a long way down the standings.

In 1987, Cooksley again represented New Zealand, the event this time staged at Unadilla in the United States. Cooksley and his team-mates, brothers Darryll and Shayne King, struggled in the sloppy mud and failed to record enough finishes to register, but it all helped to build up international experience for the Kiwis. The following year, 1988, New Zealand (with the King brothers and Darryl Atkins) finished 17th at Villars Ecot, in France. At last New Zealand was on the scoreboard.

New Zealand didn't enter a team in 1989 or 1990, but in 1991 veteran Cooksley was again called into national service. The three-man Kiwi team for the Dutch track at Valkenwaard that year consisted of Cooksley (500cc), Troy McAsey (250cc) and Atkins (125cc). They finished 20th.

In 1992 the Kiwis had their best chance to shine, with the event staged that year at Manjimup, near Perth, in Western Australia, just a short hop across the Tasman. The King brothers again teamed with Atkins, this time finishing a creditable tenth.

In Austria in 1993, at Schwanenstadt, the same Kiwi trio finished fifth. American stars Jeremy McGrath, Mike Kiedrowski and Jeff Emig won it that year, ahead of the Belgians (Marnicq Bervoets, Stefan Everts and Werner De Wit). It was the first year the Kiwi trio, as individuals, had spent the season based in Europe, contesting the motocross world championships, and that experience was starting to shine through.

With Kiwi riders taking their careers overseas in increasing numbers, and New Zealanders lining up more regularly at a GP or even American Motorcycling Association (AMA) events, the likelihood of New Zealand winning the Motocross des Nations had gone from a far-fetched dream to achievable reality.

Slovakia 1995

In 1995, Josh was based in Europe and had been making slow but steady headway on the GP scene. He was an obvious choice for the New Zealand team at the Motocross des Nations, the teenager proud to be called upon to represent his country and challenge for the event's famous prize, the Chamberlain Trophy. 'I rode a 125 at the Motocross des Nations in Sverepec, Slovakia, for the first time in 1995,' says Josh. He had been racing a Suzuki RM250 all season, but now borrowed an RM125 for the Motocross des Nations.

'It was quite exciting because the track was really cool. I had been racing the 250cc world championships, but switching back to the 125 to ride for New Zealand was pretty cool, even if it was a little bit scary at that time. I was still quite young and didn't really know how to handle that sort of pressure.'

His New Zealand team-mates were Taranaki's King brothers, Darryll and Shayne, already several years down the track of their own GP careers and able to instil a bit of extra confidence in their younger team-mate. 'The King brothers helped me out a little bit. It was a real nice time for me and very exciting.'

Despite getting a flat tyre midway through his opening race, Josh finished 15th and seventh in his two 125cc outings. With Darryll King (Kawasaki KX500) finishing third and fifth and Shayne King (KTM 250) finishing eighth and seventh, the New Zealand team wound up seventh overall, just one point behind the sixth-ranked Swedes and two points behind the fifth-placed Dutch trio.

It was an inspiring Motocross des Nations debut for Josh.

Spain 1996

The following year, in Spain, with another GP season under his wheels, Josh showed more confidence and helped move the New Zealand team up one spot, to sixth overall.

Shayne King (KTM 360), Darryll King (Honda CR250) and Josh (Suzuki RM125) were again in elite company. Defending Motocross des Nations champion Belgium had 500cc world championships runner-up Joel Smets (Husaberg FC501), 250cc world championships runner-up Marnicq Bervoets (Suzuki RM250) and 250cc world number one Stefan Everts (Suzuki RM125) to fly their flag.

The Americans were there in force too, with 250cc outdoor champion and 250cc supercross runner-up Jeff Emig (Kawasaki KX500), 250cc supercross champion and 250cc outdoor runner-up Jeremy McGrath (Honda CR250) and 125cc outdoor champion Steve Lamson (Honda CR125) waving the Stars and Stripes.

McGrath won both the 125–500 and 250–500 combined races to

set the Americans up for another win. Lamson went first and third, and Emig finished third and fifth, and that wrapped it up for them.

Shayne King, just a fortnight after being crowned 500cc world champion, finished seventh and 14th. Darryll King, who had finished fifth in the 500cc world champions that season, was eighth and seventh in his two outings, while Josh crashed out of the first race, but managed 17th on a pre-production bike in his next race.

'The track was awesome,' Josh recalls. 'There were heaps of jumps and really nice soil, but it rained all day Friday, which made it really soft. We had to make a lot of changes to the bike over the weekend. I had made a good start and was the fifth-placed 125cc rider in the day's first race [for 125 and 500 riders]. I passed Paul Malin [Britain] and Pedro Tragter [Netherlands], but I was riding too hard — I should have relaxed a bit. I crashed heavily and the bike was too damaged to continue.'

Josh got a poor start in his next race (for 125 and 250 riders). 'I was riding too tense, but got it all together in the latter stages [of the race] and passed several 250cc riders, including Australia's Craig Anderson.' Though he finished 17th overall, he was the sixth-highest-placed 125cc rider.

Belgium 1997

New Zealand finished seventh the following year at Nismes, in Belgium. Battling muddy conditions at this 35-nation showdown, the Kiwi trio of Darryll King (Husqvarna 633), Shayne King (KTM 250) and Josh Coppins (Suzuki RM125) had a tough time. Both Josh and Darryll King finished seventh in their opening race (for 125 and 500 riders respectively). 'The track was totally over-watered by the organisers,' Josh says, who had been the third-fastest 125cc rider when the track was dry and dusty for qualifying 24 hours earlier.

Josh finished 16th in the next race, for the 125cc and 250cc riders, while team-mate Shayne King was 12th. For the third race of the day (250–500), Darryll and Shayne King finished seventh and 13th respectively. The Belgian team, comprising 500cc world champion Smets, 250cc world champion Everts and 250cc world number two Bervoets, easily won the day.

England 1998

In 1998, Josh was again in New Zealand's Motocross des Nations' squad, this time scheduled for Foxhills in England. With heavy rain leading up to the event, it turned out to be an absolute quagmire, and many riders, world champions included, struggled and often failed to claw their way up one of the steep and slippery hills.

'It was particularly tough for me on the 125. I had been racing the 250cc world championships, but I was obviously demoted to the 125 for the Motocross des Nations at that time because I was the smallest guy,' Josh recalls. 'But it was good to get on the podium and really great to beat the Americans.'

Rising star for the Americans at that time was a youngster called Ricky Carmichael, in later years regarded as one of the sport's true superstars and able to command multi-million-dollar salaries from his American factory team bosses. But even in 1998, with Carmichael then just a freckle-faced 19-year-old, he was already very highly regarded, though Josh beat him on the day. 'It was so wet and muddy that, to tell the truth, I didn't know who I'd beaten until afterwards. You didn't really know where you were coming in the races. I think Carmichael crashed. I got stuck on the big hill, along with a lot of riders, but I felt no disgrace because I looked across and could see American Doug Henry and Alessio Chiodi [three-time world 125cc champion from Italy] stuck there beside me. There were about 13 of us stuck there, so I was in good company.'

Tough as it was, Josh never gave up. Each time his progress up that hill was stalled by traffic or loss of momentum, followed by a loss of balance, Josh would muscle his Suzuki out of the gluey mud, roll back to the bottom of the hill and have another crack at it.

Perseverance like this is what makes champions.

Brazil 1999

Low-budget New Zealand never made it to the 1999 edition of the great event in faraway Brazil, and the following September struggled to finish 19th overall when France hosted the spectacle at Saint Jean d'Angely.

Josh says he was 'gutted' by the Kiwi team's withdrawal from the Brazilian event. 'New Zealand riders were at that time at a high level internationally and we had the opportunity to garner a lot of publicity. That consideration wasn't only for the three team riders, but for all the Kiwi riders coming through. I think if clubs had known more about it, we'd have been there. I find it extremely hard to believe that something couldn't have been organised to raise funds. Slovakia raised enough to get to Brazil in 1999.

'It's really sad for the up-and-comers. I was sad about the damage this would do to the sport in New Zealand. I don't think people in New Zealand realised how our no-show would affect them. As a country we were right up there, a top country, producing top motocross riders. We didn't even have to qualify in 1999. We would have been riders numbered seven, eight and nine. I'm sure Daryl [Hurley] would have risen to the occasion and stepped up to the challenge. It's sad he didn't get the chance. Darryll King was not going to be around for ever, and it was guys like Hurley who needed the experience.'

Motorcycling New Zealand (MNZ) executive officer Sandra Perry was quick to defend her office and said fundraising schemes were in place, and that the June 1999 issue of *MNZ News*, posted to all clubs and licence holders, had included a plea for support from clubs and members. 'We just don't have that kind of money ourselves,' she said at the time. 'We circulated all the clubs and the response was disappointing. We received a $300 cheque from the Cambridge club just a fortnight before the event. It was too little and too late.' She also noted that MNZ had received two other donations, each for $30, from individuals.

France 2000

But New Zealand was back at the 'Motocross Olympics' a year later, albeit unable to achieve the lofty results of which the rider knew they were capable. The American trio won the French edition of the race in 2000, while the Kiwis suffered their worst-ever result. However, the New Zealand trio was in good company — the host country, France, finished a lowly 18th and Sweden was the last of the 20 countries to qualify.

With two non-finishes, the world-class New Zealand team of Darryll King (Husqvarna 633), Josh (Suzuki RM250) and Shayne King (KTM 125) never had a chance.

Shayne King's KTM 125SX was running like a rocketship and he felt comfortable after the early practice sessions, but when the gate dropped for the opening 125–500 moto, he was soon in trouble. King was brought down by another 125 rider after only half a lap. He picked the bike up, in last spot, and fought his way back to 24th. Darryll King made a good start and was in fourth place until an engine failure (tappet-adjusting bolt) forced him to retire.

For the second moto, for 125–500 riders, Shayne King was again barged off the track by the same rider in just the second corner of the race. A knock on his elbow left Shayne with no feeling in his left arm. He was also struck on the backside and a huge hole was torn in his pants, leaving a tyre burn. It was the second DNF for Team New Zealand and spelled the end to their chances.

Meanwhile, Josh was up to fourth place until a crash saw him drop two places and finish sixth. With just the third and deciding moto to come, for the 250–500 riders, New Zealand (along with France and Sweden) were unable to qualify for a result because of the pair of DNFs. Nevertheless, Darryl King battled to 11th and Josh finished behind him in 12th. Remarkably, if the New Zealanders could have managed another tenth or 11th placing, in exchange for one of their DNFs, they could still have finished as high as sixth.

Belgium 2001

The New Zealand team bounced back with a vengeance the following year. As they had done three years earlier at a muddy Foxhills, they came very close to cresting the summit, this time finishing on the podium at Belgium's breathtaking Namur circuit. 'We finished third at Namur and that was really something,' Josh says. 'The team was Shayne King, Daryl Hurley and myself. I rode well that day. I'd had a bad year and I wanted to finish the season off with a good result.

'It was just a day that went well after a crap year, basically. It was a highlight for me because I was leaving Suzuki and it was my last ride for them — my last big effort for Sylvain — and I wanted to go out on a high note. It was especially sweet to do so well at Namur. The place has an unbelievable atmosphere, but one mistake there and it's all over.

'For the first time I was the rider in the team with the best results. In the years before, Shayne and Darryll King had always produced the best individual results for the team, but now I was the rider with the best results and that was kind of cool.'

Spain 2002

The following year was another no-show from the New Zealand contingent as, sadly, budget constraints prevented the Kiwis from mustering a team and travelling to Spain. There was a terrible mix-up that year anyway, with the original host country, the United States, dropping the ball when they encountered last-minute problems whilst trying to use Indian-owned reservation land. Spain stepped up to the plate to offer their venue as a replacement, but it was all a bit muddled and hurried.

Belgium 2003

But New Zealand was soon back among the leading teams in 2003 when Shayne King, Josh and Ben Townley (the youngster making his Motocross des Nations debut) turned up to race at Zolder.

King's name hadn't been there when the New Zealand team was

originally announced for the Zolder event. For the first time in more than a decade, King brothers Darryll and Shayne weren't first-choice riders for the Kiwi squad, but 125cc specialist Daryl Hurley crashed and injured himself at round eight of the American 125cc nationals near Washington a fortnight before Zolder. When the extent of Hurley's ankle injuries were revealed, a quick rethink of the Kiwi line-up was required. A fax from California reported Hurley's injuries were so severe that he was under doctor's orders not to race for at least six weeks, and Motorcycling New Zealand rushed to the phone to call up the first reserve rider, Shayne King.

The 32-year-old King said he hadn't been disappointed to be omitted from the original squad, despite the fact he was then leading the Australian four-stroke nationals and was the reigning New Zealand 250cc and 500cc champion. 'Josh, Ben and Daryl were the men for the job that year. I was winning in Australia, and although it's another step up to compete at the GP level, I knew I still had the pace to run with the world leaders.'

And so it proved to be, with New Zealand taking its 'patched together' team to fourth place overall.

Netherlands 2004

With Ben Townley, Daryl Hurley and Josh picked to wear the Silver Fern, the New Zealand contingent had high hopes for the 2004 Motocross des Nations at the sandy Lierop circuit in the Netherlands.

The day started well for the Kiwis. The first race was won by Belgium's Stefan Everts while Josh finished third and Townley finished sixth, good enough to give the Kiwi team the preliminary four-point lead over the chasing nations. Unfortunately, that was the only race where both New Zealand riders would finish, as mechanical gremlins attacked.

Townley's bike packed up in the second race and he recorded a DNF, dropping the team to seventh overall, a position they were unable to improve upon in the final race after Josh's bike had a mechanical crisis and he was unable to finish. Belgium (Everts, Steve Ramon and

Kevin Strijbos) retained the crown, with Holland and France making it a European lock-out.

The team manager, Wellington's Mike McLeod, said at the time: 'It's very disappointing after such a good build-up and a brilliant start. Our hopes were high.'

France 2005

It was a new three-man Kiwi combination — Josh, Ben Townley and Motocross des Nations debutante Cody Cooper — that finished a fighting fourth at the 2005 edition of the great race in France. It was less than the Kiwi team had hoped for, but still a remarkable feat, with a New Zealand presence on the podium in all three races at the stony Ernee circuit in western France.

A sell-out crowd of more than 45,000 fans screamed themselves silly as the Kiwis traded blows with the glossy magazine pin-up boys from the United States, the home-town French riders and the favoured Belgians at the head of the 36-nation field. Though New Zealand as a team missed out on a podium spot, two of the three best individuals at the event were Kiwis — Josh and Ben Townley. Top dog was American champion Ricky Carmichael, who won both his races.

Unfortunately, the Motocross des Nations is a team event where five of the six individual results are added together, with the lowest score winning the day. Townley notched up a first and second, and Josh achieved a second and fourth, but Cooper's 23rd-23rd results proved costly for the Kiwi line-up.

Carmichael (MX1 Suzuki) led from start to finish in the day's first race for MX1 and MX2 bikes, but from first lap to last, he had Josh (MX1 Honda) on his tail. French former world champion Mickael Pichon (MX1 Honda) moved up from seventh on the opening lap to finish third and take the bottom step on the podium.

Meanwhile, further down the field, Cooper (MX2 Honda) was struggling. From 30th position on the first lap of 18 in the race, he had his work cut out, but cheered on by a large contingent of Kiwi fans, he fought through the pack. He had picked off seven riders before time ran out and he finished 23rd.

The 21-year-old Cooper, drafted into the Kiwi squad at the last minute, was clearly disappointed with his result, but GP team observers were nonetheless impressed with what they saw from the youngster on his European debut.

Next up was Townley (open class KTM) and Cooper again. It didn't take long for Townley to make up for an average start, surging through from fourth on the opening lap to take the lead from American vice-champion Kevin Windham (open class Honda) on lap ten. Despite the attentions of Frenchman David Vuillemin (open class Yamaha) and Belgian Steve Ramon (open class KTM), Townley kept his head, winning the race by nine seconds from Vuillemin.

Cooper, meanwhile, had matched his first race result by finishing 23rd, this time charging through from 40th and last at the start, clawing his way past several GP stars as he made spectacular progress through the field.

The day's third and final race had New Zealand GP stars Ben Townley and Josh lined up together. Josh leapt to a great start, but team-mate Townley was on the move, passing Windham and quickly latching on to Carmichael, who was again out in front.

It stayed this way to the finish, with Carmichael taking the win from Townley, with Windham ten seconds behind in third. In the meantime, Josh had had a small crash early in the race and dropped to sixth. He quickly recovered his momentum and began making headway on the group ahead. On the final lap, he pushed past Pichon to finish fourth.

It was a case of 'so near and yet so far' for Team New Zealand. Despite teams being able to drop their worst result, the Kiwis missed by just one point on an overall podium spot. The 59th annual Motocross des Nations finished with the United States on top, France second, Belgium third and New Zealand fourth.

Ben Townley ended the weekend second overall on individual classification, beaten only by double race winner Carmichael. He left a couple of days later for the United States to prepare for his 2006 season, where he would race for Kawasaki in the supercross and outdoors series.

Josh was philosophical about his weekend in France. 'I was quite happy with my results that day. I finished second and fourth and Ben rode extremely well. On the other hand, I'm a little bit disappointed because I crashed in both races and I think I could have been a bit closer to Ricky. I think we can be pretty proud of our result as a team. Cody rode really well — we couldn't have expected more from him. He jumped in to help at the last minute, and I don't think any of us could have done any better.'

England 2006

The United States searched its 290 million citizens and came up with three pretty good motocross racers — James Stewart (MX1), Ryan Villopoto (MX2) and Ivan Tedesco (open). Belgium surveyed its ten million citizens and also produced three damn fine specimens — Stefan Everts (MX1), Kevin Strijbos (MX2) and Steve Ramon (open). The French and the British did the same with their populations of 60 million each and Italy picked over its 56 million to come up with their three representatives.

As for New Zealand, we asked around our paltry four million and came up with at least six individuals who could probably have stood on the podium at the 2006 Motocross of Nations — its name now anglicised — near Winchester, in the south of England in September.

Darryll King, Shayne King and Scott Columb said they'd be happy just to watch the racing (but they'd be there and have their boots and helmets handy, if they were needed) which meant New Zealand would go with the same three-man line-up that finished fourth in France the previous season — Josh (MX1), Ben Townley (MX2) and Cody Cooper (open).

In terms of warfare, big armies might beat little armies, but when it comes to global conflict like the Motocross of Nations, size matters little. It was our three men versus theirs. Even individual results don't really matter, as the Motocross of Nations is a unique contest in this respect. It was, as usual, three riders per team with two races each, and only five results would determine which team would take the Motocross of Nations' Chamberlain Trophy as their carry-on luggage at Heathrow on the Monday morning.

And so it proved to be that the Belgians won the battles, but the Americans won the war. Even without a win to their credit, the three-man United States team did enough to clinch the title and create history by becoming the number one motocross team in the world for a record 17th time, previously sharing the honour of 16 wins with host country Great Britain.

Consistency won the day for the Americans, with Stewart (Kawasaki) twice finishing runner-up to Everts, and 17-year-old Motocross of Nations rookie Villopoto stunning the GP stars by winning the MX2 class with his second and third placings. The previous year's winning team captain for the Americans, Ricky Carmichael, was a late withdrawal because of injury, and his replacement, Tedesco, finished sixth and ninth on his open class Suzuki RMZ450 to give his side the extra points needed to wrap it up.

Everts, in his last big international appearance, went out with a bang, the ten-time world champion finishing the day unbeaten in the MX1 class as he headed the cream of the world's motocross talent, including American 'Bubba' Stewart, Josh, and the flying young Frenchman Christophe Pourcel (just a week after he'd clinched the world MX2 title).

Belgium's open class rider, Steve Ramon, won his class too, thanks to him finishing fourth and fifth in his two outings, giving Belgium the number two spot on the Motocross of Nations podium. It was a tearful third member of the Belgian team though, Strijbos, who abandoned his bike at the bottom of the big valley and trudged back to the pits in his second outing, that non-finish the one score his country could discard.

Even so, it probably would not have been enough to stop the American juggernaut, and second place was the best Belgium could hope for. In the end, Belgium finished seven points short of the podium top step.

New Zealand battled well throughout the weekend and had been holding the number two spot after the first two races, with Kiwi MX2 rider Townley again proving a Motocross of Nations revelation when he took his Kawasaki KX250F to remarkable third and fifth placings against the bigger 450cc bikes.

But a series of crashes during the weekend's final race — for Josh on the MX1 Honda CRF450 and Cooper in the open class on another Honda CRF450 supplied by Team CAS — meant a supreme final effort was needed just for the Kiwis to stay on the podium. A late-race push from Josh to get past Britain's Billy Mackenzie (Yamaha YZF450) and Tedesco, and a last-lap effort from Cooper to surge past Canada's Blair Morgan (Honda CRF450) were enough for New Zealand to finish third, another seven points back from Belgium.

For a country of only four million people, New Zealand boxed well above its weight in the motocross world. New Zealand team manager Russell Burling summed it up afterwards: 'It's a great experience for us as a country to bring our riders from three different areas in the world to this Motocross of Nations. Cody is down in the Southern Hemisphere, Ben is in America and Josh is in Europe, and that's not easy to do. We were very grateful to Mitch Payton and the Monster/Pro Circuit/Kawasaki Team, the Molson Kawasaki team and the CAS Honda team for enabling us to do this. We are a very small country and we couldn't do it without their help. It would have been impossible for us to do this type of race, and we were extremely grateful as a motocross nation. In 2005, we lost [a podium spot] by one point to Belgium. We were over the moon to achieve a podium spot in 2006.'

The Americans were the best team and Belgium's Everts was the best individual, but the Kiwis were on the podium too, and that made them pretty special. The result was New Zealand's third podium finish, following earlier third placings at Foxhills, Britain, in 1998 and third at Namur, Belgium, in 2001.

'It was a great result for us in England,' says Josh, who was the Kiwi team captain at the time. 'It was great for New Zealand and great for our federation and the young guys back at home. I struggled in the first half of the first moto and then settled down and started to ride much better with some better lines. There were many good riders in England that day, and they all wanted to do well for their countries. We came together as a team, and we had this result to show for it.'

New Zealand's results at the Motocross des Nations since 1993
1994 (Roggenburg, Switzerland): New Zealand 16th (Shayne King, Cameron Negus, Darryl Atkins)
1995 (Sverepec, Slovakia): New Zealand seventh (Darryll King, Shayne King, Josh Coppins)
1996 (Jerez, Spain): New Zealand sixth (Shayne King, Darryll King, Josh Coppins)
1997 (Nismes, Belgium): New Zealand seventh (Darryll King, Shayne King, Josh Coppins)
1998 (Foxhills, England): New Zealand third (Darryll King, Shayne King, Josh Coppins)

1999 (Indiatuba, Brazil): New Zealand did not show

2000 (Saint Jean d'Angely, France): New Zealand 19th (Darryll King, Josh Coppins, Shayne King)

2001 (Namur, Belgium): New Zealand third (Daryl Hurley, Josh Coppins, Shayne King)

2002 (Bellpuig, Spain): New Zealand did not show

2003 (Zolder, Belgium): New Zealand fourth (Shayne King, Josh Coppins, Ben Townley)

2004 (Lierop, Netherlands): New Zealand seventh (Ben Townley, Josh Coppins, Daryl Hurley)

2005 (Ernee, France): New Zealand fourth (Josh Coppins, Ben Townley, Cody Cooper)

2006 (Matterley Basin, England): New Zealand third (Josh Coppins, Ben Townley, Cody Cooper)

2007 (Budds Creek, Maryland, USA): New Zealand failed to qualify (Josh Coppins was injured and his replacement in the team, Daryl Hurley, then crashed during qualifying; Ben Townley also crashed during qualifying; the third team member was Cody Cooper)

2006: Back from the brink

For 2006, the CAS Honda line-up underwent further refinements. Jussi Vehvilainen retired, and Josh was joined in the encampment by 21-year-old Belgian rider Ken de Dycker, who was seen as his potential replacement a few more years down the line.

The early part of 2006 had promised much for Josh, but in the end he was prevented from delivering very much at all. A good build-up to the season saw him twice finish runner-up to perennial GP favourite Stefan Everts in both heats at the pre-season Pernes les Fonataine international in France in late February. It was an encouraging result and certainly augured very well for the season ahead.

French riders Mickael Pichon, Sebastien Tortelli, and MX2 rider Sebastian Pourcel — the surprise of the season's warm-up weekend — all played a big part in the fighting at Pernes les Fonataine, but it was Everts and his Kiwi nemesis who gave fans a taste of what they might expect for the 2006 world title hunt, due to start in Zolder just over a month later.

Though his pace looked good to observers at Pernes les Fonataine, Josh wasn't happy with his qualifying form, and was only the eighth-fastest around the famous French venue. 'I had a good gate pick in the first race, but I made a little mistake coming off the start which left me in fifth position,' he explains. 'I made my way to fourth immediately and then to third when Pichon stalled his bike. Pourcel was riding really well, but I passed him and then went after Stefan who had managed to holeshot, so he beat me by five seconds in the end.'

The deciding second race would be a three-way battle, with a role reversal at the start and Josh leading out of the first corner. 'I grabbed the holeshot and led for five laps or so. I decided to slow the pace a little, to let Stefan past and see what lines he was using, but then I saw that Pichon was right on him, so that plan wasn't going to work. I made a few mistakes and Stefan got by me, and he picked up the pace quite a bit, but I managed to stay with him for a good battle. This was a sign to me of the sort of things to expect in 2006.'

The Kiwi was also pleased to reap the benefit of his CAS Honda team's work and development during the race, and felt confidence in his Honda CRF450. 'We had worked a lot on the bike over the weekend and found some good suspension settings. The engine was very good, obviously, with the holeshot in the second heat. For the first race of the season I was really content with second place overall. It was also good to see Stefan pushing really hard — you don't normally see that from him so early in the season.'

But just as the Kiwi star's 2006 prospects were looking bright, Josh's world once again came tumbling down around his ears. With the eagerly awaited start of the GP season just a few days away, Josh hurt himself badly during training at the end of March and re-injured his right shoulder. It was a serious setback and would eventually sideline him for three months and derail his entire championship bid.

'I caught my right shoulder on a post. It dislocated and then went back into place straight away. I didn't even crash,' Josh explains. 'A previous injury had torn my bicep muscle which had basically torn the cap on the top of my humerus bone. It was like a bolt missing a washer. It was kind of sloppy and loose. I kept riding, thinking it wasn't real, but then my shoulder gave way again and I was forced to stop, in a lot of pain.' It was the same shoulder he had injured in a crash during a pre-season race a year earlier, in 2005 at the Hawkstone track in England.

A serious injury just two days out from the start of the season was hard for him to accept. He tried to race the opening round of the world championships at Zolder, but pulled out after making two attempts to ride during practice sessions, his shoulder still unstable, even though braced and taped. There was no way he could last the season, and he didn't want to be a rider making up the numbers — he wanted to be in the race to win. 'After five months' preparation, to be out like that so suddenly was very difficult and frustrating. I was in denial for a few days, and then I just sat back and mapped out what I had to do to get back.'

After the crash he met with orthopaedic surgeon Toon Claes, had x-rays, a scan and ultrasound, and was told there was new damage to the shoulder and only a 50-50 chance of avoiding recurring problems. 'I hate going to Dr Claes as he always looks at the x-rays and goes, "Aha . . . aha," which he normally follows up by telling me some bad news. Basically I had dislocated my shoulder and damaged the bottom part of the cuff a year earlier. When I dislocated it again, I had damaged the top part of the cuff — of course there are technical terms for what I'd done, but it all went in one ear and out the other.'

The recovery process was slow and extremely frustrating. Imagine a greyhound chained to the kennel or a lion caged. It took a long time to come back: a month in a sling, then a month of physiotherapy followed by normal training. 'We all have to deal with injury at some point. It's all part and parcel of the sport,' Josh says. 'Recovery is always hard, as all your focus goes on that part of your body. I was limited in what I could do in the gym, but I did what I could, knowing that it would help to speed up recovery and keep me in shape for my comeback. I strongly believe that if you don't use it, you lose it. My base fitness really helped my body recover faster, as well as helping me regain my mental strength.

'Being a motocross racer, it's amazing what you learn about your body. You go through so many things . . . fatigue, injury, burn-out and so on. But you very quickly work out what your body is telling you, meaning what you need to sort it out. Going to races and the training tracks with friends was also really beneficial. This really gave me time to watch and learn from the other top riders. I was looking at what lines they took on the track and their bike set-up, and I took notes on their training. All in all, I utilised my downtime to work really hard to get perspective on the sport.

'The hardest thing for me was to watch as everyone else who could challenge Everts also dropped out. First it was Pichon — out in the first race — and then Tortelli too dropped to the sidelines. Everts had no trouble dominating after that. He just backed off the pace and it was really hard for me to accept that he was able to do that, and that I couldn't be there to keep him honest.

'It was definitely a speed bump in my career. My team got together and we reassessed what needed to be done to try and recover. It was hard too, because it wasn't really that I'd made a mistake to injure myself. It was just one of those things. I didn't have a huge crash because I miscalculated something. I didn't even crash, as I never actually fell off.'

He was forced to watch helplessly as Everts won the Belgian GP and began to build towards an historic tenth world title. By midway through the season, Everts was nearly 100 points clear of his nearest challengers, Suzuki rider Kevin Strijbos (Belgium) and Kawasaki rider Tanel Leok (Estonia).

Josh was to be sidelined for three months, leaving Everts virtually unchallenged as, almost machine-like, he methodically yet skilfully increased his championship lead at each successive GP. In his time on the fringes, Josh would miss the GPs of Spain, Germany, Portugal, Japan and Bulgaria, in total skipping six events in the 15-round championship.

'Obviously my 2006 season didn't start how I planned it,' Josh says. 'I'd been working extremely hard for the six months leading up to the first GP, and I had made a lot of sacrifices to give myself and the team the best chance at the title.' Though his 2006 MX1 title bid was ruined, Josh continued to work hard in the gym. He spent many hours cycling and training with the legendary cyclist Plons, hoping those tough kilometres would once again give him an advantage over his rivals when he returned to racing. 'I wanted to be back for the British Grand Prix [round eight of the world series, on June 18], but I refused to race in England unless I felt I was ready.'

The doctor finally gave Josh the all-clear to race again, but told him there was only so much he could do in 12 days to get ready for his first world championship event of the 2006 season, the British GP at Matterley Basin, Winchester. 'I had 12 days and I hadn't ridden for three months,' Josh says. 'The 12 days I had on the bicycle didn't help a lot. There's simply no substitute for time on a motocross bike. I did a lot of cycling and running and swimming, but time on the bike was what I needed.

'I'd been watching the races and was enjoying the battles between Everts and Tortelli, but watching them lap up to fifth place or whatever, I didn't enjoy that. You know the younger guys looked OK on the easier tracks, like in Spain, but on the rougher tracks — like Zolder and Portugal — they didn't have the same speed as Everts.'

Tough talk indeed, but Josh soon backed up his sharp words with equally sharp action when he was back among the leaders at his first comeback race on 18 June in the British GP, in round eight of the series.

Considering the lack of build-up, Josh managed a creditable performance at the brand-new Matterley Basin circuit, near Winchester, south-west of London. 'The first race wasn't so bad [he finished third], but I wasn't smooth on the bike,' he said at the time. 'The second race was tough because I broke my goggles and I had a lot of dirt in my eyes [he finished fifth].' The results were good enough to put him on the podium, and even though he'd contested just one of the eight GPs at that stage, he earned enough points to slot in at 23rd overall in the series standings. It was a sparkling comeback.

Josh proved he hadn't lost his touch when he grabbed the holeshot in race one, which had 39,000 frantic spectators cheering the Kiwi on. An aggressive Steve Ramon (Belgium) made his way past Josh, only to bite the dirt a few corners later, with Josh having to overshoot the corner to avoid hitting him.

After settling into the race, he managed to pass Frenchman Pascal Leuret and Belgian Cedric Melotte, moving into second place behind championship leader Everts. Josh doggedly defended his position but a last-lap battle ensued with his CAS Honda team-mate, Belgian Ken de Dycker, with the stable-mates battling right to the finish line. Josh eventually settled for third, but pride was restored with the Kiwi coming across the line less than one second behind de Dycker.

Josh leapt to another great start in the second MX1 race of the British GP, going handlebar to handlebar with Everts into the first turn. However, the wily Belgian had the advantage of the inside line and forced Josh wide. A hectic first lap saw Josh back in fifth as he tried to keep in touch with the leaders.

But then misfortune struck and a flying rock from another rider dislodged his goggle lens. This meant Josh had to keep his distance, settling for fifth. Consistency rewarded Josh with third overall for the day and a spot on the podium, capping off a magnificent return to GP racing.

'This was an important race for the team and our sponsors, which is why we took the decision to race earlier than planned,' Josh says. 'I was far from 100 per cent fit and had problems riding at that fast pace. I was not so smooth and was fighting with the bike. I broke my goggles in the second moto and had a lot of dirt in my eyes, but I just rode my own race. It wasn't such a bad race for my first time back though.'

Now there's an understatement for you. 'Not such a bad race' translated to a podium spot, something some riders may never achieve in their entire professional career. From absolutely nowhere in the championship standings, Josh's performance at the British GP earned him 36 points, put him on the third step of the podium, and saw him suddenly appear on the rankings list in the number 23 spot.

The number 23 was significant for Josh — it had popped up much earlier in his international career. He had finished 23rd in the 250cc world championships in 1996, his second full year on the circuit. Ten years on and he was good enough to earn 23rd after just one GP.

Josh's second GP after his injury break was in Sweden and it ended with a similar result, a third and a fifth placing, although he struggled even more with his fitness after so long off the bike. 'I felt worse in Sweden than in England,' he recalls. 'In England, I was really excited to be back, and in Sweden I struggled again with my energy. I got a bad start in the opening race and [Spaniard] Jonathan Barragan got away from me. In the second race, again I just didn't have enough energy.' He was beaten by Everts, Strijbos, Ramon and Irishman Gordon Crockard.

South Africa was next on the agenda and this time Josh rode much better, finishing with two second placings and leading home everyone except for miracle man Everts. Next up it was Loket, in the Czech Republic. He finished second and third there, despite crashing in the second race. 'I crashed with Barragan in the second race and Kevin [Strijbos] got away from me. I couldn't pull him back.'

Things improved for Josh as his fitness and conditioning once again reached the level of his GP rivals. He stormed into the Belgian GP at Namur and captured two second places. Again nobody could match Everts, who bagged a pair of wins and took the GP overall, but Josh was on the second step of the podium.

After two months off and just five GPs under his belt, Josh was closing in on the top step, a rare sight in a season where Everts was seemingly unbeatable and had already clocked a remarkable winning streak of 12 GPs. But Josh broke the streak at the next event, the Irish GP at Desert Martin, round 13, in August that year, finishing second and first to Everts' first and second, the two men equal on points for the day. Not even a nibble was taken out of Everts' points advantage, but significantly, Josh was named the Irish GP winner because he'd finished better in the second leg of the event. 'Stefan took the loss really well and congratulated me. I'd just ended his GP winning streak and ruined his perfect season. It was probably my best win in my career — to do it on that track and against Stefan after he'd been undefeated all season was pretty cool stuff.

'The crowds in Ireland were awesome. I have a good following in Ireland — I do the British championship races there, and the people are really great. It was unbelievable when I got onto the podium. I also think people wanted to see Stefan get beaten — they were cheering for the underdog. I was really happy with how Stefan reacted — he was really gracious, and he said that even in defeat he was really happy for me.'

Josh recalls the race easily, a win like that staying vivid in his mind. 'Stefan sort of went past me under the yellow flag, and I lost my momentum in the first race. I wasn't prepared to let him pass me in the second one. I tried so hard in the first race and wanted to come back, but I couldn't. I was getting in all sorts of problems with the lapped riders, so thought in the second race that I was just going to push and push and not let him get me back. I was happy he took the pressure off a little and I could follow him, then I came back and felt really strong.

'In the first race I let him go — I wanted to follow him, but I couldn't because of the situation. When I passed him in the second race, it was clean. We got close a couple of times, nothing serious — we were really focused and we ride different lines anyway, so it's hard to get together.'

That day Josh clicked with the Irish track like never before. 'Off the top of the hill, on the first lap, I came out and jumped off a bump and onto a berm — it just felt so perfect. It was the sort of thing you see Stefan do in the sand and think to yourself, "I wish I could do that," but this time I did it. It was awesome, and then he [Everts] started doing it. I could triple into the whoops, and there were not many guys doing that. Even the younger guys weren't doing it, and that surprised me. I think it was because of the supercross races I'd done back in New Zealand in December, which helped with the jumping and timing.

'I knew from the first race that when Stefan and I were lapping guys like [Frenchman] Pascal Leuret and [Estonian] Avo Leok, we would be coming up on the others. When I lapped Kevin Strijbos in the second race, I knew we had lapped just about everyone. Stefan and I were so much stronger than all the other riders that day.'

The following GP at Lierpo in the Netherlands, the penultimate event on the GP calendar, was a case of 'normal service has been resumed', with Everts winning both races back to back and Josh twice finishing runner-up.

He now turned his thoughts to finishing the season strongly at the French GP in Ernee, the same venue used for the Motocross of Nations 12 months earlier. This final GP of the season was the race Josh wanted to win probably more than any in his career, with it being Everts' final GP and the fact that he stood to earn a lot of bragging rights for 2007 if he won.

But it wasn't to be. Josh made a number of mistakes and finished a disappointing sixth and second in the two races for fourth place overall. 'I really wanted to beat Everts,' Josh says. 'I also wanted to let the others know that I was going to be the guy to beat in 2007. In the first race, Pichon landed on me in the first corner, and that freaked me out a little. I also wanted to get to Everts quickly, but made a mistake and crashed again. I jumped into Jonathan Barragan and that pretty much ended my chances.'

Although the season had been a write-off from the start for Josh, he could take plenty of cheer from the fact that remarkably he had climbed on to the podium in seven of the eight GPs in the second half of 2006. He had also been the only man to beat Everts in the season in which the Belgian great had claimed his record tenth world championship crown.

'I can't take anything away from Stefan Everts. He was awesome in 2006 and definitely the best rider. It's hard to say if he would have simply stepped up a notch and still won if I'd been there throughout. He would definitely have been hard to beat, but I did beat him when I came back near the end of the season. When I did beat him, together we lapped half the field, which showed just what level he was at and the level I had to be at to beat him.

'I don't know that he would have won all the races he did if I had been there the whole time in 2006 — maybe it would have been the same result — but at least they would have been better races and a better show for the fans. I never expected to get on the podium straight away. Stefan had really dominated every race — he was riding so well. I really wanted to make a race of it when I came back to the track. I think even Stefan wanted to be in a real race too.'

Josh was offended by how easy it had been and critical that the other riders hadn't been challenging Everts. 'To come straight back and get on the podium after only having ridden a bike 12 days before the British GP was unheard of — it shouldn't happen like that. For me it was great, and a good feeling. It showed my work ethic was paying dividends.'

A quick scan of the 2006 statistics reveal something remarkable about Josh's performance once he was off the sideline and back on the bike. When you look at the number of laps led, he was second only to Everts, despite missing seven GPs. His 'laps led' tally was better than that of riders such as Strijbos, Ramon and de Dycker, who raced for the entire season.

He picked up nine runner-up finishes behind Everts in his 16 races (eight GPs) and also snared the only GP win not taken by Everts that year. In addition to Josh, the competition had also lost MX1 world number three Ben Townley (off to race in the United States) and Joel Smets (to a career-ending knee injury), and Pichon and Tortelli had followed Josh to the sidelines with injuries.

But while some journalists continued to get excited about the racing, the lap times didn't lie, and Josh was brutally honest in his analysis. 'I was happy for the younger guys — they were all getting better results — but if you are serious, you have to look at who was not racing. I mean, last year we had Stefan, Ben, Joel, Mickael and myself. Tortelli came in [from a stint of several seasons in the United States], but then was also out through injury, so you had the five fastest guys out of the running. A second or third place would really be a seventh or eighth if everyone was fit.

'If you look at the lap times from Portugal, once Tortelli went out of the race the lap times dropped like ten seconds, and still those guys couldn't catch Stefan. I understand Stefan saw Tortelli crash and his concentration went, but still, when Tortelli was out, Stefan dropped his lap times by ten seconds. People didn't look at that.'

Although he was quickly back to his best again in the second half of 2006, it was a more philosophical Josh who had been forced to contemplate life from the sidelines for that crucial opening stanza of 2006 and, at that point in his career, he knew he couldn't afford to lose another season like that. 'A wise person once told me, some people succeed because they are destined to, while most succeed because they are determined to!'

With the 2006 season just past the halfway stage, there was an announcement in the beginning of July that Josh Coppins would leave Honda and replace his old rival Everts in the Yamaha factory team.

Everts had earlier announced he would be retiring from racing at the end of 2006.

The decision to shift from CAS Honda to Rinaldi Yamaha wasn't taken lightly. 'I first spoke with Yamaha in the middle of 2005 and they approached me [in 2006] to sign the deal before I'd ridden again after my injury,' Josh says. 'This was a sign that they really believed in me. Then I told Honda of my decision.'

As for making the switch, he was philosophical. 'I'd ridden a Suzuki for 21 years before signing with Honda, and that was hard too, because I had — and still have — a great relationship with Suzuki New Zealand, as well as Jay Foreman from Suzuki in Australia. I was with Honda for almost five years, one with the Vismara team [in Italy] and four, based in England and Belgium, with CAS Honda.

'At CAS, I was like part of a family. Given that team owner Harry Ainsworth had lost his son in a motocross accident in 2001, I really admired him for maintaining his commitment to the team after such a tragic loss. I was like his adopted son. We would talk pretty much every day, mostly about random stuff like rugby, for example, but our relationship was, and still is, quite special.'

Much like leaving Suzuki years earlier, leaving CAS Honda was a big call. 'I had always wanted to ride for the Rinaldi Yamaha team. I remember when I first arrived in Europe I'd watch Andrea Bartolini on the black Yamaha and then the white Chesterfield Yamaha bikes — they were so cool. Also, Italy is my favourite country in Europe, so this made the choice easier. With Stefan leaving at the end of 2006, the time was right for me. When I told Harry and the boys [at CAS Honda] they were disappointed, naturally, but at the same time they were happy for me. They kind of knew it was coming.'

Even though the news of Josh's defection to Yamaha became public knowledge on 4 July, well before the end of the 2006 season, he was unable to ride a Yamaha publicly until the New Year. 'There is a formality you have to go through which is both legal and moral, but it's never easy leaving a team where you've had a lot of success and which was like a big family to me. It was also hard because my old team had to make adjustments and put plans in place to replace me, and all the time I was still under their awning and trying to do a job for them.'

At the Swedish GP at Udevalla on 2 July, just two days before the official Yamaha press release announcing Josh's defection, Rinaldi Yamaha's Everts clocked up two more wins and yet another overall GP victory, with fellow Belgian Steve Ramon second that day and Josh third (thanks to a third and fifth placing). At that time, it was Everts' tenth successive GP win. 'Everts and I were washing our faces prior to heading up to the podium, and I looked across to see Michele Rinaldi, my then soon-to-be Yamaha boss, who gave me a wink, as if to say, "You're good, but you're not ready to beat us yet."

'My contract officially ended with Honda on 31 December. I was released prior to that to test the new Yamaha and to train on one, but nobody was supposed to take photos of me on a Yamaha until my contract with Honda had ended.'

Josh signed a two-year contract with Rinaldi Yamaha and now had everything in place to see him through to the finish of his European racing career. With the Rinaldi factory Yamaha team to support him, Josh was content in the knowledge that he had the infrastructure in place to finally become a world champion. 'A lot of people said I had big boots to fill, but I didn't look at it like that, and I don't think Michele Rinaldi was looking at it like that either.

'He had a list of riders he considered for 2007 and I was on top of that list. I think Stefan was a great rider — there is no chance I will ever match him — but I do have the chance to win a couple of world titles for Rinaldi. Michele Rinaldi said he wanted a rider who would always push and try to get a good result for the team. I instantly knew we would get on well.'

2007: Out from Everts' shadow

IN THE 2007 season, the pressure really went on for Josh like never before. The man who had stood in Josh's way, the legendary Everts, was gone from the starting grid, but the Belgian legend still cast an enormous shadow over the sport, his presence now felt from behind the scenes as the new race manager for the KTM factory team.

Everts' job was to guide and mentor the young up-and-comers at KTM, to teach them how to win and, most importantly, as far as Josh was concerned, how to beat him. Everts was still Josh's nemesis. The Kiwi was determined to knuckle down and do what he did best — work hard, race hard and shut out the distractions, although, perhaps, now for only two more seasons.

'I am pretty sure I will stop racing the GPs in two years,' said Josh as the 2007 championship dawned. 'I enjoy it in Europe, but every top rider has ten top years, and I know I can give 100 per cent for the next two years. After that I don't know. I will have to look at the situation after the two-year contract is up — if I don't win a world title in the next two years, it might be good enough motivation to keep going. I have spent many years in Europe and that is a big part of my life, but eventually I want to go back home to New Zealand.'

Following the move to Yamaha, Josh was pleasantly surprised with the bike and team. 'It was a different feeling. I suddenly had to be a lot more professional in all areas. At CAS Honda I called the shots and the team was basically built around me. At Yamaha, the factory in Japan would move heaven and earth for me to get the best bike and the best results from me. But I also had three bosses and was expected to get results and answer to them. I guess you could say the pressure had stepped up for me. The reasons for this were that Yamaha had had a lot of success in the past, but also the press was predicting that I would take over from Everts and win everything.'

As the only man to serve up a defeat to Everts during the Belgian's final glittering 2006 season, Josh was tipped as the most likely to succeed in Everts' absence. One of the very few riders able to match Everts in the previous 18 months, Josh had also beaten the Belgian in November 2006 at the Oceania International Motocross in Taupo.

But perhaps most significant was that Josh had taken over Everts' ride in the team widely regarded as the number one in Europe, the factory-backed Rinaldi Yamaha team. The man who had most threatened Everts during his glory-filled swansong season now had the pick of Everts' bikes and back-up in 2007. 'Everyone expected me to win in 2007. After all, that's what Yamaha had hired me to do,' Josh says. 'That's what the journalists were saying and, on paper, it was probably true. But championships aren't made on paper.

'The bike at Yamaha was a factory bike, and the resources were unlimited when it came to the bike and anything about it. It's a tough job testing and training under pressure, and then there's the racing, but my Yamaha team had so much experience. Decisions like where to test and train and what races to do pre-season were all made for me. All that stuff was out of my hands, and all I had to do was focus on doing my job.

'Motocross riders appreciate the simple things, and the day I signed with Yamaha, the bosses phoned me to welcome me to the team. It's the small things like that that give a rider confidence and the knowledge that, behind the scenes and behind the desk, behind the numbers and the computer, there is an entire corporation fighting for you. I wouldn't have gone to Yamaha if Stefan Everts had stayed.

'I spoke with the Rinaldi team at the start of 2005, when Stefan was thinking then about moving, and I said I wasn't going there if Stefan stayed. With Marc de Reuver as team-mate in 2007 it was going to be different. We would be on the same level — there was no number one or number two rider in the team — Michele Rinaldi said he had no time for favouritism.

'I honestly believed that if I just kept my head down, made no stupid mistakes and got the work done, I could win. I told myself Stefan was still there, and continued to train as if he was still there, facing me. I aspired to be at the level he was at in 2006 and to dominate the way he did.'

While he would end up having to eat his words, Josh was happy to give an assessment of his rivals prior to the 2007 season. 'Steve Ramon is probably going to be my most consistent threat,' he said at the time, 'although I honestly don't think he'll have what it takes to beat me. I think I have more determination and I think I have a better bike. But Steve is always there and will always be good. Technically, he's a great rider, but I think he'll be a second- or third-placed guy again.

'Kevin Strijbos will sometimes win too. Sometimes he will win heats, but I don't think he'll have the physical condition over 15 rounds. It'll be the same with Ken de Dycker [Josh's team-mate in 2006]. He'll have the speed but not the consistency and, again, won't have the physical condition over the 15 rounds to worry me at the end. In 2006 he only had two podiums, so to say he's going to be a threat for the title after only having two podiums in his entire career is unheard of, really. In 1999 I had my first podium. In 2000 I had five or six. I'd probably had 20 or 30 up to 2004. I had maybe 40-odd podiums alone with CAS Honda, and de Dycker's had just two in his career. I think he's got a long way to go. In one of his podiums, I lapped him. He finished third at the Irish GP at Desert Martin, and I won there and lapped him in the process. It was a pretty good race for me.'

So who did Josh consider would be the biggest threat with Everts out of the picture? 'Everybody. They will all be good at different times and some individuals might win a GP or two. The biggest factor in my favour is that I will be better over the 15 rounds. Some guys will beat me at GPs, but not over 15 rounds. There are five, six or seven guys who will challenge me, week in and week out. But those same guys will have a DNF, or a crash, or finish seventh or eighth at the next event. I did only half the season in 2006 and didn't finish off the podium. That is going to be hard for them to match.

'Some of them are sand specialists, and will favour one track or another, but I can ride all conditions. I was able to finish second to Stefan in the deep sand, in front of five or six Belgians who were really good on that surface. Nobody can say, "Josh can't ride sand," or "Josh can't ride mud". I can do it all.

'I know it sounds cocky, but I can't see those guys beating me week-in and week-out. There is always that nagging thought that maybe one of them can step up, but I just can't see that happening.'

But there was criticism too of Josh's talent, or — as some would say — his lack of natural ability. 'I've heard that said, but it doesn't bother me at all,' he said. 'Every rider is different. You've got your Stefan, your Ben [Townley] and your Joel [Smets], but I'm just a steady rider. I'm not flash or anything, but my goal is to win a world title and what I look like whilst doing it doesn't really concern me. I just keep focused on what I do. I can't change that about me.'

Until the start of 2007, it had been 11 years since Josh had begun chasing the world championship. That's more than a decade of 'nearly but not quite'. When asked what he thought had been missing prior to 2007, he felt that he hadn't had the right combinations at the right time. 'I have always been in the toughest class, but in saying that, I don't offer that as an excuse. There has always been a top guy there — Stefan Everts, Joel Smets, Sebastien Tortelli, Mickael Pichon — standing in my way to the top. It's been tough for me. I've just never had the whole package until now.

'There will be no excuses for 2007. I am fit enough and strong enough. I offer no excuses for my past. I simply wasn't good enough. I think now I am good enough and that's the difference.

'If you look at someone like Stefan Everts, he's got the X factor. First of all, he's got the technique and that helps him a lot, I believe, because he saves a lot of energy, and so, when he rides, he can ride at maybe 20 per cent less effort than me and he can still get the job done. I can attack and attack and attack, and eventually he just wears me down because he's able to ride effortlessly but still at the same pace. I have to push and push and push, and it's very tiring.

'He's also made a lot of good choices in his career. He's had good people around him. Physically, mentally and technically, all the people at Yamaha have been good for him. I think a combination of all those things — and the fact that he's worked hard — is what made Stefan Everts so difficult to match or beat. I'll never be able to match his ten world titles, but I think I can win one or two. That's always been my goal and I think I have a good chance in the next two seasons to do just that.

'I'm 29 years old now, but I don't think I'm too old to be winning a world title. Every rider is different. You take someone like Ben Townley, who won a title at a young age [as a 19-year-old], or take young Frenchman Christophe Pourcel, who also won a world title as a teenager, but then take Joel Smets. He didn't start his career until quite late.' [Belgium's Smets didn't get his first motorcycle until he was aged 17, an old air-cooled Yamaha YZ490 that was given to him by his uncle. He won his first 500cc class world title in 1995, then promptly lost it to Shayne King the following year. Smets took the 500cc world title back from King in 1997, and then backed that up with world titles in 1998, 2000 and 2003. Like Everts, Smets also retired at the end of 2006.]

'So you see, everyone peaks at different times and everyone has a different shelf-life. Just because you win a title at age 16 doesn't mean you're still going to be around at age 26, although I think most guys have a ten-year shelf-life. I don't think I've really been at the top level for ten years yet. My first year at the top level was really 1999, my first year of breaking into the top ten. So, hopefully, I've still got a couple of years left in me yet to win a few world titles. I have a two-year contract [with Rinaldi Yamaha], but after that, who knows? I'm still just taking one year at a time.'

The 2007 world championship

S OMETIMES SPORT CAN be just plain cruel. The 2007 motocross world championships will be remembered as the year when not only did the fastest man not win (he finished third), but the man named as world champion never won a single GP.

If not for the waywardness of a small pebble, New Zealand's Josh Coppins would have been crowned world champion a couple of weeks before the season officially wound up in early September. Instead, the man from Motueka, his factory Yamaha team and his many loyal fans could only watch helplessly as his title hopes shrivelled up and blew away. The hard work of ten GPs, and, indeed, of all those years before that, dissolved in a gut-wrenching five-week period. With Josh unable to ride at the final round, the Dutch GP at Lierop on 2 September, his Belgian rival, Steve Ramon, took the title unchallenged.

Only weeks earlier, Josh had been the overwhelming favourite to take the world title. He had stretched his lead at the top of the MX1 world standings to 107 points over Ramon, giving him two full GP events up his sleeve, with just the final third of the season, five of the 15 rounds, remaining.

But disaster struck in round 11, in Loket in the Czech Republic, when a small stone found its way into the rear brake mechanism of Josh's bike, and he failed to score any points in the day's first of two races. Worse was to follow when his damaged brakes failed him at a crucial moment during the next race, as he attempted to slow at the bottom of a steep hill. Josh crashed and broke his shoulder blade. Forced to miss the next three rounds, he watched his lead shrink to just 12 points.

Josh returned to racing at the season's penultimate event, the British GP at Donington Park, but his bid to preserve his championship lead was short-lived when unbearable pain forced him to withdraw from racing soon after the start of the day's second race. Suddenly Josh was 14 points behind Ramon, the first time since the season began that he wasn't the holder of the championship leader's red number board.

Ramon was handed the red plate on the podium at Donington Park. He stood to the far left on the podium, not on the number one, two or three step. He'd finished only fourth overall that day in England, and yet he had now been thrust suddenly into the limelight as the champion-in-waiting. With Josh a non-starter at the final round in the Netherlands the following weekend, there was nothing to stand in the way of Ramon collecting the MX1 world title.

Though undoubtedly a hugely talented rider, many race fans cringed when Ramon took the 2007 title without winning a single GP. His team boss, Suzuki factory team owner Sylvain Geboers, was naturally delighted that both his riders had risen past Josh to finish first and second in the championship, particularly since it had never really looked likely through the first half of the season. Ironically, Geboers never won a world title during his racing career, despite winning more races than his main rival, Joel Robert, in the 1969 championships. 'I won many GPs in my career [14 in fact], but I never won a world title,' he said at the Dutch GP. 'I would swap with Steve anytime.'

Of the 15 GPs that made up the 2007 season, Josh won the most — five before that fateful round 11 — while the next best in the GP-winning stakes was Ramon's team-mate, Belgian Kevin Strijbos. But the record books now show that Ramon won the world crown for 2007, with Strijbos runner-up and Josh slipping to third.

It was not a fair reflection of his worth, and a bitter pill for Josh to swallow, frustrated that he was unable to fight for the championship in the latter stages of a season he had led so comfortably from the outset. 'I am filled with so many emotions right now,' he said at the time. 'It is difficult to explain in words how I feel. I had put so much effort into the pre-season and it all seemed to pay off with a huge lead prior to Loket. But in the end, it proved to be not enough when you get hurt like I did — that's the hard reality of motocross racing. I'm focusing already on next year and I absolutely want to grab the title then.'

For years, Josh's professionalism and mental toughness had made him the natural successor to Everts. His former boss, CAS Honda team chief Harry Ainsworth, said he would not mind if one of his riders finished second in the championship, provided it was Coppins who won the title, preferring his former charge over the 'other young, overpaid muppets'. He emphasised: 'Josh is not naturally talented as a rider, but he's got strength, and his bloody-mindedness will get him there. I don't think anybody in the pits didn't want Josh to win.'

Josh's Yamaha team boss, Carlo Rinaldi, one half of the Rinaldi family that runs the factory outfit, said the New Zealander was also the sentimental favourite to win in 2007. 'Anybody you could talk to — be they green, blue, orange or red bike fans —will all tell you they wanted Josh to win. Josh is a very hard worker. He is also very popular with the other riders and certainly deserved to win this year.'

Rinaldi's elder brother, Michele, the other half of the Yamaha factory team management, also shared Josh's disappointment. 'After [the Yamaha team] winning six consecutive world championships, we know what it feels like to win championships, but not Josh. When you can dominate like he did in the first ten rounds, it is terrible to be sidelined and see your title prospect disappear. It does not feel right. What remains positive is that we made the right decisions for 2007, and I am convinced Josh and Yamaha will be the combination to beat in 2008.'

Yamaha Europe's racing division manager, Laurens Klein Koerkamp, said it had been a difficult time. 'Josh has worked so hard for it this year, I believe harder than anybody, and because of his preparation, he dominated the first ten rounds of the championship. For all of us, it was utterly frustrating to see his 107-point lead slowly diminish.'

With Stefan Everts, Josh's nemesis from earlier seasons having retired from racing at the end of 2006 following ten years of almost total dominance in the sport, it seemed Josh's time had come. 'I had always been chasing him in 2006 — always pushing that little bit extra to keep him in my sights — and it was different in 2007,' Josh says. 'I would have been satisfied just to keep up with Stefan and not look too much beyond that. If I'd been beating him regularly and building a championship lead for myself in 2006, I might have gone into 2007 with a different mindset.'

But in 2007, he did build his own championship. 'I could see it looking at me. I was working on getting the overall situation to get as many points as possible, not necessarily trying to win every race. Anything other than a GP win was a disappointment for me in 2007 — I knew I was good enough to win races, but to keep at that level for 15 rounds . . . that was the hard thing.

'Week in and week out, I was racing different guys. In France it was Steve Ramon, in Japan it was Billy Mackenzie and Mike Brown, in Portugal it was Kevin Strijbos, in Germany it was David Philippaerts. It was as if these guys could go fast one week, but couldn't recover enough for the next GP. Ramon wasn't so aggressive in France, he just rode really well — he was going for his passes and he had better lines than me. He was racing all the Belgian and Dutch championship races, so he was sharp.'

Halfway through the season Josh had an impressive 90-point lead. 'It was hard sometimes to sit down and think: I'm going to be the world champion. I'd been working towards it for so long. At the same time I was also telling myself to get some more GP wins — I really wanted to get my GP tally up to 15 or 20. I was racing the premier class and had been for 12 years. I'd had a lot of seconds and a lot of thirds, a lot of podiums and some race wins, but I'd never led the championship before. I'd never been the best rider until 2007 — I've had a lot of strong points, but I'd never been the most talented rider and I'd had to work for it.'

Losing 'his' championship was hard for him to take. 'It's not something I expected to happen. It was just bad luck and there was nothing I could really do. I've always been a believer that you make your own luck, but honestly, with this, there wasn't a lot I could do. It's disappointing, but it was the card I was dealt and I just had to get on with life. One week after the championship, nobody was going to remember that I was the best rider of the season. They were only going to remember whether I was or was not the world champion.

'I was so disappointed I couldn't put up a better fight to the finish, to repay my fans for their loyalty. There have been a lot of people who have helped me along the way. Some have come and some have gone, but I don't think I've ever been by myself for the whole run of it. It's been a general progression since the age of four, when I started riding, and 11, when I started racing.'

Josh is now going to need that support more than ever before. Having completed a long and arduous 12 years on the GP circuit, only to have the golden chalice ripped away while in sight of the finish in 2007, it would take a very special man to line up in 2008 and give it one more shot.

The 30-year-old Kiwi is obviously a popular rider, with friends and rivals alike, but unfortunately, sport is not a popularity contest, and Josh will have to try and muster the same level of dominance when he embarks on his 2008 campaign, possibly his last crack at the elusive world title before he eventually retires from the GP scene.

Josh knows he does not need to win every race to win the world title — Ramon's 2007 effort is a starkly painful reminder of that — and history shows many titles have been won by consistency and just a little luck.

In 1969, the world championships were scored on the riders' best seven heats. In the 250cc championship, Belgium's Sylvain Geboers scored 122 points from the 12 heats that were run, while his nearest rival Joel Robert scored 102 points. With only their best seven rounds to count, it was Robert on 102 points and Geboers on 96. Joel Robert got the title. How painful must that have been for Geboers?

Sylvain was one of the greatest riders to never win a world championship, but won 14 GPs in his career. Robert won 50 GPs in his career and held the record for most GP wins, until Stefan Everts came along and smashed that record.

In 1978, Soviet rider Gennady Moisseev won just one 250cc GP from 12 rounds, achieving two first placings at the GP of Great Britain and going on to win the championship with 183 points to Sweden's Torlief Hansen's 153, when Hansen failed to score in the English and French rounds. Moisseev would eventually win 14 GPs in the 250cc class.

In 1982, American Brad Lackey won two 500cc GPs, finishing both GPs on equal points to England's Dave Thorpe and fellow American Gary Semics. Lackey was awarded the GP wins and won the championship with 228 points to Belgian Andre Vromans' 217. Lackey would win nine GPs in his career in the 500cc class.

In 1986, Dave Thorpe won just one 500cc GP, finishing with second and first placings in Holland. Thorpe won the championship by 316 points to Belgium's Andre Malherbe's 311, with Eric Geboers on 299 and Georges Jobe on 296. It was considered one of the greatest 500cc battles of all time. Thorpe would eventually win 22 500cc GPs in his career.

In 1988, Dutchman John Van Den Berk won two GPs, finishing with two first placings in Italy and a first and second in England. Van Den Berk would win the championship with 315 points to Finland's Pekka

Vehkonen, on 285. Van Den Berk would win nine GPs in his career, seven in the 125cc class and two in the 250cc class.

In 1991, Trampas Parker won two GPs in his 250 championship. The same year Belgian Georges Jobe won just one GP in the 500cc championship. Parker picked up 13 GP victories, six in the 125cc class, five in the 250cc class and two in the 500cc class. Jobe would win 28 GPs in his career, 15 in the 250cc class and 13 in the 500cc class. A year later, Jobe would win the 500cc championship, again with two GP wins. He beat England's Kurt Nicoll, who won the last three GPs with a first-third-first, three firsts, and three firsts (they ran three motos per GP in those days). Jobe still won with 550 points to Nicoll's 548. Nicoll had won five GPs in the season. Nicoll, who never won a world championship, did score 13 GP victories in his career.

And, ironically, the most recent rider before 2007 to score just a single GP victory and still win the 2003 world title was Ramon. The Suzuki factory rider won the second GP of the 2003 season and led the MX2 championship. It was bad luck for Ramon that Stefan Everts decided to join the MX2 class which he then dominated, winning eight GPs from nine starts. Frenchman Mickael Maschio won the other two GPs in that season.

Plenty of other men could, in their time, have claimed to be the fastest motocross riders in the world, yet failed to win the world title. Take, for example, Belgium's Marnicq Bervoets, Frenchman Yves Demaria, German Pit Beirer, Australian Jeff Leisk or New Zealand's Darryll King. Taranaki-born King was twice runner-up in the 500cc world championships (in 1997 and 1998) and was desperately unlucky not to win a world title. 'At the end of the day, it's the nature of sport,' King says. 'Josh definitely deserved to win it in 2007, that's the bottom line. Second place is nowhere; it's the first loser. And third is worse than that. I'm gutted for Josh. But it's sport. You're dealt these blows and a good athlete will always bounce back. I know he'll be stronger next season.

'One year I came second because I was with a new team and I simply didn't gel with the new bike, so I still think it was a great achievement to finish second that year. The next year, in 1998, I led the championship, but Joel Smets got better and better as the season progressed, and he simply caught and passed me. He deserved it that year. The following year I broke my neck. I can't compare what happened to me to what happened to Josh. What happened to Josh isn't even close to what happened to me. I can't even imagine how wrecked he feels.'

Josh clearly doesn't want to join the list of 'nearly men', riders who were extremely fast but never quite made it. Only trouble is, time is running out. It will take a special sportsman to shrug off the massive disappointment of losing and summon up the courage and drive to do it all again; to battle the elite of world motocross and beat them all as he did through the first two-thirds of 2007.

It will take a special person to lift himself for a third time from the ashes of disaster — as he did when wrongly labelled a drug cheat in 2002 and as he did again in 2003 when his bones were broken and his career seemed over, following the Phoenix supercross crash.

It will take a special man who, at the so-called twilight age of 31, will tough it out again in one of the world's most physically and mentally demanding of sports. Josh is that special man.

Risk big, win big

JOSH COPPINS HAS undergone a metamorphosis during the past decade: from a bright-eyed youth to a hardened athlete with a steely glint in his eye. And, through it all, the man from Motueka hasn't lost his down-to-earth demeanour, something that endears him to fans and sponsors alike. Sure, he accepts he's been provided one of the best motocross bikes in the world, but it's merely a tool for him to get the job done, an emotionless hunk of metal and rubber that needs constant goading, a snap here and a twist there, to make it perform.

The old equation holds true: it's always 20 per cent machine and 80 per cent man. Get the balance wrong and it ends in tears. Just ask Josh about some of the hurt he's suffered over the years and he'll point you to June 2002 and January 2003, and the heartbreaking end to his 2007 season when injury robbed him of an assured world championship — dates that stick out like sore thumbs. He's had a few of those in his time.

In 2002 it was more about suffering psychological injury when his name was tarnished after testing positive for a banned substance. His career hung in the balance, and while he was subsequently cleared, the damage was done. His season had been knocked out of skew and, despite the court ruling that cleared him of blame, some of the mud still stuck.

In January 2003 he was knocked down and considered out for the count when he crashed in a supercross in the United States. Subsequent x-rays revealed more metal and screws in his leg than there were sinew and bone.

And who can forget the high drama that came at the end of his amazing 2007 series, when he was 107 points clear of his competitors in the world championship standing, only to break his shoulder and, despite his courageous efforts to continue, was forced out of the championship that had been his for the taking.

But there have been plenty of highs too in Josh's career, from the smallest and most personally satisfying adrenaline 'hits' every time he executes a perfect pass or wins a race, to the heady and intoxicating feeling of winning a GP event.

It was a moment of warm satisfaction when, at the start of the year 2000, he graduated from a small tent and truck at the back of the paddock and was promoted to the full factory ranks, elevated to the motocross equivalent of 'Mahogany Row'. He was now a fixture along the exclusive pit lane of GP stars, a resident in one of the upmarket canvas showrooms that take centre stage on prime real estate at the forefront of the pits where all the bug-eyed, autograph-hunting fans jostle along the 'corridor of stars'.

Josh is obviously on a high when soaring 20, 30 or 40 metres across the sky, but the taciturn Kiwi has also experienced some incredible lows in his GP career. As with all those who qualify for a GP, Josh has to put his body on the line in the name of his sport.

When he launches 130 kilograms of bike off a jump, he can expect a bone-jarring thud as payback when gravity brings him back down again. When he carves too close to trackside fencing or skims too close to the steel buckles on the boots of his rivals, he can expect to draw blood — most likely his own — and he has to tape extensively to protect the skin on the palms of his hands from blistering and shredding every time he rides.

Josh commits himself fully. If he gets it wrong, it hurts. Unlike colleagues who race cars, there is no metal sheath to cocoon Josh's lean but muscular frame. A thin wrapping of fabric is often all that protects his flesh from painful bruising and bloody laceration. Carbon fibre, leather and nylon are stitched together in various combinations, meant to protect, but also to allow him freedom to move, to bend and flex. It's a fine line between form and function. Sponsors get their pound of flesh too, adorning his outfit with their logos.

And that's where some of the rewards are found. Josh is paid very well indeed, but one still has to question whether the financial rewards justify the deadly dangers he risks each time he takes a leap of faith on board what is essentially a snarling, spitting iron horse. And there's more to Josh's career than just being able to ride a motorbike.

Few people, even those imbedded in the motocross community, perhaps realise the full extent of what it means to race world championship motocross in Europe, so far from friendly faces, old schoolmates, friends and family. 'It's interesting to note that, since the end of 1999, my entire family — but mostly my parents — and Murray Thorn have had zero to do with my racing,' says Josh. 'It's like I turned a page and went my own way. Even though they had so much to do with my racing in the beginning, none of them realise what it takes to win a championship over here in Europe.

'In fact, almost the entire New Zealand population doesn't know, and that even includes the motocross fans. The effort that the manufacturer puts in, from the mechanics to the office ladies, from sponsors to the rider trainer . . . everybody puts everything into every day of the year. It is immense. It's not a job or hobby, it's a life — and that goes for everybody in your team.

'To win a championship, not only do you have to win, but you have to be smart, strong, lucky and careful, and do it year in and year out, building on what you have. Yes, I can win on a weekend, but to do it all year, with the press commitments, travelling demands, training, injuries and so on, is where it gets hard.

'My parents don't understand this — none of my friends either. To them, I'm just Josh, a guy who races bikes. And to be honest, I don't mind this because, when I come home, I'm still just Josh.'

As with any young man growing up, mistakes were made and lessons learned. But that's a process that's had to have been sped up for Josh. There's certainly more than meets the eye regarding competition at the top level.

'I was sitting in a restaurant waiting for my meal the night before a motocross event in 2006 when my phone rang,' Josh says. 'It was Graham Deans, a friend of mine from New Zealand who had brought a group of young Kiwis across to Europe to race at the world junior motocross championships in Finland. Although you can turn senior at the age of 16, in these world championships you could still be classified as a junior up to age 18. In theory that means Christophe Pourcel [the young Frenchman who won the MX2 world title in 2006] would have been eligible to race the world junior championships. Deansy told me that none of the Kiwi boys had made the cut at the world junior champs and they were pretty down about it.

'When you're a kid, you're normally pretty cocky and think you're ready to take on the world. I think they may have underestimated the speed of the Euro riders. I told Deansy that, even if they didn't qualify, it was still a worthwhile trip because the young boys now knew what they would have to work on and what they would have to work towards, and now the real work would start for them.

'I reckon that most up-and-coming Kiwi riders underestimate the level of racing outside of home. I know a few young Kiwis get a wake-up call when they cross the Tasman Sea to race in Australia. I think that's due to a couple of things. Firstly, they underestimate the past successes of Kiwi racers. They tend to think that, if they can run with Cody Cooper or Daryl Hurley back home, they should be able to keep up with the riders in Australia, or if they are close to Ben Townley or myself at a local race in New Zealand, that means they're ready for Europe. These guys often don't realise the level of commitment it takes — the training and the organisation right from day one.

'Secondly, they underestimate things like jet-lag, bike set-up, conditioning for longer races or being ready to qualify on a hot-lap system. Put them on the start line with 40 hot riders after they've had a bad qualifying time and this often leads to a bad start, a tough race, which often leads to crashes and injuries, or a bent bike. They quickly get discouraged.

'Unfortunately, training isn't just cruising the streets in your pimped-out van with your girlfriend on the seat beside you. Darryll, Shayne and Damien King are true legends of the sport, but Darryll is now 38. He shouldn't still be winning races at the top level in New Zealand — it's unheard of. We have a dozen riders in New Zealand who are professional or semi-professional, and dozens more who call themselves "professional". Darryll, Shayne and Damien are only semi-professional these days and yet all three of them, despite having families, jobs and businesses to run, are still able to win races and get the job done. The so-called pros can't. Why? Are the new boys on the block putting in the work? Sure, some of them have had injuries or other problems, but a few of them should have done better.

'OK, so Cody Cooper and Daryl Hurley were injured in 2006, but, like I said, the rest of the boys seem to be content with filling up the rest of the spots below number one or number two in New Zealand. If this is the case on their home turf, how are they meant to be doing the business abroad? I had some boys tell me that BT [Ben Townley] is where they should have been. Come on, boys! I don't care if you used to smoke him in the mini ranks — if you put in half the work he did, you would be dominating the New Zealand races.'

As far as Josh is concerned, motocross is no different from other sports.

You get out what you put in. 'More than anyone, I want to see more talented, hard-working riders coming out of New Zealand — riders who push the limits and make a few mistakes because they want it so bad, riders who sacrifice the nice things in life and who don't let girlfriends, mates and parties get in their way.'

He recalls growing up in small-town New Zealand and seeing the emphasis change over the years as 'political correctness' crept into the way we recognise achievement. And, as a self-confessed 'old school' pupil, it's not something he generally agrees with. 'I'm a big fan of competition and giving kids the chance to win. But, nowadays, kids are rewarded for participation, rather than winning, and it's making everyone soft. I argued this with my sister and she told me that things had changed — the teachers don't want anyone to be left out.' At a school prizegiving, Josh saw students given prizes for such things as 'finding lost shoes', 'bringing a pet rat to school' or 'being the loudest girl in class'.

'That's rubbish,' he says. 'Personally speaking, I never knew of any child when I was at school who was a complete dud. All of us have a gift, whether it be academically, musically or in a sporting sense. If your child is the best in school at something, the teacher should let them know about it and encourage them to really have a go at it. I think you're more likely to fall short of your potential if you're not pushed to win. People need to know when they are good at something and congratulated for it, while also encouraged to work harder at the things they are not so good at.

'I was never good at maths, but if I moved up in the class, I took a huge pride in that and made sure that all those I passed knew all about it. I was never going to be number one at maths, but every now and then I moved up because I was intent on competing and trying to be the best. For me that's been a positive thing.

'It's not just my own home town where things are changing. I guess it's a worldwide thing. But I still want to go back to Motueka and start coaching at my own motocross facility. It'll definitely be "the old school way". That way, if my students get a compliment, they'll know they definitely earned it and that will make it so much sweeter.'

Over the years Josh also had to learn how to deal with the media. It was something he'd done since the beginning, but over time it became far more complex. Managing his public profile and how the world saw him was important if he was going to continue to be attractive to sponsors, almost as important as his ability to ride the bike and win races.

The motorcycling magazine media has been pretty generous to him over the years and, in 2007 when he was considered the favourite by all those who follow the sport, he was destined to receive a few more magazine covers dedicated to his image and a few more headlines screaming his name.

'I've got a good relationship with the press and a good relationship with a lot of the magazine journalists and photographers. I've done pretty well really, especially since I was with a British team [CAS Honda] and doing the British championships. Motocross is fairly big in Britain, and there are quite a few good magazines.

'Obviously the coverage hasn't been as great at home [in New Zealand], where the sport is fairly small. Rugby tends to dominate the sports pages. The motorcycle press in New Zealand has been good to me, but not the non-motorcycle media. But that sort of suits me, to be honest, because it means I can come home and rest, without the distractions and without the media being in my face. I can come home to New Zealand and have my summer holidays and nobody bothers me too much.'

He does concede that as New Zealand doesn't provide a cent of his budget for racing, if he was to get more general media attention at home it would create more stress for him and more obligations, and he would lose his peaceful homecomings. 'I'd have to do lots of interviews and be opening bike shops or supermarkets, cutting ribbons and so on. I'm quite content with how it works for me right now.'

But Josh is also able to take an abstract view and step back and see the big picture of what all this means for the sport he loves in the country in which he grew up. 'For the sport of motorcycling, it would be better if I did get more recognition at home, because it would be better for the sport and better for the young guys coming through. That's the aspect that's kind of sad. Talking to the media is part of what I have to do, and I don't find it at all difficult.

'It gets to be a pain in the arse, though, when you come across a journalist who hasn't done his homework and starts asking dumb questions like "When did you start riding?" and "What did you ride?" and "How old were you then?" You get a bit bored with those sorts of questions. I've been asked — and answered — those basic questions many, many times before.

'But I do like it when I'm asked something a little more interesting, such as about my lifestyle. I did a parachute dive with Miss Belgium in 2006 and that was great — it was certainly something different to talk about!'

Life at the top

THE HUGE IMPROVEMENT in his riding in the past few years hasn't been something that Josh has just stumbled onto. It has come about after years of hard work and accumulating knowledge and experience. In the process, Josh became the fastest GP rider on the circuit. Just where that extra speed has come from is anyone's guess, but Josh feels it was due to the team behind him, combined with his own increasing experience.

'It's been a slow process. I don't think the fact that I have improved has anything to do with my time recovering from the injuries I had in America a few years ago. I'm just riding better than I ever was in 2002 or at any other time. I am also really confident and have changed my way of thinking. Going to the races and thinking I should win is a big difference to going and hoping to win. I go to the races now and believe I can win.'

This is a much more relaxed Josh Coppins than the one who first stepped off a plane in Europe in 1995. It's taken him a dozen years of living away from home, friends and family, dealing with alien cultures, different attitudes and strange habits, and travelling across so many international borders month after month. Now he is at the stage where he can relax and concentrate on the business of riding and racing a motorcycle.

He looks back fondly on his memories of settling into life in Europe. 'I've mostly lived in two countries since I began racing in Europe — Belgium and Italy — but I've also spent a lot of time in England, and I've raced in all the other countries of Europe. All of this has given me the chance to experience a bit of each country's strange habits, as well as their good and bad points.'

While he wouldn't have chosen to live in Belgium, that was where Suzuki's GP team was based, and he had to get used to mayonnaise on his chips, strange shop opening hours and grumpy people. 'The Belgians tend to keep to themselves. To give you an idea of what they're like, I lived in the same house for six years and never met my neighbours. Motocross is a popular sport in Belgium though, and people in Belgium really appreciate the sport and the effort that goes into it. I also like the fact that the sport of motocross is mainstream, unlike in New Zealand or Australia.

'In 2002, I rode for Honda Europe and was based in Florence, Italy. That was an awesome place, with great food and a great lifestyle.' Like any young man, food was a priority for him. 'I also liked the warm climate and long lunches, and I fitted in well. But like any European country, Italy had its own strange ways. Everything seemed to take for ever to happen. It was always "Domani, domani", which means tomorrow, tomorrow. The local espresso coffee looks like tar — it's so thick and strong. My mechanic, Fabio, knocked three or four of them back every day — just one made the hairs on the back of my neck stand up.

'Like the Belgians, though, the Italians are passionate about motocross and this is something we have in common. Each country has its good and its bad points, I guess — it's just different. At first it's a bit frustrating, but it's always a laugh.'

After more than a decade on the GP scene, Josh is a seasoned traveller and probably as much a European as he is a Kiwi. No longer a rookie, he has also hardened over the years. Gone is the 'Mister Nice Guy' on the track — Josh now works on getting inside the head of his rivals, and showing them that he is, in fact, a serious championship contender.

'I don't look back at the years I didn't win,' he says. 'I'm not like

Sebastien Tortelli, or the young Pourcel brothers — they were really quick, really young. I think I can still improve, and my career is going to be a long one. I am learning more all the time. I am better at knowing what I want from the bike, and it's been something I have had to work through slowly. I don't look back and wish I was like this before, because I wasn't.'

Josh feels he should have been winning races earlier in his 2005 season. A shoulder injury at a pre-season race in England cost him valuable time on the bike and also dented his confidence, although hard work and a tunnel vision approach saw him come good. 'I think my shoulder injury at Hawkstone Park [in England] hurt me more than I thought it would. I was only off the bike for ten days, but it took me a long time to get back to where I was.

'I was on top of the world, and I really went to the races thinking I was the best; I was prepared to stick it to Stefan Everts. Confidence-wise, it took me a long time to get that back. We got lost in the set-up of the bike, my mistakes and the team's mistakes, and now we are spot on. I am more aggressive and I feel like I can win.'

Josh also knows the CAS Honda team was a valuable part of his success, and his friendship with the team made his job more fun and easier to achieve his goals. Led by Harry Ainsworth, and with people such as Neil Prince and Nick Moores, the CAS team emerged during Josh's tenure as one of the strongest in the pit paddock. 'I remember American champion Ricky Carmichael saying how he had good people around him, and I felt the same when I was with CAS Honda. I feel the same now at Rinaldi Yamaha. Everyone in the CAS team did their job without question, and we all got along really well. We didn't race for the money; we were doing it for the results, and because we loved it. That was also important.'

Josh points out that it was a slightly different chemistry at the Rinaldi Yamaha team. 'It became more of a job, with higher expectations. I was just glad that I was able to deliver.' There developed a different chemistry too between Josh and his rivals, particularly as the sport entered a new phase with the retirement of some of its legends. 'Mickael Pichon retired and so did Sebastien Tortelli, Stefan Everts and Joel Smets. Ben Townley moved to America.

'There is a whole different look to the riders who line up alongside me now. When I was battling with any of those four or five riders, I knew I could trust what they were doing. You could race close with them. In this new era, things are a little bit different. These new riders will quite happily crash and burn for a win. They're not prepared to back off and say, "Hey, I only need to finish second or third here — I just need the points." They will say, "Either I am going to win or I'm going to crash trying." That's quite hard for me because I'm not used to that. But then that's why I managed to get a 90-point lead by halfway through the 2007 season.

'All my rivals show good speed, and they all have good teams behind them and good bikes underneath them, but they can't do it week in and week out. The mental side of the sport is very important. You start the season feeling great, but by mid-season, you'll pick up the odd injury. It's getting through the things like that — getting through the bad times — that's the tough part.

'Often, three-quarters of the way through the season, you'll get fatigued — riders suffer from blood problems because they're working too hard. You need to be confident in yourself and strong in the head to say to yourself that you don't need to practise today, that you'll be strong enough on the weekend. It's all about being fresh. You can't doubt yourself.'

It's this sort of sports psychology that plays a large part in shaping a champion. It's sometimes more than mind over matter — if you don't mind hurting yourself, it doesn't matter — and the brain can be a powerful tool in the armoury of any top sportsperson. Champion riders may sometimes seem aloof and distant or perhaps seem to act a little superior; often, when interviewed, they seem brash and conceited. But it would be a mistake to think they are this shallow.

The truth is that they must possess an unwavering self-confidence if they are to succeed. A successful rider must be able to harness a powerful machine, react swiftly to sudden dangers, skilfully steer the motorcycle through high-speed traffic and over impossible terrain, and beat 30 or 40 other sportsmen who are similarly blessed.

If they don't honestly believe they are the best, then they probably never will be. To admit that their rival is favoured to win at a track can become a self-fulfilling prophecy. Confidence breeds confidence.

Josh sums it up: 'You can't afford to doubt yourself. That is where Stefan Everts was so strong.'

Where to from here?

ALTHOUGH JOSH IS undecided about what he will do once the European phase of his life wraps up, he's definitely ruled out the United States as a possible destination. 'That's not the place for me. I'll be 31 by the time I finish in Europe, and the only option in the States for me would be an outdoor-only contract for a year.'

Without a big budget and a decent bike, racing in the United States would probably be a futile exercise for Josh, not that there's anything he has to prove to anybody anyway. But nor is he likely to take the 'pipe and slippers' option and go 'cold turkey' from racing motocross at a high level. 'I think there's more chance of me racing in Australia as a wind-down year after Europe,' he says. 'I'm definitely racing in 2008 in Europe, but it depends on whether I want to stay on for another year or stop, spend a year in Australia, and then settle back in New Zealand after that.

'The hardest thing for me would be to race a bike that's less than a factory machine. A stock motocross bike is, for me at least, totally unrideable because I've been spoilt and have always had things the way I like them with the bike. Yamaha made the bike for me exactly the way I like it, so to ride a stock bike would be very hard. Everything on a factory bike is hand-made or crafted just for me — all the little things, like the grip diameter, the grip compound, the footpeg height, the footpeg width and length, the seat height and even the foam they use in the seat.

'Those are the things that are more important than the engine, exhaust or suspension. A good rider can ride around those things, but when you actually sit on the bike, it's the way you feel, the things that you feel, the things that you touch — the pull ratio on the levers, the brakes, the seat. The day I hang up my boots as a professional but keep riding as a recreational rider is going to be a nightmare. I'll be hard to live with because I'll always be complaining.'

Regardless of when he finally does hang up his helmet, the world of motorcycles — and motocross in particular — will never be far away. Even in Motueka, a long way from the mechanics, the workshops and support of a European team, Josh has remarkable facilities, and this is where he'll put something back into the sport with his dream of training future generations.

'I've got 22 hectares near Motueka. It was a deer farm, but basically I bought it before the property boom, so I was quite lucky. I built a house on it in 2004 and now we're building workshops. We had sheep grazing there in 2005, but now we have cows. My sister and my girlfriend — when she's out in New Zealand with me — ride horses; we've got two. I'm quite heavily involved now with real estate, which is going pretty well. I can't see myself staying in Europe after the racing. I do enjoy it there and I've got a lot of friends over there, but I'll be back in New Zealand eventually.'

Looking ahead to the future, his crystal ball-gazing sees him as more than just a happy farmer at the tip of New Zealand's South Island, but perhaps the owner-operator (and head coach, of course) of a motocross centre of excellence.

'I can't wait until I come back and have a few more animals. It's a nice spot and we're building it up at the moment to make it better. I'd like to get it to the stage where I can run motocross coaching and training schools in the future. I'd really like to tie up something with the bike manufacturers or importers to support this. How many families can afford to buy a new bike and send their kids to me at Motueka for motocross lessons? Families don't have endless amounts of money. I want to make it so that the kid down the road can come — not just the kid from the rich family. I want it so that they can all come and enjoy it. I don't want to put so much pressure on the kids. They should be there to enjoy it. They need to come and learn about the bikes, learn about the riding, learn basic skills and enjoy themselves.

'This is my way of putting something back into the sport. I didn't have any pressure put on me. Even when I was riding badly, my dad would tell me I was riding well. That's all he'd ever say. I got to know that, even when I rode badly, he'd give me encouragement and be positive. He doesn't like to watch motocross much. He gets too nervous. I think I would too, if I had a child racing. I get nervous watching a supercross event, especially when I see my cousin riding. He's been riding only a year and I know the pain if you get hurt — I don't want to see him get hurt.'

By setting up a motocross training school on his Motueka property, Josh knows he can pass on the skills he's learned from a long and illustrious career, perhaps teaching a few young New Zealanders how to race safely, to enjoy themselves, and maybe even to become the world champions of tomorrow.

Fact file

Born 11 March 1977

CAREER FIRSTS

1st MX race, 1988 at Mapua, near Nelson, New Zealand (aged 11)

1st GP ride, 29 August 1993, 125cc GP Manjimup, Australia (aged 16)

1st full GP season in 1995 (aged 18)

1st call-up to the Motocross des Nations in Slovakia in 1995

1st offered factory GP ride, Suzuki, 2000

1st GP win, Isle of Wight, 2004

1992

Suzuki

1st 14–15 years, junior 85cc motocross

1st 14–15 years, junior 85cc supercross

1993

Suzuki

1st junior 125cc at New Zealand Motocross Grand Prix at Woodville on the Saturday and raced senior expert class on the Sunday (first event as a senior)

1st New Zealand 125cc support class

World champs:

1st GP ride, 125cc class at Manjimup, Australia (finishing 16, 17 and 18 in the three races)

1994

Suzuki

Injured at round one of the NZ championships at Pukekohe (anterior cruciate ligament, left knee, out for four months)

2nd 250cc New Zealand supercross championships

2nd 125cc New Zealand supercross championships

1995

Suzuki

3rd NZ 250cc motocross championships

1st 250cc NZ supercross championships

1st 125cc NZ supercross championships

World champs:

Privateer Suzuki RM250, previous year's models leased from the factory

Team-mates: Werner de Wit and Marnicq Bervoets

Mechanic: Glenn Bayly, Tauranga

41st 250cc world championships (racing bike number 77)

7th Motocross des Nations (Sverepec, Slovakia, with Darryll King and Shayne King)

1996

Suzuki

3rd NZ 250cc motocross championships

1st Woodville MX GP feature

2nd 250cc NZ supercross championships

2nd 125cc NZ supercross championships

World champs:

Privateer Suzuki RM250, previous year's models leased from the factory

Team-mates: Werner de Wit and Marnicq Bervoets

Mechanic: Glenn Woodman (Waikanae, NZ)

23rd 250cc world championships

6th Motocross des Nations (Jerez, Spain, teamed with Darryll King and Shayne King)

1997

Suzuki

1st 250cc NZ supercross championships

1st 125cc NZ supercross championships

1st 226–250cc NZ four-stroke championships

1st 251–350cc NZ four-stroke championships

World champs:

Privateer Suzuki RM250, factory lease

Team-mates: Werner de Wit and Marnicq Bervoets

Mechanic: Blair Selfe (Oamaru, NZ)

17th 250cc world championships

7th Motocross des Nations (Nismes, Belgium, teamed with Darryll King and Shayne King)

1998

Suzuki

1st 250cc NZ supercross championships

1st 125cc NZ supercross championships

1st 250cc NZ motocross championships (first Suzuki MX title win in NZ since 1989)

1st 125cc NZ motocross championships (first Suzuki MX title win in NZ since 1989)

World champs:

Privateer Suzuki RM250, factory lease

Team-mates: Werner de Wit and Marnicq Bervoets

Mechanic: Blair Selfe (Oamaru, NZ)

13th 250cc world championships

3rd Motocross des Nations (Foxhills, Britain, teamed with Darryll King and Shayne King)

1999

Suzuki

1st Woodville MX GP feature (winner of Roddy Shirriffs memorial title)

1st 250cc NZ supercross championships

1st 125cc NZ supercross championships

1st Taupo, Labour Weekend (winner of Nicky Smith memorial race)

World champs:

Privateer Suzuki RM250

Team-mates: Leon Giesbers and Brian Jorgensen

Mechanic: Blair Selfe (Oamaru, NZ)

7th 250cc world championships (highest placed Suzuki rider)

Motocross des Nations (Indiatuba, Brazil — no New Zealand team entered)

2000

Suzuki

1st Woodville MX GP feature (winner of Roddy Shirriffs memorial title)

1st 250cc NZ supercross championships

1st 125cc NZ supercross championships

Did not attend New Zealand motocross nationals

World champs:

Factory Suzuki RM250

Team-mate: Mickael Pichon (France)

Mechanic: Blair Selfe (Oamaru, NZ)

4th 250cc world championships

19th Motocross des Nations (St Jean d'Angely, France, teamed with Darryll King and Shayne King)

2001

Suzuki

2nd Woodville MX GP feature

World champs:

Factory Suzuki RM250

Team-mate: Mickael Pichon (France)

Mechanic: Blair Selfe (Oamaru, NZ)

6th 250cc world championships

3rd Motocross des Nations (Namur, Belgium, teamed with Daryl Hurley and Shayne King)

2002

Honda

3rd Taupo, Labour Weekend Nicky Smith memorial race

World champs:

Vismara Honda CR250

Team-mates: Pit Bierer (Germany) and Andrea Bartolini (Italy)

Mechanic: Fabio Santoni (Italy)

2nd 250cc world championships

Motocross des Nations (Bellpuig, Spain — no New Zealand team entered)

2003

Honda

11th British MX1 champs (injured for first half of season)

World champs:

CAS factory Honda CR250

Team-mates: Gordon Crockard (Ireland), Yoshitaka Atsuta (Japan) and Jussi Vehvilainen (Finland)

Mechanic: Fabio Santoni (Italy)

12th MX GP world championships

4th Motocross des Nations (Zolder, Belgium, teamed with Shayne King and Ben Townley) — first ride on the CRF450 four-stroke

2004

Honda

1st British MX1 champs

World champs:

CAS factory Honda CRF450

Team-mates: Yoshitaka Atsuta (Japan) and Jussi Vehvilainen (Finland)

Mechanic: Fabio Santoni (Italy)

3rd MX1 world championships

7th Motocross des Nations (Lierop, Netherlands, teamed with Ben Townley and Daryl Hurley)

2005

Honda

4th 125cc NZ supercross championships (did not complete series)

1st British MX1 champs

World champs:

CAS factory Honda CRF450

Team-mate: Jussi Vehvilainen (Finland)

Mechanic: Fabio Santoni (Italy)

  2nd MX1 world championships

  4th Motocross des Nations (Ernee, France, teamed with Ben Townley and Cody Cooper)

2006

Honda

  1st at round one of NZ supercross championships (125cc and open classes)

World champs:

CAS factory Honda CRF450

Team-mate: Ken de Dycker (Belgium)

Mechanic: Fabio Santoni (Italy)

  7th MX1 world championships (due to pre-season injury contested eight out of 15 GPs)

  3rd Motocross of Nations (Winchester, England, teamed with Ben Townley and Cody Cooper)

2007

Yamaha

  1st at round one of NZ supercross championships (125cc class)

World champs:

Rinaldi factory Yamaha YZF450

Team-mate: Marc de Reuver (Netherlands)

Mechanic: Fabio Santoni (Italy)

  3rd MX1 world championships

ArtScroll Mesorah Series®

Rabbi Nosson Scherman / Rabbi Meir Zlotowitz

General Editors

הגדה-של-פסח

CHASSIDIC
MASTERS

by
Rabbi Shalom Meir Wallach

hAGGADAh
OF ThE

Published by

Mesorah Publications, ltd

in conjunction with

ArtScroll/Jerusalem, ltd.
ארטסקרול/ירושלים בע"מ

A TVUNAH PUBLICATION

FIRST EDITION
First Impression . . . February, 1990

Published and Distributed by
MESORAH PUBLICATIONS, Ltd.
Brooklyn, New York 11232

Distributed in Israel by
MESORAH MAFITZIM / J. GROSSMAN
Rechov Harav Uziel 117
Jerusalem, Israel

Distributed in Europe by
J. LEHMANN HEBREW BOOKSELLERS
20 Cambridge Terrace
Gateshead, Tyne and Wear
England NE8 1RP

Distributed in Australia & New Zealand by
GOLD'S BOOK & GIFT CO.
36 William Street
Balaclava 3183, Vic., Australia

Distributed in South Africa by
KOLLEL BOOKSHOP
22 Muller Street
Yeoville 2198
South Africa

ISBN:
0-89906-222-9 (hard cover)
0-89906-223-7 (paperback)

Typography by CompuScribe at ArtScroll Studios, Ltd.
4401 Second Avenue / Brooklyn, N.Y. 11232 / (718) 921-9000

Printed in the United States of America by Moriah Offset
Bound by Sefercraft, Quality Bookbinders, Ltd. Brooklyn, N.Y.

בחר ה׳ ביעקב

Тhis volume is dedicated
in memory of

הרב יעקב ב״ר אליעזר קיפפעל זצ״ל
Rabbi Jacob Kiffel זצ״ל
נפטר במוצאי שבת קודש ט״ו סיון תשמ״ט / June 18, 1989

He was a 'brand rescued from fire' —
but the flame of his soul was never extinguished.

Orphaned and alone from the age of twelve,
he wandered from Poland through Siberia to France.
Always determined to be near Torah and its scholars,
and longing to become a talmid chochom himself.

He succeeded.

He came to America to learn, but by personal example
he became a rosh yeshiva of inspiration.
He taught joy, faith, fulfillment in Torah,
devotion to rebbayim, loyalty to friends.

All his life his smile and wit illuminated his surroundings
and inspired his comrades. A profoundly devoted husband
and father, he raised a generation of b'nei Torah
who are worthy of his hopes.

Snuffed out suddenly while still bright and vibrant,
his memory remains the light of his stricken family
and a model for all who knew him.

תנצב״ה

Publisher's Preface

The chassidic story and the chassidic insight into a verse or commandment have become staples of Jewish life and thought. scores of Chassidism's great leaders have become household words, and their stories and parables have given new dimensions to our understanding of life and our mission as Jews. This book mines that rich treasury of literature and tradition, and applies it to the *Haggadah*.

From an almost infinite library of commentary and tales, Rabbi Shalom Meir Wallach has assembled a new commentary on the *Haggadah*. As the Talmud teaches, one who exerts himself in the study of Torah will find success. Rabbi Wallach has exerted himself and he has found the material to create an enlightening and fascinating book that is not only a commentary on the *Haggadah*, but makes interesting and informative reading all year round.

In addition, this book offers an essay that explains and illustrates the major significance of stories in Chassidic teaching and life. And, not surprisingly, the essay itself is filled with meaningful stories.

The art of anthology is a delicate and demanding one. It demands taste, breadth, and writing skill. Rabbi Wallach has all three, and that is why this book was a runaway success in its original Hebrew edition in Israel. We are grateful to him for making this work available to the English-reading Jewish public. To Yaakov Petroll, who translated, is a scholar of consummate skill whose work has become familiar to ArtScroll readers. So is Rabbi Shlomo Fox-Ashrei, who edited. It is our privilege to make their work available to the English-reading Torah public. They have all rendered a valuable service to tens of thousands of people.

Once more it is our pleasure to acknowledge the Director of ArtScroll Jerusalem, Reb Shmuel Blitz for coordinating this major project in the same efficient, dedicated manner that he brings to all of ArtScroll's book from Israel. He is a major force in the field of Torah Judaica and we are proud that he has been a key factor in the ArtScroll Series since its earliest Years.

Introduction
Chasidim and the Chasidic Tale

The movement of Chasidus was founded some two hundred and fifty years ago by the sainted Ba'al Shem Tov, R' Yisrael of Mezhibuz. In a short period it conquered by storm most of greater Poland and Galitzia, and wide areas of Russia and Lithuania. Thereafter it spread to Rumania and Hungary. The disciples of the Ba'al Shem, and their disciples after them, founded dynasties of rebbes (*admorim*) who led tens of thousands of chasidim and created chasidic courts by the hundreds, each unique, each with its traditions and character, each with its teachings and its tales.

What was the message which the Ba'al Shem brought to the world? What was original in Chasidus?

The standard answer is that it turned to the masses, to the simple folk, who felt neglected and rejected. By placing emphasis on the heart and its intentions, by stressing the elements of joy and devotion, it made the common people stand up tall. In practice, this led to purposeful intention (כַּוָּנָה) in prayer, to song and dance, to the cohesion of the group and the all-inclusive embrace of all orders of society. Taken as a whole, it was a novel application of the remark of *Chazal*:

> The one who does more, and the one who does less, are equal, provided that each directs his heart towards Heaven (*Berachos* 5b).

"A Jew preoccupied on a market day, running about here and there, buying and selling, of a sudden might raise his eyes heavenward and, heart all atwitter, cry out, 'Oh my! The sun will soon set and I have not yet offered up my *minchah* prayer.' He seeks a secluded corner and prays in haste and confusion. And, nevertheless," the Ba'al Shem Tov would say, "angels and seraphim tremble before this prayer!"

And there is the well-known story of the *Ne'ilah* (Concluding Prayer) on a particular Yom Kippur. The Ba'al Shem prayed at great length and strove mightily to do away with an accusation brought in the court of heaven, an accusation which would lead to the passing of a terrible

decree. His disciples, too, felt what was happening and joined their prayers to his in moving plea. Tears fell from their eyes in full rivulets and the cries echoed and re-echoed from the vault of the *beis midrash* — but went unanswered. The heavenly charge, as yet, stood ground; the gates of compassion were sealed.

Among those present was a villager, who could barely pray, and his son, who did not know how to read or write. The lad looked and looked at the congregation pouring its heart out to the Creator. His heart groaned within him; he longed to share in the prayer, but could not. "Yet there is something I can do, Master of the world," said the youngster. Out of his pocket came a reed pipe. He put it to his lips and let loose a sharp, high, shrill whistle.

All stood shocked and silent. And then the Ba'al Shem Tov broke out in song with a happy melody. That piercing note which came by way of a shepherd's pipe from the innermost recesses of a youngster's heart had torn through the barriers on high, drawing up all the prayers in its wake. The prosecution was silenced; the impending decree dismissed.

❀ ❀ ❀

The foregoing is all true. But we will be distorting and oversimplifying the picture if we say that it represents the total message of Chasidus.

Not for this alone did the Ba'al Shem receive Torah from Achiah of Shiloh, the teacher of Eliyahu HaNavi (as his disciple, the author of the *Toledos Yaakov Yosef* of Polno'e, bears witness; *Parashas Balak*). Not for this alone was he found worthy of the hidden light of Torah which enabled him to see from one end of the world to the other (by witness of his grandson, author of *Degel Machaneh Efraim*; *Parashas Bereishis*). Not for this alone did he realize tremendous achievements when his soul rose to heaven, night after night (as the Gaon of Vilna bears witness in *Keser Rosh*). Once, indeed, he remarked to his grandson in explaining the verse: "It (the Torah) is not in the heavens . . . nor on the far side of the ocean" (*Devarim* 30:12-13), "I swear to you that there is one who learns the Torah from the Holy One, Himself — not from an angel or a seraph — *in the heavens*. And he is not certain at any time that he will not be banished in the next moment to the abyss — *on the far side of the ocean*" (concluding passage of *Degel Machaneh Efraim*).

Chasidus is, essentially, a two-sided coin. On the one hand it turns to the masses. It encourages them; it presents a face of joy to them. But on the other hand it seeks out the exceptional among men, opening before them deep and hidden treasures of the mind. Upon them it makes

limitless demands. The Ba'al Shem claimed that the snatched and hurried prayer of the preoccupied few shook the angels and seraphim. Yet, his disciple the Maggid of Zlotchov would say, "My *sin* of praying three times a day is more than enough. For is *that* how one prays to his Creator?" And R' Elimelech of Lizensk was convinced that it would be necessary to fashion a new *Gehinnom* for him; the existing one, he thought, was insufficient for someone of his failings. He once was asked, "Does the Rebbe truly believe that? We see his acts of devotion. 'If flame befalls the cedars, what fate awaits the moss clinging to the walls?' What awaits us?"

"The fates are not comparable," said the Rebbe. "A man hit by a large club receives a blow, but nothing more. If, however, he is pierced by a sharp needle, it penetrates farther and farther within."

❀ ❀ ❀

How was Chasidus able to maneuver between, or embrace, both of these positions; to appeal to the masses and make demands of an elite; to be simple and joyous, yet profound and severe? There were schools of Chasidus that found a road of the golden mean. The Ba'al Shem attracted the common folk, but also gave guidance to superior disciples — the Maggid of Mezritch, R' Pinchas of Kuritz, the authors of the *Hafla'ah*, of *Meir Nesivim*, the Maggid of Ostraha and others. His successor, the Maggid of Mezritch, followed in his footsteps. He concentrated a group of the great about himself, among whom were to be found R' Elimelech of Lizensk, R' Zusha of Hanipoli, R' Shmelke of Nikolsburg, R' Pinchas of Frankfurt, R' Levi Yitzchak of Berdichev, and the author of the *Tanya*, R' Shneur Zalman of Liadi. Yet, at one and the same time, he threw open his doors to the masses. So, too, his disciple, R' Elimelech of Lizensk, who counted the Chozeh of Lublin, the Maggid of Kuzhnitz, the Rebbe of Apta and R' Menachem Mendel of Riminov among his disciples. And after him, the Chozeh of Lublin at whose 'table' sat four hundred 'wearers of the white' (that was the dress of rebbes of those days) and along with them, the common folk streamed to him to receive his blessing and be delivered from their ordeals.

But there were schools of chasidic thought, great and well known, who tended to follow one of the two paths and did not walk in both. Pshischa split off from Lublin. The Yehudi of Pshischa, disciple though he was of the Chozeh of Lublin, drew about himself a circle of the elite, dove down to the depths of the soul and brought them up to the heights of the spirit. R' Bunim of Pshischa, who succeeded him, refined his approach. His way brought upon itself the anger of the other courts which

attempted to denounce it at the great wedding in Ostilla, attended by hundreds of *admorim*. Only the wisdom of the disciples of Pshischa, with the Chidushei HaRim of Gur at their head, saved the day and repelled the charges of the accusation. This school of thought reached its zenith under the fierce guidance of the Rebbe (Fiery Angel) of Kotzk, who asked that forty men follow him into the forest. They would call out, "Hashem is God," and He would rain down *manna* for them.

And in contrast there were those courts which found it proper to descend to the masses, to lead them and aid them. By the nature of things, there were clashes between the two philosophies; between the piercing brilliance of Kotzk and the innumerable, clearly visible miracles of the sainted Zaide of Radoshitz; between the profundities and the mystical ways of Breslav and the amazing acts of marvel of the Shpole Zaide.

When the picture is taken as a whole, however, chasidism was multi-faceted. Elevated minds could be found side by side with simple folk at every chasidic court. Each found his place therein; each rose to the heights he could scale, led and directed by the rebbe in the light of the philosophy of his particular school of thought and the traditions of his dynasty — be it the world of pensive thought of Chabad or the world of images and "aspects" (בְּחִינוֹת) of Breslav; the world of allusions (רְמָזִים) of Ruzhin, or that of the penetrating remark of Kotzk; that of the biting satire of Ropshitz, or the world of fiery enthusiasm of Karlin.

❦ ❦ ❦

The two-sided character of Chasidus is also reflected in its creative works, both written and oral. The profound words of Torah, the lofty thoughts which are a full treasure-house of the mind are to be found in hundreds of works of Chasidus over the generations; they are directed to the intellectual elite. Some were, right from the start, unintelligible to, and not meant for, a broader, general audience; the contents of *Heichal HaBrachah* of Komarna and *Toras Avraham* of Slonim fall into such a category.

Others read easily, as if they could be understood without effort. It is their like that the Rebbe of Polno'e had in mind when he remarked of the sayings of the Ba'al Shem quoted in his work, "They are like the stars in heaven which seem so tiny and are really, each in itself, a world and its entirety." When R' Nachman of Breslav first received his great disciple-to-be, R' Nasan, he told him about a disciple of the Ba'al HaTanya who heard one saying from his master and expounded upon it for eight years. Indeed, this was what R' Nasan, himself, did in

composing the *Likutei Halachos* on the teachings of his own master. The introduction to *Noam Elimelech* promises that everyone will understand what is written in it at his particular level. So it appears. Yet his disciple, the Rebbe of Riminov, claimed, "Angels and seraphim labor to the point of exhaustion, before they comprehend a passage in this work." Such are the seemingly simple.

Men of intellect refresh themselves, then, from wells of thought which are bottomless. What of the masses, the simple folk? On the surface, it would seem that the tales were fashioned for them. They passed from mouth to mouth, from father to son. They were told and retold at gatherings of friends, at *kiddushim* and *melavei malkah*. They often tell of the miracles brought about by the *tzaddikim*, showing their powers, fostering belief in them, and they encourage the listeners themselves to achieve greater heights.

At times this was clearly expressed:

Nor is such an attitude limited to chasidic circles only. The pre-eminent sage, the *Aderes* (R' Eliahu David Rabinowitz-Te'omim, Rabbi of Yerushalayim and before then of Ponoviezh and Mir), of Lithuanian stock, wrote a warm approbation in particular to *Eser Kedushos*, a work on the miraculous deeds of ten rebbes. There, he lists the stories of the wondrous acts of the *Tanna'im* and *Amora'im* which are mentioned in the *gemara* — the *Tanna'im* and *Amora'im* of whom it is said, "The least among them could revive the dead" (*Avodah Zara* 10b); "If the *tzaddikim* wished to do so, they could create the world" (*Sanhedrin* 65b).

Such an attitude is also reflected in *Chazal* when they say that there is no age that does not have *tzaddikim* of the stature of our forefather Avraham (*Succah* 54b); that a man must declare, "When will my deeds approach those of my forefathers, Avraham, Yitzchak and Yaakov?" (*Tanna D'vei Eliahu* 24). From this perspective, it could be said that the first "chasidic tales" are those related in *Bereishis*.

But we will err greatly if we see the tale of the *tzaddik* as folklore only, even if we view it as folklore with an ethical purpose. If its sole reason for being were to instill and strengthen our belief in *tzaddikim*, that would be sufficient. As the Rebbe of Sanz, the Divrei Chaim said, "I do not know whether or not the tales of wonders are true. But this I do know. The *tzaddikim* had it within their power to accomplish such wonders" (*Mekor Chaim*). True or make-believe, they have a moral force. The chasidic tale, however, goes far beyond this.

It must! For the young Menachem Mendel, who was to become the Rebbe of Kotzk, was first drawn to Chasidus by the stories. The Kotzker symbolizes trenchant genius and opposition to tales of the miraculous.

David HaMelech said : "Our forefathers in Egypt did not pay attention to understand (לֹא הִשְׂכִּילוּ) Your wonders" (*Tehillim* 106:7). The Fiery Angel of Kotzk interpreted the verse as saying that Israel in Egypt did not reach their heights of understanding by contemplating the miracles (he treated wonders — נִפְלְאוֹתֶיךָ — as the subject, and forefathers — אֲבוֹתֵינוּ — as the object): "Your wonders did not make our forefathers in Egypt understand." Yet it was he who said, "I became a chasid because of an old man in my town. He told tales of *tzaddikim*. He told and told, and I listened and listened."

It was not the wondrous which spoke to the heart of the keen youth. He paid scant attention to such matters. When he arrived in Lublin, he bought a small pocketknife before entering the presence of the Chozeh of Lublin for the first time. "Did you come to Lublin to buy a pocket-knife?" asked the Chozeh with a smile.

Then and there he answered, "Rebbe, you will not win me over with your holy sight (*ruach hakodesh*). I have come to learn, not to be impressed!"

No! It was not the wondrous which drew him. But the old man knew how to tell the stories and Menachem Mendel knew how to listen. For there is something to hear in the chasidic tale. One must bend an ear and know how to listen. In the town of Yaritchov there was a well-known fool called Peretz. One day R' Shalom of Kaminka teasingly asked him, "Why don't you get married?"

"Why should a man marry?" said Peretz.

"What a question!" said R' Shalom. "To have children."

"If I want children, I'll travel to the Rebbe of Belz and ask that he bless me with children," declared the fool.

When he told the story over, R' Chaim of Sanz would say, "Do you think that R' Shalom wished to mock the fool? Certainly not! He wished to teach us that just as the *tzaddik's* blessing for children will not take effect unless one has a wife, so too, the chasid, who comes to the rebbe to draw up the spiritual by the bucketful, should know that he will gain nothing if he does not himself become involved in the study of Torah and in devotion to *Hashem* (*Rabbenu HaKadosh MiSanz* III 86).

The story was to be seen on at least two levels. It entered the mind as well as the ears.

The chasidic tale must be examined closely. It has not been transmitted from generation to generation without reason. The outer form, which makes it attractive, is designed to preserve its contents and message. Nor is that lesson and inner meaning always evident.

It is told that someone once wished to repeat a saying of R' David of

Lelov to the Chiddushei HaRim of Gur. "Don't tell me," said the Rebbe, "what they said, we are unable to comprehend."

The tales present uplifting examples; they have an appeal to the mind. But there is something more.

They have a special force; they awaken remembrance of the merit of the *tzaddikim* and bring about deliverance by sheer faith. "Through the words and through the recollection of the miracle the very force of the miracle is aroused and continues to have effect. That is why it is a *mitzvah* to tell over the story of the Exodus from Egypt" (The Rebbe of Lutzk in his *Divros Shlomo* on the Book of *Esther*).

The following story told by the Rebbe of Ruzhin shows us that this is the way *tzaddikim* themselves viewed the stories:

> Once a matter of life-or-death came before the Ba'al Shem Tov. The Rebbe ordered that a wax candle be made. He went to the forest with it, affixed it to a tree, appealed to the Holy One with special prayers and names, and brought forth deliverance. Years passed and a similar incident presented itself to his disciple, my grandfather, the Maggid of Mezritch, who followed in the Ba'al Shem's path. He, too, had a candle made, went into the forest near the very same tree and said, "I do not know what thoughts and purposeful intentions (כַּוָּנוֹת) the Ba'al Shem had. But I affix this candle, relying on those intentions." His act was accepted in Heaven and salvation followed. Years later, when R' Moshe Leib of Sasov faced a like problem he said, "I don't know where the forest or the tree is, but I will retell the tale and may Hashem help." And help came (*Knesses Yisrael* 23).

The tale presents uplifting examples; it provides food for thought; it has an ongoing life of its own.

Even when the true meaning escapes us, the story works its magic. R' Nachman of Breslav once said, "I see that my words of Torah are not affecting you. I shall start to tell you stories." Stories affect us all. The *Haggadah* says: "Even if we were all men of wisdom (חֲכָמִים), understanding (נְבוֹנִים), experience (זְקֵנִים), and knowledge of the Torah (יוֹדְעִים אֶת הַתּוֹרָה), it would still be an obligation upon us to tell about the Exodus from Egypt." For, as the Tzemach Tzedek of Lubavitch says, wisdom (חָכְמָה), understanding (בִּינָה), and knowledge (דַעַת) do not and can not reach places which the story enters. It makes its way by another path, indirectly, into the innermost recesses of the soul.

❀　❀　❀

The chasidic tale is not only the legacy of the simple; it belongs to all. Each one understands it at his own level. As the Rebbe of Radomsk puts it:

> *Chazal* say that the common talk of the servants of the Patriarchs is more important than the Torah of their children (*Bereishis Rabbah* 60; Eliezer tells his story to Rivkah's family at length and it is a repeated version, whereas many *mitzvos* and *halachos* are written in brief, or only alluded to in the Torah). They are important because the tales of the servants of the Patriarchs become Torah for the sons (*Tiferes Shlomo*, *Chanukah*).

HAGGADAH
OF THE
CHASSIDIC
MASTERS

בדיקת חמץ

The *chametz* search is initiated with the recitation of the following:

הֲרֵינִי מוּכָן וּמְזוּמָּן לְקַיֵּם מִצְוַת עֲשֵׂה וְלֹא תַעֲשֶׂה שֶׁל בְּעוּר חָמֵץ. לְשֵׁם
יְחוּד קֻדְשָׁא בְּרִיךְ הוּא וּשְׁכִינְתֵּהּ, עַל יְדֵי הַהוּא טָמִיר וְנֶעְלָם, בְּשֵׁם
כָּל יִשְׂרָאֵל. וִיהִי נֹעַם אֲדֹנָי אֱלֹהֵינוּ עָלֵינוּ, וּמַעֲשֵׂה יָדֵינוּ כּוֹנְנָה עָלֵינוּ,
וּמַעֲשֵׂה יָדֵינוּ כּוֹנְנֵהוּ:

בָּרוּךְ אַתָּה יהוה אֱלֹהֵינוּ מֶלֶךְ הָעוֹלָם, אֲשֶׁר
קִדְּשָׁנוּ בְּמִצְוֹתָיו, וְצִוָּנוּ עַל בְּעוּר חָמֵץ.

Upon completion of the *chametz* search, the *chametz* is wrapped well and set aside
to be burned the next morning and the following declaration is made. The declaration
must be understood in order to take effect; one who does not understand the Aramaic
text may recite it in English, Yiddish or any other language. Any *chametz* that will be
used for that evening's supper or the next day's breakfast or for any other purpose prior
to the final removal of *chametz* the next morning is not included in this declaration.

כָּל חֲמִירָא וַחֲמִיעָא דְּאִכָּא בִרְשׁוּתִי, דְּלָא
חֲמִתֵּהּ וּדְלָא בְעַרְתֵּהּ וּדְלָא יְדַעְנָא לֵהּ,
לִבָּטֵל וְלֶהֱוֵי הֶפְקֵר כְּעַפְרָא דְאַרְעָא.

יְהִי רָצוֹן מִלְּפָנֶיךָ, יהוה אֱלֹהֵינוּ וֵאלֹהֵי אֲבוֹתֵינוּ, שֶׁתְּזַכֵּנוּ לַחֲזֹר וּלְחַפֵּשׂ
בְּנִגְעֵי בָּתֵּי הַנֶּפֶשׁ, אֲשֶׁר נוֹאַלְנוּ בַּעֲצַת יִצְרֵנוּ הָרָע, וּתְזַכֵּנוּ לָשׁוּב בִּתְשׁוּבָה
שְׁלֵמָה לְפָנֶיךָ, וְאַתָּה בְּטוּבְךָ הַגָּדוֹל תְּרַחֵם עָלֵינוּ. עָזְרֵנוּ אֱלֹהֵי יִשְׁעֵנוּ עַל
דְּבַר כְּבוֹד שְׁמֶךָ, וְתַצִּילֵנוּ מֵאִסּוּר חָמֵץ, אֲפִילוּ בְּכָל שֶׁהוּא, בְּשָׁנָה זוֹ וּבְכָל
שָׁנָה כָּל יְמֵי חַיֵּינוּ. אָמֵן, כֵּן יְהִי רָצוֹן:

בִּעוּר חמץ

יְהִי רָצוֹן מִלְּפָנֶיךָ, יהוה אֱלֹהֵינוּ וֵאלֹהֵי אֲבוֹתֵינוּ, כְּשֵׁם שֶׁאֲנִי מְבַעֵר הֶחָמֵץ
מִבֵּיתִי וּמֵרְשׁוּתִי, כַּךְ יהוה אֱלֹהֵינוּ וֵאלֹהֵי אֲבוֹתֵינוּ תְּבַעֵר כָּל הַחִיצוֹנִים
וְאֶת רוּחַ הַטֻּמְאָה תְּבַעֵר מִן הָאָרֶץ, וְאֶת יִצְרֵנוּ הָרָע תַּעֲבִירֵהוּ מֵאִתָּנוּ,
וְתִתֶּן לָנוּ לֵב בָּשָׂר לְעָבְדְּךָ בֶּאֱמֶת, וְכָל הַסִּטְרָא אַחֲרָא וְכָל הָרִשְׁעָה כְּלָּה
כֶּעָשָׁן תִּכְלֶה, וְתַעֲבִיר מֶמְשֶׁלֶת זָדוֹן מִן הָאָרֶץ, וְכָל הַמַּעֲיקִים לַשְּׁכִינָה
תְּבַעֲרֵם בְּרוּחַ מִשְׁפָּט, כְּשֵׁם שֶׁהֶעֱבַרְתָּ אֶת מִצְרַיִם וְאֶת אֱלֹהֵיהֶם בַּיָּמִים
הָהֵם וּבַזְּמַן הַזֶּה. אָמֵן:

The following declaration, which includes all *chametz* without exception, is to be made
after the burning of leftover *chametz*. It should be recited in a language which one
understands. When *Pesach* begins on *Motzaei Shabbos*, this declaration is made on
Shabbos morning. Any *chametz* remaining from the *Shabbos* morning meal is flushed
down the drain before the declaration is made.

SEARCH FOR CHAMETZ

The *chametz* search is initiated with the recitation of the following:

Behold, I am prepared and ready to perform the positive and negative commandments of removing chametz. For the sake of the unification of the Holy One, Blessed is He, and His Presence, through Him Who is hidden and inscrutable — [I pray] in the name of all Israel. May the pleasantness of my Lord, our God, be upon us — may He establish our handiwork for us; our handiwork may He establish.

Blessed are You, Hashem, our God, King of the universe, Who has sanctified us by His commandments, and commanded us concerning the removal of chametz.

Upon completion of the *chametz* search, the *chametz* is wrapped well and set aside to be burned the next morning and the following declaration is made. The declaration must be understood in order to take effect; one who does not understand the Aramaic text may recite it in English, Yiddish or any other language. Any *chametz* that will be used for that evening's supper or the next day's breakfast or for any other purpose prior to the final removal of chametz the next morning is not included in this declaration.

Any chametz which is in my possession which I did not see, and remove, nor know about, shall be nullified and become ownerless, like the dust of the earth.

May it be Your will, Hashem, our God and the God of our forefathers, that You enable us to explore and search out our spiritual maladies, which we have acquired by following the advice of our Evil Inclination; that You enable us to return in complete repentance before You; and may You, in Your abundant beneficence have mercy upon us. Assist us, O God of our salvation, for the sake of Your Name's glory, and rescue us from transgressing the prohibition of chametz in the slightest degree, this year and every year, for all the days of our lives. Amen. So may it be.

BURNING THE CHAMETZ

May it be Your will, Hashem, our God and the God of our forefathers, that just as I have removed the chametz from my house and my property, so may You, Hashem, our God and the God of our forefathers, remove all the external influences, and the spirit of defilement from the earth; cause our Evil Inclination to leave us, and give us a heart of flesh to serve You with sincerity; may all the forces of the "Other Side" and all evil evaporate like smoke; may the realm of wantonness pass from the earth; and may You remove, in the spirit of justice, all that impede the Divine Presence; just as You removed Egypt and its idols in those days at this season. Amen.

The following declaration, which includes all *chametz* without exception, is to be made after the burning of leftover *chametz*. It should be recited in a language which one understands. When *Pesach* begins on *Motzaei Shabbos*, this declaration is made on *Shabbos* morning. Any *chametz* remaining from the *Shabbos* morning meal is flushed down the drain before the declaration is made.

כָּל חֲמִירָא וַחֲמִיעָא דְּאִכָּא בִרְשׁוּתִי, דַּחֲזִתֵּהּ וּדְלָא חֲזִתֵּהּ, דַּחֲמִתֵּהּ וּדְלָא חֲמִתֵּהּ, דְּבִעַרְתֵּהּ וּדְלָא בִעַרְתֵּהּ, לִבָּטֵל וְלֶהֱוֵי הֶפְקֵר כְּעַפְרָא דְאַרְעָא.

יְהִי רָצוֹן מִלְּפָנֶיךָ, יהוה אֱלֹהֵינוּ וֵאלֹהֵי אֲבוֹתֵינוּ, שֶׁתְּרַחֵם עָלֵינוּ וְתַצִּילֵנוּ מֵאִסּוּר חָמֵץ, אֲפִילוּ מִכָּל שֶׁהוּא, לָנוּ וּלְכָל בְּנֵי בֵיתֵנוּ וּלְכָל יִשְׂרָאֵל, בְּשָׁנָה זוֹ וּבְכָל שָׁנָה וְשָׁנָה כָּל יְמֵי חַיֵּינוּ. וּכְשֵׁם שֶׁבִּיעַרְנוּ הֶחָמֵץ מִבָּתֵּינוּ וְשֵׂרַפְנוּהוּ, כֵּן תְּזַכֵּנוּ לְבַעֵר הַיֵּצֶר הָרָע מִקִּרְבֵּנוּ תָּמִיד כָּל יְמֵי חַיֵּינוּ, וּתְזַכֵּנוּ לְדַבֵּק בְּךָ וּבְתוֹרָתְךָ וְאַהֲבָתְךָ וּלְדַבֵּק בְּיֵצֶר הַטּוֹב תָּמִיד, אֲנַחְנוּ וְזַרְעֵנוּ וְזֶרַע זַרְעֵנוּ מֵעַתָּה וְעַד עוֹלָם. כֵּן יְהִי רָצוֹן, אָמֵן:

עירוב תבשילין

It is forbidden to prepare on *Yom Tov* for the next day even if that day is the Sabbath. If, however, Sabbath preparations were started before *Yom Tov* began, they may be continued on *Yom Tov*. *Eruv tavshilin* constitutes this preparation. A matzah and any cooked food (such as fish, meat or an egg) are set aside on the day before *Yom Tov* to be used on the Sabbath and the blessing is recited followed by the declaration [made in a language understood by the one making the *eruv*]. If the first days *of Pesach* fall on Thursday and Friday, an *eruv tavshilin* must be made on Wednesday.
[In *Eretz Yisrael*, where only one day *Yom Tov* is in effect, the *eruv* is omitted.]

בָּרוּךְ אַתָּה יהוה אֱלֹהֵינוּ מֶלֶךְ הָעוֹלָם, אֲשֶׁר קִדְּשָׁנוּ בְּמִצְוֹתָיו, וְצִוָּנוּ עַל מִצְוַת עֵרוּב.

בְּהָדֵין עֵרוּבָא יְהֵא שָׁרֵא לָנָא לַאֲפוּיֵי וּלְבַשּׁוּלֵי וּלְאַצְלוּיֵי וּלְאַטְמוּנֵי וּלְאַדְלוּקֵי שְׁרָגָא וּלְתַקָּנָא וּלְמֶעְבַּד כָּל צָרְכָּנָא, מִיּוֹמָא טָבָא לְשַׁבַּתָּא לָנָא וּלְכָל יִשְׂרָאֵל הַדָּרִים בָּעִיר הַזֹּאת.

הדלקת נרות

The candles are lit and the following blessings are recited.
When *Yom Tov* falls on *Shabbos*, the words in parentheses are added.

בָּרוּךְ אַתָּה יהוה אֱלֹהֵינוּ מֶלֶךְ הָעוֹלָם, אֲשֶׁר קִדְּשָׁנוּ בְּמִצְוֹתָיו, וְצִוָּנוּ לְהַדְלִיק נֵר שֶׁל [שַׁבָּת וְשֶׁל] יוֹם טוֹב.

בָּרוּךְ אַתָּה יהוה אֱלֹהֵינוּ מֶלֶךְ הָעוֹלָם, שֶׁהֶחֱיָנוּ וְקִיְּמָנוּ וְהִגִּיעָנוּ לַזְּמַן הַזֶּה.

Any chametz which is in my possession which I did or did not see, which I did or did not remove, shall be nullified and become ownerless, like the dust of the earth.

May it be Your will, HASHEM, our God and the God of our forefathers, that You be merciful with us and rescue us from transgressing the prohibition of chametz even in the slightest degree — us, our entire household, and all of Israel — this year and every year, for all the days of our lives. And just as we have removed the chametz from our houses and burnt it, so may You enable us to remove the Evil Inclination from within us eternally, all the days of our lives; may You enable us to cleave to You, to Your Torah, and to Your love, and to cleave to the Good Inclination eternally — us, our children, and our children's children — from now and forever. So may it be. Amen.

ERUV TAVSHILIN

It is forbidden to prepare on *Yom Tov* for the next day even if that day is the Sabbath. If, however, Sabbath preparations were started before *Yom Tov* began, they may be continued on *Yom Tov*. *Eruv tavshilin* constitutes this preparation. A matzah and any cooked food (such as fish, meat or an egg) are set aside on the day before *Yom Tov* to be used on the Sabbath and the blessing is recited followed by the declaration [made in a language understood by the one making the *eruv*]. If the first days *of Pesach* fall on Thursday and Friday, an *eruv tavshilin* must be made on Wednesday.
[In *Eretz Yisrael*, where only one day *Yom Tov* is in effect, the *eruv* is omitted.]

Blessed are You, HASHEM, our God, King of the universe, Who sanctified us by His commandments and commanded us concerning the commandment of eruv.

Through this eruv may we be permitted to bake, cook, fry, insulate, kindle flame, prepare for, and do anything necessary on the festival for the sake of the Sabbath — for ourselves and for all Jews who live in this city.

LIGHTING THE CANDLES

The candles are lit and the following blessings are recited.
When *Yom Tov* falls on *Shabbos,* the words in parentheses are added.

Blessed are You, HASHEM, our God, King of the universe, Who has sanctified us through HIs commandments, and commanded us to kindle the flame of the (Sabbath and the) festival.

Blessed are You HASHEM, our God, King of the universe, Who has kept us alive, sustained us, and brought us to this season.

❦ Preparing for the Seder

The Seder preparations should be made in time for the Seder to begin as soon as the synagogue services are finished. It should not begin before nightfall, however. Matzah, bitter herbs and several other items of symbolic significance are placed on the Seder plate in the arrangement shown below.

ג' מצות
3 MATZOS

Matzah — Three whole matzos are placed one atop the other, separated by a cloth or napkin. Matzah must be eaten three times during the Seder, by itself, with maror, and as the afikoman. Each time, the minimum portion of matzah for each person should have a volume equivalent to half an egg. Where many people are present, enough matzos should be available to enable each participant to receive a proper portion.

Maror and **Chazeres** — Bitter herbs are eaten twice during the Seder, once by themselves and a second time with matzah. Each time a minimum portion, equal to the volume of half an egg, should be eaten.

The Talmud lists several vegetables that qualify as maror, two of which are put on the Seder plate in the places marked Chazeres and maror. Most people use romaine lettuce (whole leaves or stalks) for Chazeres, and horseradish (whole or grated) for maror, although either may be used for the mitzvah of eating maror later in the Seder.

Charoses — The bitter herbs are dipped into charoses (a mixture of grated apples, nuts, other fruit, cinnamon and other spices, mixed with red wine). The charoses has the appearance of mortar to symbolize the lot of the Hebrew slaves, whose lives were embittered by hard labor with brick and mortar.

Z'roa [Roasted bone] and **Beitzah** [Roasted egg] — On the eve of Passover in the Holy Temple in Jerusalem, two sacrifices were offered and their meat roasted and eaten at the Seder feast. To commemorate these two sacrifices we place a roasted bone (with some meat on it) and a roasted hard-boiled egg on the Seder plate.

The egg, a symbol of mourning, is used in place of a second piece of meat as a reminder of our mourning at the destruction of the Temple — may it be rebuilt speedily in our day.

Karpas — A vegetable (celery, parsley, boiled potato) other than bitter herbs completes the Seder plate. It will be dipped in salt water and eaten. (The salt water is not put on the Seder plate, but it, too, should be prepared beforehand, and placed near the Seder plate.)

קַדֵּשׁ

Kiddush should be recited and the Seder begun as soon after synagogue services as possible — however, not before nightfall. Each participant's cup should be poured by someone else to symbolize the majesty of the evening, as though each participant had a servant.

הֲרֵינִי מוּכָן וּמְזוּמָּן לְקַדֵּשׁ עַל הַיַּיִן, וּלְקַיֵּם מִצְוַת כּוֹס רִאשׁוֹן מֵאַרְבַּע כּוֹסוֹת. לְשֵׁם יִחוּד קֻדְשָׁא בְּרִיךְ הוּא וּשְׁכִינְתֵּיהּ, עַל יְדֵי הַהוּא טָמִיר וְנֶעְלָם, בְּשֵׁם כָּל יִשְׂרָאֵל. וִיהִי נֹעַם אֲדֹנָי אֱלֹהֵינוּ עָלֵינוּ, וּמַעֲשֵׂה יָדֵינוּ כּוֹנְנָה עָלֵינוּ, וּמַעֲשֵׂה יָדֵינוּ כּוֹנְנֵהוּ:

קַדֵּשׁ / Kaddesh

Shpole Zaide   It is customary for teachers of the very young to have their tender pupils memorize the key words which give the order of the Seder (קַדֵּשׁ וּרְחַץ וְכוּ') along with their traditional interpretations.

Once, on the evening of the Seder, the *Shpole Zaide* asked his little son to recite the key aloud. The youngster began, "*Kaddesh* — when the father comes from the *beis knesses*, the synagogue, on the evening of the Seder, he must immediately recite *kiddush*."

His father waited for him to continue, but the child said that the teacher had not taught him anything further on this point. And so, his father taught him the conclusion: "so that the youngsters won't fall asleep, but will ask the *Ma Nishtannah* (the Four Questions)."

On the following day, the teacher was present at the Rebbe's *tish* (table) and the Rebbe asked him, "Why didn't you teach the children the concluding remarks?"

"I didn't want to have them go to the trouble," said the teacher, "especially since it isn't a very important reason. For even a man who has no children recites the *kiddush* immediately on his arrival from the *beis knesses*."

The Rebbe became angry, "Are you the one to judge which reason is important and which is not? Are you wiser than all the other teachers? How did you dare change the version that has been taught for generations? Let me tell you what those who lived before us alluded to with this statement.

"*When the father* — that is our Father in Heaven — *comes from the beis knesses on the evening of the Seder* and sees how his children, the people of Israel, have severed themselves from the life of the everyday and the darkness and troubles of the Exile, how they have come to the *beis knesses* to pray before Him and praise Him for their Redemption; when He sees this, *He must immediately say kiddush* — He must renew the *kiddushin*, the marriage bond between Himself and ourselves, and take us out of exile; *so that the youngsters won't fall asleep* — so that we don't sink into a deep slumber in our Exile; *but will ask the Ma Nishtannah, why is this night different from all other nights* — why is this night, this Exile, longer than all the other exiles."

When he had said this, the Zaide burst into torrential weeping and all

KADDESH

Kiddush should be recited and the Seder begun as soon after synagogue services as possible — however, not before nightfall. Each participant's cup should be poured by someone else to symbolize the majesty of the evening, as though each participant had a servant.

Behold, I am prepared and ready to recite the Kiddush over wine, and to fulfill the mitzvah of the first of the Four Cups. For the sake of the unification of the Holy One, Blessed is He, and His Presence, through Him Who is hidden and inscrutable — [I pray] in the name of all Israel. May the pleasantness of my Lord, our God, be upon us — may He establish our handiwork for us; our handiwork may He establish.

---

present wept along with him. The Zaide came to himself and said, "Now we must give our Father some joy; we must show Him that His child can dance in the darkness, too." And he ordered them to sing a melody and began to dance, as was his holy way (*Sipurei Chasidim*).

קַדֵּשׁ וּרְחַץ / Kaddesh Urechatz

Tiferes Shmuel

On the first *Pesach* after he had become Rebbe, the *Tiferes Shmuel of Alexander* remarked: "The order of the seder is *kaddesh urechatz* — say the *kiddush* (קִידּוּשׁ) the prayer of sanctification of the Festival, and then wash hands. Should not the order have been the reverse? First wash — a man should wash himself clean of sin — and then rise and become holy (יִתְקַדֵּשׁ).

"If, however, we think in terms of a parable, we can understand the order. Not everyone is permitted to enter the palace of a king. Even those who have been invited to do so must make preparations, they must dress properly. And they can only go in at the appointed hour. If a man should enter without an invitation, without preparing himself — in sackcloth, or at an hour other than the one assigned — he would be severely punished.

"But if the man was fleeing from a band of murderous robbers, and would rush into the palace to save his life, no one would hold him blameworthy or punish him.

"On the evening of the first Seder in Egypt, Israel was sunk in the depths of impurity and corruption and was about to sink into the final depth and be completely assimilated. They were forced to leap up and out of the abyss into the palace of the King of kings to save themselves. They sanctified themselves (*kaddesh*) first, so to speak, and only afterwards went through stages of preparation; through the counting of the forty-nine days of the *omer*. That was the *urechatz*, the washing away of the sins" (*Eser Zechuyos* 20).

הֲרֵינִי מוּכָן / Behold, I am prepared

R' Chaim of Sanz

R' Chaim of Sanz was on his way to prayers. He reached the *beis midrash*, turned about, and retraced his steps. The *Rav of Barniv* followed him. R' Chaim returned home, remained

(וַיְהִי עֶרֶב וַיְהִי בֹקֶר)

יוֹם הַשִּׁשִּׁי: וַיְכֻלּוּ הַשָּׁמַיִם וְהָאָרֶץ וְכָל צְבָאָם. וַיְכַל אֱלֹהִים בַּיּוֹם הַשְּׁבִיעִי מְלַאכְתּוֹ אֲשֶׁר עָשָׂה, וַיִּשְׁבֹּת בַּיּוֹם הַשְּׁבִיעִי מִכָּל מְלַאכְתּוֹ אֲשֶׁר עָשָׂה. וַיְבָרֶךְ אֱלֹהִים אֶת יוֹם הַשְּׁבִיעִי וַיְקַדֵּשׁ אֹתוֹ, כִּי בוֹ שָׁבַת מִכָּל מְלַאכְתּוֹ אֲשֶׁר בָּרָא אֱלֹהִים לַעֲשׂוֹת.[1]

there for a brief period and, once more, started on his way to the *beis midrash*. When he noticed the *Rav of Barniv*, he said, "Do you know why I returned home? A man must mentally prepare himself before fulfilling any *mitzvah*. Walking to the *beis midrash* is itself a *mitzvah*. And because I was so concerned with preparing myself for prayer, I neglected to think that I was about to perform the *mitzvah* of walking to the *beis midrash*. That is why I returned home."

He raised his voice and added, "Now, behold, I am walking to the *beis midrash* to pray!" (*Otzar HaSipurim* VI:11).

וַיְכֻלּוּ / (Thus the heaven and the earth) were finished

R' Avraham Yaakov of Sadigur   Several free-thinking, 'enlightened' Jews (*maskilim*) had arranged among themselves to be present at the *tish* (table) of *R' Avraham Yaakov of Sadigur* to scoff and mock him when he would say *kiddush* over the wine.

When they arrived, the Rebbe's face lit up with pleasure. "How fitting it is to say *kiddush* now," he said. When we pronounce the passage of *vayechulu* (וַיְכֻלּוּ), we bear witness to the creation of the heaven and earth and the dominion of the Holy One over His world. Testimony is only relevant when doubts are cast and protest is raised. Let us stand before those who protest, and bear witness out loud."

And with that, he began the *kiddush* (*Imrei Tzaddikim* 4).

בָּרוּךְ אַתָּה ה' / Blessed are You, Hashem

R' Shlomo Leib of Lentchena   Once when *R' Shlomo Leib of Lentchena* uttered the name of Hashem in the blessing over the wine during *kiddush*, he was beset by fear. All his limbs trembled, the cup fell from his hand, and the wine spilled. The cup was refilled and he completed *kiddush* in a loud voice as was his custom.

Subsequently, he did not hold the cup in his free unsupported hand, but would place his hand on the arm rest of the chair and the cup would be placed within it (*Eser Ataros* 8).

(And there was evening and there was morning)

The sixth day. Thus the heaven and the earth were finished, and all their array. On the seventh day God completed His work which He had done, and He abstained on the seventh day from all His work which He had done. God blessed the seventh day and hallowed it, because on it He abstained from all His work which God created to make.[1]

---

1. *Bereishis* 1:31-2:3.

R' Aaron Leib of Premishlan One of the chasidim of *R' Aaron Leib of Premishlan* begged of the Rebbe that he might behold Eliyahu HaNavi, at least in a dream. The Rebbe gave his promise.

Some time later, the chasid dreamt that Eliyahu had come to his home. In his great excitement and joy, he did not know how to receive Eliyahu or what to offer him. He asked his wife to serve cake for the Prophet's pleasure. Eliyahu looked at him and said, "Fie! Do you think I would pronounce the great and awesome name of Hashem in a blessing on mere physical goods?"

That short statement filled the chasid with such fear and dread, that, for the rest of his life, whenever he would open his mouth to make a blessing, his teeth chattered in terror (*Rachamei Av*).

מֶלֶךְ הָעוֹלָם / King of the universe

R' Chaim of Sanz The *Rav of Barniv* very much wished to see how *R' Chaim of Sanz* awoke from sleep. He begged the Rebbe's *shammash* (personal attendant) to allow him to enter the Rebbe's bed chamber and was granted permission.

Towards morning, the Rebbe arose with a lion's roar* and cried out loudly, "I say praise before You (*Modeh Ani*), King." He repeated the word *King* several times until he said with a heartrending groan, "I don't yet feel the King's presence — " and he broke off and did not complete the *Modeh Ani*. He washed his hands, made the morning blessings and the blessings of the Torah — all while sitting on his bed — and instructed his *gabbai* to bring a *gemara*. He learned with fervor for some two hours, closed the *gemara*, ran his hand across his chest and said, "Ah! Now I know and feel that He is King," and he concluded the prayer, *"living and existing, Who has mercifully returned my soul to me, great is Your faithfulness"* (*Otzar HaSipurim* II:14).

[*lion's roar* — The opening words of the *Shulchan Aruch* are: He should be powerful like a lion to arise in the morning (*Orach Chaim* 1:1).]

סַבְרִי מָרָנָן וְרַבָּנָן וְרַבּוֹתַי:

בָּרוּךְ אַתָּה יהוה אֱלֹהֵינוּ מֶלֶךְ הָעוֹלָם, בּוֹרֵא
פְּרִי הַגָּפֶן:

בָּרוּךְ אַתָּה יהוה אֱלֹהֵינוּ מֶלֶךְ הָעוֹלָם, אֲשֶׁר
בָּחַר בָּנוּ מִכָּל עָם, וְרוֹמְמָנוּ מִכָּל לָשׁוֹן,
וְקִדְּשָׁנוּ בְּמִצְוֹתָיו. וַתִּתֶּן לָנוּ יהוה אֱלֹהֵינוּ בְּאַהֲבָה
[שַׁבָּתוֹת לִמְנוּחָה וּ]מוֹעֲדִים לְשִׂמְחָה, חַגִּים וּזְמַנִּים
לְשָׂשׂוֹן, אֶת יוֹם [הַשַּׁבָּת הַזֶּה וְאֶת יוֹם] חַג הַמַּצּוֹת
הַזֶּה, זְמַן חֵרוּתֵנוּ [בְּאַהֲבָה] מִקְרָא קֹדֶשׁ, זֵכֶר
לִיצִיאַת מִצְרָיִם, כִּי בָנוּ בָחַרְתָּ וְאוֹתָנוּ קִדַּשְׁתָּ
מִכָּל הָעַמִּים, [וְשַׁבָּת] וּמוֹעֲדֵי קָדְשֶׁךָ [בְּאַהֲבָה וּבְרָצוֹן]
בְּשִׂמְחָה וּבְשָׂשׂוֹן הִנְחַלְתָּנוּ. בָּרוּךְ אַתָּה יהוה,
מְקַדֵּשׁ [הַשַּׁבָּת וְ]יִשְׂרָאֵל וְהַזְּמַנִּים.

בָּרוּךְ אַתָּה יהוה אֱלֹהֵינוּ מֶלֶךְ הָעוֹלָם, בּוֹרֵא מְאוֹרֵי
הָאֵשׁ.

בָּרוּךְ אַתָּה יהוה אֱלֹהֵינוּ מֶלֶךְ הָעוֹלָם, הַמַּבְדִּיל בֵּין
קֹדֶשׁ לְחוֹל, בֵּין אוֹר לְחֹשֶׁךְ, בֵּין יִשְׂרָאֵל
לָעַמִּים, בֵּין יוֹם הַשְּׁבִיעִי לְשֵׁשֶׁת יְמֵי הַמַּעֲשֶׂה. בֵּין
קְדֻשַּׁת שַׁבָּת לִקְדֻשַּׁת יוֹם טוֹב הִבְדַּלְתָּ, וְאֶת יוֹם
הַשְּׁבִיעִי מִשֵּׁשֶׁת יְמֵי הַמַּעֲשֶׂה קִדַּשְׁתָּ, הִבְדַּלְתָּ
וְקִדַּשְׁתָּ אֶת עַמְּךָ יִשְׂרָאֵל בִּקְדֻשָּׁתֶךָ. בָּרוּךְ אַתָּה יהוה,
הַמַּבְדִּיל בֵּין קֹדֶשׁ לְקֹדֶשׁ.

מוֹעֲדִים לְשִׂמְחָה / *Appointed times for gladness*

R' Avraham Shalom of Stropkov   *R' Avraham Shalom of Stropkov wondered how it was possible to rejoice in
the midst of our bitter exile. He answered his question by way of a parable:*

On all nights other than Friday, begin here;
on Friday night include all passages in parentheses.

By your leave, my masters and teachers:

Blessed are You, HASHEM, our God, King of the universe, Who creates the fruit of the vine.

Blessed are You, HASHEM, our God, King of the universe, Who has chosen us from all nations, exalted us above all tongues, and sanctified us with His commandments. And You, HASHEM, our God, have lovingly given us (Sabbaths for rest), appointed times for gladness, feasts and seasons for joy, (this Sabbath and) this Feast of Matzos, the season of our freedom (in love,) a holy convocation in memoriam of the Exodus from Egypt. For You have chosen and sanctified us above all peoples, (and the Sabbath) and Your holy festivals (in love and favor), in gladness and joy have You granted us as a heritage. Blessed are You, HASHEM, Who sanctifies (the Sabbath,) Israel, and the festive seasons.

On Saturday night, add the following two paragraphs:

Blessed are You, HASHEM, our God, King of the universe, Who creates the illumination of the fire.

Blessed are You, HASHEM, our God, King of the universe, Who distinguishes between sacred and secular, between light and darkness, between Israel and the nations, between the seventh day and the six days of activity. You have distinguished between the holiness of the Sabbath and the holiness of a Festival, and have sanctified the seventh day above the six days of activity. You distinguished and sanctified Your nation, Israel, with Your holiness. Blessed are You, HASHEM, who distinguishes between holiness and holiness.

A servant of a king was once suspected of treason and thrown into prison to await his sentence. While sitting in his dark cell, the door flew open and the king walked in. The king ordered a bountiful table set before the prisoner and ordered him to eat, sing, and be merry. The king, thereupon, left the cell and the door swung shut once more.

If the servant had been dull witted, he would have said to himself, "The

On all nights conclude here:

בָּרוּךְ אַתָּה יהוה אֱלֹהֵינוּ מֶלֶךְ הָעוֹלָם, שֶׁהֶחֱיָנוּ
וְקִיְּמָנוּ וְהִגִּיעָנוּ לַזְּמַן הַזֶּה.

*The wine should be drunk without delay while reclining on the left side.
It is preferable to drink the entire cup, but at the very least,
most of the cup should be drained.*

וּרְחַץ

The head of the household — according to many opinions, all participants in the
Seder — washes his hands as if to eat bread, [pouring water from a cup, twice on the
right hand and twice on the left] but without reciting a blessing.

כַּרְפַּס

All participants take a vegetable other than maror and dip it into salt-water. A piece
smaller in volume than half an egg should be used. The following blessing is recited
[with the intention that it also applies to the maror which will be eaten during the
meal] before the vegetable is eaten.

בָּרוּךְ אַתָּה יהוה אֱלֹהֵינוּ מֶלֶךְ הָעוֹלָם, בּוֹרֵא
פְּרִי הָאֲדָמָה.

---

king is mocking me. He casts me into prison and commands me to rejoice!
What cruelty! And if my king and judge is cruel, I am doubly miserable!''

But he was clever and thought, ''The king is wise and knows my state of
mind. He is not in the habit of making sport of his subjects, certainly not of
those pining away in prison. He wishes to see for himself if I am really one
of his admirers and have been slandered. He is observing me through some
slit to see if I have confidence in him and will obey his command and rejoice,
trusting that I will be freed because I rely on his mercy.'' Then, he ate in joy
and sang praises of the kindness of the king and his goodness.

The king witnessed this and summoned the judges, so that they, too,
could see that the prisoner was among his admirers. And on the day of
judgment the king raised him above all his ministers. Israel is the servant in
prison . . . (*Divrei Shalom*).

כַּרְפַּס / Karpas

R' Yissachar Dov of Belz The *Rebbe of Kretchnif* told the following story:
A chasid brought a sack of carrots to *R'
Yissachar Dov of Belz* to be used as *karpas* during the Seder. He parted from
the Rebbe and left for home. R' Yissachar Dov gave orders that the sack of
carrots be burned with the *chametz*. Despite the astonishment of all

On all nights conclude here:

Blessed are You, HASHEM, our God, King of the universe, Who has kept us alive, sustained us, and brought us to this season.

The wine should be drunk without delay while reclining on the left side.
It is preferable to drink the entire cup, but at the very least,
most of the cup should be drained.

URECHATZ

The head of the household — according to many opinions, all participants in the Seder — washes his hands as if to eat bread, [pouring water from a cup, twice on the right hand and twice on the left] but without reciting a blessing.

KARPAS

All participants take a vegetable other than maror and dip it into salt-water. A piece smaller in volume than half an egg should be used. The following blessing is recited [with the intention that it also applies to the maror which will be eaten during the meal] before the vegetable is eaten.

Blessed are You, HASHEM, our God, King of the universe, Who creates the fruits of the earth.

---

present, no one questioned his instructions.

A few hours passed and the man who had brought the carrots appeared; he was very disturbed. His maidservant had asked him if he was pleased with the carrots, since they were large and appealing to the eye! She even revealed the secret of her success. She had, she said, watered the plants with beer.

Her master had been horrified. "Beer is *chametz*," he had thought. "The carrots are forbidden for *Pesach* and the Rebbe, heaven forbid, will use them for *karpas*." He had immediately saddled his horse and ridden full gallop to Belz. They calmed him and told him that the carrots had been burned with the *chametz*.

To the chasidim the incident seemed to be a miracle. But the Rebbe said, "I did not order the carrots burned because I knew that they had been watered with beer. How could I have known that? But I did know that it is forbidden to introduce changes which alter the ways of our fathers. When the carrots were brought for *karpas*, I thought to myself, 'When did the generations gone by ever use carrots for *karpas*? Something is not quite right here!' That is why I had them burned."

The Rebbe of Kretchnif concluded his narration with, "See how adherence to ancestral customs prevented a violation of eating *chametz* on *Pesach*" (*Arba'ah Arazin* 92).

יַחַץ

The head of the household breaks the middle matzah in two. He puts the smaller part back between the two whole matzos, and wraps up the larger part for later use as the afikoman. Some briefly place the afikoman portion on their shoulders, in accordance with the Biblical verse recounting that Israel left Egypt carrying their matzos on their shoulders, and say בְּבֶהָלוּ יָצָאנוּ מִמִּצְרָיִם, 'In haste we went out of Egypt.'

מַגִּיד

The broken matzah is lifted for all to see as the head of the household begins with the following brief explanation of the proceedings.

הִנְנִי מוּכָן וּמְזוּמָן לְקַיֵּם הַמִּצְוָה לְסַפֵּר בִּיצִיאַת מִצְרַיִם. לְשֵׁם יִחוּד קֻדְשָׁא בְּרִיךְ הוּא וּשְׁכִינְתֵּיהּ, עַל יְדֵי הַהוּא טָמִיר וְנֶעְלָם, בְּשֵׁם כָּל יִשְׂרָאֵל. וִיהִי נֹעַם אֲדֹנָי אֱלֹהֵינוּ עָלֵינוּ, וּמַעֲשֵׂה יָדֵינוּ כּוֹנְנָה עָלֵינוּ, וּמַעֲשֵׂה יָדֵינוּ כּוֹנְנֵהוּ:

הָא לַחְמָא עַנְיָא דִּי אֲכָלוּ אַבְהָתָנָא בְּאַרְעָא דְמִצְרָיִם. כָּל דִּכְפִין יֵיתֵי וְיֵכוֹל, כָּל דִּצְרִיךְ יֵיתֵי וְיִפְסַח. הָשַׁתָּא הָכָא, לְשָׁנָה הַבָּאָה בְּאַרְעָא דְיִשְׂרָאֵל. הָשַׁתָּא עַבְדֵי, לְשָׁנָה הַבָּאָה בְּנֵי חוֹרִין.

יַחַץ / Yachatz

Tzemach Tzedek   At the Seder of the *Tzemach Tzedek*, the Rebbe of Lubavitch, one of those present, after breaking the middle matzah, measured the pieces against each other to see which was the bigger and would serve as *afikoman*. On seeing this, the Rebbe remarked, "If an object must be measured to determine whether it is great, then even something small may be greater than it" (*Sipurei Chasidim II 315*).

[The Rebbe was making a general statement about greatness and great men. Greatness which only can be determined in comparison with others is not true greatness.]

מַגִּיד / Maggid

Avnei Nezer   The *Rebbe of Sochachov*, author of *Avnei Nezer*, noted that the Aramaic translation of Onkelos renders וְהִגַּדְתָּ לְבִנְךָ – *you shall tell your son* (*Shemos* 13:8) as: וּתְחַוֵּי לְבִנְךָ, which may be understood as: *you should show your son*. We are to *show* him the Exodus, have him *see* it, in a sense, not merely tell him about it (*Neos Deshe* II p. 189).

[The usual translation of הַגֵּד in Aramaic is חַוֵּי. The point is not that we have an unusual translation but that the Aramaic חַוֵּי besides meaning *tell* also means *see*.]

YACHATZ

The head of the household breaks the middle matzah in two. He puts the smaller part back between the two whole matzos, and wraps up the larger part for later use as the afikoman. Some briefly place the afikoman portion on their shoulders, in accordance with the Biblical verse recounting that Israel left Egypt carrying their matzos on their shoulders, and say בְּבֶהָלוּ יָצָאנוּ מִמִּצְרַיִם, 'In haste we went out of Egypt.'

MAGGID

Behold, I am prepared and ready to fulfill the mitzvah of telling the story of the Exodus from Egypt. For the sake of the unification of the Holy One, Blessed is He, and His Presence, through Him Who is hidden and inscrutable — [I pray] in the name of all Israel. May the pleasantness of my Lord, our God, be upon us — may He establish our handiwork for us; our handiwork may He establish.

The broken matzah is lifted for all to see as the head of the household begins with the following brief explanation of the proceedings.

This is the bread of affliction that our fathers ate in the land of Egypt. Whoever is hungry — let him come and eat! Whoever is needy — let him come and celebrate Pesach! Now, we are here; next year may we be in the Land of Israel! Now, we are slaves; next year may we be free men!

יֵיתֵי וְיִפְסַח / Let him come and celebrate Pesach

R' Yissachar Ber of Radoshitz

Before the world recognized his greatness, R' Yissachar Ber of Radoshitz was very poor. One year, he did not even have a slice of bread to divide into the ten small pieces, customarily placed about the house prior to the Search for Leaven (בְּדִיקַת חָמֵץ), which the one who conducts the search seeks out while looking for chametz in general. To fulfill the mitzvah in the most proper fashion, he was forced to break his practice of not borrowing from another.

On the following morning, though he was able to perform the mitzvah of ridding his home of leaven in the full sense of the commandment, he was far from being able to look forward to "in the evening you shall eat matzos" (Shemos 12:18); his larder was completely bare.

In mid-afternoon two men arrived at his home in a magnificent carriage and asked for his whereabouts. His wife said that he was in the beis midrash and asked if she could be of help. They replied that they were from Germany and were here for the festival. Since they were meticulous in observing Pesach with all its strict rulings, and had heard that the rebbe was pious and God fearing, they would like to spend the festival with him. The rebbetzin sighed and said that there was no food in the house. She need not be concerned about that, they answered, as they had brought all that was

The Seder plate is removed and the second of the four cups of wine is poured. The youngest present asks the reasons for the unusual proceedings of the evening.

מַה נִּשְׁתַּנָּה הַלַּיְלָה הַזֶּה מִכָּל הַלֵּילוֹת?

שֶׁבְּכָל הַלֵּילוֹת אָנוּ אוֹכְלִין חָמֵץ וּמַצָּה, הַלַּיְלָה הַזֶּה – כֻּלּוֹ מַצָּה.

שֶׁבְּכָל הַלֵּילוֹת אָנוּ אוֹכְלִין שְׁאָר יְרָקוֹת, הַלַּיְלָה הַזֶּה – מָרוֹר.

necessary with them in the carriage. With that, they forthwith set the table in a grand manner and went off to pray.

At the end of the prayers, they turned to the Rebbe and asked that they be allowed to be his guests.

"You certainly may," said the Rebbe, "but I have prepared nothing."

"If we don't find anything, we won't eat," they said.

They walked home together and found light and joy in the house and a table set for a king. The Rebbe asked his wife if she had abided by his prohibition not to request alms from anyone. "Yes!" she said. "These guests brought all this with them." The Rebbe gave praise to Hashem and rejoiced in his guests whom he found to be exceptionally wise scholars of the Torah. They conducted the Seder in happiness and retold the story of the Exodus through the entire night. And, in a like manner, they spent the night of the second Seder, which is held in the lands of the Diaspora. After *havdalah*, at the close of *Yom Tov*, the guests went out — and failed to return. The Rebbe sought them everywhere in town but could not find them.

For *Shavuos*, the Rebbe of Radoshitz traveled to his master, the *Chozeh of Lublin*. The Chozeh asked him about his state of affairs and the Rebbe told him of his strained conditions and of the miracle which had occurred to him on *Pesach*.

"Do you know who your important guests were?" said the Chozeh. "They were the angels Michael and Gavriel! How fortunate you are. From now on, you will prosper and the years of want will pass away, never to return!"

And so it was. From that time forward, the name of the Rebbe of Radoshitz became known to the world and his fame spread afar (*Otzar HaSipurim* XVII:18).

יֵיתֵי / Let him come

R' Ze'ev Wolf of Strikov

R' Ze'ev Wolf of Strikov asked, "Why do we open the door when we say *Pour Your wrath* (שְׁפֹךְ חֲמָתְךָ) after the meal, and not before the meal when we recite the

The Seder plate is removed and the second of the four cups of wine is poured. The youngest present asks the reasons for the unusual proceedings of the evening.

Why is this night different from all other nights?

1. On all other nights we may eat chametz and matzah, but on this night — only matzah.

2. On all other nights we eat many vegetables, but on this night — we eat maror.

---

formula *whoever is hungry let him come and eat* (כָּל דִּכְפִין יֵיתֵי וְיֵכוֹל)? How can we invite guests, if the door is kept locked?"

And he answered, "*Whoever is hungry etc.* has a non-physical aspect. For, on the evening of the Seder, the gate to high spiritual attainments lies open. Not only can they be acquired, but we are invited to enter and receive them in overflowing measure — *whosoever is hungry let him come*! But there is a single prior condition which must be met. We must ourselves open the door. We must show that we are not lazy."

The *Rebbe of Kotzk* explained a *gemara* in a similar vein: Rabban Gamliel declared that if a man's inner spiritual self did not match his outward mode of behavior, he was to be barred from entering the *beis midrash*. And he posted a watchman to enforce his decree (*Berachos* 28a). Yet how could the watchman gauge a man's true personality?

In practice the watchman gave entry to no one. Whoever climbed the wall and entered via the window showed that his inner self complemented his outer one; he truly wished to learn (*Zer Zahav*).

מַה נִּשְׁתַּנָּה / Why [is this night] different

| Ba'al HaHafla'ah | *R' Pinchas*, the author of the *Hafla'ah*, was asked why we pose questions on *Pesach* and not on *Succos*, when |

many changes are also introduced and we leave our permanent homes for the temporary structure of the *succah*.

"On *Pesach*," he answered, "when the ever-troubled, ever-pursued Jew sits down to his table, as if free, and sees the beautiful dishes set before him, as if he is a lord and master, he asks, in amazement, 'Why is this night different?'

"But on *Succos*, he enters a tottery *succah*. That is in keeping with, and normal to, the bitter life of Exile. There is no reason for amazement" (*Chasidim Mesaprim* I:525).

| R' Yissachar Dov of Belz | *R' Yissachar Dov of Belz* did many things, out of the ordinary, on the evening of the Seder, so |

that his son (who later became R' Aharon of Belz) should be aroused to question him. But the youngster asked not a word.

"Don't my actions seem strange to you?" asked the father.

שֶׁבְּכָל הַלֵּילוֹת אֵין אָנוּ מַטְבִּילִין אֲפִילוּ פַּעַם אֶחָת, הַלַּיְלָה הַזֶּה – שְׁתֵּי פְעָמִים.

שֶׁבְּכָל הַלֵּילוֹת אָנוּ אוֹכְלִין בֵּין יוֹשְׁבִין וּבֵין מְסֻבִּין, הַלַּיְלָה הַזֶּה – כֻּלָּנוּ מְסֻבִּין.

The Seder plate is returned. The matzos are kept uncovered as the *Haggadah* is recited in unison. The *Haggadah* should be translated if necessary, and the story of the Exodus should be amplified upon.

עֲבָדִים הָיִינוּ לְפַרְעֹה בְּמִצְרָיִם, וַיּוֹצִיאֵנוּ יהוה אֱלֹהֵינוּ מִשָּׁם בְּיָד חֲזָקָה וּבִזְרוֹעַ נְטוּיָה. וְאִלּוּ לֹא הוֹצִיא הַקָּדוֹשׁ בָּרוּךְ הוּא אֶת אֲבוֹתֵינוּ מִמִּצְרָיִם, הֲרֵי אָנוּ וּבָנֵינוּ וּבְנֵי בָנֵינוּ מְשֻׁעְבָּדִים הָיִינוּ לְפַרְעֹה בְּמִצְרָיִם. וַאֲפִילוּ כֻּלָּנוּ חֲכָמִים, כֻּלָּנוּ נְבוֹנִים, כֻּלָּנוּ זְקֵנִים, כֻּלָּנוּ יוֹדְעִים אֶת הַתּוֹרָה, מִצְוָה עָלֵינוּ לְסַפֵּר בִּיצִיאַת מִצְרָיִם. וְכָל הַמַּרְבֶּה לְסַפֵּר בִּיצִיאַת מִצְרַיִם, הֲרֵי זֶה מְשֻׁבָּח.

מַעֲשֶׂה בְּרַבִּי אֱלִיעֶזֶר וְרַבִּי יְהוֹשֻׁעַ וְרַבִּי אֶלְעָזָר בֶּן עֲזַרְיָה וְרַבִּי עֲקִיבָא וְרַבִּי טַרְפוֹן שֶׁהָיוּ מְסֻבִּין בִּבְנֵי בְרַק, וְהָיוּ מְסַפְּרִים בִּיצִיאַת מִצְרָיִם כָּל אוֹתוֹ הַלַּיְלָה. עַד שֶׁבָּאוּ תַלְמִידֵיהֶם וְאָמְרוּ לָהֶם, רַבּוֹתֵינוּ הִגִּיעַ זְמַן קְרִיאַת שְׁמַע שֶׁל שַׁחֲרִית.

"Father, I don't question anything you do!" answered the boy (*Admorei Belz* IV:23).

כֻּלָּנוּ זְקֵנִים / (If) we were all men of experience

R' Nachman of Tulshin R' Nachman of Tulshin was asked, "Why do the Sages say that the minds of the learned (*talmidei chachamim*) become more settled the older they become, and the minds of the ignorant become sillier and sillier with advancing age?"

"Once," he answered, "I traveled aboard the wagon of a gentile driver who stopped at every tavern along the way to have a drink. We once passed

3. On all other nights we do not dip even once, but on this night — twice.

4. On all other nights we eat either sitting or reclining, but on this night — we all recline.

The Seder plate is returned. The matzos are kept uncovered as the Haggadah *is recited in unison. The* Haggadah *should be translated if necessary, and the story of the Exodus should be amplified upon.*

We were slaves to Pharaoh in Egypt, but HASHEM our God took us out from there with a mighty hand and an outstretched arm. Had not the Holy One, Blessed is He, taken our fathers out from Egypt, then we, our children, and our children's children would have remained enslaved to Pharaoh in Egypt. Even if we were all men of wisdom, understanding, experience, and knowledge of the Torah, it would still be an obligation upon us to tell about the Exodus from Egypt. The more one tells about the Exodus, the more he is praiseworthy.

It happened that Rabbi Eliezer, Rabbi Yehoshua, Rabbi Elazar ben Azaryah, Rabbi Akiva, and Rabbi Tarfon were reclining (at the Seder) in Bnei Brak. They discussed the Exodus all that night until their students came and said to them: 'Our teachers, it is [daybreak] time for the reading of the morning Shema.'

---

the ruins of a one-time tavern. He halted, entered the broken-down building, and remained there for a long time. When he returned I asked him, 'All right! I can understand your wanting to visit a tavern for a drink, but why did you go into the ruins?'

" 'I went in,' said the driver, 'to think about the old days, when this tavern was full of life, and to remember the first-class, strong whiskey they sold here.'

"That story teaches us the difference between the wise *talmidei chachamim* and the ignorant. The ignorant waste their youth carousing and become addicted to following their desires. In old age, their bodies become 'ruins' and they cannot kick up their heels as they did in the past. Then it is that they spend their time in fruitless longing. The wise, however, in contrast, war against their desires while young, in order to serve Hashem. In old age, when the body is weak and the desires no longer have their former

אָמַר רַבִּי אֶלְעָזָר בֶּן עֲזַרְיָה, הֲרֵי אֲנִי כְּבֶן שִׁבְעִים שָׁנָה, וְלֹא זָכִיתִי שֶׁתֵּאָמֵר יְצִיאַת מִצְרַיִם בַּלֵּילוֹת, עַד שֶׁדְּרָשָׁהּ בֶּן זוֹמָא, שֶׁנֶּאֱמַר, לְמַעַן תִּזְכֹּר אֶת יוֹם צֵאתְךָ מֵאֶרֶץ מִצְרַיִם כֹּל יְמֵי חַיֶּיךָ.[1] יְמֵי חַיֶּיךָ הַיָּמִים, כֹּל יְמֵי חַיֶּיךָ הַלֵּילוֹת. וַחֲכָמִים אוֹמְרִים, יְמֵי חַיֶּיךָ הָעוֹלָם הַזֶּה, כֹּל יְמֵי חַיֶּיךָ לְהָבִיא לִימוֹת הַמָּשִׁיחַ.

בָּרוּךְ הַמָּקוֹם, בָּרוּךְ הוּא. בָּרוּךְ שֶׁנָּתַן תּוֹרָה לְעַמּוֹ יִשְׂרָאֵל, בָּרוּךְ הוּא. כְּנֶגֶד אַרְבָּעָה בָנִים דִּבְּרָה תוֹרָה: אֶחָד חָכָם, וְאֶחָד רָשָׁע, וְאֶחָד תָּם, וְאֶחָד שֶׁאֵינוֹ יוֹדֵעַ לִשְׁאוֹל.

---

force, they are able to serve Hashem in peace and quiet; nothing troubles them" (*Avaneha Barzel* 62).

לְמַעַן תִּזְכֹּר . . . כֹּל יְמֵי חַיֶּיךָ
That you may remember . . . all the days of your life

R' Elazar Menachem of Lelov

R' Elazar Menachem of Lelov:
When a man peruses a book while at his table and, at the end of the meal, before returning it to its place, shakes off the crumbs which have fallen into it, [so that there will be no *chametz* in his books when *Pesach* comes,] he fulfills, in this way, in all the days of the year, the commandment *that you remember the day on which you went out of the land of Egypt all the days of your life* (Devarim 16:3) (*Likutei Divrei David* 29).

כֹּל יְמֵי חַיֶּיךָ הַלֵּילוֹת
The addition of the word "all" includes the nights as well

Lev Same'ach

The *Lev Same'ach of Alesk* showed exceptional devotion in his service to Hashem during *Succos* and, most particularly so, during the *hakafos*, when the Torah scrolls are carried about in dance. Even in old age, he did not change his conduct by a hair.

The local gentile judge was told about his wondrous behavior and came to the *beis knesses*. He remained until after the *hakafos*, witnessing the lengthy dancing. After accompanying the Rebbe home he said, "I was present during the dancing. Had I not seen it, I would not believe it. Your act of devotion

Rabbi Elazar ben Azaryah said: I am like a seventy-year-old man, but I could not succeed in having the Exodus from Egypt mentioned every night, until Ben Zoma expounded it: 'In order that you may remember the day you left Egypt all the days of your life.'[1] The phrase 'the days of your life' would have indicated only the days; the addition of the word 'all' includes the nights as well. But the Sages declare that 'the days of your life' would mean only the present world; the addition of 'all' includes the era of the Messiah.

Blessed is the Omnipresent; Blessed is He. Blessed is the One Who has given the Torah to His people Israel; Blessed is He. Concerning four sons does the Torah speak: a wise one, a wicked one, a simple one, and one who is unable to ask.

---

1. *Devarim* 16:3.

stands beyond the bounds of nature! I would suggest that, in your old age, you leave such tiring service to your sons, or at least, that of the evening, and that Your Honor should devote yourself to the service by day."

The Rebbe rose from his place and declared with great fervor: "In the presence of Hashem, one must show his devotion by day and by night, when one is young and when one is old!"

The judge was so overcome upon hearing this that he fell over backwards. With difficulty he stood up and said to those present, "I think you should leave the Rebbe; he is still under the effect of his devotions."

Such were the impressions of a non-Jew (*Or Chadash* ch. 6).

אֶחָד חָכָם / *A wise one*

R' Simchah Bunim

R' Simchah Bunim of Pshischa said:

Each one of the two hundred and forty-eight positive commandments of the Torah tells you, "Be a wise man." Each one of its three hundred and sixty-five prohibitions says, "Do not be a fool."

His disciple, *R' Menachem Mendel of Kotzk,* said:

I have evidence that it is possible to be a righteous fool. The *gemara* tells us that the angel who has been appointed to oversee pregnancy takes the soul and places it before the Holy One and asks, "What will happen to this soul? Will it be the soul of a poor man or a rich man; a wise man or a fool?" He does not ask whether it is destined for a righteous man or a wicked man, because that depends on the future free choice of the individual. Thus, it is

entirely possible that a man will be born a fool, but by proper choice and self-development he will be righteous.

There you have it — the combination that makes up a righteous fool (*Siach Sarfei Kodesh* I:257).

R' Naftali Tzvi of Ropshitz
R' Naftali Tzvi of Ropshitz was very wise, very perceptive and keen witted. Once his master, the *Chozeh of Lublin*, said to him, "The Torah commands us: *You shall be innocent* (תָּמִים) *with Hashem, your God (Devarim* 18:13); it does not demand: you shall be wise!"

"True, Rebbe," said R' Naftali, "but one needs exceptional wisdom to reach such innocence" (*Or Yesharim* p.229).

אֶחָד חָכָם, וְאֶחָד רָשָׁע / A wise one, a wicked one

R' Tzvi Hirsch of Ziditchov
R' Michel of Sambur said in the name of his uncle *R' Tzvi Hirsch of Ziditchov*:

Why did the compiler of the *Haggadah* place the wicked son next to the wise son and not at the end of the list of four sons?

Had the wicked son stood next to and after the simple son or the one who is unable to ask, he would influence them and ruin them, before the wise man could foil his plans. But he is placed next to the wise son who can keep an eye on him and cut him down (*Eser Kedushos Tinyana* 34).

R' Tzvi Elimelech of Dinov
Once, on the evening of the Seder, *R' Tzvi Elimelech of Dinov* passed through the town to see how the common folk conducted the Seder. When he reached the window of one simple man, he heard him recite the paragraph of the Four Sons.

Each time he said the word *one* — a wise *one*, a wicked *one* — he read the word *one* (אֶחָד) in full voice and lengthened the final syllable, as is done when reading the *one* (אֶחָד) in *Hear O Israel, Hashem is our God, Hashem is One* of the *Shema*. The Rebbe was exceptionally pleased and said, "This man has turned the Four Sons into the declaration of faith of the *Shema*."

R' Yissachar Dov of Belz said that when his father, *R' Yehoshua of Belz*, heard the above, his face changed color several times.

"I understood," said R' Yissachar Dov, "that the tale reflected very important matters, indeed. Man, because of the physical aspect of his nature, is liable to sin. But he can overcome this side of himself by accepting the Majesty of Heaven. The Rebbe of Dinov meant that through the agency of the One (אֶחָד) of the *Shema*, all of the Four Sons can be corrected" (*Haggadah Imrei Kodesh Belz* p. 58).

אֶחָד תָּם / A simple one

Ba'al Shem Tov

The *Yesod Ha'Avodah* of *Slonim* in the name of *R' Noach of Lechovitz*:

The *Ba'al Shem Tov* once told his disciples, "After all that I have gained in the upper realms in terms of spiritual understanding of the foundations of Torah and its *mitzvos*, and after all the pleasure I have derived from such understanding, I put it all aside and grasp onto simple faith; I am a simpleton and believe.

"And although it is stated: *The simpleton believes everything* (*Mishlei* 14:15), it is also stated: *Hashem guards the simpletons* (*Tehillim* 116:6) (*Yesod Ha'Avodah*).

R' Bunim of Pshischa

The chasidus of Pshischa plumbed the depths of the soul. First and foremost, it demanded that a man not fool himself. Once the Rebbe asked his chasidim, "Tell me! Who is a chasid?"

"A chasid (literally a pious man)," they answered, "is one who goes beyond what is demanded by the letter of the law."

"Well then," said the Rebbe, "the law requires that you not fool your fellow man. And the chasid does not fool even himself; that goes beyond the letter of the law."

A young man was to be found in the town of Pshischa who did fool himself. He imagined that he had ascended far up the ladder of holiness and purity and was not far from the rung on which he would be thought worthy of Divine revelation and prophecy.

R' Chanoch Henoch of Alexander wished to teach him a lesson. One day the young man found a 'note from Heaven' on his seat, giving detailed practices of holiness and purity and asceticism on an impossibly high plane. It was signed by 'The Angel פילד.'

The young man was excited by the note and sought to know who the angel *Fild* was and what his position was in the heavenly hosts. He approached the Rebbe, *R' Bunim of Pshischa*, and showed him the note. The Rebbe understood who was behind the affair and summoned *R' Chanoch Henoch*. When he arrived, the Rebbe said, "This young man would like to know who the angel *Fild* is, the one who signed the note."

R' Chanoch answered, "His name is made up of the first letters of the words in the verse (*Mishlei* 14:15): פֶּתִי יַאֲמִין לְכָל דָּבָר, *The fool believes everything*!" (*Siach Sarfei Kodesh* III:1; IV:152).

חָכָם, רָשָׁע, תָּם / A wise one, a wicked one, a simple one

Divrei Chaim

One day, the *Divrei Chaim of Sanz* stood by the window looking out. A man passed by. The Rebbe tapped on the window and motioned him in. When he entered, the Rebbe asked, "Tell

[41] THE PESACH HAGGADAH

חָכָם מָה הוּא אוֹמֵר? מָה הָעֵדֹת וְהַחֻקִּים וְהַמִּשְׁפָּטִים אֲשֶׁר צִוָּה יהוה אֱלֹהֵינוּ אֶתְכֶם?[1] וְאַף אַתָּה אֱמָר לוֹ כְּהִלְכוֹת הַפֶּסַח, אֵין מַפְטִירִין אַחַר הַפֶּסַח אֲפִיקוֹמָן.

רָשָׁע מָה הוּא אוֹמֵר? מָה הָעֲבֹדָה הַזֹּאת לָכֶם?[2] לָכֶם וְלֹא לוֹ, וּלְפִי שֶׁהוֹצִיא אֶת עַצְמוֹ מִן

me! If you found a purse filled with gold coins, would you return it to its owner?"

"Certainly, Rebbe," said the man. "I would return it immediately."

"You're a fool," said the Rebbe, and dismissed him.

Once more, he stood at the window and motioned to another passing man to enter. He put the same question to him.

"I'm not such a fool as to return a purse full of gold coins that fell into my hand," said the man.

"You are wicked," said the Rebbe, and sent him off.

Once again, he returned to the window, and beckoned to a third man to come in. And once again, he asked his question.

"How can I give an answer to the Rebbe?" said the man. "Do I know what will happen at such a moment? Will I have it in myself to suppress my evil desire (יֵצֶר הָרָע)? I hope that Hashem would help me overcome and help me return the lost object to its owner."

"You are a wise man," said the Rebbe, "that is how one should answer" (*Mekor Chaim* 166).

אֵין מַפְטִירִין . . . אֲפִיקוֹמָן / One may not eat dessert

R' Yissachar Dov of Belz   Just as it is not permitted to taste anything after eating the portion of the *Pesach* sacrifice, so that the aftertaste of the sacrifice remain in the mouth, in a like manner, speak to the wise son of matters which will leave a taste with him forever (*Admorei Belz III* 150).

רָשָׁע / The wicked son

R' Naftali Tzvi of Ropshitz   R' Naftali Tzvi of Ropshitz was asked why new *Haggados* are printed year in year out.

"The wicked son of last year," he replied, "seems to be a righteous man this year, in the light of the rapid decline of the generations" (*Chasidim Mesaprim* II:130).

The wise son — what does he say? 'What are the testimonies, decrees, and ordinances which HASHEM, our God, has commanded you?'[1] Therefore explain to him the laws of the Pesach offering: that one may not eat dessert after the final taste of the Pesach offering.

The wicked son — what does he say? 'Of what purpose is this work to you?'[2] He says, 'To you,' thereby excluding himself. By excluding himself

---

1. *Devarim* 6:20.   2. *Shemos* 12:26

מַה הָעֲבֹדָה הַזֹּאת לָכֶם? לָכֶם וְלֹא לוֹ

Of what purpose is this work to you? . . . thereby excluding himself

Akeidas Yitzchak — *Chazal* interpret the *to you* (לָכֶם) of the verse which speaks of work permitted on the festivals (*Shemos* 12:16) as referring 'to all your needs' (*Beitzah* 28b).

The wicked son throws out his *to you* in a like manner. He says, ''All the eating that you engage in on the evening of the Seder is *to you* — to fill your bellies, and *not for Him* (וְלֹא לוֹ), for the Holy One.''

In seeing things this way he 'denies the basic principle of Judaism' (כָּפַר בָּעִיקָּר). For the basic principle is to ''know Him in all your ways'' and ''let all your actions be for the sake of heaven.'' If he does not eat with a sense of sanctity, *blunt his teeth* (הַקְהֵה אֶת שִׁנָּיו). Why does he need teeth? After all, eating was not conceived except as a service in the name of Hashem (*Tiferes Rabboseinu Me'Alexander* 171).

Chida — The *Chida* (Chaim Yosef David Azulai) once met a man without a beard and asked him why he shaved.

''Just as I was born without a beard,'' said the man, ''I continue to live without one.''

''Now,'' said the Chida, ''I understand what is meant by *therefore, blunt his teeth* which is found in the *Haggadah* with reference to the wicked son. Just as he was born without teeth, thus he should remain, without teeth'' (*Otzar HaSipurim* VIII:14).

R' Yechezkel Michelson — An adherent of the freethinkers, the so-called enlightened ones (*maskilim*), complained to R' Yechezkel Michelson of Plonsk:

''Why does the compiler of the *Haggadah* tell us to blunt the teeth of the wicked son? The question of the wicked son appears in the Torah with an answer directly following: *And it will be when your sons will say to you,*

הַכְּלָל, כָּפַר בְּעִקָּר – וְאַף אַתָּה הַקְהֵה אֶת
שִׁנָּיו וֶאֱמָר לוֹ, בַּעֲבוּר זֶה עָשָׂה יהוה לִי בְּצֵאתִי
מִמִּצְרָיִם.[1] לִי וְלֹא לוֹ, אִלּוּ הָיָה שָׁם לֹא הָיָה
נִגְאָל.

תָּם מָה הוּא אוֹמֵר? מַה זֹּאת? וְאָמַרְתָּ אֵלָיו,
בְּחֹזֶק יָד הוֹצִיאָנוּ יהוה מִמִּצְרַיִם מִבֵּית
עֲבָדִים.[2]

'What is this service to you?' And you will say, 'This is the Pesach sacrifice to Hashem' (Shemos 12:26-27)."

"You have ignored the great difference between the two questions," said R' Yechezkel. "The Torah put the question in the plural, in the mouths of a band of wicked men. Such a gang is dangerous and they must be answered with restraint.

"But the *Haggadah* speaks in the singular, of a lone wicked man who throws off the yoke of submission to Heaven. Concerning him, we are told, 'Rise and blunt his teeth' " (*Sichas Chulin Shel Talmidei Chachamim*, p.47).

R' Yisrael of Salant   *R' Yisrael of Salant* once arrived together with several Torah leaders of Lithuania to meet with the *Chidushei HaRim* and discuss how they might combat the plots of the free-thinking *maskilim*. Some suggested the gentle arts of persuasion. But the Gerer Rebbe, in contrast, pushed for a strong hand and open warfare.

"I wonder," said one of the rabbis with a smile, "why the *tzaddikim* of Poland don't direct their thoughts against the *maskilim* while pronouncing the blessing against the slanderers (וְלַמַּלְשִׁינִים) in the *Shemoneh Esrei*. Their prayer would bring the enemy down in defeat."

On the spot, the Rebbe answered, "If the *maskilim* would limit themselves to only thinking about us when they say the blessing which follows, *for the tzaddikim and the pious* etc. . . . . (עַל הַצַּדִּיקִים), we would only need to think about them in the blessing against the slanderers. But now that they have arisen in battle against us, we must return their blows in double measure" (*Hamaor Hagadol*, p. 244).

כָּפַר בְּעִקָּר – הַקְהֵה אֶת שִׁנָּיו
He denies the basic principle of Judaism — blunt his teeth

R' Baruch of Mezhibuz   One of the chasidim once heard that the wife of R' Baruch of Mezhibuz was complaining about the family being in debt. He, together with a friend, made the rounds of the

from the community of believers, he denies the basic principle of Judaism. Therefore, blunt his teeth and tell him: 'It is because of this that HASHEM did so for me when I went out of Egypt.'[1] 'For me,' but not for him — had he been there, he would not have been redeemed.

The simple son — what does he say? 'What is this?' Tell him: 'With a strong hand did HASHEM take us out of Egypt, from the house of bondage.'[2]

1. *Shemos* 13:8.   2. 13:14.

neighboring villages and brought the *rebbetzin* a sum sufficient to cover the debts.

While they spent the *Shabbos* with the Rebbe, he remarked during the meal, "*Ribbono Shel Olam* (Master of the world), help this man who helped me pay my debts and give him so many and so many thousands of rubles.

"I suggest that You take the sum from someone whose actions are bad and give them to this man. But if You think that man will complain that You have caused him such great damage, I have a further suggestion. Take it from one who denies God's existence (כֹּפֵר בְּעִיקָר). Since he denies You, he won't complain to You."

And all things turned out according to the Rebbe's blessings. Throughout his life, the chasid never had less than the sum the Rebbe had specified (*Mekor Baruch* 7).

Seraph of Moglenitza   The *Fiery Angel (Seraph) of Moglenitza* told of a man who had come to him with a request that he speak to him and drive out thoughts of heresy.

"I cannot agree to speak of these matters, at all," said the Rebbe. "For we are warned by Shlomo HaMelech to stay at a distance from the doorstep of the house of heresy.

"Should you argue that I must speak of these things to save the soul of a member of Israel, I say that you cannot help him by violating a directive of the Sages!" (*Toledos HaNiflaos* 113).

לִי וְלֹא לֹו / For me, but not for him

R' Avraham Yaakov of Sadigura   R' Moshe David Gutman, the personal attendant (*shammash*) of R' Avraham Yaakov of Sadigura, would stand at his post each evening until the Rebbe would bid him "good night" and go to bed. At times, when the Rebbe was buried in his thoughts and the hour was late, R' Moshe David would cause

וְשֶׁאֵינוֹ יוֹדֵעַ לִשְׁאוֹל, אַתְּ פְּתַח לוֹ. שֶׁנֶּאֱמַר, וְהִגַּדְתָּ לְבִנְךָ בַּיּוֹם הַהוּא לֵאמֹר, בַּעֲבוּר זֶה עָשָׂה יהוה לִי בְּצֵאתִי מִמִּצְרָיִם.[1]

יָכוֹל מֵרֹאשׁ חֹדֶשׁ, תַּלְמוּד לוֹמַר בַּיּוֹם הַהוּא. אִי בַּיּוֹם הַהוּא, יָכוֹל מִבְּעוֹד יוֹם, תַּלְמוּד לוֹמַר בַּעֲבוּר זֶה. בַּעֲבוּר זֶה לֹא אָמַרְתִּי אֶלָּא בְּשָׁעָה שֶׁיֵּשׁ מַצָּה וּמָרוֹר מֻנָּחִים לְפָנֶיךָ.

---

a slight noise, by moving a table or chair, to remind the Rebbe that he should take a brief rest.

One night, many hours had passed; the Rebbe paced back and forth, caught up in his thoughts. The attendant moved the chairs and tapped on the windows, without success. Finally, not long before dawn, he girded up his courage, approached the Rebbe and said, "Will the Rebbe please excuse me, but the sun will soon be up and you have not yet rested."

"For you it is easy," said the Rebbe. "You can sleep in peace. But what am I to do? I had a visitor today for whom my soul finds no solution. Should I include him as part of Israel? I find that bitter as gall; he is frightfully polluted. Shall I drive him out of Israel? I find that very difficult; after all, he is a Jew!" (*Eser Oros* 9).

אַתְּ פְּתַח לוֹ / *You must initiate for him*

Chozeh of Lublin   A man's mouth is called a door (פֶּתַח) as the prophet says: "Guard the doors of your mouth" (*Michah* 7:5). I and *R' Zusha of Hanipoli* once went in to see the *great Maggid of Mezritch*. The Maggid commented, "Yaakov Yitzchak, you forgot to lock the door." When I heard that, I took it upon myself to refrain from speech for seven years (*Or Haniflaos*, p.13).

וְהִגַּדְתָּ לְבִנְךָ / *You shall tell your son*

R' Yehoshua of Belz   The Torah has attached a precondition to the retelling of the story of the Exodus to children — "Words that flow from the heart enter the heart." In order to fix the story in the hearts of children, the fathers must first fix it in their own hearts. On this point the Torah says: "That you may tell in the ears of your son and the son of your son what I did in Egypt and of the signs which I put upon them — and you will know that I am Hashem" (*Shemos* 10:2). In order to tell over the story to your children you must first know that I am Hashem! (*Ohel Yehoshua* 14).

As for the son who is unable to ask, you must initiate the subject for him, as it is stated: You shall tell your son on that day: 'It is because of this that HASHEM did so for me when I went out of Egypt.'[1]

One might think that the obligation to discuss the Exodus commences with the first day of the month of Nissan, but the Torah says: 'You shall tell your son on that day.' But the expression 'on that day' could be understood to mean only during the daytime; therefore the Torah adds: 'It is because of this that HASHEM did so for me when I went out of Egypt.' The pronoun 'this' implies something tangible, thus, 'You shall tell your son' applies only when matzah and maror lie before you — at the Seder.

1.*Shemos* 13:8.

מֻנָּחִים לְפָנֶיךָ *[When matzah and maror] lie before you*

R' Yissachar Dov of Belz

After *R' Yissachar Dov of Belz* had finished his Seder, he passed through the streets of town to hear how the common folk observed it. From one of the houses burst forth the voice of a householder calling out fervently:

"*This* (זֶה) implies only when matzah and *maror* are associated by marriage before you." (He mistakenly said מְחוּתָּנִים, *mechutanim*, rather than מֻנָּחִים, *munachim*.)

The Rebbe's attendant laughed, but the Rebbe nodded his head and said, "He's right! Matzah and *maror* are really associated by marriage.

"Imagine a rich man who has an accomplished daughter and wishes to marry her off. He finds an accomplished young man, but he is exceptionally poor. He buys him handsome clothes and wishes to have the marriage feast immediately. The young man asks for a delay so that he can make preparations for a proper wedding meal. The rich man is impatient and has the meal commence, using the dry bread in the young man's larder.

"With the passage of time, the young man acts impertinently towards his father-in-law. The rich man draws forth some of the rags which his son-in-law wore in the past and says, 'Do you remember from what state I saved you?' The young man in turn produces a piece of the dry bread and says, 'But you should remember that you wanted me and you couldn't wait.'

מִתְּחִלָּה, עוֹבְדֵי עֲבוֹדָה זָרָה הָיוּ אֲבוֹתֵינוּ, וְעַכְשָׁו קֵרְבָנוּ הַמָּקוֹם לַעֲבוֹדָתוֹ. שֶׁנֶּאֱמַר, וַיֹּאמֶר יְהוֹשֻׁעַ אֶל כָּל הָעָם, כֹּה אָמַר יהוה אֱלֹהֵי יִשְׂרָאֵל, בְּעֵבֶר הַנָּהָר יָשְׁבוּ אֲבוֹתֵיכֶם מֵעוֹלָם, תֶּרַח אֲבִי אַבְרָהָם וַאֲבִי נָחוֹר, וַיַּעַבְדוּ אֱלֹהִים אֲחֵרִים. וָאֶקַּח אֶת אֲבִיכֶם אֶת אַבְרָהָם מֵעֵבֶר הַנָּהָר, וָאוֹלֵךְ אוֹתוֹ בְּכָל אֶרֶץ כְּנָעַן, וָאַרְבֶּה אֶת זַרְעוֹ, וָאֶתֶּן לוֹ אֶת יִצְחָק. וָאֶתֵּן לְיִצְחָק אֶת יַעֲקֹב וְאֶת עֵשָׂו, וָאֶתֵּן לְעֵשָׂו אֶת הַר שֵׂעִיר לָרֶשֶׁת אוֹתוֹ, וְיַעֲקֹב וּבָנָיו יָרְדוּ מִצְרָיִם.[1]

בָּרוּךְ שׁוֹמֵר הַבְטָחָתוֹ לְיִשְׂרָאֵל, בָּרוּךְ הוּא. שֶׁהַקָּדוֹשׁ בָּרוּךְ הוּא חִשַּׁב אֶת הַקֵּץ, לַעֲשׂוֹת כְּמָה שֶׁאָמַר לְאַבְרָהָם אָבִינוּ בִּבְרִית בֵּין הַבְּתָרִים, שֶׁנֶּאֱמַר, וַיֹּאמֶר לְאַבְרָם, יָדֹעַ תֵּדַע כִּי גֵר יִהְיֶה זַרְעֲךָ בְּאֶרֶץ לֹא לָהֶם, וַעֲבָדוּם

"So, too, the Holy One shows us the *maror*, the bitter herbs, which remind us of the bitter servitude from which He delivered us. We, in turn, show Him the matzah, which did not have sufficient time to rise because He was in such a hurry to save us.

"Indeed the matzah and *maror* are *mechutanim*" (*Admorei Belz* III 209).

מַתְחִיל בִּגְנוּת וּמְסַיֵּם בְּשֶׁבַח
He begins with shame and concludes with the praiseworthy

R' Nachum of Slonim [This is the mishnaic directive as to the format for telling the story of the Exodus; *Mishnah Pesachim* 10:4.]

R' Nachum of Slonim, one of the elders of the disciples of the *Zaide of Lechovitz*, told the following to the *Yesod Ha'Avodah of Slonim*:

While studying the *Avos D' R' Nasan* (Ch. 21), I came across the passage which states that R' Akiva, in teaching his students, recalled his childhood. I imagined that the passage would note that R' Akiva was saddened when he

Originally our ancestors were idol worshipers, but now the Omnipresent has brought us near to His service, as it is written: Joshua said to all the people, 'So says HASHEM, God of Israel: Your fathers always lived beyond the Euphrates River, Terach the father of Avraham and Nachor, and they served other gods. Then I took your father Avraham from beyond the river and led him through all the land of Canaan. I multiplied his offspring and gave him Yitzchak. To Yitzchak I gave Yaakov and Esav; to Esav I gave Mount Seir to inherit, but Yaakov and his children went down to Egypt.'[1]

Blessed is He Who keeps His pledge to Israel; Blessed is He! For the Holy One, Blessed is He, calculated the end of bondage in order to do as He said to our father Avraham at the Covenant between the Parts, as it is stated: He said to Avram, 'Know with certainty that your offspring will be aliens in a land not their own, they will serve them

---

1. *Yehoshua* 24:2-4.

---

remembered the years which had passed wastefully. But to my amazement, the recollection of the past caused R' Akiva to rejoice over his later years and he said, "I praise You, Hashem, my God, that You have given me, as my lot, to be among those who sit in the *beis midrash*."

This teaches us that whoever succeeds to improve later in life should not be saddened by his early days. On the contrary, he should rejoice and be encouraged by the good he has found in the end (*Ma'asei Avos*, ch. 4).

וָאוֹלֵךְ אוֹתוֹ בְּכָל אֶרֶץ כְּנָעַן / *I led him through all the land of Canaan*

Imrei Emes   When the *Imrei Emes* of Gur visited *Eretz Yisrael* in 5692 (1932), he traveled by land via Turkey, Syria and Lebanon. He arrived in the country by way of Rosh Hanikrah.

When asked if the journey had not been tiring, he answered tersely, as usual, "One must try all the ways" (*Perek Zichronos Lehagrash Ginzburg*).

[The everyday talk (שִׂיחַת חוּלִין) of the great serves as guidelines for behavior in, and attitudes to, life in general. The Rebbe meant to indicate that one must exhaust every possible approach, whatever the matter at hand.]

וְעִנּוּ אֹתָם, אַרְבַּע מֵאוֹת שָׁנָה. וְגַם אֶת הַגּוֹי אֲשֶׁר
יַעֲבֹדוּ דָּן אָנֹכִי, וְאַחֲרֵי כֵן יֵצְאוּ בִּרְכֻשׁ גָּדוֹל.[1]

The matzos are covered and the cups lifted as the following paragraph is proclaimed joyously. Upon its conclusion, the cups are put down and the matzos are uncovered.

וְהִיא שֶׁעָמְדָה לַאֲבוֹתֵינוּ וְלָנוּ, שֶׁלֹּא אֶחָד
בִּלְבַד עָמַד עָלֵינוּ לְכַלּוֹתֵנוּ. אֶלָּא שֶׁבְּכָל
דּוֹר וָדוֹר עוֹמְדִים עָלֵינוּ לְכַלּוֹתֵנוּ, וְהַקָּדוֹשׁ בָּרוּךְ
הוּא מַצִּילֵנוּ מִיָּדָם.

צֵא וּלְמַד מַה בִּקֵּשׁ לָבָן הָאֲרַמִּי לַעֲשׂוֹת לְיַעֲקֹב
אָבִינוּ, שֶׁפַּרְעֹה לֹא גָזַר אֶלָּא עַל הַזְּכָרִים,
וְלָבָן בִּקֵּשׁ לַעֲקוֹר אֶת הַכֹּל. שֶׁנֶּאֱמַר:

דָּן אָנֹכִי / *I execute judgment*

R' Abish of Tchernovitz — R' Abish of Tchernovitz was a simple, perfect soul. When his Rebbe, R' Yisrael of Ruzhin, escaped from a Russian jail and went into exile, R' Abish asked him, in all innocence, why he did not punish the czar for all that he had suffered, and have him dethroned.

"Do you believe that Hashem directs the world?" asked the Rebbe.

"Certainly!" said R' Abish.

"Do you believe in the miracle of the Exodus from Egypt and the Ten Plagues?"

"Without a doubt."

"Well, then, when I see that the all-powerful Holy One chooses to contain Himself, despite the evil behavior of the czar, I follow in His footsteps and control myself" (*Irin Kaddishin*, end of Part III).

וְאַחֲרֵי כֵן יֵצְאוּ בִּרְכֻשׁ גָּדוֹל
And afterwards they shall leave with great possessions

R' Meir of Premishlan — R' Meir of Premishlan was asked, "We place *maror* on the Seder plate in memory of the bondage; *charoses* in memory of the mortar; *matzah* in memory of the bread of poverty. Why do we not have a symbol to remind us of the great possessions with which we left Egypt?"

"It is only right that we do as we do," said the Rebbe. "The *maror* is a memento of the servitude and we still have traces of that today. But we place

and they will oppress them four hundred years; but also upon the nation which they shall serve will I execute judgment, and afterwards they shall leave with great possessions.'[1]

The matzos are covered and the cups lifted as the following paragraph is proclaimed joyously. Upon its conclusion, the cups are put down and the matzos are uncovered.

It is this that has stood by our fathers and us. For not only one has risen against us to annihilate us, but in every generation they rise against us to annihilate us. But the Holy One, Blessed is He, rescues us from their hand.

Go and learn what Lavan the Aramean attempted to do to our father Yaakov! For Pharaoh decreed only against the males, Lavan attempted to uproot everything, as it is said:

―――――
1. *Bereishis* 15:13-14.

---

no symbol of the great possessions because there is nothing left of them" (*Bircas Chaim* II, p.112).

צֵא וּלְמַד מַה בִּקֵשׁ לָבָן הָאֲרַמִּי לַעֲשׂוֹת

Go and learn what Lavan the Aramean attempted to do

Tiferes Shlomo　　A young man came before the *Tiferes Shlomo of Radomsk* and told him that he was at present occupied with the study of the Torah and supported by his father-in-law. But his father-in-law was trying to convince him to go into trade.

"*Go and learn* (צֵא וּלְמַד)," the Rebbe directed him. "Go to the *beis midrash* and continue to learn Torah. For your father-in-law is trying to do to you what *Lavan the Aramean attempted to do to our father Yaakov* (מַה בִּקֵשׁ לְבָן הָאֲרַמִּי לַעֲשׂוֹת לְיַעֲקֹב אָבִינוּ). Lavan sent Yaakov to herd sheep rather than allow him to be a *dweller in tents* * (יוֹשֵׁב אֹהָלִים) (*Ateres Shlomo*, p.95).

[*dweller in tents — a student in the *beis midrash*.]

R' Hillel of Eibshutz　　A son-in-law once summoned his father-in-law to a *din torah* (a rabbinical trial), because he refused to pay for his support and allow him to study, as he had promised.

The father-in-law argued that his son-in-law should support himself by the work of his own hands, following the dictum of the *Mishnah*: "Torah is good when it goes together with the way of the world" (that is, work — *Avos* 2:2).

אֲרַמִּי אֹבֵד אָבִי, וַיֵּרֶד מִצְרַיְמָה וַיָּגָר שָׁם בִּמְתֵי
מְעָט, וַיְהִי שָׁם לְגוֹי, גָּדוֹל עָצוּם וָרָב.[1]

וַיֵּרֶד מִצְרַיְמָה – אָנוּס עַל פִּי הַדִּבּוּר.

וַיָּגָר שָׁם – מְלַמֵּד שֶׁלֹּא יָרַד יַעֲקֹב אָבִינוּ
לְהִשְׁתַּקֵּעַ בְּמִצְרַיִם, אֶלָּא לָגוּר שָׁם. שֶׁנֶּאֱמַר,
וַיֹּאמְרוּ אֶל פַּרְעֹה, לָגוּר בָּאָרֶץ בָּאנוּ, כִּי אֵין מִרְעֶה
לַצֹּאן אֲשֶׁר לַעֲבָדֶיךָ, כִּי כָבֵד הָרָעָב בְּאֶרֶץ כְּנָעַן,
וְעַתָּה יֵשְׁבוּ נָא עֲבָדֶיךָ בְּאֶרֶץ גֹּשֶׁן.[2]

בִּמְתֵי מְעָט – כְּמָה שֶׁנֶּאֱמַר, בְּשִׁבְעִים נֶפֶשׁ
יָרְדוּ אֲבֹתֶיךָ מִצְרַיְמָה, וְעַתָּה שָׂמְךָ יהוה אֱלֹהֶיךָ
כְּכוֹכְבֵי הַשָּׁמַיִם לָרֹב.[3]

They argued their case before *R' Hillel of Eibshutz* who said, "True, the *mishnah* is clear. But it is preferable that your son-in-law study and be learned in the entire Torah and be remiss in this one *mishnah*, rather than that he maintain this single *mishnah* and be ignorant in the entire Torah" (*Maskil el Dal* III 2).

וְלָבָן בִּקֵּשׁ לַעֲקוֹר אֶת הַכֹּל
Lavan attempted to uproot everything

R' Yaakov Aryeh   *R' Aharon Menachem Mendel of Radzimin* said:
When I was a little boy and we reached this part of the *Haggadah*, my sainted grandfather *R' Yaakov Aryeh* put me on his lap and said to me, "Know that there is a simple, direct, evil nature (יֵצֶר הָרָע) who pushes men to sin. His name is *Pharaoh*. We can hope to escape him, because he attacks openly. And even if we fail in our encounter, God forbid, there is hope that we will repent.

"But there is an evil nature whom we call *Lavan the Aramean* (אֲרַמִּי), because he fools us (מִרְמָה — treating אֲרַמִּי as if derived from the root רמה), and dresses up in white (לָבָן) like a righteous man, a *tzaddik*. He persuades a man that a particular sin is not a sin, but a *mitzvah*. We are liable to overlook the trap and, not seeing it as a sin, fail to repent.

"Of him, my child, it is said that he wishes to *uproot* everything" (*Chasidim Mesaprim* III 451).

An Aramean attempted to destroy my father. Then he descended to Egypt and sojourned there, with few people; and there he became a nation — great, mighty and numerous.[1]

Then he descended to Egypt — compelled by Divine decree.

He sojourned there — this teaches that our father Yaakov did not descend to Egypt to settle, but only to sojourn temporarily, as it says: They (the sons of Yaakov) said to Pharaoh: 'We have come to sojourn in this land because there is no pasture for the flocks of your servants, because the famine is severe in the land of Canaan. And now, please let your servants dwell in the land of Goshen.'[2]

With few people — as it is written: With seventy persons, your forefathers descended to Egypt, and now HASHEM, your God, has made you as numerous as the stars of heaven.[3]

---

1. *Devarim* 26:5.   2. *Bereishis* 47:4.   3. *Devarim* 10:22.

אֲרַמִּי אֹבֵד אָבִי
An Aramean attempted to destroy my father

Chidushei HaRim — Once, a grandson of one of the great *tzaddikim* visited Gur. He assumed that the Rebbe, the *Chidushei HaRim,* would show him great honor, because of his illustrious grandfather, and when he presented himself, he gave his family connections in full.

The Rebbe glared at him and thundered, "The Torah states: *an Aramean destroyed my father!** If a man fools himself, in the end, he destroys the favorable account which exists through the merit of his father.

"Not only is this so, but that very merit becomes a stumbling block to him. At the end of the list of punishments for our sins in the Passage of Rebuke (תּוֹכֵחָה), it is said: *and I shall remember My covenant with Yaakov and also My covenant with Yitzchak, and also My covenant with Avraham (Vayikra* 26:42). The sainted *Sh'lah* interprets this as one of the reasons for punishment. The Holy One says, 'You had such ancestors and this is what you look like?'

"That is why in our prayers we say 'our God and the God of our fathers' (in the first paragraph of the *Shemoneh Esrei,* for example). If we ourselves

---

[*An Aramean etc. The Gerer Rebbe interpreted *Arami* (ארמי) as if derived from רמה — to fool.]

וַיְהִי שָׁם לְגוֹי – מְלַמֵּד שֶׁהָיוּ יִשְׂרָאֵל מְצֻיָּנִים
שָׁם.
גָּדוֹל עָצוּם – כְּמָה שֶׁנֶּאֱמַר, וּבְנֵי יִשְׂרָאֵל פָּרוּ
וַיִּשְׁרְצוּ וַיִּרְבּוּ וַיַּעַצְמוּ בִּמְאֹד מְאֹד, וַתִּמָּלֵא הָאָרֶץ
אֹתָם.[1]

---

are worthy, then, and only then, may we join the merits of our fathers to ourselves" (*HaMaor HaGadol* ch. 35).

מְצֻיָּנִים שָׁם / *(The Israelites were) distinctive there*

R' Simchah Bunim of Pshischa

Distinctive there: They did not change their names, language, or dress.

A freethinker, a *maskil*, wished to vex *R' Simchah Bunim of Pshischa* and said, "Did Avraham wear a *shtreimel* (the fur hat worn by the chasid on *Shabbos*) and a silk *kapote* (the caftan-like garb of the chasid)?"

"I don't know exactly what he wore," said the Rebbe. "But this I do know. He looked about to see what the gentiles wore and took up a different mode of dress" (*Siach Sarfei Kodesh*).

Chidushei HaRim

Rashi has written (in *parashas Chukas*) that the Amalekites who came to do battle with Israel spoke Canaanite, so that they would not be identified and Israel would not be able to pray for their downfall. And, indeed, when they saw this strange people, who spoke the tongue of Canaan and wore the dress of Amalek, Israel prayed without mentioning a specific nation but said: "If you give *this nation* into my hand, I will destroy their cities" (*Bamidbar* 21:2).

However, the Torah itself, as *R' Yehoshua of Belz* has noted, does not call them Amalekites, but Canaanites: "And the Canaanites heard . . . and did battle with Israel" (ibid. v. 1). This indicates, he said, how much a man changes his essential self when he changes his language.

The *Chidushei HaRim of Gur* wondered why the Amalekites did not change both their dress and speech. Had they done so, they would have fooled Israel completely.

This teaches us, he said, that had they adopted both the dress and speech of Canaan, they would have not only appeared, but would actually have become Canaanites (*Ohel Yehoshua* 25; *Siach Sarfei Kodesh* I 522).

Chidushei HaRim

When the government decreed that Jews were to learn the national language and were not to wear

There he became a nation — this teaches that the Israelites were distinctive there.

Great, mighty — as it says: And the Children of Israel were fruitful, increased greatly, multiplied, and became very, very mighty; and the land was filled with them.[1]

---

1. *Shemos* 1:7.

---

distinctive dress, the *Chidushei HaRim* saw this as an act of religious persecution which should be opposed even to the point of martyrdom.

At the time, Sir Moses Montefiore of England was passing through Poland on his way to Russia where he wished to confer with the czar on behalf of his fellow Jews. The Chidushei HaRim thought of meeting with Sir Moses to convince him to request that the decree be abolished.

When the *Rebbe of Kotzk* heard of the Gerer Rebbe's plans, he commented that he was certain that nothing would come of the meeting with Montefiore.

In Posen, he said, the freethinking *maskilim* had stirred up the feelings of the authorities against the longstanding, Orthodox form of Jewish education. The Orthodox wished to present a written defense of their traditional system of education, but could not find one of their own to pen it in elegant German. They turned to one of the *maskilim* and paid him to draft a letter.

R' Akiva Eiger, the Rabbi of Posen, however, thought that the letter would not be effective. He quoted the verse: "Do not put your trust in princes, in a man who does not possess salvation" (*Tehillim* 146:3), and interpreted it to mean 'in a man who is not himself saved through his action.' "The writer of the letter, the *maskil*, is an opponent of traditional education," said R' Akiva Eiger. "He is not trying to save himself. How could a letter written by him persuade the authorities to abolish the decree?"

Montefiore himself, said the Kotzker, wore modern dress and spoke foreign languages. Why should he agree to speak on behalf of traditional costume and Yiddish?

And when Montefiore did meet with the Chidushei HaRim he said, "I don't know why you stubbornly insist on wearing bear-fur hats. And as far as language is concerned, I have proof that Jews spoke foreign tongues. Mordechai understood the conversation of King Achashverosh's guards and was thus able to reveal their plot and deliver his people."

"But that, to the contrary," replied the Chidushei HaRim, "shows that Jews did not speak the language of the country. That is why the guards ignored Mordechai's presence. They knew that Jews spoke only their own

language. They did not realize that Mordechai, because he was a member of the Sanhedrin, knew other languages."

"At least, you admit," said Montefiore, "that there is a need for someone to know foreign languages."

"Yes," said the Rebbe, "and my lord, you, with your mastery of languages, fill that need."

In the final analysis, Montefiore did not prove helpful. Deliverance from the decree came through the Chidushei HaRim's own strong opposition. The authorities imprisoned him. The Jews came out in stormy protest, so much so, that there was fear of revolt. The Rebbe was freed and the decree annulled (*Siach Sarfei Kodesh*).

R' Mordechai of Nadvornah

R' Mordechai of Nadvornah told the following story:

"I was once traveling to a particular place for *Shabbos* and sent a wagon with my baggage on ahead; I traveled separately, on Friday. Time rushed by, and I was forced to remain for *Shabbos* in a tiny village lacking my *Shabbos* outfit. I summoned a tailor and ordered him to fashion a *shtreimel*, immediately, from thirteen wide pieces of goat hide, since that was what was available in the hamlet.

"You can well imagine how I looked in that *shtreimel* and how everyone stared at me, but it was inconceivable to me that a Jew could go through a *Shabbos* without a *shtreimel* on his head."

At the time the Rebbe told the story, the Rabbi of Neupest was present in the audience. He and the members of his community had always followed the custom of German Jewry in their mode of dress. The Rebbe asked, "Rabbi of Neupest, did you understand [the significance of] my remark?"

When the Rabbi of Neupest returned home, he ordered a *shtreimel* and a chasidic coat to be made up for himself (*Sha'ar HaOsios*, p. 12).

R' Yissachar Dov of Belz

In Belz the chasidim would wear their shirts open at the collar, and their pants (breeches) gathered and tied at the knee, inserted into long socks. A chasid once came in a new style: shirt buttoned up to the neck; pants with legs open and down to the shoes.

R' Yissachar Dov of Belz smiled and said, "When a chasid comes to the rebbe, the rebbe tries to pass on to him the fear of Hashem. He can do so in plenty through the open shirt collar. And since the pants are fastened below, that feeling remains with the chasid. But with the new style of dress, it is very hard to instill the fear of God into the heart through the fastened collar. And if one succeeds in getting anything in, it tumbles down and out through the open pants' legs" (*Admorei Belz* III:311).

שֶׁלֹּא שִׁנּוּ אֶת שְׁמָם / They did not change their name

Ahavas Yisrael　　In one of the communities near Kolmaya there was a rabbi called R' Meir of whom it was said that he gave his stamp of approval to products of doubtful *kashrus* in return for money. When the *Ahavas Yisrael of Vizhnitz* visited the town, members of the community lodged complaints against the rabbi and he promised to attend to matters, in his way.

When the rabbi appeared before him, the Rebbe said, ''We all know that at the close of the *Shemoneh Esrei* prayer, we say a verse, the first and last letters of which correspond to the first and last letters of our names. This is to help us remember our names on the Final Judgment Day.

''I've often wondered, who is it that would not remember his name? Each of us hears his name tens of times a day. If someone should argue that in our fear and confusion before the Divine Judge we might forget our names, why would we not forget the verse, too?

''The verse is not meant for those who have taken non-Jewish names. Such Jews don't pray and don't say the verse.

''The verse is probably meant for rabbis. They don't usually hear their names, because they are addressed by their title — Rabbi — and they must be reminded of their names through a verse. Your verse is: מִפִּקּוּדֶיךָ אֶתְבּוֹנָן עַל כֵּן שָׂנֵאתִי כָּל אֹרַח שָׁקֶר, 'My contemplation of Your commands makes me hate every path of falsehood (*Tehillim* 119:104).' This verse will remind you of your name on the Final Day of Judgment, if you repeat it continually.''

The rabbi, who was astute, caught the hint and stopped taking the bribes and lending his stamp of approval to invalid products (*Kedosh Yisrael* II).

Tzemach Tzedek　　The *Tzemach Tzedek of Lubavitch*:
It is said that Israel had sunk to the forty-ninth, the all but final, depth of impurity in Egypt. Had they descended to the fiftieth, and bottom level, they could not have been saved.

The preservation of their distinctive name, language and dress prevented them from falling to the ultimate depth. But today, they have changed their name, language and dress; they are at the lowest state possible, that fiftieth depth. How can they be redeemed?

Fortunately, the present and the age of servitude in Egypt differ in one important factor. In Egypt, Israel had not yet received the Torah. They could have been assimilated completely. But after the Torah has been given, redemption is possible even from the abyss of the fiftieth depth of impurity (*Siach Sarfei Kodesh* IV 203).

וָרָב – כְּמָה שֶׁנֶּאֱמַר, רְבָבָה כְּצֶמַח הַשָּׂדֶה נְתַתִּיךְ, וַתִּרְבִּי וַתִּגְדְּלִי וַתָּבֹאִי בַּעֲדִי עֲדָיִים, שָׁדַיִם נָכֹנוּ וּשְׂעָרֵךְ צִמֵּחַ, וְאַתְּ עֵרֹם וְעֶרְיָה; וָאֶעֱבֹר עָלַיִךְ וָאֶרְאֵךְ מִתְבּוֹסֶסֶת בְּדָמָיִךְ, וָאֹמַר לָךְ, בְּדָמַיִךְ חֲיִי, וָאֹמַר לָךְ, בְּדָמַיִךְ חֲיִי.[1]

וַיָּרֵעוּ אֹתָנוּ הַמִּצְרִים, וַיְעַנּוּנוּ, וַיִּתְּנוּ עָלֵינוּ עֲבֹדָה קָשָׁה.[2]

וַיָּרֵעוּ אֹתָנוּ הַמִּצְרִים – כְּמָה שֶׁנֶּאֱמַר, הָבָה נִתְחַכְּמָה לוֹ, פֶּן יִרְבֶּה, וְהָיָה כִּי תִקְרֶאנָה מִלְחָמָה, וְנוֹסַף גַּם הוּא עַל שֹׂנְאֵינוּ, וְנִלְחַם בָּנוּ, וְעָלָה מִן הָאָרֶץ.[3]

רְבָבָה כְּצֶמַח הַשָּׂדֶה נְתַתִּיךְ
I made you as numerous as the plants of the field

R' Moshe of Kubrin

R' Moshe of Kubrin said:
The Holy One said, "I begged of you, Israel, that as you developed you should be 'as the plants of the field.' The more mature the stalks of grain are, the fuller and heavier are their heads, and the lower they bend under the weight. The heavier a tree is with fruit, the more bowed are its branches.

"But the opposite has occurred — וַתִּרְבִּי וַתִּגְדְּלִי, *you grew and developed* — you have stood overly erect with excessive pride; וְאַתְּ עֵרֹם וְעֶרְיָה, *and you were naked and bare* — you had no reason for the pride, for you were empty of fruit" (*Bircas Chaim* II, p. 131).

וַתִּרְבִּי / *You developed*

Divrei Chaim

The *Divrei Chaim of Sanz* said:
"A man imagines that he has grown (וַתִּרְבִּי — *you developed*); that he is worthy of being a rebbe. He convinces himself that he is a great man (וַתִּגְדְּלִי — *you have grown great*). He thinks he is adorned with *mitzvos* (וַתָּבֹאִי בַּעֲדִי עֲדָיִים — *you were bedecked with jewelry*); that he nurtures disciples with his words of Torah (שָׁדַיִם נָכֹנוּ — *prepared to nurture*). But in truth," he would say bitterly, "*you are naked and bare* (וְאַתְּ עֵרֹם וְעֶרְיָה) — he is bare of Torah, bare of *mitzvos*, hollow and empty. How far a man can lie to, and fool, himself!" (*Mekor Chaim* 100).

Numerous — as it says: I made you as numerous as the plants of the field; you developed and grew, and were bedecked with jewelry, beautiful of figure; and your hair grown long; but you were naked and bare. And I passed over you and saw you downtrodden in your blood and I said to you: 'Through your blood shall you live!' And I said to you: 'Through your blood shall you live!'[1]

The Egyptians did evil to us and afflicted us; and imposed hard labor upon us.[2]

The Egyptians did evil to us — as it says: Let us deal with them wisely lest they multiply and, if we happen to be at war, they may join our enemies and fight against us and then leave the country.[3]

_____
1. Yechezkel 16:7,6.   2. Devarim 26:6.   3. Shemos 1:10.

בְּדָמַיִךְ חֲיִי / Through your blood shall you live

Divrei Chaim

The Divrei Chaim of Sanz said:
A man once usurped another's livelihood. He rented the tavern, which had been previously rented out to the other, from the local landlord.

The man who had lost his livelihood complained to R' Chaim, and the Rebbe summoned the one who had appropriated the rights to the tavern and reproached him.

But he tried to justify himself. "Rebbe," he said, "the previous tenant of the tavern is a sinner, a wicked, evil man. It is a good deed, a *mitzvah*, to bury him!"

The Rebbe smiled and replied, "And who told you that it is a *mitzvah* to bury the wicked? I'll bring you proof to the contrary.

"The *midrash* says that the wicked of Israel died in Egypt, during the three days of the plague of darkness, and were buried then, so that the Egyptians would not witness their death. After the plague had passed, Hashem took note that Israel was bare of *mitzvos*; they had nothing in their favor that would make them worthy of deliverance. And so He granted them two *mitzvos* involving blood — circumcision and the offering of the *pesach* sacrifice (with its placing of the blood on the doorposts and the lintel), as it is stated: *And I said to you, Through your blood you shall live! And I said to you, Through your blood you shall live! (Yechezkel 16:6).*

"But you would have it that it is a *mitzvah* to bury the wicked. If so, Israel would have had bundle upon bundle of *mitzvos*. There you have it, explicit proof that it is not a *mitzvah* to bury a wicked man.

וַיְעַנּוּנוּ – כְּמָה שֶׁנֶּאֱמַר, וַיָּשִׂימוּ עָלָיו שָׂרֵי
מִסִּים, לְמַעַן עַנֹּתוֹ בְּסִבְלֹתָם, וַיִּבֶן עָרֵי מִסְכְּנוֹת
לְפַרְעֹה, אֶת פִּתֹם וְאֶת רַעַמְסֵס.[1]

וַיִּתְּנוּ עָלֵינוּ עֲבֹדָה קָשָׁה – כְּמָה שֶׁנֶּאֱמַר, וַיַּעֲבִדוּ
מִצְרַיִם אֶת בְּנֵי יִשְׂרָאֵל בְּפָרֶךְ.[2]

וַנִּצְעַק אֶל יהוה אֱלֹהֵי אֲבֹתֵינוּ, וַיִּשְׁמַע יהוה
אֶת קֹלֵנוּ, וַיַּרְא אֶת עָנְיֵנוּ, וְאֶת עֲמָלֵנוּ,
וְאֶת לַחֲצֵנוּ.[3]

וַנִּצְעַק אֶל יהוה אֱלֹהֵי אֲבֹתֵינוּ – כְּמָה שֶׁנֶּאֱמַר,
וַיְהִי בַיָּמִים הָרַבִּים הָהֵם, וַיָּמָת מֶלֶךְ מִצְרַיִם, וַיֵּאָנְחוּ
בְנֵי יִשְׂרָאֵל מִן הָעֲבֹדָה, וַיִּזְעָקוּ, וַתַּעַל שַׁוְעָתָם אֶל
הָאֱלֹהִים מִן הָעֲבֹדָה.[4]

וַיִּשְׁמַע יהוה אֶת קֹלֵנוּ – כְּמָה שֶׁנֶּאֱמַר, וַיִּשְׁמַע
אֱלֹהִים אֶת נַאֲקָתָם, וַיִּזְכֹּר אֱלֹהִים אֶת בְּרִיתוֹ אֶת
אַבְרָהָם, אֶת יִצְחָק, וְאֶת יַעֲקֹב.[5]

וַיַּרְא אֶת עָנְיֵנוּ – זוֹ פְּרִישׁוּת דֶּרֶךְ אֶרֶץ, כְּמָה
שֶׁנֶּאֱמַר, וַיַּרְא אֱלֹהִים אֶת בְּנֵי יִשְׂרָאֵל, וַיֵּדַע
אֱלֹהִים.[6]

"Now, then, if you give the man back his livelihood, well and good. If you do not, yours will be a bitter end!" (*Mekor Chaim* 428).

מִן הָעֲבוֹדָה וַיִּזְעָקוּ / (And the Children of Israel groaned) because of the servitude and cried

R' Chanoch Henoch of Alexander   After the death of the *Chidushei HaRim of Gur*, his chasidim wished to crown R' Chanoch Henoch as their Rebbe, whereupon he told the following:

"A butcher was once butchering the carcass of an animal on Friday. Time passed as he cut and cut, until night fell. The butcher suddenly took note that *Shabbos* had arrived and dashed out of his shop at a run, to the *beis*

And afflicted us — as it says: They set taskmasters over them in order to oppress them with their burdens; and they built Pisom and Raamses as treasure cities for Pharaoh.[1]

They imposed hard labor upon us — as it says: The Egyptians subjugated the Children of Israel with hard labor.[2]

We cried out to HASHEM, the God of our fathers; and HASHEM heard our cry and saw our affliction, our burden and our oppression.[3]

We cried out to HASHEM, the God of our fathers — as it says: It happened in the course of those many days that the king of Egypt died; and the Children of Israel groaned because of the servitude and cried; their cry because of the servitude rose up to God.[4]

HASHEM heard our cry — as it says: God heard their groaning, and God recalled His covenant with Avraham, with Yitzchak, and with Yaacov.[5]

And saw our affliction — that is the disruption of family life, as it says: God saw the Children of Israel and God took note.[6]

---

1. *Shemos* 1:11. 2. 1:13. 3. *Devarim* 26:7. 4. *Shemos* 2:23. 5. 2:24. 6. 1:11.

---

knesses; the congregation was singing *Lecha Dodi*.* The butcher let loose a groan. It wasn't really the butcher's groan but a groan of the 'eternal Jew' within him.

"When the verse says, 'and the *Children of Israel* groaned because of the servitude,' it means to tell us that the 'child of Israel' within each of them groaned when he realize how deeply he had sunk into servitude. And then the Torah says: וַיֵּדַע אֱלֹקִים — *Elokim took note* (*Shemos* 2:25) — the Holy One filled them with knowledge (דַּעַת).

"Only after the groan (וַיֵּאָנְחוּ), which showed an awareness of their involvement in the material, and only after they had acquired knowledge (וַיֵּדַע), can the Torah return to speak of Moshe: 'And Moshe was herding the flock of Yisro (ibid. 3:1)' — only then could He send the redeemer to them (*Siach Sarfei Kodesh*).

Lecha Dodi; The song composed by R' Shlomo Alkabetz, for the first part of the *Shabbos* evening prayer, *kabalas Shabbos*.

וְאֶת עֲמָלֵנוּ – אֵלּוּ הַבָּנִים, כְּמָה שֶׁנֶּאֱמַר, כָּל הַבֵּן הַיִּלּוֹד הַיְאֹרָה תַּשְׁלִיכֻהוּ, וְכָל הַבַּת תְּחַיּוּן.[1]

וְאֶת לַחֲצֵנוּ – זוֹ הַדְּחַק, כְּמָה שֶׁנֶּאֱמַר, וְגַם רָאִיתִי אֶת הַלַּחַץ אֲשֶׁר מִצְרַיִם לֹחֲצִים אֹתָם.[2]

וַיּוֹצִאֵנוּ יהוה מִמִּצְרַיִם בְּיָד חֲזָקָה, וּבִזְרֹעַ נְטוּיָה, וּבְמֹרָא גָּדֹל, וּבְאֹתוֹת וּבְמֹפְתִים.[3]

וַיּוֹצִאֵנוּ יהוה מִמִּצְרַיִם – לֹא עַל יְדֵי מַלְאָךְ, וְלֹא עַל יְדֵי שָׂרָף, וְלֹא עַל יְדֵי שָׁלִיחַ, אֶלָּא הַקָּדוֹשׁ בָּרוּךְ הוּא בִּכְבוֹדוֹ וּבְעַצְמוֹ. שֶׁנֶּאֱמַר, וְעָבַרְתִּי בְאֶרֶץ מִצְרַיִם בַּלַּיְלָה הַזֶּה, וְהִכֵּיתִי כָל בְּכוֹר

עֲמָלֵנוּ, אֵלּוּ הַבָּנִים / Our burden — refers to the children

R' Yisrael of Ruzhin

When R' Yisrael of Ruzhin was in prison, he sent his mother a message saying that she was responsible for his detention.

Her son, she explained, had once told her that Heaven informed him that it was within his power to bring an elevated soul into the world, a soul so elevated that its like had not existed for a thousand years. But he would have to accept suffering to do so. He had asked her whether he should agree to the condition.

"What does a father not do for his children?" she had answered.

He had agreed to accept the suffering and the future Rebbe of Hosyatin had been born. Now that he was in prison, he wished to remind his mother of her advice, so that she not be grieved (Sha'ar HaOsios, p. 8).

Yehudi Hakadosh of Pshischa

In the way of the world, a man is involved in his occupation, in business, sunken into his concerns. He doesn't have a moment free for Torah and prayer. When he is questioned about it, he answers that all of his efforts are directed to making a livelihood and bringing up his son to Torah, mitzvos and good deeds. But that son when he grows up also throws himself into the whirlwind of livelihood and he, too, doesn't have a moment to spare for himself, concerned as he is to raise his son up to Torah.

How I would love to meet that son, the end product of the chain of generations, for whom all his forebears toiled to raise him up to Torah!

The Torah alludes to this process: "These are the offspring of Noach; Noach was a righteous man; pure in his generation" (Bereishis 6:9). Noach decided

Our burden — refers to the children, as it says: Every son that is born you shall cast into the river, but every daughter you shall let live.[1]

Our oppression — refers to the pressure expressed in the words: I have also seen how the Egyptians are oppressing them.[2]

Hashem brought us out of Egypt with a mighty hand and with an outstretched arm, with great awe, with signs and wonders.[3]

Hashem brought us out of Egypt — not through an angel, not through a seraph, not through a messenger, but the Holy One, Blessed is He, in His glory, Himself, as it says: I will pass through the land of Egypt on that night; I will slay all the firstborn in the

---

1. *Shemos* 1:22.   2. 3:9.   3. *Devarim* 26:8.

---

that rather than labor on behalf of his children, who would then labor on behalf of their children, who would labor on behalf of their children, he would labor for himself; he himself would be righteous (*Nifleos HaYehudi* 33a).

This seems to be a development of *Rashi* based on the *midrash*: *"These are the offspring of Noach etc.* This teaches you that the important offspring of the righteous are their good deeds" (*Rashi* to *Bereishis* 6:9).

כָּל הַבֵּן הַיִּלּוֹד / Every son that is born

| R' Yissachar Ber of Radoshitz | There was once a large crowd at the house of R' Yissachar Ber of Radoshitz, and |

they caused a considerable commotion. The Rebbe, concerned about their disturbing his wife's rest, hushed them up.

"You should know," he said, "that she has a large share in my Torah and my devotion to Hashem.

"When I was a young man, I found that I could not make ends meet. I gathered some goods and made the rounds from town to town to earn a livelihood. But I thought to myself, 'Is this the purpose for my existence? Was I born into the world to spend the time on the roads going from town to town?' And then the verse 'Every son that is born you shall cast into the river' (*Shemos* 1:22) came to mind. As *Chazal* say, 'Water can only mean Torah' — every man should be in the water, preoccupied with the water of Torah.

"You will ask, perhaps, 'What will we eat?' The Torah itself gives us the answer in the last part of the verse: 'but every daughter, you should let live. — the woman will busy herself in providing the livelihood.

"Immediately, I turned about and made my way home. Upon arrival, I

בְּאֶרֶץ מִצְרַיִם מֵאָדָם וְעַד בְּהֵמָה, וּבְכָל אֱלֹהֵי מִצְרַיִם אֶעֱשֶׂה שְׁפָטִים, אֲנִי יהוה.[1]

וְעָבַרְתִּי בְאֶרֶץ מִצְרַיִם בַּלַּיְלָה הַזֶּה – אֲנִי וְלֹא מַלְאָךְ. וְהִכֵּיתִי כָל בְּכוֹר בְּאֶרֶץ מִצְרַיִם – אֲנִי וְלֹא שָׂרָף. וּבְכָל אֱלֹהֵי מִצְרַיִם אֶעֱשֶׂה שְׁפָטִים – אֲנִי וְלֹא הַשָּׁלִיחַ. אֲנִי יהוה – אֲנִי הוּא, וְלֹא אַחֵר.

בְּיָד חֲזָקָה – זוֹ הַדֶּבֶר, כְּמָה שֶׁנֶּאֱמַר, הִנֵּה יַד יהוה הוֹיָה בְּמִקְנְךָ אֲשֶׁר בַּשָּׂדֶה, בַּסּוּסִים בַּחֲמֹרִים בַּגְּמַלִּים בַּבָּקָר וּבַצֹּאן, דֶּבֶר כָּבֵד מְאֹד.[2]

וּבִזְרֹעַ נְטוּיָה – זוֹ הַחֶרֶב, כְּמָה שֶׁנֶּאֱמַר, וְחַרְבּוֹ שְׁלוּפָה בְּיָדוֹ, נְטוּיָה עַל יְרוּשָׁלָיִם.[3]

וּבְמֹרָא גָּדֹל – זוֹ גִּלּוּי שְׁכִינָה, כְּמָה שֶׁנֶּאֱמַר, אוֹ הֲנִסָּה אֱלֹהִים לָבוֹא לָקַחַת לוֹ גוֹי מִקֶּרֶב גּוֹי, בְּמַסֹּת, בְּאֹתֹת, וּבְמוֹפְתִים, וּבְמִלְחָמָה, וּבְיָד חֲזָקָה, וּבִזְרוֹעַ נְטוּיָה, וּבְמוֹרָאִים גְּדֹלִים, כְּכֹל אֲשֶׁר עָשָׂה לָכֶם יהוה אֱלֹהֵיכֶם בְּמִצְרַיִם לְעֵינֶיךָ.[4]

---

repeated my thoughts to my wife. She agreed to earn our living, to take up my route, going from town to town. I entered the *beis midrash* to sink myself into the Torah. Now you can understand how much I owe to her" (*Nifleos HaSaba Kadisha* 12b).

אֲנִי ה' / I, Hashem

R' Yoel of Tshaploh   R' Yoel of Tshaploh was a disciple of *R' Menachem Mendel of Vitebsk* and *R' Shlomo of Karlin*. When they passed away, he became a disciple of *R' Mordechai of Lechovitz*. Once, he felt an overwhelming longing for his master, and saddling his horse, he rode off to Lechovitz. On arriving, he tied the horse to a peg and made his way to the Rebbe's study. He knocked on the door. The Rebbe asked, "Who's there?" To which R' Yoel answered, "I."

The Rebbe called out loudly, "Who can allow himself to say *I*? *I, Hashem; it is I and no other*. It is only fitting for the Holy One to use *I*!"

R' Yoel immediately mounted his horse and returned home. He felt that he had received what he needed (*Ma'asei Avos* 97).

land of Egypt from man to beast; and upon all the gods of Egypt will I execute judgments; I, HASHEM.[1]

'I will pass through the land of Egypt on that night' — I and no angel; 'I will slay all the firstborn in the land of Egypt' — I and no seraph; 'And upon all the gods of Egypt will I execute judgments' — I and no messenger; 'I, HASHEM' — it is I and no other.

With a mighty hand — refers to the pestilence, as it is stated: Behold, the hand of HASHEM shall strike your cattle which are in the field, the horses, the donkeys, the camels, the herds, and the flocks — a very severe pestilence.[2]

With an outstretched arm — refers to the sword, as it says: His drawn sword in His hand, outstretched over Jerusalem.[3]

With great awe — alludes to the revelation of the Shechinah, as it says: Has God ever attempted to take unto Himself a nation from the midst of another nation by trials, miraculous signs, and wonders, by war and with a mighty hand and outstretched arm and by awesome revelations, as all that HASHEM your God did for you in Egypt, before your eyes?[4]

---

1. *Shemos* 12:12.   2. 9:3.   3. *I Divrei Hayamim* 21:16.   4. *Devarim* 4:34.

וּבְמֹרָא גָּדֹל / *With great awe*

R' Mordechai David of Dombrova
_____

R' Mordechai David of Dombrova visited his master, the *Chozeh of Lublin,* and attended his Seder. The Chozeh looked at him when he said the passage: *with great awe alludes to the revelation of the Shechinah.* R' Mordechai was seized by a great fear; all his limbs shook, and, in his terror, he felt that his teeth were being shaken loose. He prayed to Hashem that his teeth remain in his mouth, so that he might eat the *matzah-of-mitzvah* and the afikoman (*Kerem HaChasidus* III 68).

בְּאֹתוֹת וּבְמֹפְתִים / *With signs and wonders*

R' Eliezer Ze'ev of Kretchnif
_____

A *maskil* impertinently asked *R' Eliezer Ze'ev of Kretchnif,* "Why did Israel witness obvious signs and miracles during the Exodus and upon crossing the Red

וּבְאֹתוֹת – זֶה הַמַּטֶּה, כְּמָה שֶׁנֶּאֱמַר, וְאֶת הַמַּטֶּה הַזֶּה תִּקַּח בְּיָדֶךָ, אֲשֶׁר תַּעֲשֶׂה בּוֹ אֶת הָאֹתֹת.[1]

וּבְמֹפְתִים – זֶה הַדָּם, כְּמָה שֶׁנֶּאֱמַר, וְנָתַתִּי מוֹפְתִים בַּשָּׁמַיִם וּבָאָרֶץ

As each of the words דָּם, blood; אֵשׁ, fire; and עָשָׁן, smoke, is said, a bit of wine is removed from the cup, with the finger or by pouring.

דָּם וָאֵשׁ וְתִמְרוֹת עָשָׁן.[2]

דָּבָר אַחֵר – בְּיָד חֲזָקָה, שְׁתַּיִם. וּבִזְרֹעַ נְטוּיָה, שְׁתַּיִם. וּבְמֹרָא גָדֹל, שְׁתַּיִם. וּבְאֹתוֹת, שְׁתַּיִם. וּבְמֹפְתִים, שְׁתַּיִם. אֵלּוּ עֶשֶׂר מַכּוֹת שֶׁהֵבִיא הַקָּדוֹשׁ בָּרוּךְ הוּא עַל הַמִּצְרַיִם בְּמִצְרַיִם, וְאֵלּוּ הֵן:

Sea, but today, we experience nothing of the sort?"

"I remember," said the Rebbe, "when the Rumanians conquered Siget, they had a victory parade to display their power — regiment upon regiment of troops and long columns of weapons, tanks and artillery. Twenty years have passed since then and no further parade has been staged. Why?

"At the time of the conquest, the government had to show its power to the people in order to impress its might upon them. But once they witnessed that power and strength, why should they march by, through the city streets, in their military masses?" (Sha'ar HaOsios, p. 118).

וְאֶת הַמַּטֶּה הַזֶּה תִּקַּח בְּיָדֶךָ / Take this staff in your hand

R' Nachman of Breslav　　When R' Nachman of Breslav gave his discourse Trust in Hashem (Likutei Maharan 79), which explains that the staff of Moshe represents the freedom of choice which allows a man to turn to one side of an issue or the other, he walked about in his house, here and there, as was his custom, holding his staff in hand and said, "And the staff of Elokim in my hand" (Shemos 17:9). He emphasized my hand, as if to say that he was the master of his choice and had the staff in his hand, and could turn it in whatever direction he desired.

Fortunate is he who has gained such a state! (Chayei Maharan 36).

אֲשֶׁר תַּעֲשֶׂה בּוֹ אֶת הָאֹתֹת
That you may perform the miraculous signs with it

R' Shmuel Abba of Zichlin　　The verse (Shemos 4:17) alludes to the role of the signs and wonders performed by the

With signs — refers to the miracles performed with the staff as it says: Take this staff in your hand, that you may perform the miraculous signs with it.[1]

With wonders — alludes to the blood, as it says: I will show wonders in the heavens and on the earth

As each of the words דָּם, blood; אֵשׁ, fire; and עָשָׁן, smoke, is said, a bit of wine is removed from the cup, with the finger or by pouring.

Blood, fire, and columns of smoke.[2]

Another explanation of the preceding verse: [Each phrase represents two plagues,] hence: mighty hand — two; outstretched arm — two; great awe — two; signs — two; wonders — two. These are the ten plagues which the Holy One, Blessed is He, brought upon the Egyptians in Egypt, namely:

---

1. *Shemos* 4:17. 2. *Yoel* 3:3.

---

tzaddik in order to arouse others to an awareness of Hashem and have them return to Him in *teshuvah*.

Think! Who needs a staff? The healthy do not need it. And it does not help a sick man confined to bed with suffering. But it does serve as an aid to the man who is not completely well and yet, not bound to a bed.

So too, signs and wonders will not bring the man who is mortally ill in spirit, who does not believe in God at all and denies His existence, to have faith. Nor does the man who is strong and healthy in his faith have need of the signs. It is the man of shaky faith who is helped by the wonders. They are the strong staff on which he can support his faith.

The verse alludes to this: *Take this staff in your hand* — take the nature of the staff into consideration when you are to *perform the miraculous signs with it* (*Lahav Esh* 30).

אֵלּוּ עֶשֶׂר מַכּוֹת
These are the ten plagues

R' Pesach Slonimski of Meitchet

When R' Pesach Slonimski of Meitchet came before R' Avraham, the Zaide of Slonim for the first time, he told him of the bitterness he felt, because he was troubled in matters of faith. He had presented his problems to several *tzaddikim* and they had given him satisfying answers. But as soon as he arrived home, the questions had resurfaced. He was unable to fix the ideas in his heart.

"Pharaoh of Egypt asked questions," said the Rebbe, " 'Who is Hashem

As each of the plagues is mentioned, a bit of wine is removed from the cup.
The same is done by each word of Rabbi Yehudah's mnemonic.

דָּם. צְפַרְדֵּעַ. כִּנִּים. עָרוֹב. דֶּבֶר. שְׁחִין. בָּרָד. אַרְבֶּה. חֹשֶׁךְ. מַכַּת בְּכוֹרוֹת.

רַבִּי יְהוּדָה הָיָה נוֹתֵן בָּהֶם סִמָּנִים:

דְּצַ״ךְ ● עֲדַ״שׁ ● בְּאַחַ״ב.

The cups are refilled. The wine that was removed is not used.

רַבִּי יוֹסֵי הַגְּלִילִי אוֹמֵר: מִנַּיִן אַתָּה אוֹמֵר שֶׁלָּקוּ הַמִּצְרִים בְּמִצְרַיִם עֶשֶׂר מַכּוֹת וְעַל הַיָּם לָקוּ חֲמִשִּׁים מַכּוֹת? בְּמִצְרַיִם מָה הוּא אוֹמֵר, וַיֹּאמְרוּ הַחַרְטֻמִּם אֶל פַּרְעֹה, אֶצְבַּע אֱלֹהִים הוּא.[1] וְעַל הַיָּם מָה הוּא אוֹמֵר, וַיַּרְא יִשְׂרָאֵל אֶת הַיָּד הַגְּדֹלָה אֲשֶׁר עָשָׂה יהוה בְּמִצְרַיִם, וַיִּירְאוּ הָעָם אֶת יהוה, וַיַּאֲמִינוּ בַּיהוה

---

that I must heed his voice?' Moshe's answers were the plagues — a plague
after the first question; another plague after the second question."

And so it happened to R' Pesach. His body was afflicted with sores equal
in number to his questions. Thereafter he was not troubled by questions and
grew close in body and soul to his Rebbe (*Ma'asei Avos* 156).

דְּצַ״ךְ עֲדַ״שׁ בְּאַחַ״ב / D'Tzach Adash B'Achav

Chozeh of Lublin *Riaz* heard the following from his master, the *Rabbi of Barniv*, who heard it from his grandfather, *R' Eliezer of Tzikov*, who had witnessed the incident when he accompanied his father, *R' Naftali of Ropshitz*, to spend *Pesach* with the *Chozeh of Lublin*:

When the Chozeh reached the abbreviations *D'tzach etc.*, he said, "*Dreit sich a Deitch b'Achav* (a German wanders about *Achav*)." The company present was astonished and the Rebbe of Ropshitz suggested, "The Rebbe should look into the *Haggadah* and go over the passage." The Chozeh looked into the *Haggadah* and said in a loud voice, "*Dreit sich a Deitch b'Achav*," again, to the amazement of all present.

The first day of *Pesach* passed, and that evening (מוֹצָאֵי יוֹם טוֹב), *R' Shimon Oderberger of Germany*, known as R' Shimon Deitch (the German), arrived. When he descended the wagon and went to greet the Rebbe, the Chozeh

1. Blood 2. Frogs 3. Vermin 4. Wild Beasts
5. Pestilence 6. Boils 7. Hail 8. Locusts 9. Darkness
10. Plague of the Firstborn.

Rabbi Yehudah abbreviated them
by their Hebrew initials:
D'TZACH, ADASH, B'ACHAV

Rabbi Yose the Galilean said: How does one derive that the Egyptians were struck with ten plagues in Egypt, but with fifty plagues at the Sea? — Concerning the plagues in Egypt the Torah states: The magicians said to Pharaoh, 'It is the finger of God.'[1] However, of those at the Sea, the Torah relates: Israel saw the great 'hand' which Hᴀsʜᴇᴍ laid upon the Egyptians, the people feared Hᴀsʜᴇᴍ and they believed in Hᴀsʜᴇᴍ and in His

---

1. *Shemos* 8:15.

---

said, "I felt, and shared in, your suffering while saying the *Haggadah*."

When R' Shimon left the Chozeh, they asked him, "What happened to you on the night of the Seder, and how did you get here so quickly from home?"

R' Shimon told them that he had been traveling to Lublin for *Pesach* and when he reached the hamlet of Achav, not far from Lublin, a wagon wheel broke. By the time it was repaired, it was too late to travel to Lublin and he was forced to remain in the village for *yom tov*. During the Seder, he thought of the Chozeh conducting the Seder with his pious company and how here he was in the village, unable to be among them. Overcome by his misery, he stopped his recitation of the *Haggadah*, went out, and wept greatly.

That was when the Rebbe could not contain himself and had said in pain, "*Dreit sich a Deitch b'Achav*" (*Otzar HaSipurim* V:5).

וַיַּרְא יִשְׂרָאֵל . . . וַיַּאֲמִינוּ / *Israel saw . . . and they believed*

Chidushei HaRim   *Israel saw the great 'hand' which Hashem laid upon the Egyptians.* But even after they had seen, the Torah tells us: *and they believed in Hashem.* They had yet to reach the level of faith. This shows us that believing is greater than seeing (*Siach Sarfei Kodesh* I 406).

וּבְמֹשֶׁה עַבְדּוֹ.[1] כַּמָּה לָקוּ בְאֶצְבַּע? עֶשֶׂר מַכּוֹת. אֱמוֹר מֵעַתָּה, בְּמִצְרַיִם לָקוּ עֶשֶׂר מַכּוֹת, וְעַל הַיָּם לָקוּ חֲמִשִּׁים מַכּוֹת.

R' Mordechai of Lechovitz   One of the chasidim of *R' Mordechai of Lechovitz* was the business partner of a *misnaged* (opponent of chasidus). The chasid convinced his partner to accompany him to the Rebbe.

When they arrived, the Rebbe was in the middle of a meal. The *misnaged* looked on and was very impressed. When asked why he was so impressed, he said, "You can actually see how he eats in holiness — it is like the act of devotion of the *kohen gadol* (the High Priest) in the *Beis HaMikdash!*"

The chasid was taken aback by the answer. He entered the Rebbe's chamber and asked, "How is it that my friend was fortunate to see on his first visit that which I have as yet not seen?"

"Nothing to wonder at," said the Rebbe. "He is a *misnaged* and must be shown; you are a chasid and must believe!" (*Sipurei Chasidim, Mishpatim*)

וַיַּאֲמִינוּ / *They believed*

R' Tzvi Elimelech of Dinov   I have been told by those who heard him that *R' Meshulam Zusha* said that he did not expect a reward in the world-to-come for the period in which he served Hashem after he already knew the truth of His greatness; he hoped for a reward for serving Hashem in faith, in the tradition which he received from his fathers (*Agra D'Pirka* 3).

R' Yitzchak Isaac of Komarna   The *Ba'al Shem* would tell the story that, when he was young, his teacher, the Prophet *Achiah HaShiloni*, taught him the Holy Names — their meaning, their use and how to teach them. Since he was as yet little, he wished to see if he could truly use them. He placed a cloth on the Dniester River and crossed the river on it by the power of a Holy Name. He had done *teshuvah* for this act all his days and fasted to correct the fault. He finally succeeded in correcting it in the following way. He was once forced to cross the Dniester to save his life from the Turkish army. He placed his prayer sash (*gartel*) on the river and crossed without using any Holy Name — but through great faith in God. He was thus favored because he had studied Torah for its own sake, and because his soul clung to the Creator at all times (*Notzer Chesed* ch. 86).

servant Moshe.[1] How many plagues did they receive with the finger? Ten! Then conclude that if they suffered ten plagues in Egypt [where they were struck with a finger], they must have been made to suffer fifty plagues at the sea [where they were struck with a whole hand].

---

1. *Shemos* 14:31.

R' Yitzchak of Neschiz

An epileptic once begged of *R' Yitzchak of Neschiz* that he be cured. The Rebbe refused to help him. The man placed all his money before him and said, "Take what you will for a *pidyon*."

"Believe me," said the Rebbe, "you can be cured, but you lack faith; that's what's missing. You heard that there is a rebbe in Neschiz who works wondrous cures, and you came. Yet, in all truth, it is Hashem alone Who brings redemption, not I. When you believe in Him, you shall be cured.

"I will tell you a story; listen and pay attention. A villager was once robbed. He came to the *Maggid of Koszhnitz* to ask for a blessing that he be delivered from his trouble.

" 'Believe me,' said the Maggid, 'I did not rob you. The members of my family can bear witness that I was home all that day.'

"The man and his wife begged the Maggid to bless them that the stolen goods be returned, and the husband gave a gold coin as a *pidyon*.

" 'I want more,' said the Maggid. The man put down three gold coins and the Maggid asked for more and more and finally he said, 'I want sixty gold coins.' They gave forty, then agreed to fifty, but the Maggid stood by his demand. 'Nothing less than sixty,' he said.

"At that, his wife scooped up the pile of coins from the table and said to her husband, 'Let's go. Hashem can bring us help, without our giving away all this!'

"When he heard this the Maggid said, 'You have already been helped. Know that it was difficult to fulfill your request, because you trusted in me and forgot Hashem. Now, that you have remembered Him, that in itself saves you. Leave only the single gold coin which you first gave me' " (*Zikaron Tov*, Inyanei Tzedakah 25).

וּבְמֹשֶׁה עַבְדּוֹ / And in His servant Moshe

Ba'al HaTanya

The *Ba'al HaTanya* once saw his son wearing expensive clothing. "How is it that a poor fellow like yourself can allow himself to have such an expensive outfit made up?" he asked.

"I am not poor," replied his son. "My dowry is safely deposited with a

wealthy man and I am your son and eat at your table."

"My son, what a man does not have in his house cannot be taken into consideration. And though you eat at my table, one never knows what tomorrow will bring."

Not very long afterwards, the rich man, with whom the dowry was deposited, lost everything in his possession, including the young man's money. War broke out with France and the Rebbe and his household were forced to leave their place of residence. The Rebbe's son saw that all had been foreseen by his father and asked, "Why didn't you expressly tell me to ask for the return of the dowry?"

"Many years ago," said the Rebbe, "in my wanderings I came upon a tavern, where drunken gentiles were rolling about. I asked the tavern keeper, who was a Jew, for a room in which I might pray the evening prayer (*ma'ariv*).

"After I had prayed, the taverner said to me, 'Rebbe, I would like your advice.' I replied, 'Believe me! I am not a rebbe and I am lacking in advice!' To which he answered, 'As far as I am concerned you are a *tzaddik* like all the *tzaddikim* and I have confidence in your advice.'

"I thought to myself, 'True, I am not a rebbe, but perhaps I will be able to give him good advice.' I asked him what it was that troubled him.

"He told me that the tavern had been in the family for five generations. However, many of the villagers had left for other parts and his earnings had dwindled. He had, therefore, rented a tavern in a neighboring village. The establishment there was flourishing. Yet he had qualms about leaving his ancestral heritage, and he returned to it each night to sleep. On the other hand, he was concerned lest his newly founded establishment, uninhabited by night, might be liable to theft. Should he leave this tavern completely and move to the other, or continue to maintain both?

"I listened and answered that a man's place is where he finds his livelihood. Since it was in the other village, he ought to move there. He thanked me, and while I was as yet eating my evening meal, he packed all his belongings and loaded them onto a wagon. He wished to travel in the dead of night. But I was very weary, and begged of him that he wait until daylight. He agreed to stay the night and prepared a bed for me.

"When I rose in the morning, he brought me a hot drink and urged me to travel with them to the new tavern and bless him with prosperity.

"We started out. His wife glanced back and saw a column of smoke rising in the village. We turned about and retraced our steps and found the tavern being consumed by a raging fire.

"Heaven had decreed that all the belongings of the tavern keeper be destroyed. But, because of his hospitality and faith in *tzaddikim*, he had been given a reprieve. For the verse וְצַדִּיק בֶּאֱמוּנָתוֹ יִחְיֶה, 'the righteous man, in his faith shall live' (*Chavakuk* 2:4), may be interpreted, 'Through his faith in the *tzaddik* a man will live.'

"And you, my son, if you had put your faith in *tzaddikim*, like that tavern keeper, you would have run to ask for your dowry as soon as I dropped my hint."

The *Yismach Yisrael* of Alexander retold the story to his chasidim on the day before *Rosh Hashanah* and added the following:

"That is what is meant by the passage in the prayers on the Days of Awe, 'עֵצָתוֹ אֱמוּנָה, His advice is faith.' The advice of Hashem by which He saves a man is through faith in Hashem and His servant Moshe" (Introduction to *Tiferes Yisrael*).

Tiferes Shmuel of Alexander

I remember that when I was a youngster my sainted father was once teaching Torah to the townsmen of Turchin. He reached the verse: "And Yehoshua bin Nun was full of the spirit of wisdom because Moshe had placed his hands upon him and the Children of Israel hearkened to him" (*Devarim* 34:9). The wisdom of Yehoshua, he explained, flowed from two sources. There was a heavenly factor from above — "because Moshe had placed his hands upon him." And there was a human factor, from below — the belief in the wise (*emunas chachamim*) which the Children of Israel had with regard to him (*Tiferes Shlomo* 203).

R' Yisrael of Ruzhin

R' Yisrael of Ruzhin asked the chasid Reb Yaakovke of Yarishov, "Did you know *R' Baruch of Mezhibuz*?"

"I did not really *know* him, but I *believed* in his holiness," answered Reb Yaakovke, wisely.

The Rebbe was pleased by his answer and said, "That is, indeed, as it should be!

"When Israel went out of Egypt, they reached the heights of human understanding of Hashem. The maidservant who witnessed the crossing of the Red Sea saw that which the prophet Yechezkel did not see in his vision. It was then that the Evil Desire (יֵצֶר הָרָע) came upon them and tried to sway them and lead them into error. 'You have already seen everything,' he said. 'You have grasped it all. You have reached the limit of understanding.' But they were not led astray. They knew that much, as yet, lay hidden and that they were in need of simple faith. That is why the Torah tells us that, just at that point in time, 'They believed in Hashem.'

"And the verse continues: 'and in His servant Moshe.' For just as a man must realize that, as far as his belief in Hashem is concerned, no matter how much he grasps the greatness and lofty transcendence of the Creator, he has not reached an infinitesimal part of understanding, so he must know that he cannot grasp the exalted loftiness of the *tzaddik*. The more we understand the heights of his holiness, the more we must believe that he immeasurably surpasses our grasp" (*Sipurei Tzaddikim* 81).

רַבִּי אֱלִיעֶזֶר אוֹמֵר. מִנַּיִן שֶׁכָּל מַכָּה וּמַכָּה שֶׁהֵבִיא הַקָּדוֹשׁ בָּרוּךְ הוּא עַל הַמִּצְרִים בְּמִצְרַיִם הָיְתָה שֶׁל אַרְבַּע מַכּוֹת? שֶׁנֶּאֱמַר, יְשַׁלַּח בָּם חֲרוֹן אַפּוֹ – עֶבְרָה, וָזַעַם, וְצָרָה, מִשְׁלַחַת מַלְאֲכֵי רָעִים.[1] עֶבְרָה, אַחַת. וָזַעַם, שְׁתַּיִם. וְצָרָה, שָׁלֹשׁ. מִשְׁלַחַת מַלְאֲכֵי רָעִים, אַרְבַּע. אֱמוֹר מֵעַתָּה, בְּמִצְרַיִם לָקוּ אַרְבָּעִים מַכּוֹת, וְעַל הַיָּם לָקוּ מָאתַיִם מַכּוֹת.

רַבִּי עֲקִיבָא אוֹמֵר. מִנַּיִן שֶׁכָּל מַכָּה וּמַכָּה שֶׁהֵבִיא הַקָּדוֹשׁ בָּרוּךְ הוּא עַל הַמִּצְרִים בְּמִצְרַיִם הָיְתָה שֶׁל חָמֵשׁ מַכּוֹת? שֶׁנֶּאֱמַר, יְשַׁלַּח בָּם חֲרוֹן אַפּוֹ, עֶבְרָה, וָזַעַם, וְצָרָה, מִשְׁלַחַת מַלְאֲכֵי רָעִים.[1] חֲרוֹן אַפּוֹ, אַחַת. עֶבְרָה, שְׁתַּיִם. וָזַעַם, שָׁלֹשׁ. וְצָרָה, אַרְבַּע. מִשְׁלַחַת מַלְאֲכֵי רָעִים, חָמֵשׁ. אֱמוֹר מֵעַתָּה, בְּמִצְרַיִם לָקוּ חֲמִשִּׁים מַכּוֹת, וְעַל הַיָּם לָקוּ חֲמִשִּׁים וּמָאתַיִם מַכּוֹת.

כַּמָּה מַעֲלוֹת טוֹבוֹת לַמָּקוֹם עָלֵינוּ.

אִלּוּ הוֹצִיאָנוּ מִמִּצְרַיִם,

דַּיֵּנוּ. וְלֹא עָשָׂה בָהֶם שְׁפָטִים,

אִלּוּ עָשָׂה בָהֶם שְׁפָטִים,

דַּיֵּנוּ. וְלֹא עָשָׂה בֵאלֹהֵיהֶם,

אִלּוּ עָשָׂה בֵאלֹהֵיהֶם,

דַּיֵּנוּ. וְלֹא הָרַג אֶת בְּכוֹרֵיהֶם,

אִלּוּ הָרַג אֶת בְּכוֹרֵיהֶם,

דַּיֵּנוּ. וְלֹא נָתַן לָנוּ אֶת מָמוֹנָם,

Rabbi Eliezer said: How does one derive that every plague that the Holy One, Blessed is He, inflicted upon the Egyptians in Egypt was equal to four plagues? — for it is written: He sent upon them his fierce anger: wrath, fury, and trouble, a band of emissaries of evil.[1] [Since each plague in Egypt consisted of] 1) wrath, 2) fury, 3) trouble and 4) a band of emissaries of evil, therefore conclude that in Egypt they were struck by forty plagues and by the sea two hundred!

Rabbi Akiva said: How does one derive that each plague that the Holy One, Blessed is He, inflicted upon the Egyptians in Egypt was equal to five plagues? — For it is written: He sent upon them His fierce anger, wrath, fury, trouble, and a band of emissaries of evil.[1] [Since each plague in Egypt consisted of] 1) fierce anger, 2) wrath, 3) fury, 4) trouble and 5) a band of emissaries of evil, therefore conclude that in Egypt they were struck by fifty plagues and by the sea two hundred and fifty!

The Omnipresent has bestowed
so many favors upon us!

Had He brought us out of Egypt, but not executed judgments against the Egyptians,
it would have sufficed us.

Had He executed judgments against them, but not upon their gods,   it would have sufficed us.

Had He executed judgments against their gods, but not slain their firstborn,
it would have sufficed us.

Had He slain their firstborn, but not given us their wealth,   it would have sufficed us.

---

1. *Tehillim* 78:49.

אִלּוּ נָתַן לָנוּ אֶת מָמוֹנָם,

וְלֹא קָרַע לָנוּ אֶת הַיָּם, דַּיֵּנוּ.

אִלּוּ קָרַע לָנוּ אֶת הַיָּם,

וְלֹא הֶעֱבִירָנוּ בְּתוֹכוֹ בֶּחָרָבָה, דַּיֵּנוּ.

אִלּוּ הֶעֱבִירָנוּ בְּתוֹכוֹ בֶּחָרָבָה,

וְלֹא שִׁקַּע צָרֵינוּ בְּתוֹכוֹ, דַּיֵּנוּ.

אִלּוּ שִׁקַּע צָרֵינוּ בְּתוֹכוֹ,

וְלֹא סִפֵּק צָרְכֵּנוּ בַּמִּדְבָּר

אַרְבָּעִים שָׁנָה, דַּיֵּנוּ.

נָתַן לָנוּ אֶת מָמוֹנָם
(Had He) given us their wealth

Avnei Nezer Once, on *Shabbos Shirah,* while the chasidim were drinking and toasting each other at the table (*tish*) of the *Avnei Nezer*, one of those present complained to the Rebbe of the difficulty he had in earning a living and commented that he would like to have *"the loot of the sea."

"Certainly, if you will be on the exalted plane of Israel as they stood on the shore of the Red Sea, after crossing through the parted waters, then you will also have the loot of the sea," replied the Rebbe (*Abir HaRoim* II 338).

סִפֵּק צָרְכֵּנוּ בַּמִּדְבָּר
(Had He) provided for our needs in the desert

R' Meir Shalom of Kalishin R' Meir Shalom of Kalishin was asked what's involved when chasidim crown a rebbe to be their leader.

"We find in holy *sefarim*," he said, "that everything is to be classified as 'world' (עוֹלָם), 'year' (שָׁנָה) or 'soul' (נֶפֶשׁ). In other words, everything fits into a category of place (world), time (year), or personality (soul).

"The Children of Israel in the desert were in a dry and desolate place and yet drew the *Shechinah* (Divine Presence) to encamp there. That is with respect to *world* or place. As far as *year* or time is concerned, we find that the rabbinical court (בֵּית דִּין) is appointed to sanctify the new moon. Heaven follows the court's decision and grants its sanctity.

[* *The loot of the sea* — the silver, gold, and other valuables of the Egyptian army drowned in the Red Sea, which the sea cast upon its shores to be gathered by Israel.]

Had He given us their wealth, but not split the Sea for us,   it would have sufficed us.

Had He split the Sea for us, but not led us through it on dry land,   it would have sufficed us.

Had He led us through on dry land, but not drowned our oppressors in it,

       it would have sufficed us.

Had He drowned our oppressors in it, but not provided for our needs in the desert for forty years,

       it would have sufficed us.

"And when Israel chooses a leader — that falls within the category of *soul* or personality. Then, too, Hashem allows his Divine Presence to rest upon that man" (*Gan Hadasim* 18).

R' Yitzchak Isaac of Komarna   The *Ba'al Shem Tov* and a disciple once, during a journey, found themselves in a desolate, dry area. Water was not to be found for many miles about. The disciple felt parched and said to his master, "I am very thirsty." The Ba'al Shem said not a word. When the disciple saw how dangerously thirsty he was, he said, "Master, I am thirsty to the point of collapse."

"Do you believe," said the Ba'al Shem, "that when the Holy One created the universe, He envisioned your dire straits and prepared water for you to drink?"

The disciple did not reply immediately, but pondered the matter. He, then, answered, "I truly believe that."

"Wait a while," said the Ba'al Shem.

They went on and came upon a non-Jew carrying two large pitchers of water on his shoulders. They gave him a few small coins and he gave them to drink.

"Why are you carrying water in this barren dessert?" asked the Ba'al Shem.

"My noble owner has gone mad," said the man, "and sent me to draw water from a distant well. I must carry the water three miles and have no idea why."

"Just contemplate Divine Providence," said the Ba'al Shem to his disciple. "Hashem, for your sake, created a nobleman who would go mad, so that you might have water. And Hashem ordained this in His providence at the moment the world was created" (*Nesiv Mitzvosecha; Nesiv HaYichud* 3:1).

אִלּוּ סִפֵּק צָרְכֵּנוּ בַּמִּדְבָּר
אַרְבָּעִים שָׁנָה,
וְלֹא הֶאֱכִילָנוּ אֶת הַמָּן, **דַּיֵּנוּ.**
אִלּוּ הֶאֱכִילָנוּ אֶת הַמָּן,
וְלֹא נָתַן לָנוּ אֶת הַשַּׁבָּת, **דַּיֵּנוּ.**
אִלּוּ נָתַן לָנוּ אֶת הַשַּׁבָּת,
וְלֹא קֵרְבָנוּ לִפְנֵי הַר סִינַי, **דַּיֵּנוּ.**

הַמָּן / The Manna

Chozeh of Lublin

The *Chozeh of Lublin* once taught, ''The Torah tells us that the *Manna* (מָן) was given its name 'because they did not know what it was' (מַה הוּא — *Shemos* 16:15). And that was because it was spiritual food, food that the angels, who serve Hashem, eat. Those who ate it rose from day to day, higher and higher, so much so that a man could not recognize his friend from one day to the next and would ask, 'Who is he (מִי הוּא)?'

''Indeed, even today, there is a young man here who wanders among the trees and no one really knows him. Tomorrow all will ask, 'Who is he?'

R' David of Lelov, who was present, went out to see who it was that was wandering among the trees and found *R' Simchah Bunim of Pshischa* (*Siach Sarfei Kodesh* I 209).

R' Chanoch Henoch of Alexander

R' Chanoch Henoch of Alexander was asked why chasidim *snatch at and partake of the food of the dishes the rebbe tastes.

''Every man draws down food to himself in accordance with his spiritual essence (*shoresh*, lit. 'root'),'' said the Rebbe. ''When Israel went up out of Egypt they reached a lofty, heavenly state and were found worthy of eating *Manna*, 'the bread of heaven.' The *tzaddik* is heavenly in nature and his food, too, is of the same sort as *Manna*'' (*Siach Sarfei Kodesh* IV 83).

[*snatch at and partake of the food etc. This is the practice of eating *she'irayim*, the 'leftovers', so to speak, of the rebbe. The comment of the Rebbe of Alexander is not a homiletic bon mot, pure and simple. It has halachic overtones. The Talmud says: Whosoever enjoys a meal in which a wise man (תַּלְמִיד חָכָם) participates is like one who enjoys the brightness of the *Shechinah* (*Berachos* 64a; see, too, the Rambam's positive instruction to endeavor to eat with *talmidei chachamim* — *Hilchos De'os* 6:2).]

Had He provided for our needs in the desert for forty years, but not fed us the Manna,
it would have sufficed us.

Had He fed us the Manna, but not given us the Shabbos,
it would have sufficed us.

Had He given us the Shabbos, but not brought us before Mount Sinai,
it would have sufficed us.

Chidushei HaRim "Behold I will rain down for you bread from Heaven ... that I might test them whether they will walk in My Torah, or not" (*Shemos* 16:4).

What test is involved with the eating of *Manna*?

Chazal tell us: "This is the way of Torah — you shall eat bread with salt, and drink water in small measure" (*Avos* 6:4). They have also said: "Before a man prays that the words of the Torah will enter his innards, he should first pray that delicacies will not enter his innards." For the pursuit of fine foods and pleasures runs counter to the life of Torah.

The *Manna* had a special characteristic; in eating it, one could taste any food he desired. This presented a great test. For those who wished to rise in the realm of Torah must not desire to taste anything, but only to sustain life (*Siach Sarfei Kodesh* IV 62).

נָתַן לָנוּ אֶת הַשַּׁבָּת / *(Had He) given us the Shabbos*

Akeidas Yitzchak of Alexander The *mashgiach* (spiritual supervisor) of the *yeshiva* of Slobodka, *R' Avraham Grodzinski*, visited the *Akeidas Yitzchak* of Alexander. In the course of their conversation the Rebbe asked, "The *gemara* says: The Holy One said to Moshe, 'I have a fine gift in My treasure house called *Shabbos*. I would like to give it to Israel. Go and inform them!' What is there about *Shabbos* which make it a mystery that needs revelation?

"Once a poor man came to my sainted grandfather. My grandfather had nothing else to give him and so took the jewelry of the *rebbetzin* and gave that. When his wife heard of this, she ran after the man. After she had caught up to him, she said, 'The jewels are very valuable. Be aware of that, and don't sell them cheaply!'

"The Holy One sent Moshe to tell Israel, 'Be aware that *Shabbos* is a valuable gift; don't change it into nothing more than a steaming bowl of *cholent* and a slice of spicy *kugel'* " (*Vaya'al Moshe*).

Chidushei HaRim The *Chidushei HaRim of Gur* reproached his chasidim regarding the sanctity of the Sabbath:

אִלּוּ קֵרְבָנוּ לִפְנֵי הַר סִינַי,
וְלֹא נָתַן לָנוּ אֶת הַתּוֹרָה,
דַּיֵּנוּ.

The *Shabbos* is like a great rebbe, a great teacher. Just as Rabban Gamliel proclaimed that whoever had an inner self unlike his outer show, who thought one way and acted differently, was to be denied entry into the *beis midrash* to hear the Torah discourse, so too, he whose inner and outer self do not correspond to each other is not allowed to enter *Shabbos*.

I am also denied entry, but the difference between me and you is that I stand at the door and am aware that I am barred from coming in. You, however, stand from afar and do not even knock (*Or*, p. 46).

R' Chaim of Sanz　　It was forbidden by law to cut down timber in the royal forest which grew about the city of Vienna. But a wealthy lumber dealer and some senior officials had made an illegal pact allowing him to fell trees there. As a result, he earned huge profits. But he gained the envy of his competitors who informed upon him to the authorities. His house was surrounded in the dark of night, a unit of police arrested him, and he was spirited off. His wife searched for him for four months, but learned nothing of his whereabouts.

In her misery, she traveled to *R' Chaim of Sanz*. The Rebbe said that if her husband would promise to observe *Shabbos* properly, he would be freed. The woman said she had no way of securing her husband's promise, for she had no idea where he was being held. But the Rebbe told her to go home in peace and, on the way home, she would find out where he was.

The woman boarded the train and bitterly bemoaned her fate. Opposite her sat a senior officer who asked her why she wept. After she told him her tale, he revealed that he was the commandant of the prison in which her husband was to be found. He arranged to have her meet with her husband and she told him of the Rebbe's condition. The man hesitated, for the lumberyards of all his rivals were open on *Shabbos*. Finally, he came to the conclusion that it was better to close his establishment once a week on *Shabbos* rather than languish in prison all seven days of the week.

His wife went and informed the Rebbe of her husband's decision and the Rebbe told her that she might return home untroubled. Her husband, he said, was already free and awaiting her (*Rabbeinu HaKadosh MiSanz* 295).

לִפְנֵי הַר סִינַי / *Before Mount Sinai*

R' Shlomo of Radomsk　　*R' Shlomo of Radomsk* did not wish to be a rebbe. Once, just before *Shavuos*, when he saw large crowds of chasidim arriving, he rose and traveled to *R' Yechezkel of Kuzhmir* to spend the festival in his presence.

Had He brought us before Mount Sinai, but not given us the Torah, it would have sufficed us.

The *Rebbe of Kuzhmir* was surprised to see him and reproached him saying, "You cannot abandon an assembly of Hashem and leave them like a flock of sheep without a shepherd. The Torah tells us that Moshe Rabbenu 'descended from the mountain to the people.' This teaches us, says *Rashi*, that he did not occupy himself, after coming down from Sinai, with his private interests *(Shemos 19:14)*.

"Now what private interests would Moshe have had in the desert? The answer is that each man of Israel was preparing himself to receive the Torah. In all likelihood, Moshe too would have wished to sanctify and purify himself like an angel. But he was a faithful shepherd and did not turn to his private interests of the spirit; he descended from the mountain to the people. You, however, left the people to attend to your own needs and to sanctify yourself."

The Rebbe of Radomsk heard the reproach and replied, then and there, "True! But Moshe even when he descended to the people was, as yet, at the foot of Mount Sinai. I also came here, to Mount Sinai" *(Nifleos HaTiferes Shlomo* 118).

סִינַי / *Mount Sinai*

R' Tzvi Hirsch Gidziler

R' Tzvi Hirsch Gidziler was exceptionally humble, truly insignificant in his own eyes. Once *R' Moshe of Lelov* visited him and found it difficult to remain indoors because of the smell of fresh hides which had been placed on the stove to dry.

"Why are these hides here?" he asked. "After all, you spend your time in learning and devotion to Hashem."

"True!" said R' Hirsch. "But my children earn their livelihood by the sale of hides and they find it more convenient to dry them here, in my house."

"*Chazal* tell us, indeed," said the Rebbe of Lelov, "that the Holy One gave the Torah on Mount Sinai, a *lowly* hill, so that we might learn from the act, the importance of modesty. But why then did He not give the Torah in a valley? The Torah shows us, thereby, that there is a limit to humility. A man must be something of a hill or mountain and not allow himself to be trampled upon by others" *(Likutei Divrei David* 49).

קֵרְבָנוּ לִפְנֵי הַר סִינַי . . . נָתַן לָנוּ אֶת הַתּוֹרָה / (Had He) brought us before Mount Sinai . . . (Had He) given us the Torah

R' Moshe Leib of Sasov

I was once in Lublin for *Succos*. The *Chozeh of Lublin* went to the *succah* to fulfill the *mitzvah* of *esrog* and *lulav*. All the chasidim followed, and I went along with them. For the space of a whole hour, he burned and trembled with visible enthusiasm. The chasidim followed suit in their excitement, moving to and fro, quaking

אִלּוּ נָתַן לָנוּ אֶת הַתּוֹרָה,
וְלֹא הִכְנִיסָנוּ לְאֶרֶץ יִשְׂרָאֵל, דַּיֵּנוּ.
אִלּוּ הִכְנִיסָנוּ לְאֶרֶץ יִשְׂרָאֵל,
וְלֹא בָנָה לָנוּ אֶת בֵּית הַבְּחִירָה, דַּיֵּנוּ.

in great fear. I, for my part, sat quietly on a bench, waiting for the Rebbe to end his preliminary preparations. I did not want to give preference to the secondary over the more important but wished to concentrate on the Rebbe as he pronounced the blessing. It is impossible to describe his exaltation then.

My attitude is alluded to in the Torah. "And the entire people saw the sounds and torches and the blast of the *shofar* and the smoking mountain" (*Shemos* 20:15). They saw the preliminaries to the giving of the Torah and were very excited by them: "And the people saw and moved" (ibid.). Moshe on the other hand, 'approached the fog where *Elokim* was' (ibid. 20:18); he was not overcome by the outward phenomena at Sinai, but reached towards the inner core of the Ten Commandments to receive the Torah itself (*Likutei Maharil, Yisro* s.v. וכל).

נָתַן לָנוּ אֶת הַתּוֹרָה / (Had He) given us the Torah

Chidushei HaRim The Holy One gave us the Torah. By the Law (*halachah*) a giver should give in good measure, and whoever gives his fellow a field surrounded by other fields also grants him a path of entry to the field. If Hashem gave us the Torah, he most certainly granted each of us the path, the power and ability to reach the Torah (*Siach Sarfei Kodesh* I 407).

Divrei Chaim of Sanz A descendant of *tzaddikim* once chanced to be in the presence of the *Divrei Chaim of Sanz* on *Shavuos*. This grandchild had nothing about him in the way of Torah learning nor the good manners (דֶּרֶךְ אֶרֶץ) which should surpass learning. He was full of pride and the demand for honor because of his family tree.

"Do you know, " the Rebbe asked him, "why the days before *Shavuos* are called illustrious days (הַיָּמִים הַמְיוּחָסִים)?"

The grandchild of the illustrious did not know.

"Before the Torah was given," said the Rebbe, "the pedigreed, the wellborn, were important. After *Shavuos*, after the Torah had been given, however, the importance passed over to those who are learned in Torah and are graced with good manners (דֶּרֶךְ אֶרֶץ). Being wellborn is no longer sufficient" (*Kol Hakasuv LeChaim*, p. 126).

Had He given us the Torah, but not brought us
into the Land of Israel,   it would have sufficed us.

Had He brought us into the Land of Israel, but not
built the Temple for us,   it would have sufficed us.

לְאֶרֶץ יִשְׂרָאֵל / Into the Land of Israel

R' Binyamin David of Ostrowa

R' Binyamin David of Ostrowa was in charge of the monies collected for *Eretz Yisrael*. When he was once in the presence of *R' Yechezkel of Kuzhmir*, the Rebbe asked him, "Why is the Holy Land called *Eretz Yisrael*, the Land of Israel? After all, it was promised to all our forefathers, to Avraham and Yitzchak, as well as to Yisrael."

"Had it been named after Avraham and Yitzchak," said R' Binyamin David, "Yishmael and Esav would also have a share in it. That is why it has received the name of our forefather Yaakov only."

"No!" said the Rebbe. "It is named *Yisrael* because only one who acts like a *Yisraeli*, a Jew, and observes the *mitzvos* and upholds the Torah has a share in the Land" (*Siach Sarfei Kodesh* V, p. 8).

R' Yoel of Satmar

R' Yosef Tzvi Dushinsky, the Rav of *Yerushalayim,* told *R' Yoel of Satmar* that he had been questioned by a British board of inquiry about the immigration of non-observant Jews. He had said that one could not tell in advance who was non-observant. The answer had aroused the ire of the secular Zionists and the Mizrachi. For it implied that those who declared that they were non-observant should not be permitted to immigrate.

The Rebbe of Satmar smiled and said, "Perhaps they are of the same opinion as Rav Hai Gaon."

The conversation was cut short abruptly. Those who had been present, wishing to know to what the Rebbe had alluded, came and asked him. He showed them the *Aruch* under the entry *eser* (עֶשֶׂר — ten), which notes that the *mishnah* in *Keilim* (1:6-9) lists ten degrees of holiness of place which do not include the holiness of *Eretz Yisrael,* although it appears in the *mishnah* (it is the eleventh item). Rav Hai Gaon is cited by the *Aruch* as saying that *Eretz Yisrael* stands apart from the others. For all the other places, because of their holiness, deny entry to people bearing certain types of impurity. But *Eretz Yisrael*, though it is holy, is accessible to even the impure (*Olamos Shacharvu* 60).

הִכְנִיסָנוּ לְאֶרֶץ יִשְׂרָאֵל / (Had He) brought us into the Land of Israel

R' Avraham Dov of Avritch

A man who had been sent from Tzefas, in the Holy Land, to gather funds for his

עַל אַחַת כַּמָּה, וְכַמָּה טוֹבָה כְפוּלָה וּמְכֻפֶּלֶת לַמָּקוֹם עָלֵינוּ. שֶׁהוֹצִיאָנוּ מִמִּצְרַיִם, וְעָשָׂה בָהֶם שְׁפָטִים, וְעָשָׂה בֵאלֹהֵיהֶם, וְהָרַג אֶת בְּכוֹרֵיהֶם, וְנָתַן לָנוּ אֶת מָמוֹנָם, וְקָרַע לָנוּ אֶת הַיָּם, וְהֶעֱבִירָנוּ בְתוֹכוֹ בֶּחָרָבָה, וְשִׁקַּע צָרֵינוּ בְּתוֹכוֹ, וְסִפֵּק צָרְכֵּנוּ בַּמִּדְבָּר אַרְבָּעִים שָׁנָה, וְהֶאֱכִילָנוּ אֶת הַמָּן, וְנָתַן לָנוּ אֶת הַשַּׁבָּת, וְקֵרְבָנוּ לִפְנֵי הַר סִינַי, וְנָתַן לָנוּ אֶת הַתּוֹרָה, וְהִכְנִיסָנוּ לְאֶרֶץ יִשְׂרָאֵל, וּבָנָה לָנוּ אֶת בֵּית הַבְּחִירָה, לְכַפֵּר עַל כָּל עֲוֹנוֹתֵינוּ.

community visited the city of *R' Avraham Dov of Avritch* and spoke wonders in praise of *Eretz Yisrael*. He described the air, the landscape, flowers and fruits. In language rich in expression, he pictured the holy places and gravesites of the *tzaddikim*. His enthusiasm knew no bounds, until he finally bubbled over and said, "Rebbe, what can I say? Why should I go on? Even the rocks of *Eretz Yisrael* are pearls and precious stones of all sorts!"

The Rebbe who had already previously pined to go up to the Holy Land could no longer find peace. He left his city and his flock of chasidim, went up to Israel, and settled in Tzefas.

Sometime afterwards the funds gatherer returned home from his travels. He came before the Rebbe and asked with interest, "Well, then, has the Rebbe found what he hoped to see?"

"The land is, indeed, very, very, good," said the Rebbe. "The holy places, the graves of the *tzaddikim*, the Western Wall, the tomb of Rachel, the air — the air of *Eretz Yisrael* grants wisdom — everything is exceptional. But when you said the rocks were pearls, that was an exaggeration."

The man reacted strongly and said, "Rebbe, whoever is found worthy sees it!"

The Rebbe rose without a word, and closeted himself in his room. For an entire year he did not leave that room. For an entire year he secluded himself and devoted himself to his Maker, through study and prayer, cut off from the world. When the year drew to a close, he emerged and invited the residents of Tzefas to a feast of thanksgiving.

All sat, filled with curiosity, desirous to hear why the Rebbe had lived in enforced solitude and why he had called upon them to gather for this feast. The Rebbe proclaimed, "Indeed, the statement is correct. The rocks *are*

Thus, how much more so, should we be grateful to the Omnipresent for all the numerous favors He showered upon us: He brought us out of Egypt; executed judgments against the Egyptians; and against their gods; slew their firstborn; gave us their wealth; split the Sea for us; led us through it on dry land; drowned our oppressors in it; provided for our needs in the desert for forty years; fed us the Manna; gave us the Shabbos; brought us before Mount Sinai; gave us the Torah; brought us to the Land of Israel; and built us the Temple, to atone for our sins.

pearls; whoever is found worthy sees it."

Those present did not understand him and so he told them about the collector of funds and what the man had said. "In all my life," he said, "no one ever spoke to me with such force. I felt that Heaven had put the words on his lips in order to encourage me to reach such a state. I closed myself off in my room; I sanctified and purified myself. And, indeed, my eyes were opened. I bear true witness before you. The rocks of Israel are precious stones and shine with the luster of pearls" (*Pri Kodesh Hillulim* 111).

R' Mordechai Shlomo of Boyan   On his first visit to *Eretz Yisrael*, *R' Mordechai Shlomo of Boyan* was received by his chasidim in Haifa. Five of his followers entered the car that took him to Tel Aviv. During the two-hour ride, the Rebbe did not say a word, but looked out the window with great concentration.

One of the chasidim could not contain himself and asked, "Tell us, master, what is there to be seen from the window?"

To which the Rebbe replied, "Of *Eretz Yisrael* it is said that 'the eyes of Hashem, your God, are upon it' (*Devarim* 11:12). Certainly, then, *we* ought to look at it" (*Demu'ios Hod* III 252).

R' Yisrael of Ruzhin   A chasid wished to go up to the Holy Land. "Know that *Eretz Yisrael* is like a feather bed, a down quilt," said his rebbe, *R' Yisrael of Ruzhin*. "In the cold of a winter night, a man crawls under the quilt. At first it is cold. Only with time does it grow warmer and warmer. For the quilt is not of itself warm; it gathers up the warmth of a man's body and warms him, in turn, all the more.

"So it is with the Holy Land. If a man of fire comes to live in her, she adds the heat of holiness to him in his devotion. But to the cold soul, she remains as cold as she was before" (*Ner Yisrael* I 164).

רַבָּן גַּמְלִיאֵל הָיָה אוֹמֵר. כָּל שֶׁלֹּא אָמַר
שְׁלֹשָׁה דְבָרִים אֵלּוּ בַּפֶּסַח,
לֹא יָצָא יְדֵי חוֹבָתוֹ, וְאֵלּוּ הֵן,

פֶּסַח. מַצָּה. וּמָרוֹר.

פֶּסַח שֶׁהָיוּ אֲבוֹתֵינוּ אוֹכְלִים בִּזְמַן שֶׁבֵּית
הַמִּקְדָּשׁ הָיָה קַיָּם, עַל שׁוּם מָה? עַל שׁוּם
שֶׁפָּסַח הַקָּדוֹשׁ בָּרוּךְ הוּא עַל בָּתֵּי אֲבוֹתֵינוּ
בְּמִצְרָיִם. שֶׁנֶּאֱמַר, וַאֲמַרְתֶּם, זֶבַח פֶּסַח הוּא
לַיהוה, אֲשֶׁר פָּסַח עַל בָּתֵּי בְנֵי יִשְׂרָאֵל בְּמִצְרַיִם
בְּנָגְפּוֹ אֶת מִצְרַיִם, וְאֶת בָּתֵּינוּ הִצִּיל, וַיִּקֹּד הָעָם
וַיִּשְׁתַּחֲווּ.[1]

פֶּסַח מַצָּה וּמָרוֹר / *Pesach — the Pesach offering;*
matzah — the unleavened bread; maror — the bitter herbs

Chidushei HaRim   *Matzah* is meant to remind us of freedom, while
maror is meant to remind us of the bondage which
preceded that freedom. Why, then, is *matzah* referred to before *maror*?

R' Simchah Bunim of Pshischa gave the following parable:

A king had an only son whom he loved and upon whom he lavished every
favor. The son, however, was an ingrate and rebelled against his father who,
forthwith, banished him. Years passed and the king was moved to pity for
his son. He sent one of his ministers to seek him out and bring him back.
The minister inquired and investigated. He found the prince in an
out-of-the-way village, barefoot, dressed in tatters and drinking himself silly
in the local tavern. The minister approached him and asked him how he was.

"Marvelous," answered the youth. "If I had a sheepskin jacket and a pair
of boots no one could be happier."

The minister wept to hear to what depths the once-pampered prince had
fallen.

Thus it is that David HaMelech in speaking of Egypt and the Exodus says:
"And He saw in what straits they were — when He heard their song"
(*Tehillim* 106:44). They were mired in the muck of bondage, and yet they
sang. For the nadir of servitude is the coming to terms with the state of
degradation.

We eat the *matzah* before the *maror*, because Israel was totally unaware

R
abban Gamliel used to say: Whoever has not
explained the following three things on Passover
has not fulfilled his duty, namely; PESACH — the
Pesach offering; MATZAH — the unleavened bread;
MAROR — the bitter herbs.

P
esach — Why did our fathers eat a Pesach
offering during the period when the Temple
stood? — Because the Holy One, Blessed is He,
passed over the houses of our fathers in Egypt, as it
is written: You shall say: 'It is a Pesach offering for
HASHEM, Who passed over the houses of the Children
of Israel in Egypt when He struck the Egyptians and
spared our houses; and the people bowed down and
prostrated themselves.'[1]

---

1. *Shemos* 12:27.

---

of the bitterness of servitude indicated by the *maror* until they were worthy
of the light of deliverance alluded to by the *matzah*. They truly tasted
redemption before they felt their bondage (*Siach Sarfei Kodesh* I 244).

אֲשֶׁר פָּסַח עַל בָּתֵּי בְּנֵי יִשְׂרָאֵל /
Who passed over the houses of the Children of Israel

R' Moshe Leib of Sasov   *R' Moshe Leib of Sasov* loved his fellow Jews
and would often say to his chasidim, "Would
that you would love the righteous man, the *tzaddik*, as much as the Holy
One loves the least of those in Israel."

Once, when he visited his master, *R' Elimelech of Lizensk*, his rebbe gave
him the honor of speaking.

"The Torah tells us," he said, "that *Hashem* 'passed over the houses of
the Children of Israel in Egypt.' Are we to take this in a literal sense? How
can we? His glory fills the entire world. We must rather imagine that when
Hashem came upon the home of an Israelite living in an Egyptian
neighborhood, He would skip (פָּסַח) and dance, so to speak, and say with
joy, 'A Jew lives here! A Jew lives here!' " (*Chidushei HaRamal*).

אֲשֶׁר פָּסַח / *Who passed over*

R' Baruch of Mezhibuz   The Holy One demands of man that he make
the greatest of efforts possible before He extends
His help. As *Chazal* put it:

When a man sanctifies himself slightly, Heaven makes him very holy; he
sanctifies himself on earth and Heaven above sanctifies him (*Yoma* 39a).

The middle matzah is lifted and displayed while the following paragraph is recited.

מַצָּה זּוֹ שֶׁאָנוּ אוֹכְלִים, עַל שׁוּם מָה? עַל שׁוּם
שֶׁלֹּא הִסְפִּיק בְּצֵקָם שֶׁל אֲבוֹתֵינוּ
לְהַחֲמִיץ, עַד שֶׁנִּגְלָה עֲלֵיהֶם מֶלֶךְ מַלְכֵי הַמְּלָכִים
הַקָּדוֹשׁ בָּרוּךְ הוּא וּגְאָלָם. שֶׁנֶּאֱמַר, וַיֹּאפוּ אֶת
הַבָּצֵק אֲשֶׁר הוֹצִיאוּ מִמִּצְרַיִם עֻגֹת מַצּוֹת כִּי לֹא
חָמֵץ, כִּי גֹרְשׁוּ מִמִּצְרַיִם, וְלֹא יָכְלוּ לְהִתְמַהְמֵהַּ,
וְגַם צֵדָה לֹא עָשׂוּ לָהֶם.¹

The maror is lifted and displayed while the following paragraph is recited.

מָרוֹר זֶה שֶׁאָנוּ אוֹכְלִים, עַל שׁוּם מָה? עַל שׁוּם
שֶׁמֵּרְרוּ הַמִּצְרִים אֶת חַיֵּי אֲבוֹתֵינוּ
בְּמִצְרָיִם. שֶׁנֶּאֱמַר, וַיְמָרְרוּ אֶת חַיֵּיהֶם, בַּעֲבֹדָה
קָשָׁה, בְּחֹמֶר וּבִלְבֵנִים, וּבְכָל עֲבֹדָה בַּשָּׂדֶה, אֵת
כָּל עֲבֹדָתָם אֲשֶׁר עָבְדוּ בָהֶם בְּפָרֶךְ.²

בְּכָל דּוֹר וָדוֹר חַיָּב אָדָם לִרְאוֹת אֶת עַצְמוֹ
כְּאִלּוּ הוּא יָצָא מִמִּצְרַיִם. שֶׁנֶּאֱמַר,
וְהִגַּדְתָּ לְבִנְךָ בַּיּוֹם הַהוּא לֵאמֹר, בַּעֲבוּר זֶה עָשָׂה

If one works at it and makes the tiring effort, help will come from Heaven. The Holy One says to Israel, "Make for me a single crack of an opening with *teshuvah*, just the width of the point of a needle, and I will make an opening for you through which carts and wagons may pass" (*Shir HaShirim Rabba* 5:2 para. 2).

But in Egypt Israel had sunken to the forty-ninth depth of impurity and were falling lower and lower. They were almost at the point of complete assimilation. Therefore, Hashem hastened their redemption. He did not wait until they gave Him a crack of an opening the width of a needle point, lest He be too late.

And thus the verse says: "and Hashem passed over the doorway" (*Shemos* 12:23) — He waived the opening of the "door" on our part. The Redemption came about completely through His initiative (*Butzina Dinehora* 1).

The middle matzah is lifted and displayed while the following paragraph is recited.

Matzah — Why do we eat this unleavened bread? — Because the dough of our fathers did not have time to become leavened before the King of kings, the Holy One, Blessed is He, revealed Himself to them and redeemed them, as it is written: They baked the dough which they had brought out of Egypt into unleavened bread, for it had not fermented, because they were driven out of Egypt and could not delay, nor had they prepared any provisions for the way.[1]

The maror is lifted and displayed while the following paragraph is recited.

Maror — Why do we eat this bitter herb? — Because the Egyptians embittered the lives of our fathers in Egypt, as it says: They embittered their lives with hard labor, with mortar and bricks, and with all manner of labor in the field: whatever service they made them perform was with hard labor.[2]

In every generation it is one's duty to regard himself as though he personally had gone out of Egypt, as it is written: You shall tell your son on that day: 'It was because of this that HASHEM did

1. *Shemos* 12:39. 2. 1:14.

וְגַם צֵדָה לֹא עָשׂוּ לָהֶם

Nor had they prepared any provisions for the way

R' Simchah Bunim of Pshischa

R' Simchah Bunim of Pshischa:
The condition for the Redemption from Egypt was that Israel leave their homes, abandon all their possessions and make their way into the desert. Such is not the practice which is in fashion today. But man must realize that that is the way of redemption, that is the way which leads to the receiving of the Torah (*Siach Sarfei Kodesh* I 48).

יהוה לִי, בְּצֵאתִי מִמִּצְרָיִם.[1] לֹא אֶת אֲבוֹתֵינוּ
בִּלְבַד גָּאַל הַקָּדוֹשׁ בָּרוּךְ הוּא, אֶלָּא אַף אוֹתָנוּ גָּאַל
עִמָּהֶם. שֶׁנֶּאֱמַר, וְאוֹתָנוּ הוֹצִיא מִשָּׁם, לְמַעַן הָבִיא
אֹתָנוּ לָתֶת לָנוּ אֶת הָאָרֶץ אֲשֶׁר נִשְׁבַּע לַאֲבוֹתֵינוּ.[2]

The matzos are covered and the cup is lifted and held until it is to be drunk.
According to some customs, however, the cup is put down after the following
paragraph, in which case the matzos should once more be uncovered.

לְפִיכָךְ אֲנַחְנוּ חַיָּבִים לְהוֹדוֹת, לְהַלֵּל, לְשַׁבֵּחַ,
לְפָאֵר, לְרוֹמֵם, לְהַדֵּר, לְבָרֵךְ, לְעַלֵּה,
וּלְקַלֵּס, לְמִי שֶׁעָשָׂה לַאֲבוֹתֵינוּ וְלָנוּ אֶת כָּל הַנִּסִּים
הָאֵלּוּ, הוֹצִיאָנוּ מֵעַבְדוּת לְחֵרוּת, מִיָּגוֹן לְשִׂמְחָה,
וּמֵאֵבֶל לְיוֹם טוֹב, וּמֵאֲפֵלָה לְאוֹר גָּדוֹל, וּמִשִּׁעְבּוּד
לִגְאֻלָּה, וְנֹאמַר לְפָנָיו שִׁירָה חֲדָשָׁה, הַלְלוּיָהּ.

הַלְלוּיָהּ הַלְלוּ עַבְדֵי יהוה, הַלְלוּ אֶת שֵׁם
יהוה. יְהִי שֵׁם יהוה מְבֹרָךְ, מֵעַתָּה
וְעַד עוֹלָם. מִמִּזְרַח שֶׁמֶשׁ עַד מְבוֹאוֹ, מְהֻלָּל שֵׁם
יהוה. רָם עַל כָּל גּוֹיִם יהוה, עַל הַשָּׁמַיִם כְּבוֹדוֹ. מִי

הַלְלוּ עַבְדֵי ה' / *Praise, you servants of Hashem*

Fiery Angel of Moglenitza　　One day the *Fiery Angel of Moglenitza*
entered the *beis midrash* and stopped to listen
to his disciple *R' Yissachar Ber of Volbroz* learning aloud with burning
enthusiasm. The others noticed the Rebbe and fell silent. When R' Yissachar
Ber sensed the quiet, he lifted his eyes and saw his Rebbe standing over him.
He immediately closed the *sefer* and rose in awe.

"Is it proper to give preference to a man of flesh and blood, and honor
him over the Torah?" asked the Fiery Angel.

R' Yissachar Dov asked permission to speak and said, "We find one verse
which places praise of Hashem prior to praise of Hashem's servants (הַלְלוּ אֶת
שֵׁם ה', הַלְלוּ עַבְדֵי ה'; *Tehillim* 135:1), whereas another verse has the reverse
order (הַלְלוּ עַבְדֵי ה', הַלְלוּ אֶת שֵׁם ה'; *Tehillim* 113:1). This teaches us that the

for "me" when I went out of Egypt.'[1] It was not only our fathers whom the Holy One redeemed from slavery; we, too, were redeemed with them, as it is written: He brought "us" out from there so that He might take us to the land which He had promised to our fathers.[2]

The matzos are covered and the cup is lifted and held until it is to be drunk. According to some customs, however, the cup is put down after the following paragraph, in which case the matzos should once more be uncovered.

Therefore it is our duty to thank, praise, pay tribute, glorify, exalt, honor, bless, extol, and acclaim Him Who performed all these miracles for our fathers and for us. He brought us forth from slavery to freedom, from grief to joy, from mourning to festivity, from darkness to great light, and from servitude to redemption. Let us, therefore, recite a new song before Him! Halleluyah!

Halleluyah! Praise, you servants of HASHEM, praise the Name of HASHEM. Blessed be the Name of HASHEM from now and forever. From the rising of the sun to its setting, HASHEM's Name is praised. High above all nations is HASHEM, above the heavens is His

---

1. *Shemos* 13:8.   2. *Devarim* 6:23.

---

honor due to *tzaddikim*, Hashem's servants, is equal to the honor due Hashem" (*Ohel Yissachar* 23).

[This is an imaginative interpretation (דְּרָשָׁה) of the verses. Each verse is a *single*, and similar, command to the servants of Hashem to praise Hashem. The verb of command (הַלְלוּ) is merely repeated. For each הַלְלוּ in the verse the object is אֶת שֵׁם ה'. R' Yissachar Ber — and he was not alone — treats the עַבְדֵי ה' as an object of הַלְלוּ and those addressed are the public in general. In this fashion, each verse consists of *two* commands: Praise Hashem, praise the servants of Hashem (*Tehillim* 113:1); Praise the servants of Hashem, praise Hashem (*Tehillim* 135:1). Although this interpretation of *Tehillim* is original, equating the honoring of one's teacher with honoring Hashem exists in *Chazal* and has halachic bearing; see *Rambam, Hilchos Talmud Torah*, 5:1.]

רָם עַל כָּל גּוֹיִם יהוה, עַל הַשָּׁמַיִם כְּבוֹדוֹ. מִי
כַּיהוה אֱלֹהֵינוּ, הַמַּגְבִּיהִי לָשָׁבֶת. הַמַּשְׁפִּילִי
לִרְאוֹת, בַּשָּׁמַיִם וּבָאָרֶץ. מְקִימִי מֵעָפָר דָּל,
מֵאַשְׁפֹּת יָרִים אֶבְיוֹן. לְהוֹשִׁיבִי עִם נְדִיבִים, עִם
נְדִיבֵי עַמּוֹ. מוֹשִׁיבִי עֲקֶרֶת הַבַּיִת, אֵם הַבָּנִים
שְׂמֵחָה, הַלְלוּיָהּ.[1]

בְּצֵאת יִשְׂרָאֵל מִמִּצְרָיִם, בֵּית יַעֲקֹב מֵעַם
לֹעֵז. הָיְתָה יְהוּדָה לְקָדְשׁוֹ, יִשְׂרָאֵל
מַמְשְׁלוֹתָיו. הַיָּם רָאָה וַיָּנֹס, הַיַּרְדֵּן יִסֹּב לְאָחוֹר.
הֶהָרִים רָקְדוּ כְאֵילִים, גְּבָעוֹת כִּבְנֵי צֹאן. מַה לְּךָ
הַיָּם כִּי תָנוּס, הַיַּרְדֵּן תִּסֹּב לְאָחוֹר. הֶהָרִים תִּרְקְדוּ
כְאֵילִים, גְּבָעוֹת כִּבְנֵי צֹאן. מִלִּפְנֵי אָדוֹן חוּלִי
אָרֶץ, מִלִּפְנֵי אֱלוֹהַ יַעֲקֹב. הַהֹפְכִי הַצּוּר אֲגַם מָיִם,
חַלָּמִישׁ לְמַעְיְנוֹ מָיִם.[2]

According to all customs the cup is lifted and the matzos covered
during the recitation of this blessing.

בָּרוּךְ אַתָּה יהוה אֱלֹהֵינוּ מֶלֶךְ הָעוֹלָם, אֲשֶׁר
גְּאָלָנוּ וְגָאַל אֶת אֲבוֹתֵינוּ מִמִּצְרָיִם,
וְהִגִּיעָנוּ הַלַּיְלָה הַזֶּה לֶאֱכָל בּוֹ מַצָּה וּמָרוֹר. כֵּן יהוה
אֱלֹהֵינוּ וֵאלֹהֵי אֲבוֹתֵינוּ, יַגִּיעֵנוּ לְמוֹעֲדִים וְלִרְגָלִים
אֲחֵרִים הַבָּאִים לִקְרָאתֵנוּ לְשָׁלוֹם, שְׂמֵחִים

הַמַּשְׁפִּילִי לִרְאוֹת / **Yet deigns to look**

R' Levi Yitzchak of Berdichev

When *R' Levi Yitzchak of Berdichev* was
once on a trip, the wagon driver noticed a
bale of fodder lying by the wayside. No one was in sight. He halted and
jumped down, intending to take the bale, when he heard the Rebbe
suddenly shout, ''They're watching! They're watching!''

above all nations is HASHEM, above the heavens is His glory. Who is like HASHEM, our God, Who is enthroned on high, yet deigns to look, upon the heaven and earth? He raises the destitute from the dust, from the trash heaps He lifts the needy — to seat them with nobles, with nobles of His people. He transforms the barren wife into a glad mother of children. Halleluyah![1]

When Israel went forth from Egypt, Yaakov's household from a people of alien tongue, Yehudah became His sanctuary, Israel His dominion. The Sea saw and fled; the Jordan turned backward. The mountains skipped like rams, and the hills like young lambs. What ails you, O Sea, that you flee? O Jordan, that you turn backward? O mountains, that you skip like rams? O hills, like young lambs? Before HASHEM's presence — tremble, O earth, before the presence of the God of Yaakov, Who turns the rock into a pond of water, the flint into a flowing fountain.[2]

According to all customs the cup is lifted and the matzos covered during the recitation of this blessing.

Blessed are You, HASHEM, our God, King of the universe, Who redeemed our ancestors from Egypt and enabled us to reach this night that we may eat matzah and maror. So, HASHEM, our God and God of our fathers, bring us also to future Festivals and holidays in peace, gladdened in the

---

1. *Tehillim* 113.   2. 114.

The driver dropped the fodder in fright, climbed onto the wagon and whipped up the horses. A long moment later, he peered about and saw no one. "Who was looking?" he asked in wonder.

"The Holy One, Blessed is He!" said the Rebbe (*Chasidim Mesaprim* III 814).

בְּבִנְיַן עִירֶךְ וְשָׂשִׂים בַּעֲבוֹדָתֶךָ, וְנֹאכַל שָׁם מִן
הַזְּבָחִים וּמִן הַפְּסָחִים [מִן הַפְּסָחִים וּמִן הַזְּבָחִים] אֲשֶׁר
יַגִּיעַ דָּמָם עַל קִיר מִזְבַּחֲךָ לְרָצוֹן. וְנוֹדֶה לְךָ שִׁיר
חָדָשׁ עַל גְּאֻלָּתֵנוּ וְעַל פְּדוּת נַפְשֵׁנוּ. בָּרוּךְ אַתָּה
יהוה, גָּאַל יִשְׂרָאֵל.

הֲרֵינִי מוּכָן וּמְזֻמָּן לְקַיֵּם מִצְוַת כּוֹס שֵׁנִי מֵאַרְבַּע כּוֹסוֹת. לְשֵׁם יִחוּד קֻדְשָׁא
בְּרִיךְ הוּא וּשְׁכִינְתֵּיהּ, עַל יְדֵי הַהוּא טָמִיר וְנֶעְלָם, בְּשֵׁם כָּל יִשְׂרָאֵל. וִיהִי
נֹעַם אֲדֹנָי אֱלֹהֵינוּ עָלֵינוּ, וּמַעֲשֵׂה יָדֵינוּ כּוֹנְנָה עָלֵינוּ, וּמַעֲשֵׂה יָדֵינוּ כּוֹנְנֵהוּ:

בָּרוּךְ אַתָּה יהוה אֱלֹהֵינוּ מֶלֶךְ הָעוֹלָם, בּוֹרֵא פְּרִי
הַגָּפֶן.

The second cup is drunk while leaning on the left side
— preferably the entire cup, but at least most of it.

גָּאַל יִשְׂרָאֵל / *Who has redeemed Israel*

R' Avraham of Sadigura

Each year on the evening when the Search for Leaven (בְּדִיקַת חָמֵץ) is made, on the night before *Pesach*, R' Avraham of Sadigura told the following story:

In a village, not far from the city of Kolbasov, lived a Jew who rented the tavern from the local lord in whose estate the village lay. His affairs did not prosper and he was unable to pay the rent. The landlord warned him once, then again. And on the morning of the *Shabbos* before *Pesach* (*Shabbos HaGadol*), he sent his servants to vandalize the tavern keeper's home, as a warning. They spilled the pail of slops on the ground, overturned the pot of *cholent*, broke the table and smashed the dishes. They left confusion and destruction behind them, and a family shocked and weeping.

The taverner thought to soften his suffering and went to the city to listen to the sermon of the *Ohev Yisrael of Apta*, who served, at the time, as the *rav* of Kolbasov. When he came to the *beis knesses*, the *rav* was in the midst of his talk and he heard him say, "There are two blessings: one with a concluding phrase in the past tense — 'He Who *redeemed* Israel' (גָּאַל יִשְׂרָאֵל), which we say on the evening of the *Seder*, when we recite the *Haggadah*, and also just prior to the *Shemoneh Esrei* in every prayer-service; the other, which ends in the present tense — 'He Who *redeems* Israel' (גּוֹאֵל יִשְׂרָאֵל), is the seventh blessing of the *Shemoneh Esrei*, the blessing which begins 'Look upon our afflictions' (רְאֵה נָא בְעָנְיֵנוּ).

(On *Motzaei Shabbos* the phrase in parentheses substitutes for the preceding phrase.)

rebuilding of Your city, and joyful at Your service. There we shall eat of the offerings and Pesach sacrifices (of the Pesach sacrifices and offerings) whose blood will gain the sides of Your altar for gracious acceptance.We shall then sing a new song of praise to You for our redemption and for the liberation of our souls. Blessed are You, HASHEM, Who has redeemed Israel.

Behold, I am prepared and ready to fulfill the mitzvah of the second of the Four Cups. For the sake of the unification of the Holy One, Blessed is He, and His Presence, through Him Who is hidden and inscrutable — [I pray] in the name of all Israel. May the pleasantness of my Lord, our God, be upon us — may He establish our handiwork for us; our handiwork may He establish.

Blessed are You, HASHEM, our God, King of the universe, Who creates the fruit of the vine.

The second cup is drunk while leaning on the left side
— preferably the entire cup, but at least most of it.

"The first speaks of the redemption that was, the deliverance from the exile of Egypt and the receiving of the Torah at Sinai. The second refers to the redemption which occurs at all times, so that, even if there is a Jew in some village who cannot manage to pay the rent on time and the landlord sends his Cossacks to overturn his house, even for such a Jew, the Holy One brings forth redemption and rescues him from his suffering."

The taverner heard this and was filled with joy. He returned home happily and sang, "The Rebbe said, 'He Who redeems Israel!' The Rebbe said, 'He Who redeems Israel!' " While he was in this mood, the landlord's servants arrived. Their master wished to see if the Jew had learned his lesson. The servants came back with an odd tale. The Jew was singing and dancing.

The landlord summoned the taverner and the Jew appeared before him with a shining countenance, certain that the words of the Rebbe would be made manifest. The landlord was convinced that the Jew had become mad from his sufferings. He felt compassion and said, "Moshke, why are you such an unfortunate? You are a pauper. You can't pay your debt and you don't even have money to buy spirits on which you might make a profit."

"What shall I do, then?" said the taverner.

"I'll tell you what to do. I'll give you a letter for the distillery, telling them to sell you spirits on credit. You'll sell at a profit, save a bit and pay your debt."

רחצה

The hands are washed for matzah and the following blessing is recited. It is preferable to bring water and a basin to the head of the household at the Seder table.

בָּרוּךְ אַתָּה יהוה אֱלֹהֵינוּ מֶלֶךְ הָעוֹלָם, אֲשֶׁר קִדְּשָׁנוּ בְּמִצְוֹתָיו, וְצִוָּנוּ עַל נְטִילַת יָדָיִם.

The taverner followed his suggestion and, in the short span of the few days between *Shabbos HaGadol* and the day before *Pesach*, he sold a huge amount of whiskey which netted a profit large enough to both pay the landlord and buy all his needs for the festival, with a liberal hand.

On the day before *Pesach* he tied money into a kerchief, came to the Rebbe and said, "Rebbe, I have brought the money of 'He Who *redeems* Israel' " (*Sipurei Chasidim, Moadim*, p. 267).

R' Yissachar Dov of Belz

R' Yissachar Dov of Belz would go out into the streets of town after completing his own Seder, to see how the common folk conducted theirs.

Once, he heard a simple Jew ending the blessing 'He Who redeemed Israel' (גָּאַל יִשְׂרָאֵל) with great fervor and immediately launching into *Shemoneh Esrei*.

The Rebbe's attendant burst out laughing, but the Rebbe said with great feeling, "He joined the blessing of redemption (גְּאוּלָה) to the *Shemoneh Esrei* prayer (תְּפִילָה) with purposeful intention (בַּוָּנַת הַלֵּב) and his prayer will be received in Heaven! He is childless and now he will have children!" (*Admorei Belz* III 207).

[The last of the blessings of the *Shema*, immediately prior to the *Shemoneh Esrei* of the morning prayers, ends with גָּאַל יִשְׂרָאֵל. The *halachah* requires that *Shemoneh Esrei* follow it without interruption — not even a pause (*Shulchan Aruch, Orach Chaim* 111). The Rebbe saw a good omen in the man's mistake.]

רָחְצָה / *Rachtzah*

R' Chanoch Henoch of Alexander

R' Chanoch Henoch of Alexander:

When I first came to my master, *R' Menachem Mendel of Kotzk*, he said, "Come and I will teach you the meaning of *chasid*. The chasid constantly asks himself, 'Why?' just as the *gemara* often asks, 'What is the reason (מַאי טַעְמָא)?' "

I did not understand what the Rebbe wanted to say.

Some days later, I was about to wash my hands, in order to eat and, suddenly, I remembered the Rebbe's remarks. I began to think about the

RACHTZAH

The hands are washed for matzah and the following blessing is recited. It is preferable to bring water and a basin to the head of the household at the Seder table.

Blessed are You, HASHEM, our God, King of the universe, Who has sanctified us with His commandments, and has commanded us concerning the washing of the hands.

---

nature of the *mitzvah* which I was about to perform; about its purpose. I contemplated the thought that I was about to fulfill the *mitzvah* in the presence of the Divine. I stood, thus, for some two hours, washing-cup in hand, gripped by my thoughts. After I fully realized the great favor the Holy One had shown us when He sanctified us through His *mitzvos* and when He commanded us to wash hands, I made the blessing.

Would that I might have the fortune to make the blessing thus, today! (*Siach Sarfei Kodesh* I 556).

[*When he sanctified . . . to wash hands.* This is in effect the formula of the blessing itself: אֲשֶׁר קִדְּשָׁנוּ בְּמִצְוֹתָיו וְצִוָּנוּ עַל נְטִילַת יָדָיִם. R' Chanoch Henoch felt the full import of the blessing that day. It transcended its formulaic bounds for him.]

נְטִילַת יָדָיִם / *The washing of hands*

R' Sar Shalom of Belz	*R' Sar Shalom of Belz* told the following story:

Not long ago, an evil man, a totally corrupt man, lived not far from our city. He was truly wicked and there was not a single sin which he had not committed, all with an air of defiance (לְהַכְעִיס). There was a lone *mitzvah*, a rabbinic *mitzvah* which he observed strictly, throughout his life; he would always wash his hands before meals.

Once, in the Intermediate Days (חוֹל הַמּוֹעֵד) of *Pesach*, he had to take a trip to a town some twenty miles distant. He saddled his horse and took several matzos with him. Whether he did so because he did not wish to eat *chametz*, I do not know. But he did take matzos for fare on the road. After having ridden several miles, he felt hungry, but did not wish to eat without first washing his hands. For he said, "I have committed all the sins in the world and not fulfilled *mitzvos*. But, since I have kept this single *mitzvah*, throughout my days, why should I give it up now?"

He rode on for some four miles and found that he no longer had any strength, due to his fasting. He sought here and there, but found no source of water. Then, he remembered that a path led off the road to a well. The well, however, was frequented by fierce bandits. He said to himself, "If I stay here, I will die a drawn-out, agonizing death from hunger. If I get there, the bandits will slay me. It's all one and the same. I prefer to die by their hands on a full stomach. But I will not eat without first washing my hands."

He rode to the well. Whether he said the blessing over the matzos

מוֹצִיא

The following two blessings are recited over matzah; the first is recited over matzah as food, and the second for the special *mitzvah* of eating matzah on the night of Pesach. [The latter blessing is to be made with the intention that it also apply to the 'sandwich' and the afikoman.]

הִנְנִי מוּכָן וּמְזוּמָן לְקַיֵּם מִצְוַת אֲכִילַת מַצָּה. לְשֵׁם יִחוּד קֻדְשָׁא בְּרִיךְ הוּא וּשְׁכִינְתֵּיה, עַל יְדֵי הַהוּא טָמִיר וְנֶעְלָם, בְּשֵׁם כָּל יִשְׂרָאֵל. וִיהִי נְעַם אֲדֹנָי אֱלֹהֵינוּ עָלֵינוּ, וּמַעֲשֵׂה יָדֵינוּ כּוֹנְנָה עָלֵינוּ, וּמַעֲשֵׂה יָדֵינוּ כּוֹנְנֵהוּ:

The head of the household raises all the matzos on the Seder plate and recites the following blessing:

בָּרוּךְ אַתָּה יהוה אֱלֹהֵינוּ מֶלֶךְ הָעוֹלָם, הַמּוֹצִיא לֶחֶם מִן הָאָרֶץ.

The bottom matzah is put down and the following blessing is recited while the top (whole) matzah and the middle (broken) piece are still raised.

מַצָּה

בָּרוּךְ אַתָּה יהוה אֱלֹהֵינוּ מֶלֶךְ הָעוֹלָם, אֲשֶׁר קִדְּשָׁנוּ בְּמִצְוֹתָיו, וְצִוָּנוּ עַל אֲכִילַת מַצָּה.

(הַמּוֹצִיא), I do not know. But I do know that he did not eat without washing. The bandits soon arrived, robbed him of his money and killed him.

In the heavens above, there was a great stir and commotion. A man had risked his life and knowingly put himself into mortal danger for the sake of a *mitzvah* of rabbinic force. This *mitzvah* had been so dear in his eyes, even though he had high-handedly transgressed and committed all possible sins.

Judgment was passed in his favor and he was granted a place in the light of life in Gan Eden.

Think and give your hearts over to imagine what will be the judgment of the man who observes the entire Torah — in all its principles and particulars (*Dover Shalom* 48).

Ba'al Shem Tov Before he was revealed to the world at large, the *Ba'al Shem* would wander in solitude in the mountains about Okop. Once, robbers who were active in the area saw him approach a deep ravine. He was sunken in thought and unaware of the danger. They were certain that he would plunge into the abyss. But, to their amazement, the hill opposite moved and joined the hill on which the Ba'al Shem was walking; the canyon disappeared. The robbers realized that they were in the presence of a holy man. They approached and said, "Master, we know of a short route to *Eretz Yisrael*, through caves. If you so wish, come with us and we will show you the way."

MOTZI

The following two blessings are recited over matzah; the first is recited over matzah as food, and the second for the special *mitzvah* of eating matzah on the night of Pesach. [The latter blessing is to be made with the intention that it also apply to the 'sandwich' and the afikoman.]

The head of the household raises all the matzos on the Seder plate and recites the following blessing:

Behold, I am prepared and ready to fulfill the mitzvah of eating matzah. For the sake of the unification of the Holy One, Blessed is He, and His Presence, through Him Who is hidden and inscrutable — [I pray] in the name of all Israel. May the pleasantness of my Lord, our God, be upon us — may He establish our handiwork for us; our handiwork may He establish.

Blessed are You, HASHEM, our God, King of the universe, Who brings forth bread from the earth.

The bottom matzah is put down and the following blessing is recited while the top (whole) matzah and the middle (broken) piece are still raised.

MATZAH

Blessed are You, HASHEM, our God, King of the universe, Who has sanctified us with His commandments, and has commanded us concerning the eating of matzah.

They came to a deep, muddy marsh. A narrow plank was laid across it. The robbers passed over it. Yet, when the Ba'al Shem wished to cross, he sensed that he would be in terrible danger. He turned about to retrace his steps, but thought to himself, "I have certainly not come to this spot in vain!" And, lo and behold, there on the edge of the marsh sat a huge frog. He asked the frog, "Who are you?"

The frog told him that for the past five hundred years the soul of a wise man, a *talmid chacham*, had been interred within him. Even the sainted *Ari* who had made whole all the damaged souls had not been able to find the means to redeem this one and had put him far away in a place unfrequented by men, so that none should redeem him.

The Ba'al Shem asked what his sin had been. He answered that he had, one single time, treated the washing of hands before meals disparagingly and not washed properly. Satan had pointed an accusing finger, but had been told that a man cannot be indicted for a single transgression. However, since a sin tends to drag a further sin along in its wake, if he could cause the man to fall into an additional sin, he would be punished for this one, too. If the man would remember Hashem and sin no more, he would be cleansed of this sin, also. Satan tried him with another temptation and he did not resist. One sin brought on another and he violated almost the entire Torah. Because the first cause of all the sins was that of treating the washing of

Each participant is required to eat an amount of matzah equal in volume to an egg. Since it is usually impossible to provide a sufficient amount of matzah from the two matzos for all members of the household, the other matzos should be available at the head of the table from which to complete the required amounts. However, each participant should receive a piece from each of the top two matzos. The matzos are to be eaten while reclining on the left side and without delay; they need not be dipped in salt.

מָרוֹר

The head of the household takes a half-egg volume of maror, dips it into charoses, and gives each participant a like amount. The following blessing is recited with the intention that it also apply to the maror of the 'sandwich'. The maror is eaten without reclining, and without delay.

הִנְנִי מוּכָן וּמְזֻמָּן לְקַיֵּם מִצְוַת אֲכִילַת מָרוֹר. לְשֵׁם יִחוּד קֻדְשָׁא בְּרִיךְ הוּא וּשְׁכִינְתֵּיה, עַל יְדֵי הַהוּא טָמִיר וְנֶעְלָם, בְּשֵׁם כָּל יִשְׂרָאֵל. וִיהִי נְעַם אֲדֹנָי אֱלֹהֵינוּ עָלֵינוּ, וּמַעֲשֵׂה יָדֵינוּ כּוֹנְנָה עָלֵינוּ, וּמַעֲשֵׂה יָדֵינוּ כּוֹנְנֵהוּ:

בָּרוּךְ אַתָּה יהוה אֱלֹהֵינוּ מֶלֶךְ הָעוֹלָם, אֲשֶׁר קִדְּשָׁנוּ בְּמִצְוֹתָיו, וְצִוָּנוּ עַל אֲכִילַת מָרוֹר.

---

hands lightly, upon his death his soul had found its way into a frog which is constantly in water. He had been placed in an out-of-the-way spot, lest a Jew pass by and pronounce a blessing, or have a good thought, as this would redeem the souls which had been removed to that place.

The Ba'al Shem repaired the damage to the soul and raised it up; the frog fell dead (*Shivchei HaBesht* 49).

עַל אֲכִילַת מַצָּה /
Concerning the eating of matzah

Sainted Yehudi of Pshischa The Sainted Yehudi (Jew) of Pshischa was powerful by nature. Once, on a visit to his master, the *Chozeh of Lublin*, there were those who wished to see how strong he really was. Many of the chasidim sat on one end of a table ten cubits long and a hands-width thick. The Yehudi leaned his weight on the other end and lifted them all up in the air. When his pipe was once clogged he blew through it to clean it, and the pipe shattered.

Yet, despite his bodily strength, and though he did not suffer from ill health, his teeth fell out in his youth. This was because of the fear of God which shook him when he said the *Shema*. One lone tooth remained and he called it 'the wicked one,' since it had not been stirred to fall out in fear of its Creator. He could not forgive that solitary tooth, until he remembered that it would help him in eating the matzah. That thought made him relent (*Niflaos HaYehudi* 5:8).

Each participant is required to eat an amount of matzah equal in volume to an egg. Since it is usually impossible to provide a sufficient amount of matzah from the twomatzos for all members of the household, the other matzos should be available at the head of the table from which to complete the required amounts. However, each participant should receive a piece from each of the top two matzos. The matzos are to be eaten while reclining on the left side and without delay; they need not be dipped in salt.

MAROR

The head of the household takes a half-egg volume of maror, dips it into charoses, and gives each participant a like amount. The following blessing is recited with the intention that it also apply to the maror of the 'sandwich'. The maror is eaten without reclining, and without delay.

Behold, I am prepared and ready to fulfill the mitzvah of eating maror. For the sake of the unification of the Holy One, Blessed is He, and His Presence, through Him Who is hidden and inscrutable — [I pray] in the name of all Israel. May the pleasantness of my Lord, our God, be upon us — may He establish our handiwork for us; our handiwork may He establish.

Blessed are You, HASHEM, our God, King of the universe, Who has sanctified us with His commandments, and has commanded us concerning the eating of maror.

מָרוֹר / *Maror*

R' Nachman of Breslav

R' Nachman of Breslav told the following story: A Jew and a German set out on a tour. Their money ran out while they were on the road and they no longer had provisions. This happened just on the eve of *Pesach* and the Jew said to the German, "I'll teach you some of the Jewish customs of *Pesach*. In the evening we'll go to a synagogue. Jews are a compassionate people. They will take pity on us and invite us to be guests at their *Seder*." He taught him about *kiddush*, about washing hands before the meal and other matters. But he forgot to tell him that *maror* is eaten before the meal.

In the evening they went to a synagogue and one householder invited the Jew and, another, assuming that his friend, too, was a Jew, invited the German.

The German came to the *Seder* after not having eaten the entire day. In the beginning of the evening they gave him a small portion of *karpas* dipped in salt water — hardly a satisfying morsel. And then they began reciting and reciting. He waited impatiently for them to end the recitation of the *Haggadah* and begin the meal. Finally, they washed hands and gave him a piece of matzah and he was happy. His friend, the Jew, had told him that this signaled the beginning of the meal. Now, they would serve fish and meat and other good things. And then, they passed him a portion of a vegetable. He bit into it. His mouth was filled with a bitter taste; his eyes watered. Certain that this

כּוֹרֵךְ

The bottom (thus far unbroken) matzah is now taken. From it, with the addition of other matzos, each participant receives a half-egg volume of matzah with an equal-volume portion of maror (dipped into charoses which is shaken off). The following paragraph is recited and the 'sandwich' is eaten while reclining.

זֵכֶר לְמִקְדָּשׁ כְּהִלֵּל. כֵּן עָשָׂה הִלֵּל בִּזְמַן שֶׁבֵּית הַמִּקְדָּשׁ הָיָה קַיָּם. הָיָה כּוֹרֵךְ (פֶּסַח) מַצָּה וּמָרוֹר וְאוֹכֵל בְּיַחַד. לְקַיֵּם מַה שֶּׁנֶּאֱמַר, עַל מַצּוֹת וּמְרֹרִים יֹאכְלֻהוּ.[1]

was the promised, looked-for meal, and that this was all that would be offered, he picked himself up and ran in anger from the table shouting, "Cursed Jews, after all the long Seder, you give such bitter food." He took himself to the synagogue to await his friend and reproach him for his "good advice."

Some time later his friend approached, happy and sated with food and drink. He asked the German how it had gone and the German gave vent to bitter disappointment. "Silly fool!" said the Jew. "What a pity! Had you waited but a bit longer, you would have enjoyed all the good things, just as I did."

The path of devotion to Hashem and drawing close to the true *tzaddik* is of a similar nature. After all the toil, when one is close to the goal, some bitterness enters the picture, to purify the body. Whoever bears it patiently and waits yet a bit, experiences all sorts of pleasures and feels a sense of vitality (*Avaneha Barzel*).

Yismach Yisrael of Alexander   It is important to accept suffering with love for Hashem (יִסּוּרִים שֶׁל אַהֲבָה). *Chazal* have alluded to this in saying: "If one swallows matzah (without first chewing and tasting it), he has fulfilled the *mitzvah*; if he swallows *maror*, he has not" (*Pesachim* 115b).

Maror was meant to be chewed well (*Chasidim Mesaprim* I 520).

מוֹצִיא, מַצָּה, מָרוֹר, כּוֹרֵךְ
Motzi, Matzah, Maror, Korech

Divrei Chaim of Sanz   *The Divrei Chaim of Sanz* was weak and sickly during the last year of his life and it was with exceptional sacrifice of self that he fulfilled the *mitzvos* of the Seder.

When he ate the matzah he said, "I wish to show and teach my children how one must really make a physical sacrifice for each and every *mitzvah*." Then, he took the *maror* and said, "I wish to show and teach my children that they are obliged to sacrifice themselves even for a *mitzvah* ordained by *Chazal* and not only those which appear in the Torah." Finally, he took up the *korech*

KORECH

The bottom (thus far unbroken) matzah is now taken. From it, with the addition of other matzos, each participant receives a half-egg volume of matzah with an equal-volume portion of maror (dipped into charoses which is shaken off). The following paragraph is recited and the 'sandwich' is eaten while reclining.

In remembrance of the Temple we do as Hillel did in Temple times: he would combine (the Pesach offering,) matzah and maror in a sandwich and eat them together, to fulfill what is written in the Torah: They shall eat it with matzos and bitter herbs.[1]

_____
1. *Bamidbar* 9:11.

---

and ate it with the last of his strength, saying, "I wish to teach my children that one must make a sacrifice [not only for a *mitzvah*], but even for a custom (מִנְהָג)" (*Yisrael Saba*).

כְּזַיִת מִן הַמָּרוֹר / An olive's volume of maror

Divrei Chaim of Sanz   A chasid of Dinov suffered from mortal lung disease and traveled to the capital city of Vienna for medical advice. The doctors told him that his disease could not be cured, because the lung was not in its normal position. It was pushed to the side and was filled with phlegm which could not be drained and would cause decay. They suggested that he hurry home, lest he die among strangers.

The man started on his journey homeward with a broken heart. His way passed through Sanz and he thought to himself. "Since the *Divrei Chaim* [R' Chaim of Sanz] is famous as a great scholar and *halachic* authority, I will ask him what I should do about the eating of *maror* in the forthcoming Seder. I am unable to eat the required amount of *maror* , a *kezais* (כְּזַיִת). Am I however required to eat a lesser portion and should I pronounce a blessing over it?"

The Rebbe listened to his question. "It is said," he replied, "that *maror* is a 'healing food.' You should be able to eat the full prescribed amount and be healed."

After the man left the Rebbe's presence he remembered that the *Zohar* does not say that *maror* is a healing food, but rather, matzah. The *Divrei Chaim* had obviously made an error. And, with that thought, he pushed the incident out of his mind.

On the night of the Seder when the moment for eating *maror* arrived, the sick man took the tiniest portion of bitter herbs. He immediately began to cough strenuously, weakening himself greatly. "If my end is come," he cried out, "let me at least fulfill the *mitzvah* properly!" He took the full portion of *maror* and ate it. As soon as he swallowed the *kezais* (כְּזַיִת), the cough grew worse and his whole body shook dreadfully. His family became frightened and ran to fetch the doctor. But the doctor was himself conducting a Seder and did not come running. When he did arrive, he found the patient asleep.

שולחן עורך

The meal should be eaten in a combination of joy and solemnity, for the meal, too, is a part of the Seder service. While it is desirable that *zemiros* and discussion of the laws and events of Pesach be part of the meal, extraneous conversation should be avoided. It should be remembered that the *afikoman* must be eaten while there is still some appetite for it. In fact, if one is so sated that he must literally force himself to eat it, he is not credited with the performance of the *mitzvah* of afikoman. Therefore, it is unwise to eat more than a moderate amount during the meal.

צפון

From the *afikoman* matzah (and from additional matzos to make up the required amount), a half-egg-volume portion — according to some, a full egg's volume portion — is given to each participant. It should be eaten before midnight, while reclining, without delay, and uninterruptedly. Nothing may be eaten or drunk after the *afikoman* (with the exception of water and the like) except for the last two Seder cups of wine.

הִנְנִי מוּכָן וּמְזוּמָן לְקַיֵּם מִצְוַת אֲכִילַת אֲפִיקוֹמָן. לְשֵׁם יִחוּד קוּדְשָׁא בְּרִיךְ הוּא וּשְׁכִינְתֵּיה, עַל יְדֵי הַהוּא טָמִיר וְנֶעְלָם, בְּשֵׁם כָּל יִשְׂרָאֵל. וִיהִי נֹעַם אֲדֹנָי אֱלֹהֵינוּ עָלֵינוּ, וּמַעֲשֵׂה יָדֵינוּ כּוֹנְנָה עָלֵינוּ, וּמַעֲשֵׂה יָדֵינוּ כּוֹנְנֵהוּ:

He was told that the man had become exhausted from coughing, had fallen onto the bed and dropped off into slumber. The doctor said that rest was good for him and that he should not be awakened.

He slept until a late hour the following day and when the doctor came to examine him, he was amazed. The patient was completely cured. The force of the cough and the shuddering of his body had jarred the lung and it had returned to its normal position. The phlegm had been able to drain out.

The *maror* had indeed been, as the Rebbe of Sanz had said, a "healing food" (*Divrei Yechezkel Shraga* 143).

שֻׁלְחָן עוֹרֵךְ / Shulchan Aruch, Set the Table

Divrei Chaim of Sanz

The *Gaon of Rava*, author of *Derech HaMelech*, a commentary on the *Rambam*, decided to visit the *Divrei Chaim of Sanz*. When he arrived he found the Rebbe at a meal with his chasidim. It was the Rebbe's practice to conduct a formal public meal (*tish*) daily.

When the Rebbe saw him he said, "R' Berish'l of Lublin (for thus the *Gaon* was called in his youth) probably imagined that in Sanz he will find us attempting to understand a difficult passage in the *Mishneh LaMelech* (a work on the Rambam). And here he comes upon us busied with roast meat and gravy."

The Gaon answered, without hesitation, "And what would I have found had I had the fortune to come upon the *Kohen HaGadol*, the High Priest in the *Beis HaMikdash*? Would I not have found him busy with roast meat and gravy?"

SHULCHAN ORECH

The meal should be eaten in a combination of joy and solemnity, for the meal, too, is a part of the Seder service. While it is desirable that *zemiros* and discussion of the laws and events of Pesach be part of the meal, extraneous conversation should be avoided. It should be remembered that the *afikoman* must be eaten while there is still some appetite for it. In fact, if one is so sated that he must literally force himself to eat it, he is not credited with the performance of the *mitzvah* of *afikoman*. Therefore, it is unwise to eat more than a moderate amount during the meal.

TZAFUN

From the *afikoman* matzah (and from additional matzos to make up the required amount), a half-egg-volume portion — according to some, a full egg's volume portion — is given to each participant. It should be eaten before midnight, while reclining, without delay, and uninterruptedly. Nothing may be eaten or drunk after the *afikoman* (with the exception of water and the like) except for the last two Seder cups of wine.

Behold, I am prepared and ready to fulfill the mitzvah of eating the afikoman. For the sake of the unification of the Holy One, Blessed is He, and His Presence, through Him Who is hidden and inscrutable — [I pray] in the name of all Israel. May the pleasantness of my Lord, our God, be upon us — may He establish our handiwork for us; our handiwork may He establish.

The answer pleased the Rebbe. (From the Letter of the *Rabad of Strasbourg*, opening lines of *Pitchah Zuta*.)

צָפוּן / Tzafun, The Hidden — Eating the Afikoman

Tiferes Shmuel of Alexander   My father once gave me the portion of afikoman and said, "Tzafun — Hide it!" Perhaps he was alluding to the verse: "I have hidden (צָפַנְתִּי) Your word in my heart, that I might not sin" (*Tehillim* 119:11). When a man conceals his achievements and does not bring them forth into the open, they become implanted in his heart.

The Tiferes Shmuel once commented on a *tzaddik* of his day who had strange patterns of behavior. "True," he said, "it is good and becoming that one should act modestly, hide his light and be unknown. But *Chazal* have said: 'One does not keep food warm (on *Shabbos*) by concealing it in manure — זָבָל' (*mishnah, Shabbos* 4:1) — a man should not conceal himself through strange and odd practices" (*Tiferes Yisrael* 364;374).

בָּרֵךְ / Barech, Recite Bircas HaMazon, Grace After Meals

Chidushei HaRim   The *Chidushei HaRim of Gur* once asked an aged chasid, R' Abish by name, "What did you hear from the lips of our master, *the Rebbe of Kotzk*?"

"I heard him say," said the chasid, "that he wondered why people did not become God fearing through their reciting of the after-the-meal blessings (בִּרְכַּת הַמָּזוֹן). For it was through a post-meal blessing that our forefather

בָּרֵךְ

The third cup is poured and Bircas HaMazon (Grace After Meals) is recited. According to some customs, the Cup of Eliahu is poured at this point.

שִׁיר הַמַּעֲלוֹת, בְּשׁוּב יהוה אֶת שִׁיבַת צִיּוֹן, הָיִינוּ כְּחֹלְמִים. אָז יִמָּלֵא שְׂחוֹק פִּינוּ וּלְשׁוֹנֵנוּ רִנָּה, אָז יֹאמְרוּ בַגּוֹיִם, הִגְדִּיל יהוה לַעֲשׂוֹת עִם אֵלֶּה. הִגְדִּיל יהוה לַעֲשׂוֹת עִמָּנוּ, הָיִינוּ שְׂמֵחִים. שׁוּבָה יהוה אֶת שְׁבִיתֵנוּ, כַּאֲפִיקִים בַּנֶּגֶב. הַזֹּרְעִים בְּדִמְעָה בְּרִנָּה יִקְצֹרוּ. הָלוֹךְ יֵלֵךְ וּבָכֹה נֹשֵׂא מֶשֶׁךְ הַזָּרַע, בֹּא יָבֹא בְרִנָּה, נֹשֵׂא אֲלֻמֹּתָיו.¹

If three or more males, aged thirteen or older, participated in the meal, the leader is required to formally invite the others to join him in the recitation of Grace after Meals. Following is the 'Zimun,' or formal invitation.

הִנְנִי מוּכָן וּמְזוּמָן לְקַיֵּם מִצְוַת עֲשֵׂה שֶׁל בִּרְכַּת הַמָּזוֹן, כַּכָּתוּב, וְאָכַלְתָּ וְשָׂבָעְתָּ וּבֵרַכְתָּ אֶת יהוה אֱלֹהֶיךָ עַל הָאָרֶץ הַטֹּבָה אֲשֶׁר נָתַן לָךְ:

The leader begins:

רַבּוֹתַי מִיר וֶועלֶען בֶּענְטְשֶׁען.or רַבּוֹתַי נְבָרֵךְ.

The group responds:

יְהִי שֵׁם יהוה מְבֹרָךְ מֵעַתָּה וְעַד עוֹלָם.²

The leader continues:

יְהִי שֵׁם יהוה מְבֹרָךְ מֵעַתָּה וְעַד עוֹלָם.²

If ten men join in the Zimun, the words (in parentheses) are included.

בִּרְשׁוּת מָרָנָן וְרַבָּנָן וְרַבּוֹתַי, נְבָרֵךְ (אֱלֹהֵינוּ) שֶׁאָכַלְנוּ מִשֶּׁלּוֹ.

The group responds:

בָּרוּךְ (אֱלֹהֵינוּ) שֶׁאָכַלְנוּ מִשֶּׁלּוֹ וּבְטוּבוֹ חָיִינוּ.

The leader continues:

בָּרוּךְ (אֱלֹהֵינוּ) שֶׁאָכַלְנוּ מִשֶּׁלּוֹ וּבְטוּבוֹ חָיִינוּ.

The following line is recited if ten men join in the Zimun.

בָּרוּךְ הוּא וּבָרוּךְ שְׁמוֹ.

Avraham would bring his guests to take shelter under the wings of the Divine Presence. After they had eaten and drunk he would say, 'Bless the

BARECH

The third cup is poured and Bircas HaMazon (Grace After Meals) is recited. According to some customs, the Cup of Eliahu is poured at this point.

A song of Ascents. When HASHEM brings back the exiles to Zion, we will have been like dreamers. Then our mouth will be filled with laughter, and our tongue with glad song. Then will it be said among the nations: HASHEM has done great things for us, and we rejoiced. Restore our captives, HASHEM, like streams in the dry land. Those who sow in tears shall reap in joy. Though the farmer bears the measure of seed to the field in tears, he shall come home with joy, bearing his sheaves.[1]

If three or more males, aged thirteen or older, participated in the meal, the leader is required to formally invite the others to join him in the recitation of Grace after Meals. Following is the 'Zimun,' or formal invitation.

Behold, I am prepared and ready to fulfill the mitzvah of Grace after Meals, as it is written: 'And you shall eat and you shall be satisfied and you shall bless HASHEM, Your God, for the good land which He gave you.'

The leader begins:
Gentlemen, let us bless.

The group responds:
Blessed is the Name of HASHEM from this moment and forever![2]

The leader continues:
Blessed is the Name of HASHEM from this moment and forever![2]

If ten men join in the Zimun, the words (in parentheses) are included.
With the permission of the distinguished people present, let us bless [our God] for we have eaten from what is His.

The group responds:
Blessed is [our God] He of Whose we have eaten and through Whose goodness we live.

The leader continues:
Blessed is [our God] He of Whose we have eaten and through Whose goodness we live.

The following line is recited if ten men join in the Zimun.
Blessed is He and Blessed is His Name.

1. Tehillim 126.   2. 113:2.

בָּרוּךְ אַתָּה יהוה אֱלֹהֵינוּ מֶלֶךְ הָעוֹלָם, הַזָּן אֶת
הָעוֹלָם כֻּלּוֹ, בְּטוּבוֹ, בְּחֵן בְּחֶסֶד
וּבְרַחֲמִים, הוּא נֹתֵן לֶחֶם לְכָל בָּשָׂר, כִּי לְעוֹלָם
חַסְדּוֹ.[1] וּבְטוּבוֹ הַגָּדוֹל, תָּמִיד לֹא חָסַר לָנוּ, וְאַל
יֶחְסַר לָנוּ מָזוֹן לְעוֹלָם וָעֶד. בַּעֲבוּר שְׁמוֹ הַגָּדוֹל,
כִּי הוּא אֵל זָן וּמְפַרְנֵס לַכֹּל, וּמֵטִיב לַכֹּל, וּמֵכִין

One from Whose goods you have eaten!' "

"These are words of Torah fit for a rebbe," said the Chidushei HaRim.
"But I wonder that men do not become God fearing from the very eating
itself. For the verse bears witness: 'The ox knows its owner and the donkey
the manger of its master' (Yeshayahu 1:3)" (Siach Sarfei Kodesh V 9).

הוּא נֹתֵן לֶחֶם / He gives nourishment

R' Mordechai of Neschiz   R' Mordechai of Neschiz once asked his
chasid, R' Velvel, "Where do you take the bread
from?"

"From the shelf upon which it lies," he said.

"And who puts it there?" asked the Rebbe.

"My wife, after she has baked it."

"You have answered foolishly," said the Rebbe. "For had you mentioned
Him Who truly gives bread — nourishment, you would have been blessed
with wealth and a liberal livelihood" (Zikaron Tov, Conclusion, no. 8).

R' Zusha of Hanipoli   Each morning, after prayers, R' Zusha of Hanipoli
would say, "Master of the world, Zusha is very
hungry and wishes to eat. Please furnish him with his food." When his
shammash (attendant) would hear this, he would enter and serve him
refreshments, a portion of cake and drink.

One day, the shammash thought to himself, "Why doesn't the Rebbe ask
me to bring him his food? Why does he turn to the Holy One with his
request?" He decided that he would not serve the Rebbe unless he was
asked to do so directly.

That morning, R' Zusha immersed himself in the mikveh before prayers as
was his custom. It was a rainy day and the roads of Hanipoli were muddy. A
path of narrow planks had been placed from one end of the street to the
other to allow passageway. R' Zusha was pacing along the planks on his way
to the beis knesses when, there in front of him, he saw a stranger, a visitor in
town, walking towards him. The stranger saw an elderly, slight Jew hurrying
in his direction. The desire to play a prank seized him and he pushed R'

Blessed are You, HASHEM, our God, King of the universe, Who nourishes the entire world, in His goodness — with grace, with kindness, and with mercy. He gives nourishment to all flesh, for His kindness is eternal.[1] And through His great goodness, we have never lacked, and may we never lack, nourishment, for all eternity. For the sake of His Great Name, because He is God Who nourishes and sustains all, and benefits all, and He prepares

1. *Tehillim* 136:25.

Zusha off the plank and into the mud. R' Zusha fell, dirtying his clothes, picked himself up without a word, and continued on his way. The stranger laughed heartily at the comical sight and could not stop laughing all the way to his lodgings. There, he told the innkeeper of the prank he had played.

When, in answer to his host's question, he had described the man whom he had pushed off the plank, the innkeeper smote his hands and said, "Oh my! What have you done? You shoved the Rebbe, R' Zusha, into the mud." The visitor shook and trembled. R' Zusha was known as a holy man of God. "Woe is me!" he cried out in fear, "What shall I do?"

"Listen to me," said his host. "R' Zusha spends a long time at his prayers and afterwards takes refreshments. Take some good-tasting pastry and quality liquor. Bring them to him as a present and ask his pardon. I'm positive that, righteous and modest as he is, he will forgive you wholeheartedly."

R' Zusha finished his prayers, took off his *tefillin* and said, "Master of the world, Zusha is very hungry and wishes to eat. Please furnish him with his food."

The *shammash* heard him and didn't make a move. "If the Rebbe turns to Hashem, let Hashem bring him refreshments," he thought.

The door suddenly opened and in walked a stranger bearing a tray of pastry and liquor. He entered the Rebbe's room and placed the tray before R' Zusha.

It was now evident to the *shammash* that it was not he who provided the Rebbe with food, but the Holy One (*Sipurei Tzaddikim* 74).

לְכָל בָּשָׂר / To all flesh

R' Yitzchak of Vurka Wagon drivers fall into two categories. There is the wagon driver whom Hashem wishes to sustain and so provides him with a horse and wagon. Then there is the horse that Hashem wishes to sustain and so provides him with a driver.

Both drivers may gain an equal livelihood. But in one instance, the horse

מָזוֹן לְכָל בְּרִיּוֹתָיו אֲשֶׁר בָּרָא. כָּאָמוּר: פּוֹתֵחַ אֶת
יָדֶךָ, וּמַשְׂבִּיעַ לְכָל חַי רָצוֹן. בָּרוּךְ אַתָּה יהוה, הַזָּן
אֶת הַכֹּל.

נוֹדֶה לְךָ יהוה אֱלֹהֵינוּ, עַל שֶׁהִנְחַלְתָּ לַאֲבוֹתֵינוּ
אֶרֶץ חֶמְדָּה טוֹבָה וּרְחָבָה. וְעַל
שֶׁהוֹצֵאתָנוּ יהוה אֱלֹהֵינוּ מֵאֶרֶץ מִצְרַיִם, וּפְדִיתָנוּ
מִבֵּית עֲבָדִים, וְעַל בְּרִיתְךָ שֶׁחָתַמְתָּ בִּבְשָׂרֵנוּ, וְעַל
תּוֹרָתְךָ שֶׁלִּמַּדְתָּנוּ, וְעַל חֻקֶּיךָ שֶׁהוֹדַעְתָּנוּ, וְעַל
חַיִּים חֵן וָחֶסֶד שֶׁחוֹנַנְתָּנוּ, וְעַל אֲכִילַת מָזוֹן
שָׁאַתָּה זָן וּמְפַרְנֵס אוֹתָנוּ תָּמִיד, בְּכָל יוֹם וּבְכָל עֵת
וּבְכָל שָׁעָה.

וְעַל הַכֹּל יהוה אֱלֹהֵינוּ אֲנַחְנוּ מוֹדִים לָךְ,
וּמְבָרְכִים אוֹתָךְ, יִתְבָּרַךְ שִׁמְךָ בְּפִי

---

works for the driver; in the other, the driver toils his entire life for the horse.

That is what the *midrash means: If man is found to be worthy, he is told, "You were created before the angels." If he is unworthy, he is told, "A fly preceded you, a mosquito preceded you, etc." (*Bereishis Rabbah* 8:1) — you were created so that the mosquitoes may feed on your blood (*Gedulas HaTzaddikim* II 3).

פּוֹתֵחַ אֶת יָדֶךָ, וּמַשְׂבִּיעַ לְכָל חַי רָצוֹן / *You open Your hand, and satisfy the desire of every living thing*

R' Pinchas of Koritz

A young man suffered from a serious illness which got progressively worse. He had been to many *tzaddikim*, but had not been cured. He came to *R' Pinchas of Koritz*, who assured him that he would get better. And so it turned out.

R' Pinchas said, "It is not that I stand on a higher plane than the others. They proceeded in a direct manner, while I made use of a roundabout path.

[* The *midrash* turns on the meaning of the puzzling verse: 'You fashioned me *first* and *last*' (אָחוֹר וָקֶדֶם צַרְתָּנִי — *Tehillim* 139:5). The particular view cited by the Rebbe is that of R' Shimon ben Lakish who takes *first* as referring to man's soul, which is, to him, the "spirit of *Elokim* which hovers above the waters" (*Bereishis* 1:2) and existed prior to the rest of Creation. *Last* refers to man's body which was created at the end of the sixth day of Creation (*Siach Sarfei Kodesh* V 24).]

food for all of His creatures which He has created. As it is said: 'You open Your hand, and satisfy the desire of every living thing.'[1] Blessed are You, HASHEM, Who nourishes all.

We thank You, HASHEM, our God, because You have given to our forefathers as a heritage a desirable, good and spacious land; because You removed us, HASHEM, our God, from the land of Egypt and You redeemed us from the house of bondage; for Your covenant which You sealed in our flesh; for Your Torah which You taught us and for Your statutes which You made known to us; for life, grace, and kindness which You granted us; and for the provision of food with which You nourish and sustain us constantly, in every day, in every season, and in every hour.

For all, HASHEM, our God, we thank You and bless You. May Your Name be blessed by the mouth of

1. *Tehillim* 145:16.

At first, like them, I tried to enter through the Gates of Healing and found them locked. I turned and made my way to the Gates of Sustenance (פַּרְנָסָה) and found them open. I prevailed upon Heaven to grant the sick man a livelihood. I then returned to the Gates of Healing and presented a statement of the *gemara*. *Chazal* say that the verse, 'You open Your hand and satisfy the desire of every living thing' (*Tehillim* 145:16) implies that 'when Heaven grants satisfaction (שׂוֹבַע), it does so for the living.' This statement presented a just claim for the sick man which could not be disregarded. The Gates of Healing were opened and he was granted health and life" (*Be'eros HaMayim* 81).

וְעַל הַכֹּל . . . אֲנַחְנוּ מוֹדִים לָךְ
For all . . . we thank You

R' Yaakov Shimshon of Shpitivka

R' Yaakov Shimshon of Shpitivka went up to *Eretz Yisrael* in 5559 (1799). When he saw the extreme poverty of the chasidim there, he set out to gather funds for them, in the far lands of the west. In his journeyings, he reached the home of a wise elder. When the man learned that R' Yaakov Shimshon hailed from Poland, he asked him if he knew *R' Baruch of Mezhibuz*. R'

כָּל חַי תָּמִיד לְעוֹלָם וָעֶד . כַּכָּתוּב, וְאָכַלְתָּ וְשָׂבָעְתָּ,
וּבֵרַכְתָּ אֶת יהוה אֱלֹהֶיךָ, עַל הָאָרֶץ הַטֹּבָה
אֲשֶׁר נָתַן לָךְ.[1] בָּרוּךְ אַתָּה יהוה, עַל הָאָרֶץ וְעַל
הַמָּזוֹן.

רַחֵם יהוה אֱלֹהֵינוּ עַל יִשְׂרָאֵל עַמֶּךָ, וְעַל
יְרוּשָׁלַיִם עִירֶךָ, וְעַל צִיּוֹן מִשְׁכַּן כְּבוֹדֶךָ,
וְעַל מַלְכוּת בֵּית דָּוִד מְשִׁיחֶךָ, וְעַל הַבַּיִת הַגָּדוֹל
וְהַקָּדוֹשׁ שֶׁנִּקְרָא שִׁמְךָ עָלָיו. אֱלֹהֵינוּ אָבִינוּ רְעֵנוּ
זוּנֵנוּ פַּרְנְסֵנוּ וְכַלְכְּלֵנוּ וְהַרְוִיחֵנוּ, וְהַרְוַח לָנוּ יהוה
אֱלֹהֵינוּ מְהֵרָה מִכָּל צָרוֹתֵינוּ. וְנָא אַל תַּצְרִיכֵנוּ
יהוה אֱלֹהֵינוּ, לֹא לִידֵי מַתְּנַת בָּשָׂר וָדָם, וְלֹא לִידֵי

Yaakov Shimshon realized that the wise elder was a holy man who was
aware of R' Baruch through Divine intuition (רוּחַ הַקֹּדֶשׁ). He answered that he
did, indeed, know him and he was his submissive servant. His host asked
that he repeat something of R' Baruch's Torah. Although he had never in all
his days forgotten anything that his Rebbe had said, he now forgot all that he
had ever heard. He felt terrible and the elderly *rav* wept that he had not had
the good fortune to hear Torah of truth.

Finally, R' Yaakov Shimshon said, ''I have remembered a small grain of my
Rebbe's teachings.

''The Men of the Great Synod (אַנְשֵׁי כְּנֶסֶת הַגְּדוֹלָה) put 'We thank You
Hashem' (נוֹדֶה לָךְ) into the *Bircas HaMazon* . We say that we thank Him for
giving us the Holy Land, for taking us out of Egypt, for the covenant of
circumcision, for the Torah etc., and we end with* 'and above everything,
Hashem our God we thank You etc.' (וְעַל הַכֹּל). We say, in effect, 'above
everything else we must thank You for being Hashem, our God — that we
are fortunate enough to approach Your faith.' ''

When the *rav* heard this he exclaimed in wonder, ''Is this a 'small grain'?
It is a profound thought.'' And he proceeded to expand on the topic through
the hidden paths of the Torah for three days, until R' Yaakov Shimshon's
mind could no longer embrace his words (*Mekor Baruch* 12).

[**And above everything* (וְעַל הַכֹּל). R' Baruch treated עַל not in the sense of *for*, or *on account
of*, but in the sense of *above*. He saw ה' אֱלֹקֵינוּ not as a form of address — we thank You,
Hashem, our God — parallel to *You* (לָךְ), but as part of a phrase modifying *thank* (מוֹדִים) — we
thank You for being Hashem.]

all the living, continuously for all eternity. As it is written: 'And you shall eat and you shall be satisfied and you shall bless HASHEM, your God, for the good land which He gave you.'[1] Blessed are You, HASHEM, for the land and for the nourishment.

Have mercy HASHEM, our God, on Israel Your people; on Jerusalem, Your city, on Zion, the resting place of Your Glory; on the monarchy of the house of David, Your anointed; and on the great and holy House upon which Your Name is called. Our God, our Father — tend us, nourish us, sustain us, support us, relieve us; HASHEM, our God, grant us speedy relief from all our troubles. Please, make us not needful — HASHEM, our God — of the gift of human hands nor of their

---

1. *Devarim* 8:10.

כַּכָּתוּב . . . וּבֵרַכְתָּ
As it is written . . . and you shall bless

Maggid of Mezritch   The *Maggid of Mezritch* cautioned his disciples to take greater pains with the thoughtful purpose (כַּוָּנָה) with which they pronounced the after-the-meal blessing, *Bircas HaMazon*, than that with which they approached prayer (תְּפִלָּה). For prayer was ordained by the Rabbis, whereas the after-the-meal blessing is expressly dictated by the Torah *(Toledos Aharon, Shoftim)*.

לֹא לִידֵי מַתְּנַת בָּשָׂר וָדָם
Not . . . of the gift of human hands

R' Yaakov Aryeh of Radzimin   In the days of his want, *R' Yaakov Aryeh of Radzimin* went about in tatters. He grew in Torah and devotion to Hashem without any awareness of his material state. A chasid, R' Yissachar Dov Horvitz, provided him with handsome, befitting clothing.

"What are these for?" asked R' Yaakov Aryeh.

"It is not becoming for you to go about like a pauper," was the answer.

"What!" said the rebbe. "Should I be ashamed of the poverty which is Hashem's gift and adorn myself with the gift which comes from a man of flesh and blood?"

And he did not accept them *(Chasidim MeSaprim* I 296).

הַלְוָאָתָם, כִּי אִם לְיָדְךָ הַמְּלֵאָה הַפְּתוּחָה הַקְּדוֹשָׁה
וְהָרְחָבָה, שֶׁלֹּא נֵבוֹשׁ וְלֹא נִכָּלֵם לְעוֹלָם וָעֶד.

On Shabbos add the following paragraph.

רְצֵה וְהַחֲלִיצֵנוּ יהוה אֱלֹהֵינוּ בְּמִצְוֹתֶיךָ, וּבְמִצְוַת יוֹם
הַשְּׁבִיעִי הַשַּׁבָּת הַגָּדוֹל וְהַקָּדוֹשׁ הַזֶּה, כִּי יוֹם זֶה
גָּדוֹל וְקָדוֹשׁ הוּא לְפָנֶיךָ, לִשְׁבָּת בּוֹ וְלָנוּחַ בּוֹ בְּאַהֲבָה
כְּמִצְוַת רְצוֹנֶךָ, וּבִרְצוֹנְךָ הָנִיחַ לָנוּ יהוה אֱלֹהֵינוּ, שֶׁלֹּא
תְהֵא צָרָה וְיָגוֹן וַאֲנָחָה בְּיוֹם מְנוּחָתֵנוּ, וְהַרְאֵנוּ יהוה
אֱלֹהֵינוּ בְּנֶחָמַת צִיּוֹן עִירֶךָ, וּבְבִנְיַן יְרוּשָׁלַיִם עִיר קָדְשֶׁךָ,
כִּי אַתָּה הוּא בַּעַל הַיְשׁוּעוֹת וּבַעַל הַנֶּחָמוֹת.

אֱלֹהֵינוּ וֵאלֹהֵי אֲבוֹתֵינוּ, יַעֲלֶה, וְיָבֹא, וְיַגִּיעַ,
וְיֵרָאֶה, וְיֵרָצֶה, וְיִשָּׁמַע, וְיִפָּקֵד, וְיִזָּכֵר,

וְלֹא לִידֵי הַלְוָאָתָם / Nor of their loans

R' Menachem Mendel of Riminov

A chasid came before R' Menachem Mendel of Riminov and asked that the Rebbe pray that he find favor in the eyes of a particular lord, so that the lord would agree to give him a loan.

"I cannot pray that you receive a loan from a non-Jew," said the Rebbe, "because that is one of the curses contained in the Passage of Rebuke (תּוֹכֵחָה) — 'he (the non-Jew) will lend to you' (Devarim 28:44). I can only pray that you won't need a loan" (Ateres Menachem 32).

וַאֲנָחָה / Or lament (sigh, groan)

R' Yissachar Ber of Radoshitz

In my youth I took upon myself a self-imposed exile. In my wanderings, I came to a hamlet and asked the local Jewish baker to put me up for the night. He made up a bed over the oven. At midnight, when the house was deep in darkness, I heard the baker sigh. The sigh was such as could break a man's entire body.

I felt miserable and depressed. If a simple village baker could sigh thus and pray at midnight over the destruction of the Beis HaMikdash and the self-concealment (הֶסְתֵּר פָּנִים) of the Divine Presence (שְׁכִינָה), how could I hold up my head? What could I say? What could I utter? Of what worth was my self-exile?

And, then, I heard his wife ask him, "What are you sighing about?"

loans, but only of Your Hand that is full, open, holy, and generous, that we not feel inner shame nor be humiliated for ever and ever.

On Shabbos add the following paragraph.

May it please You, HASHEM, our God — give us rest through Your commandments and through the commandment of the seventh day, this great and holy Shabbos. For this day is great and holy before You to rest on it and be content on it in love, as ordained by Your will. May it be Your will, HASHEM, our God, that there be no distress, grief, or lament on this day of our contentment. And show us, HASHEM, our God, the consolation of Zion, Your city, and the rebuilding of Jerusalem, City of Your holiness, for You are the Master of salvations and Master of consolations.

Our God and God of our forefathers, may there rise, come, reach, be noted, be favored, be heard, be considered, and be remembered —

"How long are you going to cook potatoes? Again and again and again! The time has come for you to make cheese blintzes," he answered (*Niflaos HaSaba Kadisha II* 43).

R' Pinchas of Koritz   *R' Pinchas of Koritz* was a seeker of truth. For seven years, he toiled to know what truth is; for seven years more, he labored to define falsehood; and for seven additional years he sought to learn how to acquire truth and avoid falsehood.

R' Shem of Kalshitz would immerse himself in the *mikveh* in the dark of each night, before he sat down to learn. He once found his *shammash* (attendant) asleep and, refraining from arousing him, went to the *mikveh* alone.

Caught up in his thoughts, he fell into a pit and broke a rib. When he was found there in the morning, he was carried home where he was abed, in pain, for many days. But, during that entire span of time, he did not emit a single groan. He was asked how he could contain himself.

He answered, "I thought of what R' Pinchas of Koritz has said, 'If a man groans more than his pain requires, that, too, reflects a tinge of falsehood' " (*Beis Rabbi* and Introduction to *Ohel Shem*).

אֱלֹהֵינוּ וֵאלֹהֵי אֲבוֹתֵינוּ / **Our God and God of our forefathers**

R' Shmuel Eliyahu of Z'volim   A son of a rebbe came before *R' Shmuel Eliyahu of Z'volim*. The Rebbe asked him,

זִכְרוֹנֵנוּ וּפִקְדוֹנֵנוּ, וְזִכְרוֹן אֲבוֹתֵינוּ, וְזִכְרוֹן מָשִׁיחַ בֶּן
דָּוִד עַבְדֶּךָ, וְזִכְרוֹן יְרוּשָׁלַיִם עִיר קָדְשֶׁךָ, וְזִכְרוֹן כָּל
עַמְּךָ בֵּית יִשְׂרָאֵל לְפָנֶיךָ, לִפְלֵיטָה לְטוֹבָה לְחֵן
וּלְחֶסֶד וּלְרַחֲמִים, לְחַיִּים (טוֹבִים) וּלְשָׁלוֹם בְּיוֹם
חַג הַמַּצוֹת הַזֶּה. זָכְרֵנוּ יהוה אֱלֹהֵינוּ בּוֹ לְטוֹבָה,
וּפָקְדֵנוּ בוֹ לִבְרָכָה, וְהוֹשִׁיעֵנוּ בוֹ לְחַיִּים טוֹבִים.
וּבִדְבַר יְשׁוּעָה וְרַחֲמִים, חוּס וְחָנֵּנוּ וְרַחֵם עָלֵינוּ
וְהוֹשִׁיעֵנוּ, כִּי אֵלֶיךָ עֵינֵינוּ, כִּי אֵל חַנּוּן וְרַחוּם
אָתָּה.[1]

"Who are you?"   "I am the son of Rebbe so-and-so," he said.

"But who are *you*?" said the Rebbe. "We say, 'Our God and God of our forefathers.' One's personal attributes are to be considered before family lineage."

R' Yisrael of Ruzhin   A noble had a faithful dog who accompanied him on all his hunting trips and kept steadfast watch over his home. Years passed; the dog grew old and could no longer perform his duty. The noble was reluctant to have him killed and thought of a solution to his problem. He had the dog wrapped in the hides of a leopard, a lion, a bear, and a wolf and had him sent into the forest.

Just then, the lion was holding forth to the other beasts and saw that, one by one, his audience was dwindling away before him. "What's happening today?" he asked the fox.

"A new king of the beasts has come to the forest," said the fox, "a combination lion, leopard, bear, and wolf."

Fear came over the lion and he said to the fox, "Go see what this king is like and return to tell me."

The fox went, bowed down before the new king and asked humbly, "Who are you, sir?"

"My great-great-grandfather was a lion," he answered proudly.

The fox bowed again and asked, "Who are you, sir?"

"My great-grandfather was a leopard."

"But who are you, sir?"

"My grandfather was a bear."

"And who are you, sir?"

"My father was a wolf."

"And who are you, sir?"

"I? I am a dog."

the remembrance and consideration of ourselves;
the remembrance of our forefathers; the remembrance of Messiah, son of David, Your servant; the
remembrance of Jerusalem, the City of Your Holiness; the remembrance of Your entire people, the
Family of Israel — before You for deliverance, for
goodness, for grace, for kindness, and for compassion, for (good) life, and for peace on this day of the
Festival of Matzos. Remember us on it, HASHEM, our
God, for goodness; consider us on it for blessing;
and help us on it for good life. In the matter of
salvation and compassion, pity, be gracious and
compassionate with us and help us, for our eyes are
turned to You, because You are God, the gracious,
and compassionate.[1]

1. *Nechemiah* 9:31.

The fox bowed mockingly and ran off to tell the lion.

Famed ancestors are like a string of zeros. If any other number stands at
the head of the row, the zeros multiply it and make it all the greater, each
one by ten-fold more than the previous zero. But if a descendant is himself
a zero, the string of zeros which stand beside him are of no use whatsoever
(*Ner Yisrael*).

R' Yechiel Meir of Ostrovtza
R' Yechiel Meir of Ostrovtza was the son
of a simple, but God-fearing, baker.
Through his native genius, his diligence, his holiness and prayers, he rose to
be one of the greatest rebbes of his generation.

He was once in the company of another rebbe who boasted of his
distinguished family tree and of the host of teachings which he had absorbed
in the household of his father.

"And my father," said the Rebbe of Ostrovtza, "was a bagel baker. I
learned one thing from him. A fresh bagel is better than an old one" (*Sichos
HaTzaddikim*).

Fiery Angel of Kotzk
When the *Fiery Angel of Kotzk* returned from his
first trip to Lublin (to the *Chozeh of Lublin*) his
father, who was an opponent (*misnaged*) of chasidus, asked him, "Is it
proper to leave the customs of one's fathers and follow new paths?"

To which his son answered, "First the verse states: 'This is *my* God and I
will declare His praise' and only then do we find: 'the God of *my father* and
I will exalt Him' (*Shemos* 15:2)" (*Sipurei Chasidim*, *Beshalach* 165).

וּבְנֵה יְרוּשָׁלַיִם עִיר הַקֹּדֶשׁ בִּמְהֵרָה בְיָמֵינוּ. בָּרוּךְ אַתָּה יהוה, בּוֹנֵה (בְּרַחֲמָיו) יְרוּשָׁלָיִם. אָמֵן.

בָּרוּךְ אַתָּה יהוה אֱלֹהֵינוּ מֶלֶךְ הָעוֹלָם, הָאֵל אָבִינוּ מַלְכֵּנוּ אַדִּירֵנוּ בּוֹרְאֵנוּ גּוֹאֲלֵנוּ יוֹצְרֵנוּ קְדוֹשֵׁנוּ קְדוֹשׁ יַעֲקֹב, רוֹעֵנוּ רוֹעֵה יִשְׂרָאֵל, הַמֶּלֶךְ הַטּוֹב וְהַמֵּטִיב לַכֹּל, שֶׁבְּכָל יוֹם וָיוֹם הוּא הֵטִיב, הוּא מֵטִיב, הוּא יֵיטִיב לָנוּ. הוּא גְמָלָנוּ הוּא גוֹמְלֵנוּ הוּא יִגְמְלֵנוּ לָעַד, לְחֵן וּלְחֶסֶד וּלְרַחֲמִים וּלְרֶוַח הַצָּלָה וְהַצְלָחָה, בְּרָכָה וִישׁוּעָה נֶחָמָה פַּרְנָסָה וְכַלְכָּלָה וְרַחֲמִים וְחַיִּים וְשָׁלוֹם וְכָל טוֹב, וּמִכָּל טוּב לְעוֹלָם אַל יְחַסְּרֵנוּ.

הָרַחֲמָן הוּא יִמְלֹךְ עָלֵינוּ לְעוֹלָם וָעֶד. הָרַחֲמָן הוּא יִתְבָּרַךְ בַּשָּׁמַיִם וּבָאָרֶץ. הָרַחֲמָן

אָבִינוּ / our Father

R' Shlomo of Zvihl — My father, R' Mordechai, supported his children after their marriage. One day, I decided that there is a Father above and I didn't need the support of my flesh-and-blood father. A day passed, then two days and the larder began to empty. Two more days passed and we had reached the point where we hungered for bread itself. I thought to myself, "Perhaps Heaven has ordained that my sustenance must come by way of my father." I sent my wife to my father and he gave her a full ruble.

At the time, two chasidim were visiting my father. They decided to pay me a visit, also, as I had celebrated my marriage only a short while earlier. One of them had taken a ruble out of his pocket to give to me as a wedding gift. Just as my wife returned with the ruble which she had received from my father, the chasid put his ruble, absentmindedly, back into his pocket.

I had been given a clear sign from Heaven: See, the ruble had already been prepared for you and it returned to where it had come from, to teach you that everything is ordained by Heaven (*Tzaddik Yesod Olam*).

Rebuild Jerusalem, the Holy City, soon in our days.
Blessed are You, HASHEM, Who rebuilds Jerusalem
(in His mercy). Amen.

Blessed are You, HASHEM, our God, King of the
universe, the Almighty, our Father, our King,
our Sovereign, our Creator, our Redeemer, our
Maker, our Holy One, Holy One of Yaakov, our
Shepherd, the Shepherd of Israel, the King Who
is good and Who does good for all. For every
single day He did good, He does good, and He
will do good to us. He was bountiful with us, He
is bountiful with us, and He will forever be bountiful with us — with grace and with kindness and
with mercy, with relief, salvation, success, blessing, help, consolation, sustenance, support, mercy,
life, peace, and all good; and of all good things may
He never deprive us.

The compassionate One! May He reign over us
forever. The compassionate One! May He be
blessed in heaven and on earth. The compassionate

אָבִינוּ מַלְכֵּנוּ / our Father, our King

Beis Aharon of Karlin

The basic task of the evil desire (יֵצֶר הָרָע) is to
make man forget that he is a King's son (*Darchei
Aharon* 24).

הָרַחֲמָן / The compassionate One

R' Tzvi Elimelech of Dinov

The *Maggid of Mezritch* lived in extreme
poverty before he was known to the world.
Once, his wife wept before him, lamenting the hunger of their children and
their lack of clothing in the bitter cold. The Maggid listened and sighed. And
in that instant he heard a voice from heaven telling him that, with that sigh,
he had lost his portion of the World-to-Come. He stood up trembling. For,
in a single moment, he had been thrust out of both worlds. He did not enjoy
this world of the here and now, for he and his family were pressed by hunger
and want. And now, he had lost access to the World-to-Come. But, in a brief
moment, he came to himself and said, "On the contrary! Now that I have
lost both worlds I can truly serve Hashem. It will now be devotion for its
own sake, solely to please my Creator." And he continued to learn with joy.

הוּא יִשְׁתַּבַּח לְדוֹר דּוֹרִים, וְיִתְפָּאַר בָּנוּ לָעַד
וּלְנֵצַח נְצָחִים, וְיִתְהַדַּר בָּנוּ לָעַד וּלְעוֹלְמֵי
עוֹלָמִים. הָרַחֲמָן הוּא יְפַרְנְסֵנוּ בְּכָבוֹד. הָרַחֲמָן הוּא

Thereupon, he was informed by Heaven that, because of his attitude, his portion in the World-to-Come was being returned to him, but with a condition attached: From that day on, he was not to sigh in compassion over his children's state, for he was not more compassionate than the Holy One (*Agra D' Firka* 22).

הָרַחֲמָן הוּא יְפַרְנְסֵנוּ / The compassionate One! May He sustain us

Chidushei HaRim   The world is topsy-turvy. A man's sustenance (*parnasah*) is in the hands of the Creator. Yet everyone pursues it and makes grand plans to obtain it. And on the other hand, it is in *man's* power to devote himself to God. Do not *Chazal* say that everything is in the hands of heaven except the fear of heaven? And on this issue, man relies on his Creator. Man expects *Him* to plant the love and fear of Hashem in his heart (*Siach Sarfei Kodesh* I 481).

R' Mordechai of Tchernobil   A number of chasidim who had spent *Shabbos* in the presence of *R' Mordechai of Tchernobil* were on their way home. They reviewed the Torah which they had heard from the Rebbe; the words gave them joy and were sweeter than honey. And they agreed among themselves that they had never experienced such a *Shabbos* in their lives.

Among them sat a frightfully ignorant innkeeper who also had a comment and said, "I never had a visit to the Rebbe like this one."

The others were astonished and asked, "What did you find special about the *Shabbos*?"

The innkeeper replied, "When I went to say my farewell to the Rebbe and receive his blessing, he asked me about my daily program. I told him that I rise early and go to the village to buy produce from the peasants. When I've finished my dealings, I return home, say the morning blessings (בִּרְכוֹת הַשַּׁחַר), and pray. The Rebbe said, 'It is not good that you put off your *tefillah* (prayers) until after you've taken care of your business affairs.' I told the Rebbe that the peasant farmers get up early to go out to their fields and if I would pray first, I would not find anyone left from whom to buy my produce."

" 'Let me tell you a story,' said the Rebbe:

A young man, when he was first married, stayed with, and was supported by, his father-in-law. His family grew and the time came for him to engage in trade. He left his family and went off to build up capital. Hiring himself out as a school teacher in the village, he saved penny after penny and, in three

One! May He be praised throughout all generations, may He be glorified through us forever to the ultimate ends, and be honored through us forever and for all eternity. The compassionate One! May He sustain us in honor. The compassionate One! May He

---

years, he amassed funds which were sufficient to enter the world of business. It was time to return home.

On a Friday afternoon, he arrived in a village not far from his town. But, he was too distant to reach home before *Shabbos* and he had to take quarters in a local inn.

What was he to do with his money? It was a handsome sum, twelve bags of gold coins and, among the gold, a single copper coin. He couldn't carry it about on his person; that was not allowed on *Shabbos;* money was *muktzeh*. If he left it in his bags, it might be stolen. Should he leave it with the innkeeper? Perhaps the man was dishonest and wouldn't give it back.

Shabbos grew closer and closer. There wasn't much time left. And the young man was God fearing and had no wish to desecrate the *Shabbos*. He finally gave the money to the innkeeper for safekeeping. But, throughout the *Shabbos*, his heart beat wildly and fear was a constant companion.

Shabbos departed, the innkeeper made *havdalah*, went to his chest and handed the twelve bags of gold coins to his guest. A heavy weight fell away from the young man's chest. He counted the bags. There were really twelve, not one missing! He then opened them up and poked about in their contents.

"What are you looking for?" asked the innkeeper.

"I had a small copper coin among the gold ones in one of the bags. I want to see if that's come back, too," said the young man.

" 'What a foolish young man he was,' said the Rebbe. 'Although all his bags of gold had been returned, he thought that the innkeeper might have stolen his piddling copper coin. And you, you act in a like manner. Each night you place your soul, your most valuable possession, in the Holy One's hand, and lie down to sleep like a corpse. You arise on the morrow and see that the Holy One has kept faith and returned your bag of gold, your soul. How then, can you doubt that He will assure you your livelihood, even if you turn to your affairs only after *tefillah*?' Thus the Rebbe spoke to me and invigorated me with his words."

"Indeed," said the other chasidim, "your profit from the *Shabbos* is greater than ours" (*Admorei Tchernobil* 205).

יְפַרְנְסֵנוּ בְּכָבוֹד / Sustain us in honor

R' Nachum of Tchernobil

R' *Nachum of Tchernobil* gave whatever he had to charity and lived in poverty. In contrast, his son R' *Mordechai of Tchernobil* lived in grand, royal style. When R'

יִשְׁבּוֹר עֻלֵּנוּ מֵעַל צַוָּארֵנוּ, וְהוּא יוֹלִיכֵנוּ קוֹמְמִיּוּת
לְאַרְצֵנוּ. הָרַחֲמָן הוּא יִשְׁלַח לָנוּ בְּרָכָה מְרֻבָּה
בַּבַּיִת הַזֶּה, וְעַל שֻׁלְחָן זֶה שֶׁאָכַלְנוּ עָלָיו. הָרַחֲמָן
הוּא יִשְׁלַח לָנוּ אֶת אֵלִיָּהוּ הַנָּבִיא זָכוּר לַטּוֹב,
וִיבַשֶּׂר לָנוּ בְּשׂוֹרוֹת טוֹבוֹת יְשׁוּעוֹת וְנֶחָמוֹת.
הָרַחֲמָן הוּא יְבָרֵךְ

Guests recite the following.
Children at their parents' table add words in parentheses.

אֶת (אָבִי מוֹרִי)בַּעַל הַבַּיִת הַזֶּה,
וְאֶת (אִמִּי מוֹרָתִי)בַּעֲלַת הַבַּיִת הַזֶּה,

Nachum heard of his son's way of life he questioned him about it.

"*Chazal* tell us," said R' Mordechai. "that *Rabbeinu HaKodesh* (R' Yehudah HaNasi) was fabulously wealthy. Yet, when he was on death's threshold, he lifted his ten fingers and said that even his little finger had not enjoyed the pleasures of this world. If *Chazal* tell us this, they certainly indicate that his is a possible road to follow in the service of the Creator."

When R' Nachum fell ill, his chasidim wished to have him brought to Kiev, to be seen by a prominent physician. But the trip would be a long and hard one, and R' Nachum was weak and suffering from pain. They sought a carriage that would ease the journey. R' Mordechai, his son, possessed just such a grand, upholstered carriage, but he had kept it out of sight of his father, who lived the simple life. The need of the hour dictated that it be used, however. The carriage was brought around, and R' Nachum was told that it had been hired from one of the gentry. R' Nachum entered it, sat down and commented, "This doesn't belong to one of the gentry. You are hiding the truth from me." They were forced to admit that it belonged to his son. "I immediately felt that it was the carriage of a *tzaddik*. Now, I see that a man can lead a holy life amid wealth and plenty" (*Admorei Tchernobil* pp. 76,93).

וְהוּא יוֹלִיכֵנוּ קוֹמְמִיּוּת לְאַרְצֵנוּ
And guide us erect to our Land

Yismach Moshe The *Yismach Moshe* lived in old, shabby, rented quarters. When his chasidim wished to buy a large, spacious home for him, he did not agree. For *Mashiach* would soon come, he said, and he had an estate prepared for him in the Holy Land, along with everyone else of Israel. Each evening, as he retired, he would lay out his festival clothes and cane near the bed, so that he need not waste a minute

break the yoke of oppression from our necks and guide us erect to our Land. The compassionate One! May He send us abundant blessing to this house and upon this table at which we have eaten. The compassionate One! May He send us Eliyahu, the Prophet — he is remembered for good — to proclaim to us good tidings, salvations, and consolations. The compassionate One! May He bless

Guests recite the following.
Children at their parents' table add words in parentheses.

(my father, my teacher) the master of this house, and (my mother, my teacher) lady of this house,

---

before greeting the *Mashiach* when he came. And he left orders with his *shammash* (attendant) to awake him, immediately, should the *Mashiach* come, so that he would not be late by even a single moment.

Before he passed away, while he lay in his bed in pain, he said, "Master of the world, You know that I am the least and worst among men. But You also know that I never lie, and now, before my death, I would certainly not lie.

"I say before You, that had I known that I would reach old age before *Mashiach* had come, I would not have been able to bear it; I would have died long ago. But heaven fooled me from day to day.

"I ask you: Isn't it overdoing it to make fun of an old man like me? I beg of You that You allow *Mashiach* to come immediately. It is clear and known to You that I do not make the request for my own good. As for me, I will waive my share and will be the offering of atonement for Israel, so that His great name may be magnified and sanctified (יְתְגַּדֵל וְיִתְקַדַּשׁ שְׁמֵהּ רַבָּא)'' *(MiGedolei HaChasidus* VIII 81-84).

הָרַחֲמָן הוּא יִשְׁלַח לָנוּ אֶת אֵלִיָּהוּ הַנָּבִיא
The compassionate One! May He send us Eliyahu, the Prophet

R' Levi Yitzchak of Berdichev

The prophet informs us: "Behold I will send Eliyahu the Prophet to you, before the coming of the great and awesome day of Hashem" (*Malachi* 3:23). How was it, then, that when R' Yehoshua ben Levi asked the *Mashiach*, "When are you coming, sir?" he answered (in the words of *Tehillim* 95:7), "Today, if you hearken to His voice" (*Sanhedrin* 98a). And, indeed, *why* must Eliyahu come a day before the *Mashiach*?

Mankind is sunken into the comings and goings of the world and preoccupied by its vanities. Eliyahu must come to sever them from their affairs and ready them to receive the *Mashiach*. However, "if you hearken to His voice" and shake yourselves free of the trivialities of the present, of your

Those eating at their own table recite the following,
adding the appropriate parenthesized phrases:

אוֹתִי (וְאֶת אִשְׁתִּי/בַּעְלִי. וְאֶת זַרְעִי)
וְאֶת כָּל אֲשֶׁר לִי.

All guests recite the following:

אוֹתָם וְאֶת בֵּיתָם וְאֶת זַרְעָם
וְאֶת כָּל אֲשֶׁר לָהֶם.

All continue here:

אוֹתָנוּ וְאֶת כָּל אֲשֶׁר לָנוּ, כְּמוֹ שֶׁנִּתְבָּרְכוּ אֲבוֹתֵינוּ
אַבְרָהָם יִצְחָק וְיַעֲקֹב בַּכֹּל מִכֹּל כֹּל, כֵּן יְבָרֵךְ
אוֹתָנוּ כֻּלָּנוּ יַחַד בִּבְרָכָה שְׁלֵמָה, וְנֹאמַר, אָמֵן.

בַּמָּרוֹם יְלַמְּדוּ עֲלֵיהֶם וְעָלֵינוּ זְכוּת, שֶׁתְּהֵא
לְמִשְׁמֶרֶת שָׁלוֹם. וְנִשָּׂא בְרָכָה מֵאֵת
יהוה, וּצְדָקָה מֵאֱלֹהֵי יִשְׁעֵנוּ, וְנִמְצָא חֵן וְשֵׂכֶל
טוֹב בְּעֵינֵי אֱלֹהִים וְאָדָם.[1]

On Shabbos add the following sentence:

הָרַחֲמָן הוּא יַנְחִילֵנוּ יוֹם שֶׁכֻּלוֹ שַׁבָּת וּמְנוּחָה לְחַיֵּי הָעוֹלָמִים.

---

own accord, then the *Mashiach* can come "today" — immediately. There
will be no need for the prior preparation by Eliyahu (*Sifsei Tzaddikim,
Beha'aloscha*).

יוֹם שֶׁכֻּלוֹ שַׁבָּת / *The day which will be completely a Shabbos*

Chidushei HaRim   *Shabbos* is a miniature World-to-Come (*Berachos*
57b). Just as a man cannot enter the World-to-Come
until he departs from this world, so, too, he cannot feel the holiness of
Shabbos unless he separates himself from the weekdays (*Siach Sarfei Kodesh*
III 142).

R' David of Lelov   *R' David of Lelov* would often say that there is no
such person as a bad Jew. If he does exist it is because
there is a non-Jew part within him. Since the *halachah* states that a non-Jew
who observes *Shabbos* deserves the death penalty, a Jew cannot enter into
the *Shabbos* with the non-Jew part of himself. He must banish it before
Shabbos arrives (ibid. I 77).

me (my wife/husband and family)
and all that is mine,

All guests recite the following:

them, their house, their family, and all that is theirs,

All continue here:

ours and all that is ours — just as our forefathers
Avraham, Yitzchak, and Yaakov were blessed in
everything, from everything, with everything. So
may He bless us all together with a perfect blessing.
And let us say: Amen!

On high, may merit be pleaded upon them and
upon us, for a safeguard of peace. May we
receive a blessing from HASHEM and just kindness
from the God of our salvation, and find favor and
good understanding in the eyes of God and man.[1]

On Shabbos add the following sentence:

The compassionate One! May He cause us to inherit
the day which will be completely a Shabbos and rest
day for eternal life.

---

1. *Mishlei* 3:4.

וּמְנוּחָה לְחַיֵּי הָעוֹלָמִים / *And rest day for eternal life*

R' Sar Shalom of Belz   Many, many people come to me, each with his bundle of troubles. Each cries out for deliverance. And each secretly complains, in his heart of hearts, against the Holy One, Who has wronged him. There is nothing new in this, for it is stated: "Man's foolishness twists his path — and his heart is angry with Hashem" (*Mishlei* 19:3). But in the time to come (לְעָתִיד לָבֹא), when the world will function as it should, and the earth will be filled with an awareness of God (דֵּעָה), everyone will see that "whatever heaven does is for the good." They will be convinced that He has directed each generation with kindness, "a God of truth without injustice, just and upright" (*Devarim* 32:4). Then Hashem will have a rest, so to speak, from the complaints of the Children of Israel. That will be *"a day which will be completely a *Shabbos* — and rest day for eternal life"* (*Dover Shalom* 68).

---

* [*A day which will be etc.* : וּמְנוּחָה לְחַיֵּי הָעוֹלָמִים is to be understood in context, as "a rest for eternal life." R' Sar Shalom takes (חַיֵּי הָעוֹלָמִים as a variant of חַי הָעוֹלָמִים, Life of the universe (Hashem) and thus gave the phrase a new interpretation.]

The words in parentheses are added on the two Seder nights in some communities.

הָרַחֲמָן הוּא יַנְחִילֵנוּ יוֹם שֶׁכֻּלּוֹ טוֹב. (יוֹם
שֶׁכֻּלּוֹ אָרוּךְ. יוֹם שֶׁצַּדִּיקִים יוֹשְׁבִים
וְעַטְרוֹתֵיהֶם בְּרָאשֵׁיהֶם וְנֶהֱנִים מִזִּיו הַשְּׁכִינָה וִיהִי
חֶלְקֵנוּ עִמָּהֶם.)

הָרַחֲמָן הוּא יְזַכֵּנוּ לִימוֹת הַמָּשִׁיחַ וּלְחַיֵּי
הָעוֹלָם הַבָּא. מִגְדּוֹל יְשׁוּעוֹת מַלְכּוֹ
וְעֹשֶׂה חֶסֶד לִמְשִׁיחוֹ לְדָוִד וּלְזַרְעוֹ עַד עוֹלָם.[1]
עֹשֶׂה שָׁלוֹם בִּמְרוֹמָיו, הוּא יַעֲשֶׂה שָׁלוֹם עָלֵינוּ
וְעַל כָּל יִשְׂרָאֵל. וְאִמְרוּ, אָמֵן.

יְראוּ אֶת יהוה קְדֹשָׁיו, כִּי אֵין מַחְסוֹר
לִירֵאָיו. כְּפִירִים רָשׁוּ וְרָעֵבוּ, וְדֹרְשֵׁי יהוה

יְזַכֵּנוּ לִימוֹת הַמָּשִׁיחַ
May He make us worthy of the days of Mashiach

R' Tzvi Elimelech of Bluzhov   *R' Tzvi Elimelech of Bluzhov sat in his succah surrounded by his chasidim. "Chazal* tell us," he said, "that the *Mashiach* will not come on a *Shabbos* or Festival (*Eruvin* 43a). How can we understand this? Here, all of Israel awaits him, all are consumed with troubles, pains and terrible tribulations — and the *Mashiach* is to pick and choose times; he will come on this day; he will not come on that day. Wonder of wonders!"

The Rebbe sat, head bowed, caught up in his thoughts. After what seemed an interminable time, he lifted his head and said, "The truth of the matter is that the *Mashiach* is shrewd. Imagine if he were to come now when we sit in company of our sainted guests, Avraham, Yitzchak, Yaakov, Moshe, Aharon, Yosef and David. When do we ever feel ourselves enveloped in such sanctity? We can veritably taste the pleasures of *Gan Eden* itself. If they were to come and tell us that *Mashiach* is here, waiting outside, we wouldn't even go out to greet him. We would choose to remain in our *Gan Eden,* in the company of our sainted guests. The *Mashiach* knows this, and therefore does not come on such days."

His disciple, the *Shomer Emunim,* explained his comments:

The Rebbe wished to give us the sense of purpose of the *mishnah* in *Avos*

The words in parentheses are added on the two Seder nights in some communities.

The compassionate One! May He cause us to inherit that day which is altogether good (that everlasting day, the day when the just will sit with crowns on their heads, enjoying the reflection of God's majesty — and may our portion be with them!).

The compassionate One! May He make us worthy of the days of Mashiach and the life of the World-to-Come. He Who is a tower of salvations to His king and does kindness for His anointed, to David and to his descendants forever.[1] He Who makes peace in His heights, may He make peace upon us and upon all Israel. Now respond: Amen!

Fear HASHEM, you — His holy ones — for there is no deprivation for His reverent ones. Young lions may want and hunger, but those who seek HASHEM

---

1. *II Shmuel* 22:51.

---

in concrete terms. The *mishnah* writes: "One hour of repentance and good deeds in this world outweighs the entire existence in the World-to-Come" (*Avos* 4:17). He wished to teach us that our soul's good and its soundness were not dependent, at all, on the coming of *Mashiach*. We are to "work" on the eve of *Shabbos* to ensure ourselves of "food" on the *Shabbos*; we are to devote ourselves to and serve *Hashem*, if we wish to have a proper reception in the World-to-Come (*Uvda D'Aharon* 85).

וּלְחַיֵּי הָעוֹלָם הַבָּא / And the life of the World-to-Come

Maggid of Kozhnitz   A merchant, a chasid of the sainted *Maggid of Kozhnitz*, was on the road one snowy, stormy night. He was to make his way through Kozhnitz. When he arrived in town, the entire city was deep in sleep. Only the Rebbe's house showed a light; the *Maggid* was up learning. The merchant knocked on the Rebbe's door and entered. The Rebbe did not at first recognize his chasid who was covered with snow from head to toe. When the snow melted and the chasid saw that he had been recognized, he wept before the Rebbe and cried out, "Rebbe, I have nothing of this world of the here and now (עוֹלָם הַזֶּה); I wander here and there, driven by, and completely submerged in, my affairs. I hope that at least I will be found worthy enough to gain the World-to-Come (עוֹלָם הַבָּא)."

לֹא יַחְסְרוּ כָל טוֹב.[1] הוֹדוּ לַיהוה כִּי טוֹב, כִּי לְעוֹלָם חַסְדּוֹ.[2] פּוֹתֵחַ אֶת יָדֶךָ, וּמַשְׂבִּיעַ לְכָל חַי רָצוֹן.[3] בָּרוּךְ הַגֶּבֶר אֲשֶׁר יִבְטַח בַּיהוה, וְהָיָה יהוה מִבְטַחוֹ.[4] נַעַר הָיִיתִי גַּם זָקַנְתִּי, וְלֹא רָאִיתִי צַדִּיק נֶעֱזָב, וְזַרְעוֹ מְבַקֶּשׁ לָחֶם.[5] יהוה עֹז לְעַמּוֹ יִתֵּן, יהוה יְבָרֵךְ אֶת עַמּוֹ בַשָּׁלוֹם.[6]

Upon completion of Bircas HaMazon the blessing over wine is recited and the third cup is drunk while reclining on the left side. It is preferable to drink the entire cup, but at the very least, most of the cup should be drained.

הַרֵינִי מוּכָן וּמְזוּמָּן לְקַיֵּם מִצְוַת כּוֹס שְׁלִישִׁי שֶׁל אַרְבַּע כּוֹסוֹת. לְשֵׁם יִחוּד קֻדְשָׁא בְּרִיךְ הוּא וּשְׁכִינְתֵּיהּ, עַל יְדֵי הַהוּא טָמִיר וְנֶעֱלָם, בְּשֵׁם כָּל יִשְׂרָאֵל. וִיהִי נֹעַם אֲדֹנָי אֱלֹהֵינוּ עָלֵינוּ, וּמַעֲשֵׂה יָדֵינוּ כּוֹנְנָה עָלֵינוּ, וּמַעֲשֵׂה יָדֵינוּ כּוֹנְנֵהוּ:

בָּרוּךְ אַתָּה יהוה אֱלֹהֵינוּ מֶלֶךְ הָעוֹלָם, בּוֹרֵא פְּרִי הַגָּפֶן.

"Monumental fool," said the Rebbe, "if you don't possess this world, which you strive so hard to gain through exhausting toil, how will you ever possess the World-to-Come, for which you do not labor at all?" (*Gedulas HaTzaddikim* 52).

וְדֹרְשֵׁי ה' לֹא יַחְסְרוּ כָל טוֹב
But those who seek Hashem will not lack any good

R' Yitzchak of Nishchiz
There was, in Apta, a great and righteous *rav* who once proclaimed in a speech that he could guarantee that anyone who would occupy himself with learning Torah would be provided with bread and *borscht* without any work or effort. A man who dug and sold clay for a living believed what he had heard, went home, sat himself in a corner by the stove, began saying *Tehillim* and refused to go to work. His wife was unable to persuade him to stop saying *Tehillim* and he did not reveal his reason to her. She thought that he had gone mad.

In order to make ends meet, she sent a man off on her husband's wagon to dig clay in his place, with the understanding that the profits would be divided between the worker and herself.

While digging, the man found a treasure chest of money which he loaded onto the wagon and covered with a matting. Before he could climb aboard, the horse ran off and returned, wagon and all, to his owner's home. Husband and wife rolled back the matting and discovered the treasure. After dividing it with the worker, they were able to live in wealth for the rest of their days (*Emunas HaTzaddikim* 155).

will not lack any good.[1] Give thanks to God for He is good; His kindness endures forever.[2] You open Your hand and satisfy the desire of every living thing.[3] Blessed is the man who trusts in HASHEM, then HASHEM will be his security.[4] I was a youth and also have aged, and I have not seen a righteous man forsaken, with his children begging for bread.[5] HASHEM will give might to His people; HASHEM will bless His people with peace.[6]

Upon completion of Bircas HaMazon the blessing over wine is recited and the third cup is drunk while reclining on the left side. It is preferable to drink the entire cup, but at the very least, most of the cup should be drained.

Behold, I am prepared and ready to fulfill the mitzvah of the third of the Four Cups. For the sake of the unification of the Holy One, Blessed is He, and His presence, through Him Who is hidden and inscrutable — [I pray] in the name of all Israel. May the pleasantness of my Lord, our God, be upon us — may He establish our handiwork for us; our handiwork may He establish.

Blessed are You, HASHEM, our God, King of the universe, Who creates the fruit of the vine.

---

1. *Tehillim* 34:10-11. 2. 136:1. 3. 145:16.
4. *Yirmeyahu* 17:7. 5. *Tehillim* 37:25. 6. 29:11.

R' Simchah Bunim of Pshischa

"Those who seek Hashem will not lack" because "everything is good" (כָּל טוֹב). They know that whatever *Hashem* does to them is only for the good (*Siach Sarfei Kodesh* II 396).

וְלֹא רָאִיתִי צַדִּיק נֶעֱזָב וְזַרְעוֹ מְבַקֶּשׁ לָחֶם
And I have not seen a righteous man forsaken,
with his children begging for bread

R' Yissachar Ber of Volbroz

After *R' Yissachar Ber of Volbroz* passed away, his chasidim wished to drape the mantle of leadership over the shoulders of his son *R' Yaakov Moshe*. But he vigorously refused to accept it, and went off to the industrial city of Lodz to find a livelihood.

While he was there, a man, who was unknown to him, entered his room and said to him, "The *tzaddik*, while alive, is worried about, and takes care of, his children. But when he leaves the world and can no longer help them, he stands before the Heavenly Throne and argues, 'Does the verse not assure us that: "I have not seen a righteous man forsaken, with his children begging bread" (*Tehillim* 37:25)? What will happen to my son?' It stands to reason that his words make an impression, and they turn to him and say, 'How do

The fourth cup is poured. According to most customs, the cup of Eliahu is poured at this point, after which the door is opened in accordance with the verse, 'It is a guarded night.' Then the following paragraph is recited.

שְׁפֹךְ חֲמָתְךָ אֶל הַגּוֹיִם אֲשֶׁר לֹא יְדָעוּךָ וְעַל מַמְלָכוֹת אֲשֶׁר בְּשִׁמְךָ לֹא קָרָאוּ. כִּי אָכַל אֶת יַעֲקֹב וְאֶת נָוֵהוּ הֵשַׁמּוּ.¹ שְׁפָךְ עֲלֵיהֶם זַעְמֶךָ

you wish your children to find sustenance?' To this he answers, 'I wish that their blessing not return unanswered and that their advice to those who turn to them always be effective.' "

The man turned to R' Yaakov Moshe and added, "Those are your provisions for the journey. From this day on, go forth and bless Israel."

R' Yaakov Moshe accepted the mantle of leadership and in later days told those who were close to him, "A rebbe is a man whom Eliahu the Prophet, himself, has placed on the chair of authority" (*Ohel Yissachar* 67).

בּוֹס שֶׁל אֵלִיָּהוּ / The cup of Eliahu

R' Yisrael of Ruzhin
One of the chasidim of *R' Yisrael of Ruzhin* was fabulously wealthy and, each year, he was accustomed to add to and embellish the cup of Eliahu by setting it with more exceptional and precious stones. However, his fortunes slipped and he became poverty stricken, so much so, that as Pesach rapidly approached, he was left without a penny. No one as yet knew of his condition and he did not wish to accept charity, "Perhaps," he said to his wife, "we should sell Eliahu's cup."

"Better that we suffer starvation rather than sell the cup which we fashioned to honor Eliahu, may he be mentioned for the good," replied his wife.

It was the eve of Pesach and the house was empty of food. The man went to the *beis midrash* long hours before the festival evening was to begin and in his absence, an honorable-looking individual arrived at his home. He was a stranger to the place, and he would like to be a guest at their *Seder,* he told the woman. When she said that the house was bare, he told her not to worry and gave her money with which to buy all that was needed with a liberal hand. After the *ma'ariv* prayers, he said, he would come to the house.

After *ma'ariv* the husband remained in the *beis knesses* until all of the congregation had left; he did not wish anyone to sense that his house was bare and unlit. When he did leave and finally approached the house, he was surprised to see light streaming from the windows. He opened the door to a table set to perfection. His wife told him of all that had occurred.

Before the man made *kiddush*, the guest entered and blessed them that they be granted wealth and all that was good; thereupon he immediately disappeared. They understood that this was not an ordinary matter and,

The fourth cup is poured. According to most customs, the cup of Eliahu is poured at this point, after which the door is opened in accordance with the verse, 'It is a guarded night.' Then the following paragraph is recited.

Pour Your wrath upon the nations that do not recognize You and upon the kingdoms that do not invoke Your Name. For they have devoured Yaakov and destroyed His habitation.[1] Pour Your

---

1. *Tehillim* 79:6-7.

---

after the festival, they traveled to the Rebbe of Ruzhin. The Rebbe told him that they had been visited by Eliahu the Prophet. Because they had taken such pains with his cup, they had been judged worthy to see him. And he had appeared twice to the woman, because it had been she who did not agree to sell the cup (*Ginzei Yisrael, L'Nechad HaRav HaKadosh MeRuzhin*).

שְׁפֹךְ חֲמָתְךָ עַל הַגּוֹיִם
Pour Your wrath upon the nations

_____
R' Aharon of Karlin

One year, while reciting the confessional prayer (*vidui*) of Yom Kippur, *R' Aharon the Great of Karlin* omitted two words. Instead of saying, "and the sins which I have committed before You erase in Your great mercy, **but not** through sufferings and evil diseases," he said, ". . . erase in Your great mercy through sufferings and evil diseases." His body immediately broke out in sores and boils and he suffered dreadful pains until Pesach. On the evening of the *Seder* when he reached the passage of "Pour Your wrath upon the nations," he stamped furiously on the floor. Immediately all the sores on his body burst open. The pus which flowed forth seeped through all his clothes and soaked his *kittel*.

The *kittel* was preserved in Stolin for many years (*Sipurei Chasidim, Moadim* 93).

פּוֹתְחִין הַדֶּלֶת / *The door is opened*

_____
R' Tzvi Elimelech of Dinov

R' Pesach, the father of *R' Tzvi Elimelech of Dinov*, once served in a hamlet as the teacher of children for a miserly, tight-fisted man. R' Pesach pitied the poor who were given nothing and sent away in shame from the miser's door. He suggested to his employer that he give charity and take it off his, R' Pesach's, salary. The miser agreed and at the end of the period for which R' Pesach had been hired, when the festival of Pesach was approaching, the employer made a reckoning. Not only did the money given for charity equal the wages, but surpassed them by five gold coins. The miser was unwilling to overlook the five coins which were owed him and since he had no money, R' Pesach left his *Shabbos* clothes with the miser as payment.

R' Pesach had been away from home for the long term of teaching and

וַחֲרוֹן אַפְּךָ יַשִּׂיגֵם.[1] תִּרְדֹּף בְּאַף וְתַשְׁמִידֵם מִתַּחַת שְׁמֵי יהוה.[2]

now, he was left without a penny to show for his efforts. He was embarrassed to return home empty handed, so he made his way to the *beis midrash*. There he met his son, Tzvi Elimelech, who ran home to tell his mother the good news: Father had arrived. R' Pesach's wife prepared a grand homecoming meal and sent her son to call her husband. Against his will, R' Pesach, countenance drooping and soul downcast, dragged his reluctant feet behind the skipping steps of his son.

On the way, a carriage dashed by and its passenger threw a purse towards them. R' Pesach picked it up and ran after the carriage shouting. But the galloping horses went even faster, and the man within paid no attention to R' Pesach's cries.

R' Pesach understood that this was not a chance affair. He opened the purse and found a sum exactly matching his wages, plus five gold coins — the sum that had been given away for charity.

On the evening of the *Seder*, which was celebrated on a grand scale, the youngster, Tzvi Elimelech, was sent to open the door when "Pour Your wrath" (שְׁפֹךְ חֲמָתְךָ) was said. "Look, Father!" he cried out. "It's the man who threw the purse from the carriage" (*Meha R' Tzvi Elimelech M'Dinov* 18).

R' Mordechai of Tchernobil R' Mordechai of Tchernobil supported the secret *tzaddikim* (צַדִּיקִם נִסְתָּרִים) of his generation and would have his chasidim contribute to this cause. The wealthy chasid, R' Chaim Mendel, was outstanding in giving great sums with a willing heart.

Once, however, he said to the Rebbe, "I have given great sums to help the secret *tzaddikim* but I have not had the fortune to know them. I am ready to give whatever sum is asked if only I might be allowed to see one of them."

Before the Rebbe had a chance to reply, R' Chaim Mendel continued, "I have a further request, Rebbe. My only son, Shalom Shachna, is a scholar (*talmid chacham*) and God fearing. Could the Rebbe bless him that he find his true match quickly?"

When the Rebbe questioned him, R' Chaim Mendel said that his son had rejected all the proposals that had been suggested to him. And what pained the father most of all was his son's hint that he would not be averse to marrying the daughter of Baruch Leib, the forest watchman — a pauper, common and unlearned. "Although," said R' Chaim Mendel, "my son is humble and of high moral standing, even humility has its limits. *Chazal* say that a man should even sell all that he has to marry the daughter of a sage. And I am, indeed, ready and willing to spend a fortune to marry my son to the wellborn daughter of a great man."

The Rebbe thought a while and answered, "My son, you have presented

anger upon them and let Your fiery wrath overtake them.[1] Pursue them with wrath and annihilate them from beneath the heavens of HASHEM.[2]

1. *Tehillim* 69:25. 2. *Eichah* 3:66.

two difficult requests. It is not in my power to grant either. The secret *tzaddikim* must be unknown; that is their essence and that is their destiny. As for the matter of a proper match for your son, it is the Holy One who sits in Heaven and joins the partners. The task is as difficult as the parting of the Red Sea. And who am I to intervene in the affair?"

After a few moments of additional thought the Rebbe said, "Listen, Chaim Mendel. I am not permitted to disclose who the secret *tzaddikim* are, but perhaps, you will be fortunate and Eliahu will reveal himself to you. It is no small matter to see Eliahu; not everyone is found worthy to do so. Come to me on the night of the *Seder* and perhaps Eliahu will reveal himself to you when the door is opened after the *Bircas HaMazon*. Perhaps, perhaps, he will appear in the guise of one of the secret *tzaddikim* — and your request will have been honored."

R' Chaim Mendel's heart quickened. He, a simple chasid, would see Eliahu? In preparation for the great event, he prayed with twice the thoughtful purpose (כַּוָּנָה) with which he usually prayed and he learned with twice the diligence (הַתְמָדָה). Before Pesach he doubled his contributions of festival needs to the poor. He was hurt that Baruch Leib, the forest watchman, had sent back the package of provisions which he had given. "A beggar putting on airs," he thought to himself. But he repressed his feelings. He had no time to harbor resentment, not when he was preparing to see the prophet Eliahu!

The evening of the *Seder* arrived. The Maggid of Tchernobil sat reclining at the table, robed in a white *kittel* edged with silver, his eight saintly sons about him. His face was radiant, his eyes shone brilliantly and pearls poured forth from his lips — explanations, interpretations, statements — all bathed in purity.

The meal had been served; they had already said the after-the-meal blessing (בִּרְכַּת הַמָּזוֹן); they were pouring the wine into Eliahu's cup and the *shammash* (attendant) was about to open the door. All eyes turned as the door swung on its hinges. Who knows who saw the prophet? But R' Chaim Mendel *did* see him!

He saw a figure of a man with shining face and smiling lips, in the opening. He was dressed like a peasant in sheepskin coat with a leather belt. He seemed to float towards the table. Suddenly, a thump was heard. Everyone stared in alarm. R' Chaim Mendel had fainted and lay stretched out on the floor. R' Chaim Mendel had seen and recognized the man in whose guise Eliahu had chosen to appear; the guise of Baruch Leib, the forest watchman.

They revived him with difficulty. When he had come to, the Rebbe

הלל

The door is closed and the recitation of the *Haggadah* is continued.

לֹא לָנוּ יהוה לֹא לָנוּ, כִּי לְשִׁמְךָ תֵּן כָּבוֹד, עַל
חַסְדְּךָ עַל אֲמִתֶּךָ. לָמָּה יֹאמְרוּ הַגּוֹיִם,
אַיֵּה נָא אֱלֹהֵיהֶם. וֵאלֹהֵינוּ בַשָּׁמַיִם, כֹּל אֲשֶׁר חָפֵץ
עָשָׂה. עֲצַבֵּיהֶם כֶּסֶף וְזָהָב, מַעֲשֵׂה יְדֵי אָדָם. פֶּה

indicated that he was to keep his silence. The figure of Eliahu had disappeared and the Rebbe, his face aglow, said, "See, R' Chaim Mendel, heaven agreed to grant you both requests. Now you will no longer be ashamed to join families with your neighbor Baruch Leib."

"Yes, indeed," thought R' Chaim Mendel, "my two requests were granted and I gained a favor which I had never had the impertinence to even dream about; I saw Eliahu" (*Beis Karlin-Stolin* 69).

Fiery Angel of Kotzk   On the evening of the *Seder*, before the recitation of 'Pour Your wrath' (שְׁפֹךְ חֲמָתְךָ), the *Fiery Angel of Kotzk* directed one of the participants to open the door. The chasid ran with speed and joy. But when he returned to his seat, his face betrayed his disappointment; he had failed to see Eliahu.

"Fool!" said the Rebbe. "Eliahu doesn't come through the door. He comes through the mind" (*Bircas Chaim* II).

לָמָּה יֹאמְרוּ הַגּוֹיִם / *Why should the nations say*

Zecher Chaim of Vishva-Vizhnitz   Our death stood before our eyes in Auschwitz. We were starved, humiliated and suffering forced labor, amidst blows and curses, till the last of our strength drained away. All of this did not touch my inner soul. But when a German screamed, "Work, work, cursed Jews, forgotten by God," my heart was torn within me, and I remembered the verse (*Tehillim* 42:4): "My tears were my bread, by day and by night, when it was said to me throughout the day, 'Where is your God?' " (*Zecher Chaim, Yalkut HaTeshuvah*, p. 288).

וֵאלֹקֵינוּ בַּשָּׁמַיִם / *Our God is in the heavens*

R' Shmuel Aba of Zichlin   In Lodz there lived a rich Jew, Mordechai by name, who had thrown off the yoke of Torah and *mitzvos*. A member of his family fell ill and, since the doctors could find no cure, he decided to travel to *R' Shmuel Aba of Zichlin* who had become famous as a wonder-worker.

In Zichlin, he waited in line among all the others who had come there and

HALLEL

The door is closed and the recitation of the *Haggadah* is continued.

Not for our sake, HASHEM, not for our sake, but for Your Name's sake give glory, for Your kindness and for Your truth! Why should the nations say, 'Where is their God now?' Our God is in the heavens; whatever He pleases, He does! Their idols are silver and gold, the handiwork of man. They have a mouth,

---

happened to be next to the great Torah scholar R' Shimshon of Lipno. Suddenly, the door to the Rebbe's chamber opened; the Rebbe came out and surveyed the line of the waiting. He approached the wealthy man and examined his expensive fur coat and, in particular, the collar, which was exceptionally handsome.

"Where did you get such a fine coat?" asked the Rebbe.

The man was in shock. Fear had seized him and he was unable to answer.

"How much did you pay for this marvelous collar?" asked the Rebbe.

"Several hundred rubles," answered the man.

The Rebbe now turned to R' Shimshon who was also wearing a coat trimmed with a fur collar. "And what did your coat cost?" he asked.

R' Shimshon mentioned a low sum.

"Why is there such a difference in price?" asked the rebbe.

Mordechai explained that his collar was fashioned from the fur of a rare animal.

"And if all the fur was removed from the two coats, would there still be such a vast difference in their values?" asked the Rebbe.

"No," said the rich man. "Then they would lose whatever worth they have."

"Is that how things are?" said the Rebbe heatedly. "Men strive so hard to attain the fur, the hair of the animal, and without it the value of the coat disappears, yet, you strive so hard to shave off the hair of your beard?" And with that, he returned to his chamber, leaving the rich man stunned.

It was Mordechai's turn to see the Rebbe. He went in and handed the Rebbe his note of request. Even before he read the note, the Rebbe asked him, "Tell me, Mordechai, what's doing in heaven?"

"Rebbe, am I, then, in heaven?" said the man in amazement.

"But you were there!" insisted the Rebbe.

"I don't know what the Rebbe means," he said.

"What are you wondering about? Certainly you were there — in heaven. For had you not been there, how would you know that there is no *gehinnom* in heaven? And I see that you are certain that there is no *gehinnom*, because you are not afraid to sin. You must have been there.

[135]   THE PESACH HAGGADAH

לָהֶם וְלֹא יְדַבֵּרוּ, עֵינַיִם לָהֶם וְלֹא יִרְאוּ. אָזְנַיִם
לָהֶם וְלֹא יִשְׁמָעוּ, אַף לָהֶם וְלֹא יְרִיחוּן. יְדֵיהֶם
וְלֹא יְמִישׁוּן, רַגְלֵיהֶם וְלֹא יְהַלֵּכוּ, לֹא יֶהְגּוּ
בִּגְרוֹנָם. כְּמוֹהֶם יִהְיוּ עֹשֵׂיהֶם, כֹּל אֲשֶׁר בֹּטֵחַ

"Now, I've never been to heaven. But I believe in what *Chazal* tell us — and the paths of heaven were clear to them. They tell us that a *gehinnom* exists and those who violate the commandments of the Torah are punished there. And that is why I am afraid to sin."

The burning words of the Rebbe shook the wealthy man and changed the whole course of his life, and he became a complete *ba'al teshuvah* (ibid. 24).

R' Levi Yitzchak of Berdichev

The father-in-law of *R' Levi Yitzchak of Berdichev* was opposed to chasidus. His son-in-law once traveled to *R' Shmelke of Nikolsburg* and stayed there for several months. Upon his return, his father-in-law said, "I won't reprimand you for joining the sect of chasidim, nor for your leaving home. What happened, happened. But let me just ask you this: Before you went you were already exceptionally learned and devoted to Hashem. What did you learn in your long absence?"

"I learned to know that there is God in heaven," said R' Levi Yitzchak.

His father-in-law smiled, summoned the gentile maid and asked her, "Tell me! Do you know that there is a God in heaven?"

"Certainly!" she said.

"The difference between us," said R' Levi Yitzchak, "is that she *says* she knows, but I *know*!" *(Siach Sarfei Kodesh* V 46).

רַגְלֵיהֶם וְלֹא יְהַלֵּכוּ / *Their feet — they cannot walk*

Divrei Chaim of Sanz

A man came before the *Divrei Chaim of Sanz* and complained of his bitter poverty. The Rebbe advised him to pull up his roots, move to a particular village and open a tavern there. The man took a trip to see the village and found a cluster of huts, isolated and unknown. He returned to the Rebbe with a complaint. "Can a living be had," he asked, "from a few gentiles who are busy in their fields? The village is off the beaten track."

But the Rebbe insisted, "Go there, and you will prosper."

The man borrowed money, bought a cask of whiskey, put his family aboard the wagon and moved to the village. When he arrived, he found a large gathering. The peasants told him, with emotion, that the cross in the church had moved. The report spread rapidly and the village became an

but cannot speak; they have eyes, but cannot see. They have ears, but cannot hear; they have a nose, but cannot smell. Their hands — they cannot feel; their feet — they cannot walk; they cannot utter a sound from their throat. Those who make them should become like them, whoever trusts

---

attraction to throngs of peasants who came on pilgrimage to the church and would drop in for a drink in the local tavern.

The poor Jew prospered and became a man of substance. He married off his children in honorable fashion and managed to save a goodly sum. And since things had gone so well, he traveled to his Rebbe and said, "Rebbe, I'm sick of staying in the village, a Jew in the company of boorish non-Jews. I've saved enough to allow me to move to the city, to pray in a *minyan* and to frequent the court of the Rebbe!"

The Rebbe agreed and the man hired a wagon to move his possessions from the village.

When he arrived in the village, he again encountered a huge gathering of stunned and agitated peasants. He was told that the local priest had suddenly taken ill and had requested that they call the priest from the neighboring village. He had confessed that many years ago, he had been peeved to serve as a priest in such a remote spot. He had moved the cross and spread the report that it had moved of itself, in order to turn the village and its church into a drawing center and thereby have his own star shine more brightly. Now that he was lying in a bed of pain he had revealed what he had done. The peasants who had been duped wished to exact punishment, but the priest forestalled them by dying.

The Jew packed his goods and left. The village once more became an isolated hamlet far off the beaten track (*Divrei Yechezkel Shraga*, pp. 141, 162).

עֵינַיִם לָהֶם וְלֹא יִרְאוּ . . . כְּמוֹהֶם יִהְיוּ עֹשֵׂיהֶם

They have eyes, but cannot see —
Those who make them should become like them

Divrei Chaim of Sanz   At the age of twenty, Yosef Shteckshtil was a delightful young man, diligent in learning, and exceptional in his knowledge of Torah; besides that, healthy and sturdy as an oak. In those days the Austrian regime was exceptionally strict about enforcing its draft laws and there was no prospect that Yosef would be freed from army service. Yosef's father took his tale of trouble and poured it forth to the *Divrei Chaim of Sanz*.

The Rebbe communed with himself and then said, "One folds."

Yosef's father didn't understand the answer, and repeated his story. The Rebbe, for his part, repeated, "One folds."

בָּהֶם. יִשְׂרָאֵל בְּטַח בַּיהוה, עֶזְרָם וּמָגִנָּם הוּא.
בֵּית אַהֲרֹן בִּטְחוּ בַיהוה, עֶזְרָם וּמָגִנָּם הוּא. יִרְאֵי
יהוה בִּטְחוּ בַיהוה, עֶזְרָם וּמָגִנָּם הוּא.

יהוה זְכָרָנוּ יְבָרֵךְ, יְבָרֵךְ אֶת בֵּית יִשְׂרָאֵל,
אֶת בֵּית אַהֲרֹן. יְבָרֵךְ יִרְאֵי יהוה,
הַקְּטַנִּים עִם הַגְּדֹלִים. יֹסֵף יהוה עֲלֵיכֶם, עֲלֵיכֶם
וְעַל בְּנֵיכֶם. בְּרוּכִים אַתֶּם לַיהוה, עֹשֵׂה שָׁמַיִם
וָאָרֶץ. הַשָּׁמַיִם שָׁמַיִם לַיהוה, וְהָאָרֶץ נָתַן לִבְנֵי
אָדָם. לֹא הַמֵּתִים יְהַלְלוּ יָהּ, וְלֹא כָּל יֹרְדֵי
דוּמָה. וַאֲנַחְנוּ נְבָרֵךְ יָהּ, מֵעַתָּה וְעַד עוֹלָם,
הַלְלוּיָהּ.

Yosef's father left, disappointed and depressed. At home he waited daily for the arrival of the induction orders. But days passed, then weeks and months. The authorities seemed to have forgotten about the existence of his son Yosef.

The young man married and had children. When they reached adulthood, he decided to go up to the Holy Land; it had been his long standing dream. He went to the Registration Office to apply for a passport. But, to his surprise, he was told that his name did not appear in the citizen rolls. R' Yosef rushed about from one clerk to another, from one official to another. Finally, they conducted a basic investigation into the matter and discovered that his name did appear in an old register where births were recorded. It had been written on the bottom line of the page; the edge of the sheet had been folded over and the fold had concealed the name. It had never been transferred anew to the draft register. Only then did they understand the Divrei Chaim's comment — "One folds" (*Dos Yiddishe Licht*).

יְבָרֵךְ יִרְאֵי ה', הַקְּטַנִּים עִם הַגְּדוֹלִים
He will bless those who fear Hashem,
the small as well as the great

R' Shlomo Leib of Lenchno   Those who fear *Hashem* will be considered blessed if the great and the small will live *together*, without the great being haughty towards the small (*Eser Ataros* 56).

in them! O Israel, trust in HASHEM; — their help and their shield is He! House of Aaron, trust in HASHEM; their help and their shield is He! You who fear HASHEM, trust in HASHEM; their help and their shield is He!

HASHEM Who has remembered us will bless — He will bless the House of Israel; He will bless the House of Aharon; He will bless those who fear HASHEM, the small as well as the great. May HASHEM increase upon you, upon you and upon your children! You are blessed of HASHEM, maker of heaven and earth. As for the heavens — the heavens are HASHEM'S, but the earth He has given to mankind. Neither the dead can praise God, nor any who descend into silence; but we will bless God from this time and forever. Halleluyah!

הַשָּׁמַיִם שָׁמַיִם לַה' וְהָאָרֶץ נָתַן לִבְנֵי אָדָם
The heavens are Hashem's, but the earth He has given to mankind

R' Chanoch Henoch of Alexander — The heavens are *Hashem's* — they are already heavenly; the earth He has given to mankind — to make it heavenly (*Siach Sarfei Kodesh* I 545).

וְהָאָרֶץ נָתַן לִבְנֵי אָדָם – לְאַחַר בְּרָכָה
But the earth He has given to mankind — after they recite the blessing (Berachos 35a)

R' Yissachar Ber of Volbroz — When *R' Yissachar Ber of Volbroz* dwelt in the shadow of his rebbe, the *Fiery Angel of Moglenitza*, he would fast from *Shabbos* to *Shabbos*. Once, when the Fiery Angel was returning from the *mikveh*, on a Wednesday, he made his way to R' Yissachar Ber's lodgings. The disciple received his master with awe and wished to serve him a cup of coffee.

"How can you serve someone with food that does not belong to you?" asked his master. "*Chazal* say that 'the earth and it's fullness is *Hashem's*' (*Tehillim* 24:1) — before man pronounces a blessing over the produce of the earth it is to be viewed as the property of God. But after man pronounces the blessing, it becomes his, for the verse says: 'the earth He has given to mankind' (ibid. 115:16). If *you* first make a blessing and taste of the food it will be yours. Only then can you serve of it to me."

אָהַבְתִּי כִּי יִשְׁמַע יהוה, אֶת קוֹלִי תַּחֲנוּנָי. כִּי הִטָּה אָזְנוֹ לִי, וּבְיָמַי אֶקְרָא. אֲפָפוּנִי חֶבְלֵי מָוֶת, וּמְצָרֵי שְׁאוֹל מְצָאוּנִי, צָרָה וְיָגוֹן אֶמְצָא. וּבְשֵׁם יהוה אֶקְרָא, אָנָּה יהוה מַלְּטָה נַפְשִׁי. חַנּוּן יהוה וְצַדִּיק, וֵאלֹהֵינוּ מְרַחֵם. שֹׁמֵר פְּתָאִים יהוה, דַּלּוֹתִי וְלִי יְהוֹשִׁיעַ. שׁוּבִי נַפְשִׁי לִמְנוּחָיְכִי, כִּי יהוה גָּמַל עָלָיְכִי. כִּי חִלַּצְתָּ נַפְשִׁי מִמָּוֶת, אֶת עֵינִי מִן דִּמְעָה, אֶת רַגְלִי מִדֶּחִי. אֶתְהַלֵּךְ לִפְנֵי יהוה, בְּאַרְצוֹת הַחַיִּים. הֶאֱמַנְתִּי כִּי אֲדַבֵּר, אֲנִי עָנִיתִי מְאֹד. אֲנִי אָמַרְתִּי בְחָפְזִי, כָּל הָאָדָם כֹּזֵב.

מָה אָשִׁיב לַיהוה, כָּל תַּגְמוּלוֹהִי עָלָי. כּוֹס יְשׁוּעוֹת אֶשָּׂא, וּבְשֵׁם יהוה אֶקְרָא.

R' Yissachar Ber said nothing in return, but made the blessing immediately and tasted the drink.

When the Rebbe left he said with astonishment to his *shammash* (attendant), "That is a true disciple. Today is Wednesday. He had but two more days to go to complete a fast from *Shabbos* to *Shabbos* which the devotional literature praises highly. Yet, he broke his fast without a word in order to serve me, because he considers me to be his Rebbe!" (*Ohel Yissachar* 23).

לֹא הַמֵּתִים יְהַלְלוּ יָ-הּ / Neither the dead can praise God

Sainted Yehudi   The *Sainted Yehudi* once felt, during a meal, that he was enjoying the food. He prayed to be afflicted with epilepsy and fell down in a convulsion. The family summoned his disciple, *R' Simchah Bunim of Pshische,* and he directed that they sing "neither the dead can praise God." They sang and the Sainted Yehudi arose, sat down to the table and finished the meal.

R' Simchah Bunim said that it was time for the *ma'ariv* prayer, to which the Rebbe replied, "When I rolled about on the ground, I had a victory over my great adversary, my body. And I decided to pray *ma'ariv*, then and there, because there was nothing to stop me in my service to Hashem. I felt very pleased with the yoke of heaven and wished to cling to the Creator and not rise again. But when I heard them singing 'neither the dead can praise God,' I decided to rise and continue to live" (*Or HaNer* p. 12).

I love Him, for HASHEM hears my voice, my supplications. As He has inclined His ear to me, so in my days shall I call. The pains of death encircled me; the confines of the grave have found me; trouble and sorrow I would find. Then I would invoke the Name of HASHEM: 'Please HASHEM, save my soul.' Gracious is HASHEM and righteous, our God is merciful. HASHEM protects the simple; I was brought low, but He saved me. Return, my soul, to your rest; for HASHEM has been kind to you. For You have delivered my soul from death, my eyes from tears, my feet from stumbling. I shall walk before HASHEM in the lands of the living. I have kept faith although I say: 'I suffer exceedingly.' I said in my haste: 'All mankind is deceitful.'

How can I repay HASHEM for all His kindness to me? I will raise the cup of salvations and the Name of

---

צָרָה וְיָגוֹן אֶמְצָא. וּבְשֵׁם ה' אֶקְרָא, אָנָּה ה' מַלְּטָה נַפְשִׁי /
*Trouble and sorrow I would find. Then I would invoke
the Name of Hashem: 'Please Hashem, save my soul'*

R' Dovid of Lelov   There are those who imagine that when they are in trouble — "trouble and sorrow I would find" — then it is the time to "invoke the name of Hashem." But when the Holy One aids them and they lack nothing, they have nothing for which to pray. David *HaMelech* begs: "Please *Hashem*, save my soul" — save me from the improper idea that only troubles can effect prayer (*Tiferes Beis David* 104).

R' Yitzchak of Bohush   The *mishnah* declares that man should bless the Holy One in the same spirit both for the good which he receives and the bad (*Berachos* 9:5). The *gemara* (*Berachos* 60b) suggests that this is derived from two passages in *Tehillim* which use the identical phrase to express praise of God: "I will raise the cup of salvations *and the name of Hashem I will invoke*" (116:13), which refers to the good which man experiences; "trouble and sorrow I would find. *Then I would invoke the name of Hashem*" (ibid. 3,4), which speaks of the bad.

However, the praise in the instance of the good appears in the same verse as the reference to the good, whereas reference to trouble, the bad, is found in one verse and the praise in the following verse. There is a break in the flow.

נְדָרַי לַיהוה אֲשַׁלֵּם, נֶגְדָה נָּא לְכָל עַמּוֹ. יָקָר בְּעֵינֵי יהוה, הַמָּוְתָה לַחֲסִידָיו. אָנָּה יהוה כִּי אֲנִי עַבְדֶּךָ, אֲנִי עַבְדְּךָ, בֶּן אֲמָתֶךָ, פִּתַּחְתָּ לְמוֹסֵרָי. לְךָ אֶזְבַּח זֶבַח תּוֹדָה, וּבְשֵׁם יהוה אֶקְרָא. נְדָרַי לַיהוה אֲשַׁלֵּם, נֶגְדָה נָּא לְכָל עַמּוֹ. בְּחַצְרוֹת בֵּית יהוה, בְּתוֹכֵכִי יְרוּשָׁלָיִם הַלְלוּיָהּ.

הַלְלוּ אֶת יהוה, כָּל גּוֹיִם, שַׁבְּחוּהוּ כָּל הָאֻמִּים. כִּי גָבַר עָלֵינוּ חַסְדּוֹ, וֶאֱמֶת יהוה לְעוֹלָם, הַלְלוּיָהּ.

הוֹדוּ לַיהוה כִּי טוֹב,   כִּי לְעוֹלָם חַסְדּוֹ.
יֹאמַר נָא יִשְׂרָאֵל,   כִּי לְעוֹלָם חַסְדּוֹ.
יֹאמְרוּ נָא בֵית אַהֲרֹן,   כִּי לְעוֹלָם חַסְדּוֹ.
יֹאמְרוּ נָא יִרְאֵי יהוה,   כִּי לְעוֹלָם חַסְדּוֹ.

This both reflects a truism and suggests a directive. One can express praise for the good immediately, in an instant response, but not so with the bad. Then, one must pause and give thought to what good is concealed within it and recognize, thereby, that whatever heaven does is only for the good. Then, and only then, is it possible to express praise (*Ner Yisrael* I 148).

הַלְלוּ אֶת ה', כָּל גּוֹיִם . . . כִּי גָבַר עָלֵינוּ חַסְדּוֹ
Praise Hashem, all nations . . . for His kindness has overwhelmed us

Chozeh of Lublin   The difficulty of the verse is well known: Why should the nations praise Hashem because His kindness overwhelmed *us*?

A non-Jew was an out-and-out anti-Semite in general, and in particular, he had an even more-burning hatred towards a chasid who was exceptional in his service to Hashem. The chasid could be found in the *beis knesses* each day, from before dawn to late at night. The Jew-hater dug a deep pit on the road where the chasid regularly walked early in the morning on his way to the *beis knesses*. He was certain that the Jew would not sense the pit in the pre-dawn dark.

The Holy One, however, arranged that the chasid receive a distinguished guest that night and the two were up to a late hour "speaking in learning."

HASHEM I will invoke. My vows to HASHEM I will pay, in the presence, now, of His entire people. Difficult in the eyes of HASHEM is the death of His devout ones. Please, HASHEM — for I am Your servant, I am Your servant, son of Your handmaid — You have released my bonds. To You I will sacrifice thanksgiving offerings, and the name of HASHEM I will invoke. My vows to HASHEM I will pay, in the presence, now, of His entire people. In the courtyards of the House of HASHEM, in your midst, O Jerusalem, Halleluyah!

Praise HASHEM, all nations; praise Him, all the states! For His kindness has overwhelmed us, and the truth of HASHEM is eternal, Halleluyah!

Give thanks to HASHEM for He is good;
His kindness endures forever!
Let Israel say: His kindness endures forever!
Let the House of Aharon say:
His kindness endures forever!
Let those who fear HASHEM say:
His kindness endures forever!

Thus, the chasid awoke later than usual — after the light of day. On his way to the *beis knesses*, he saw the pit and avoided it. The non-Jew noticed him and asked him why he had gotten up later that day. The chasid told him about his guest. And then, the gentile praised the Holy One Who had saved the chasid, without his knowledge, from death.

That is the meaning of the verse. Only the gentiles know what evils they contrive for us and how the Holy One foils their plans. We, on our part, exemplify that which *Chazal* say: "He who experiences a miracle is unaware of it" (*Nifleos HaRabi* 366).

יֹאמְרוּ נָא יִרְאֵי ה' / *Let those who fear Hashem say . . .*

Maggid of Tchernobil   They were trying times for Israel. The draft laws weighed heavily on the Jews of Russia. The soldiers of the czar would swoop down and snatch youngsters from their mother's lap. The *tzaddikim* of the time assembled in alarm and traveled to the eldest among them, to R' Mordechai, the Maggid of Tchernobil.

Some forty had gathered together and were in Tchernobil for *Shabbos*. And just as the Rebbe came to the table and was about to recite the *kiddush*,

מִן הַמֵּצַר קָרָאתִי יָּה, עָנָנִי בַמֶּרְחָב יָּה. יהוה לִי לֹא אִירָא, מַה יַּעֲשֶׂה לִי אָדָם. יהוה לִי בְּעֹזְרָי, וַאֲנִי אֶרְאֶה בְשֹׂנְאָי. טוֹב לַחֲסוֹת בַּיהוה, מִבְּטֹחַ בָּאָדָם. טוֹב לַחֲסוֹת בַּיהוה, מִבְּטֹחַ בִּנְדִיבִים. כָּל גּוֹיִם סְבָבוּנִי, בְּשֵׁם יהוה כִּי אֲמִילַם. סַבּוּנִי גַם סְבָבוּנִי, בְּשֵׁם יהוה כִּי אֲמִילַם.

a woman burst into the room and cried out in a broken voice, "Help me, Rebbe! They have taken away my only son, the apple of my eye!" All present wept, but the Rebbe, who was caught up in his devotions, moved not a whit.

The others gave a sign to *R' Moshe of Slavito*, the son of *R' Pinchas of Koritz*, to act as their spokesman. He called out in a tearful tone, "Sainted Maggid, where is Hashem's kindness (חַסְדֵי ה')?"

The Rebbe answered not a word. He made *kiddush*, broke bread and ate the required measure (כְּזַיִת). And, as all kept their silence, he began. "In *Hallel* we find," he said, " 'Let Israel say, His kindness endures forever. Let the House of Aharon say . . . Let those who fear Hashem say.' We have three categories here: There are clear acts of kindness for which all of Israel can give praise to Hashem and say, 'His kindness endures forever.' There are hidden acts of kindness which the masses of Israel see as harsh decrees. We pray that at least the 'House of Aharon,' those of the generation who are devoted to Hashem, might fathom their true meaning and see the kindness of Hashem within them. But there are edicts which are so terrible that even the servants of Hashem, the *tzaddikim*, are confused by them and see them as a sign of dread self-concealment of Hashem from the world (הֶסְתֵּר פָּנִים). Then, we pray that at least 'those who fear Hashem,' the greatest of the *tzaddikim* of the age, should understand and see Hashem's kindness within them.

"What can I do if heaven has revealed to me that even this decree is filled with heavenly kindness from the kiln of the All-present? How can I pray that it be abolished?" (*Admorei Tchernobil* 246).

R' Mordechai Menachem Mendel of Vurka

When the authorities decreed that Jews must shave off their beards, R' Moshe Kohen fled from Warsaw to the court of his rebbe, *R' Mordechai Menachem Mendel of Vurka*. *R' Yisrael of Ruzhin* had just departed this world at the time and the Rebbe remarked to his disciple, "My father and the Rebbe of Ruzhin are rejoicing now."

"Can anyone be happy in this time of trouble?" said R' Moshe, in pain.

"They see, in heaven, that all the decrees are for the good and they feel no suffering because of them," said the Rebbe.

From the straits did I call upon God; God answered me with expansiveness. HASHEM is with me, I have no fear; how can man affect me? HASHEM is with me through my helpers; therefore I can face my foes. It is better to take refuge in HASHEM than to rely on man. It is better to take refuge in HASHEM than to rely on nobles. All the nations surround me; in the Name of HASHEM I cut them down! They encircle me, they also surround me; in the Name of HASHEM I cut them down!

"But wasn't your father aware, while he was alive, that all the decrees are for the good? And yet, we saw that he was always pained by the sufferings of Israel," said the chasid.

To which the Rebbe replied, "Hearing is not seeing" (*Eser Zechuyos* 19).

R' Yitzchak of Skver   When my sainted grandfather, *R' Nachum of Tchernobil*, visited *R' Baruch of Mezhibuz*, R' Baruch asked him, "What do you think of me?"

"I think that you are truly God fearing," said R' Nachum.

Some time later, R' Baruch met *R' Levi Yitzchak of Berdichev*, and R' Baruch asked him, "What do you think of me?"

"I think that you are truly God fearing," answered R' Levi Yitzchak.

R' Baruch was happy. "Now I know that I am God fearing," he said, "because two honest and proper witnesses have said so."

"Is fear of Heaven a small thing?" asks the *gemara*. And it answers, "Yes, to Moshe it is a small matter" (*Berachos* 33b). Wonder of wonders! There are chasidim who have reached the level of our teacher Moshe, and fear of Heaven is a small matter in their eyes. R' Baruch of Mezhibuz was proud that he was said to possess it. Yet these chasidim do not find it proper to praise their rebbes for this quality. They think that it's not enough to consider him a rebbe for only such an inconsequential trait (*Ma'asios U'Ma'amarim Yekarim*).

טוֹב לַחֲסוֹת בַּה' מִבְּטֹחַ בִּנְדִיבִים
It is better to take refuge in Hashem than to rely on nobles

Fiery Angel of Kotzk   A very poor man came before the *Fiery Angel of Kotzk* and told him that he had a grown daughter to marry off, but he could not raise the dowry. The Rebbe gave him a letter for the princely, rich R' Moshe Rotenberg of Chantshin, asking him to help the bearer of the letter to the best of his ability.

The poor man wore out his legs on the journey, until he finally reached Chantshin and the wealthy home of R' Moshe; he was well received.

סַבּוּנִי כִדְבֹרִים דֹּעֲכוּ כְּאֵשׁ קוֹצִים, בְּשֵׁם יְהוָה כִּי אֲמִילַם. דָּחֹה דְחִיתַנִי לִנְפֹּל, וַיהוָה עֲזָרָנִי. עָזִּי וְזִמְרָת יָהּ, וַיְהִי לִי לִישׁוּעָה. קוֹל רִנָּה וִישׁוּעָה, בְּאָהֳלֵי צַדִּיקִים, יְמִין יְהוָה עֹשָׂה חָיִל. יְמִין יְהוָה רוֹמֵמָה, יְמִין יְהוָה עֹשָׂה חָיִל. לֹא אָמוּת כִּי אֶחְיֶה, וַאֲסַפֵּר מַעֲשֵׂי יָהּ. יַסֹּר יִסְּרַנִי יָּהּ, וְלַמָּוֶת לֹא נְתָנָנִי. פִּתְחוּ לִי שַׁעֲרֵי צֶדֶק, אָבֹא בָם אוֹדֶה יָהּ. זֶה הַשַּׁעַר לַיהוָה, צַדִּיקִים יָבֹאוּ בוֹ. אוֹדְךָ כִּי עֲנִיתָנִי, וַתְּהִי לִי לִישׁוּעָה. אוֹדְךָ כִּי עֲנִיתָנִי, וַתְּהִי לִי לִישׁוּעָה. אֶבֶן מָאֲסוּ הַבּוֹנִים, הָיְתָה לְרֹאשׁ פִּנָּה. אֶבֶן מָאֲסוּ הַבּוֹנִים, הָיְתָה לְרֹאשׁ פִּנָּה. מֵאֵת יְהוָה הָיְתָה זֹּאת, הִיא נִפְלָאת בְּעֵינֵינוּ. מֵאֵת יְהוָה הָיְתָה זֹּאת, הִיא נִפְלָאת בְּעֵינֵינוּ. זֶה הַיּוֹם עָשָׂה יְהוָה, נָגִילָה וְנִשְׂמְחָה בוֹ. זֶה הַיּוֹם עָשָׂה יְהוָה, נָגִילָה וְנִשְׂמְחָה בוֹ.

R' Moshe inquired as to his wishes and was given the Rebbe's letter. The poor man knew that the rich R' Moshe gave charity widely and generously. Now, with the letter, he would probably give far and above what was usual for him. To the poor man's surprise, he was given a single, lone ruble! He was highly insulted and complained that his expenses for the trip amounted to more than that, let alone the toil and troubles of the road. And there was the return trip. But nothing he said could move the man; he left dejected.

He began to make his way back with downcast shoulders. And lo! A grand carriage pulled up beside him and R' Moshe's face peered out. The servants descended and unloaded costly dress and many gifts; the philanthropist, in person, handed him a bag of money, sufficient to cover the costs of the wedding.

The poor man could not contain himself. "Since you intended giving so much, why did you cause me all that anguish?" he asked.

"I'll tell you," said R' Moshe. "When you came to me with the Rebbe's letter, I saw that you had forgotten that there is a God in Israel. I wanted you to be aware that it is useless to seek salvation from man; you must trust in Hashem. Now, help has come from Him, and you must give praise only to Him" (*Siach Sarfei Kodesh* IV 32).

They encircle me like bees, but they are extinguished as a fire does thorns; in the Name of HASHEM I cut them down! You pushed me hard that I might fall, but HASHEM assisted me. God is my might and my praise, and He was a salvation for me. The sound of rejoicing and salvation is in the tents of the righteous: 'HASHEM's right hand does valiantly. HASHEM's right hand is raised triumphantly; HASHEM's right hand does valiantly!' I shall not die! But I shall live and relate the deeds of God. God has chastened me exceedingly, but He did not let me die. Open for me the gates of righteousness, I will enter them and thank God. This is the gate of HASHEM; the righteous shall enter through it. I thank You for You have answered me and become my salvation. I thank You for You have answered me and become my salvation. The stone the builders despised has become the cornerstone. The stone the builders despised has become the cornerstone. This emanated from HASHEM; it is wondrous in our eyes. This emanated from HASHEM; it is wondrous in our eyes. This is the day HASHEM has made; let us rejoice and be glad on it. This is the day HASHEM has made; let us rejoice and be glad on it.

לֹא אָמוּת כִּי אֶחְיֶה / *I shall not die, but I shall live*

R' Shlomo Leib of Lenchno — The verse can be understood as follows: "I shall not die *while I live*" — while I am still alive. I will not be like the wicked who are called dead even when still alive (*Eser Ataros* 59).

[*while I live* (כִּי אֶחְיֶה). כִּי can be used as *when*; see *Rosh Hashanah* 3a and *Rashi's* commentary there. R' Shlomo Leib interpreted the כִּי here as *when* or *while*.]

פִּתְחוּ לִי שַׁעֲרֵי צֶדֶק / *Open for me the gates of righteousness*

Chidushei HaRim — "Fortunate is the man who hearkens *to me to keep guard at my doors, day by day; to guard the doorposts of my openings" (*Mishlei* 8:34). Each man must wait expectantly at the door for the moment it opens, so that he might immediately enter, before it closes once more.

---

*to me: wisdom which Chazal interpret as Torah.]

אָנָּא יהוה הוֹשִׁיעָה נָּא.

אָנָּא יהוה הוֹשִׁיעָה נָּא.

אָנָּא יהוה הַצְלִיחָה נָא.

אָנָּא יהוה הַצְלִיחָה נָא.

בָּרוּךְ הַבָּא בְּשֵׁם יהוה, בֵּרַכְנוּכֶם מִבֵּית יהוה. בָּרוּךְ הַבָּא בְּשֵׁם יהוה, בֵּרַכְנוּכֶם מִבֵּית יהוה. אֵל יהוה וַיָּאֶר לָנוּ, אִסְרוּ חַג בַּעֲבֹתִים, עַד קַרְנוֹת הַמִּזְבֵּחַ. אֵל יהוה וַיָּאֶר לָנוּ, אִסְרוּ חַג בַּעֲבֹתִים, עַד קַרְנוֹת הַמִּזְבֵּחַ. אֵלִי אַתָּה וְאוֹדֶךָּ, אֱלֹהַי אֲרוֹמְמֶךָּ. אֵלִי אַתָּה וְאוֹדֶךָּ, אֱלֹהַי אֲרוֹמְמֶךָּ. הוֹדוּ לַיהוה כִּי טוֹב, כִּי לְעוֹלָם חַסְדוֹ. הוֹדוּ לַיהוה כִּי טוֹב, כִּי לְעוֹלָם חַסְדוֹ.

הוֹדוּ לַיהוה כִּי טוֹב   כִּי לְעוֹלָם חַסְדוֹ.

הוֹדוּ לֵאלֹהֵי הָאֱלֹהִים כִּי לְעוֹלָם חַסְדוֹ.

הוֹדוּ לַאֲדֹנֵי הָאֲדֹנִים   כִּי לְעוֹלָם חַסְדוֹ.

לְעֹשֵׂה נִפְלָאוֹת גְּדֹלוֹת לְבַדּוֹ   כִּי לְעוֹלָם חַסְדוֹ.

When the gates of the heart open, one should increase his efforts in serving Hashem. For when those gates lock, it becomes very difficult to enter. That is why we plead: "Open for me the gates of righteousness," and follow it up, immediately, with "I will enter them and thank God" (*Siach Sarfei Kodesh* I 468).

לְעֹשֵׂה נִפְלָאוֹת גְּדֹלוֹת לְבַדּוֹ

To Him Who alone performs great wonders

Ba'al Shem Tov   On his way to *Eretz Yisrael* the *Ba'al Shem Tov* was detained in Constantinople. It was the eve of Pesach and the Ba'al Shem and his daughter were in the strange, foreign city. He went to the *beis midrash* to study; she took her father's shirt to the river for washing. And while scrubbing the shirt, she wept that although all the other Jews would sit down to a *Seder* in their homes that evening, she and her

Please, HASHEM, save now!
Please, HASHEM, save now!
Please, HASHEM, bring success now!
Please, HASHEM, bring success now!

Blessed is he who comes in the Name of HASHEM; we bless you from the House of HASHEM. Blessed is he who comes in the Name of HASHEM; we bless you from the House of HASHEM. HASHEM is God, He illuminated for us; bind the festival offering with cords until the corners of the Altar. HASHEM is God, He illuminated for us; bind the festival offering with cords until the corners of the Altar. You are my God, and I will thank You; my God, I will exalt You. You are my God, and I will thank You; my God, I will exalt You. Give thanks to HASHEM, for He is good; His kindness endures forever. Give thanks to HASHEM, for He is good; His kindness endures forever.

Give thanks to HASHEM for He is good,
      for His kindness endures forever.
Give thanks to the God of the heavenly powers,
      for His kindness endures forever.
Give thanks to the Lord of the lords,
      for His kindness endures forever.
To Him Who alone performs great wonders,
      for His kindness endures forever.

---

father had no place to celebrate the festival. A rich Jew passed by and saw the weeping girl; he asked why she wept and she, in turn, told him about her father's greatness and described their solitude in the great city.

"Don't cry," said the wealthy man. "You and your father are invited to be my guests." The girl led him to the Ba'al Shem and the rich man invited him to his home, gave him a room and honored him greatly.

When it was time for the *minchah* prayer, the host entered the guest room to call the Ba'al Shem. In amazement he saw the great man asleep with tears running from his eyes. Heart pounding, he stood and contemplated the sight. The Ba'al Shem woke suddenly and said with great fervor, "To Him Who alone performs great wonders," and he went off to the *beis knesses*.

When they returned home, the Ba'al Shem conducted the *Seder* with

לְעֹשֵׂה הַשָּׁמַיִם בִּתְבוּנָה   כִּי לְעוֹלָם חַסְדּוֹ.

לְרֹקַע הָאָרֶץ עַל הַמָּיִם   כִּי לְעוֹלָם חַסְדּוֹ.

לְעֹשֵׂה אוֹרִים גְּדֹלִים   כִּי לְעוֹלָם חַסְדּוֹ.

אֶת הַשֶּׁמֶשׁ לְמֶמְשֶׁלֶת בַּיּוֹם   כִּי לְעוֹלָם חַסְדּוֹ.

אֶת הַיָּרֵחַ וְכוֹכָבִים לְמֶמְשְׁלוֹת בַּלָּיְלָה

כִּי לְעוֹלָם חַסְדּוֹ.

לְמַכֵּה מִצְרַיִם בִּבְכוֹרֵיהֶם   כִּי לְעוֹלָם חַסְדּוֹ.

וַיּוֹצֵא יִשְׂרָאֵל מִתּוֹכָם   כִּי לְעוֹלָם חַסְדּוֹ.

---

emotion and sanctity, and when they reached the verse "To Him Who alone performs great wonders," he repeated it, time and again, his face radiant like a torch of fire. When they had finished reciting the *Haggadah*, the Ba'al Shem rose and said, " 'In every generation, they rise against us to annihilate us. But the Holy One, Blessed is He, rescues us from their hand!' Listen and I will tell you of the miracle that Hashem has worked on this night.

"As you know, the sultan, the Turkish ruler, has a Jewish advisor, named Moshe. Moshe has many enemies at court, and one of them accompanied the sultan to the Jewish quarter, that he might use the occasion of the festival to incite the sultan against the Jews. When they saw the sparkling lights and heard the happy voices, the sultan asked what it was all about, and this enemy of the Jews vilified them and their festivals. He said that their customs differed from those of the rest of the populace and they held themselves apart from all others. This led to a denouncement of the sultan's advisor, Moshe, as a traitor who was prepared to make a pact with the sultan's enemies and hand the kingdom over into their hands. And his fellow Jews would be the first to side with those enemies. It would be in the best interests of His Highness, the sultan, he said, to banish the Jews from the realm and hang Moshe, the advisor, that all might hear and fear! The sultan was persuaded; he removed his signet ring and gave it to the enemy of the Jews that he might sign and seal the decree of banishment and the writ of execution of the advisor.

"When I saw this, I wept and pleaded before the Heavenly Throne; my prayers did not return unanswered. The sultan returned to his palace and told his mother, the dowager queen, about what had happened. She burst into tears and said, 'What have you done? Do you wish to bring destruction upon us? Remember the fate of all those who oppressed the Jews — Pharaoh and Haman and Titus! What evil have the Jews ever done to you? What crime have you found among them? They are loyal to the empire; they enrich the country with their trade and fill your coffers with their taxes. And

To Him Who made the heavens with understanding,
for His kindness endures forever.
To Him Who spread out the earth upon the waters,
for His kindness endures forever.
To Him Who made great lights,
for His kindness endures forever.
The sun for the reign of the day,
for His kindness endures forever.
The moon and the stars for the reign of the night,
for His kindness endures forever.
To Him Who smote Egypt through their firstborn,
for His kindness endures forever.
And brought Israel forth from their midst,
for His kindness endures forever.

Moshe was your father's advisor before you. He has served the court loyally and his advice has always proven sound! What have you done, my son?'

"The sultan's face fell and he said, 'Truly, I have acted foolishly. But what can I do now? I gave the Jew-hater my signet ring.'

" 'Summon Moshe,' said his mother. 'His advice will help us this time, also.'

"The sultan summoned Moshe, who, after due consideration, said, 'There is a simple solution. When my enemy comes to present the sealed edict tomorrow, let the palace guards seize him; let him be accused of stealing the ring and be executed immediately, without delay.'

"The sultan and his mother accepted the clever solution. When I saw this, I praised Hashem 'Who alone performs great wonders.' "

The next day, when the Jews assembled for prayer, they learned that the Jew-hater had arrived at the palace before daybreak, the guards found the sultan's ring on his person and he was executed. The sensational news did not surprise Moshe the advisor, nor the wealthy man who had heard about it the previous night, at the close of the *Seder* before the event had even taken place. He told all those present who it was that had been responsible, through his tears, for the miracle. Everyone turned to give praise to the Ba'al Shem. But he said, "Do not praise me. 'Give thanks to Hashem, for He is good — to Him Who alone performs great wonders!' " (*Sipurei Chasidim*).

לְעֹשֵׂה הַשָּׁמַיִם בִּתְבוּנָה / **To Him Who made the heavens**
with understanding

R' Simchah Bunim of Pshischa

Certainly the Holy One made the heavens with understanding. Did anyone ever

בְּיָד חֲזָקָה וּבִזְרוֹעַ נְטוּיָה   כִּי לְעוֹלָם חַסְדּוֹ.
לְגֹזֵר יַם סוּף לִגְזָרִים   כִּי לְעוֹלָם חַסְדּוֹ.
וְהֶעֱבִיר יִשְׂרָאֵל בְּתוֹכוֹ   כִּי לְעוֹלָם חַסְדּוֹ.
וְנִעֵר פַּרְעֹה וְחֵילוֹ בְיַם סוּף   כִּי לְעוֹלָם חַסְדּוֹ.
לְמוֹלִיךְ עַמּוֹ בַּמִּדְבָּר   כִּי לְעוֹלָם חַסְדּוֹ.
לְמַכֵּה מְלָכִים גְּדֹלִים   כִּי לְעוֹלָם חַסְדּוֹ.
וַיַּהֲרֹג מְלָכִים אַדִּירִים   כִּי לְעוֹלָם חַסְדּוֹ.
לְסִיחוֹן מֶלֶךְ הָאֱמֹרִי   כִּי לְעוֹלָם חַסְדּוֹ.
וּלְעוֹג מֶלֶךְ הַבָּשָׁן   כִּי לְעוֹלָם חַסְדּוֹ.
וְנָתַן אַרְצָם לְנַחֲלָה   כִּי לְעוֹלָם חַסְדּוֹ.
נַחֲלָה לְיִשְׂרָאֵל עַבְדּוֹ   כִּי לְעוֹלָם חַסְדּוֹ.
שֶׁבְּשִׁפְלֵנוּ זָכַר לָנוּ   כִּי לְעוֹלָם חַסְדּוֹ.
וַיִּפְרְקֵנוּ מִצָּרֵינוּ   כִּי לְעוֹלָם חַסְדּוֹ.
נֹתֵן לֶחֶם לְכָל בָּשָׂר   כִּי לְעוֹלָם חַסְדּוֹ.
הוֹדוּ לְאֵל הַשָּׁמָיִם   כִּי לְעוֹלָם חַסְדּוֹ.

---

imagine that they were sewn with needles?

The verse is not discussing the *means* by which the heavens were fashioned but their *purpose. Hashem fashioned the heavens for the sake of contemplation, so that by contemplating them, we might understand His greatness, as it is written: "Lift your eyes on high, and see who created these" (Yeshayahu 40:26) (*Siach Sarfei Kodesh* I 221).

נֹתֵן לֶחֶם לְכָל בָּשָׂר
He gives nourishment to all flesh

R' Tzvi Elimelech of Dinov

R' Tzvi Elimelech of Dinov dedicated a particular hour each day to meeting with tradesmen and merchants in his community, one at a time. Each would

---

* *purpose*. The ב can be used to express *purpose*; see *Rashi* to *Bereishis* 1:1.

With strong hand and outstretched arm,
> for His kindness endures forever.

To Him Who divided the Sea of Reeds into parts,
> for His kindness endures forever.

And caused Israel to pass through it,
> for His kindness endures forever.

And threw Pharaoh and his army into the Sea of Reeds,
> for His kindness endures forever.

To Him Who led His people through the wilderness,
> for His kindness endures forever.

To Him Who smote great kings,
> for His kindness endures forever.

And slew mighty kings,
> for His kindness endures forever.

Sichon, king of the Emorites,
> for His kindness endures forever.

And Og, king of Bashan,
> for His kindness endures forever.

And presented their land as a heritage,
> for His kindness endures forever.

A heritage for Israel, His servant,
> for His kindness endures forever.

In our lowliness He remembered us,
> for His kindness endures forever.

And released us from our tormentors,
> for His kindness endures forever.

He gives nourishment to all flesh,
> for His kindness endures forever.

Give thanks to God of the heavens,
> for His kindness endures forever.

---

present a detailed account of his income and expenses for the entire year. He was able to show each one, clear as day, that his expenses outweighed his income. This proved to them that their sustenance was not a natural phenomenon; they thus came face to face with the Divine Presence (*Eser Tzachtzachos* 28).

נִשְׁמַת כָּל חַי תְּבָרֵךְ אֶת שִׁמְךָ יהוה אֱלֹהֵינוּ וְרוּחַ כָּל בָּשָׂר תְּפָאֵר וּתְרוֹמֵם זִכְרְךָ מַלְכֵּנוּ תָּמִיד. מִן הָעוֹלָם וְעַד הָעוֹלָם אַתָּה אֵל וּמִבַּלְעָדֶיךָ אֵין לָנוּ מֶלֶךְ גּוֹאֵל וּמוֹשִׁיעַ פּוֹדֶה וּמַצִּיל וּמְפַרְנֵס וְעוֹנֶה וּמְרַחֵם בְּכָל עֵת צָרָה וְצוּקָה. אֵין לָנוּ מֶלֶךְ עוֹזֵר וְסוֹמֵךְ אֶלָּא אָתָּה. אֱלֹהֵי הָרִאשׁוֹנִים וְהָאַחֲרוֹנִים אֱלוֹהַּ כָּל בְּרִיּוֹת אֲדוֹן כָּל תּוֹלָדוֹת הַמְהֻלָּל בְּרֹב הַתִּשְׁבָּחוֹת הַמְנַהֵג עוֹלָמוֹ בְּחֶסֶד

נִשְׁמַת כָּל חַי תְּבָרֵךְ אֶת שִׁמְךָ / The soul of every living being shall bless Your name

Chozeh of Lublin   If a man, for a moment, forgets to cling to his Creator, he deserves instant death. Yet, if he clings to his Creator, night and day, then he is no different from the littlest worm which constantly does the will of its Maker. That is the purpose for which man was created. What, then, does he have to be proud of — of the fact that he is not derelict in his duty? (*Tefillah LeMoshe, Nitzavim*).

כָּל חַי / Every living being

R' Mordechai Yosef of Izbitza   A very young Gershon Henoch (later the Rebbe of Radzin) ran to the river and bumped into the erudite Rabbi of Lomaz, R' David, who was numbered among the elder chasidim of Gershon Henoch's grandfather, *R' Mordechai Yosef of Izbitza*. The elderly R' David scolded him saying, "Have respect, young man."

"Why?" asked the boy.

"Because I'm the grandson of the *Chozeh of Lublin*," said the Rabbi.

"And I'm the grandson of the Rebbe," said the youngster.

"But I'm the grandson of the Chozeh," repeated R' David.

This was a novel idea for the little boy. Was someone greater than his grandfather? He went to his grandfather in a rush and complained that the Rabbi of Lomaz had said that the Chozeh was greater than the Rebbe.

The Rebbe listened to his grandson and said, "Go back and tell R' David that there is no comparison at all between me and the Chozeh of Lublin! I don't come up to his toenails. But there is a great distinction between us. I am still among the living; I still have a desire to rise and there is still a possibility of my rising and I have hopes to reach far loftier heights" (*Admorei Izbitza-Radzin*).

The soul of every living being shall bless Your Name, HASHEM our God; the spirit of all flesh shall always glorify and exalt Your remembrance, our King. From This World to the World-to-Come, You are God, and other than You we have no king, redeemer or savior. Liberator, Rescuer, Sustainer, Answerer and Merciful One in every time of distress and anguish, we have no king, helper or supporter but You! — God of the first and of the last, God of all creatures, Master of all generations, Who is extolled through a multitude of praises, Who guides His

---

פּוֹדֶה וּמַצִּיל / Liberator, Rescuer

Fiery Angel of Moglenitza

When R' Yitzchak of Vurka was ill, messengers came to the Fiery Angel of Moglenitza begging that he pray for him. The Fiery Angel directed his chasidim to say tehillim. R' Yissachar Ber of Volbroz, the Angel's disciple, was very distressed by the plight of the Rebbe of Vurka. He prayed mightily and said, "Master of the world, mankind needs that tzaddik; and I, for what purpose do I exist? Let my plea have weight before You and let me take his place, whatever his fate may be!"

The following day a messenger reached Moglenitza informing them that the Rebbe of Vurka's state was improving. But in equal measure, weakness overcame R' Yissachar Ber. He understood that his prayer had been answered and that his life was endangered. He hurried to his Rebbe and told him about his weakness and its cause.

"In our prayers we say, 'Blessed are You Who liberate and rescue,' " said the Fiery Angel. "There is no repetition here. It indicates that the Holy One liberates one man through the intercession of his fellow. Afterwards, he saves the second man by whose prayer the sick one was rescued."

And, indeed, R' Yissachar Dov regained his strength and enjoyed a long life (Ohel Yissachar 33).

כָּל בְּרִיּוֹת / Of all creatures

R' Chaim of Sanz

The Rabbi of Litovisk was firm, unbending and fearless in the face of those who threw off the yoke of mitzvos. This caused many of the townsmen to oppose him and embitter his life. The Rabbi came before R' Chaim of Sanz and told him that he had decided to leave his position and find some other means of sustenance; he was even willing to be a woodcutter.

"What brings you to such a state?" asked the Rebbe.

"Chazal say," replied the rabbi, "that if a man does not find favor in the

וּבְרִיּוֹתָיו בְּרַחֲמִים וַיהוה עֵר, הִנֵּה לֹא יָנוּם וְלֹא
יִישָׁן הַמְעוֹרֵר יְשֵׁנִים וְהַמֵּקִיץ נִרְדָּמִים (מְחַיֶּה
מֵתִים, וְרוֹפֵא חוֹלִים, פּוֹקֵחַ עִוְרִים), וְהַמֵּשִׂיחַ
אִלְּמִים וְהַמַּתִּיר אֲסוּרִים וְהַסּוֹמֵךְ נוֹפְלִים וְהַזּוֹקֵף

eyes of men (בְּרִיּוֹת), he will not find favor before the All-present (הַמָּקוֹם)
[*Avos* 3:13]. And since I do not find favor in the eyes of men, why should I
serve as rabbi against the will of Hashem?"

The Rebbe became exceptionally angry and said, "Do you think that those
who harass you deserve the name of *men*? They are inferior to randomly
strewn rocks. The *mishnah* does not have such men in mind; it has men like
me in mind. And I am as fond of you as I am of myself! Thus, you find favor
before the All-present, too; you are highly viewed in heaven. Do not fear nor
feel dread, and Hashem will aid you to achieve peace and tranquility, calm
and security" (*Mekor Chaim*).

הַמְעוֹרֵר יְשֵׁנִים וְהַמֵּקִיץ נִרְדָּמִים / Who arouses the sleepers and awakens the slumberers

R' Shmelke of Nikolsburg — There are two categories of "sleepers":
There are those who are in a deep sleep with
regard to their devotion to Hashem (יְשֵׁנִים). They must be aroused from the
coma-like slumber which the flow of time of this world has imposed upon
them. And it is the Holy One Who arouses them (הַמְעוֹרֵר יְשֵׁנִים). But there are
those who, at times, do remember and serve Hashem, and at times, forget
him; they doze off. And the Holy One also awakens these slumberers
(וְהַמֵּקִיץ נִרְדָּמִים) (*Eretz HaChaim* 423).

R' Yehoshua of Belz — When *R' Yehoshua of Belz* reached this passage,
on the evening of the *Seder*, he would note, "When
my sainted father said these words, all the sick who needed to be healed
were saved. We, unfortunately cannot effect a cure solely with *our* speech.
We turn to Him 'Who arouses the sleepers and awakens the slumberers' to
awaken those who sleep the eternal sleep. And we beg of them that they
summon up their influence and lay *their* prayers before *Hashem* to support
the fallen and heal the sick" (*Admorei Belz* I 322).

וְרוֹפֵא חוֹלִים / (And) heals the sick

R' Mordechai of Nishchiz — A chasid who was mortally ill came before *R'
Mordechai of Nishchiz*. He had visited many
doctors and taken various medicines, but nothing had helped. He had
turned, in his desperation, to the Rebbe.

world with kindness and His creatures with mercy. HASHEM is awake, behold He neither slumbers nor sleeps. He Who arouses the sleepers and awakens the slumberers (Who resuscitates the dead, heals the sick, and gives sight to the blind), Who makes the mute speak and releases the bound; Who supports the fallen and straightens the bent (and

---

"Go to the specialist in Anipoli. He will cure you," said the Rebbe.

Without delay, the chasid went off to Anipoli. The journey was long and difficult in those days before the railroads. On his arrival he immediately inquired about the specialist.

"But there is no specialist here," said the puzzled townsmen.

"Perhaps a doctor?" asked the man.

"There's no doctor here either," they said.

"A druggist?"

"There's no druggist, either."

"No specialist, no doctor, no druggist?" said the man in amazement. "What do you people do if someone takes ill?"

"What can we do?" they said. "We put our trust in Hashem and pray that He will save us."

The man now understood to which specialist the Rebbe had sent him. And the Specialist who aided the townsmen of Anipoli would also aid him (*Sipurei Chasidim, Beshalach* 168).

R' Shlomo of Bobov A young man, who was afflicted with a severe case of tuberculosis, lived with a poor man in Sanz. Before Pesach the landlord, the poor man, wished to whitewash his house, as he did each year. However, the doctor warned him that the smell of the whitewash would hasten the young man's death, though he did not have much time to live as it was, since his lungs were badly eaten away.

The landlord ran to the *Divrei Chaim of Sanz* and told him, in anguished tones, that he could not forgo whitewashing his house for Pesach; he felt he had no choice and must turn the sick young man out.

The Rebbe was shaken by the tale and asked the man to wait a short while, until the illness would pass, and then he would be able to whitewash the house.

The doctor heard about what the Rebbe had said and laughed it to scorn. But when a few days had passed, he was forced to admit that the patient had improved. And, shortly thereafter, the sick man was found to be completely cured.

The Rebbe of Bobov asked the doctor, "Well, what do you have to say now?"

כְּפוּפִים (וְהַמְפַעֲנֵחַ נֶעְלָמִים). וּלְךָ לְבַדְּךָ אֲנַחְנוּ
מוֹדִים. אִלּוּ פִינוּ מָלֵא שִׁירָה כַּיָּם וּלְשׁוֹנֵנוּ רִנָּה
כַּהֲמוֹן גַּלָּיו וְשִׂפְתוֹתֵינוּ שֶׁבַח כְּמֶרְחֲבֵי רָקִיעַ
וְעֵינֵינוּ מְאִירוֹת כַּשֶּׁמֶשׁ וְכַיָּרֵחַ וְיָדֵינוּ פְרוּשׂוֹת
כְּנִשְׁרֵי שָׁמָיִם וְרַגְלֵינוּ קַלּוֹת כָּאַיָּלוֹת אֵין אֲנַחְנוּ

"It would seem that I was mistaken when I said the lungs were eaten away
and disintegrated," said the doctor.

"Why don't you admit, rather, that you were wrong in mocking the words
of my grandfather, the Rebbe of Sanz?" asked the Rebbe of Bobov.

"If your grandfather can create new lungs, why doesn't he make the blind
see and give speech to the dumb?" replied the doctor.

"If my grandfather were to give sight to the blind, you would have no
choice but to repent," said the Rebbe of Bobov. "However, Hashem wants
man to have free choice and choose the good of his own will. That is why the
tzaddik only performs miracles of this sort which allow the doctor to say, 'I
was mistaken in my diagnosis' " (*Mekor Chaim* 197).

פִּינוּ מָלֵא שִׁירָה / *Our mouth as full of song*

R' Tzvi Elimelech of Dinov *R' Tzvi Elimelech of Dinov* would say the
Nishmas prayer in a captivating melody, while
standing at a window of his *beis midrash*, which looked out on the valley
below. The melody was so sweet and vibrant that the gentile shepherds
would gather with their flocks to listen.

R' Tzvi Elimelech passed away, and on the first *Shabbos* after his departure
an air of sorrow rested on the *beis midrash*, an air which became seven-fold
more oppressive as they approached the *Nishmas* prayer. And then, to the
amazement of all, the sweet melody floated into the *beis midrash*.

The shepherds who had been accustomed to stand and listen had, on
their own, burst forth into song (*Rabbi Tzvi Elimelech of Dinov*, p. 166).

וְעֵינֵינוּ מְאִירוֹת / *And our eyes as brilliant*

Maggid of Mezritch The *Maggid of Mezritch* would pray alone in his
chamber. When he reached *Ein Kelokeinu* (אֵין
כֵּאלֹקֵינוּ) he would gather a bare quorum (*minyan*). When the *Chozeh of
Lublin* reached Mezritch in his youth, he too once entered the private
minyan. The Maggid said, "Bring someone else in his place; he is not
capable (בַּטְלָן)." Though they sought a substitute, they could not find one
and the Chozeh remained.

When the Maggid began to say *Ein Kelokeinu*, the Chozeh fainted and was

uncovers the hidden). And to You alone we give thanks. Were our mouth as full of song as the sea, and our tongue as full of joyous song as its multitude of waves, and our lips as full of praise as the breadth of the heavens, and our eyes as brilliant as the sun and the moon, and our hands as outspread as eagles of the sky and our feet as swift

---

revived only with great difficulty. "I said he was incapable," said the Maggid. "He just took one glimpse at the Heavenly Retinue (פְּמַלְיָא שֶׁל מָעְלָה) and fainted. It would have been better to have someone who doesn't see such sights and would not fear" (*Eser Oros* 25).

R' Yechiel Yehoshua of Biale — On a wintry *Shabbos* morning, before sunrise, when the light was still very dim, *R' Yechiel Yehoshua of Biale* asked of his grandson that he bring a *siddur* (prayerbook) so that he might say the 'for Torah-study blessings' (בִּרְכוֹת הַתּוֹרָה) and the *Shema*. His grandson did not succeed in finding the proper place in the *siddur* and was forced to approach the candle burning in the corner of the room; there he found it easily. He asked his grandfather if he wished to sit near the light, but the Rebbe said that it was not necessary. He took the *siddur,* said the blessings, turned the pages to the Thirteen Principles of Faith (י"ג עִקָּרִים), and then to the *Shema*.

His grandson was amazed. For, in his last years, the Rebbe's right eye was useless and he saw through his left eye only with difficulty. How could he read in darkness where his grandson could not see with his healthy vision?

The Rebbe took his grandson's hand lovingly and said, "Just understand! If one keeps guard over one's eyes throughout all the years, that which is holy shines forth" (*Kedushas Einayim* 343).

וְעֵינֵינוּ מְאִירוֹת כַּשֶּׁמֶשׁ וְכַיָּרֵחַ / *And our eyes as brilliant as the sun and the moon*

R' BenZion of Bobov — "Our eyes" (עֵינֵינוּ) refers to the righteous, the tzaddikim, who are called "the eyes of the assembly" (עֵינֵי הָעֵדָה). Even if they are as brilliant as the sun (שֶׁמֶשׁ) at its height, they see themselves as the moon (יָרֵחַ) only, which has no radiance of its own but reflects that of the sun. They see their power as having its source in Israel who cling to them (*Heichal Bobov* 156).

וְרַגְלֵינוּ קַלּוֹת / *And our feet (as) swift*

R' Chaim of Kosov — R' Chaim of Kosov would dance with great and saintly enthusiasm each *Shabbos* night, his face

מַסְפִּיקִים לְהוֹדוֹת לְךָ יהוה אֱלֹהֵינוּ וֵאלֹהֵי
אֲבוֹתֵינוּ וּלְבָרֵךְ אֶת שְׁמֶךָ מַלְכֵּנוּ עַל אַחַת מֵאֶלֶף
אֶלֶף אַלְפֵי אֲלָפִים וְרִבֵּי רְבָבוֹת פְּעָמִים הַטּוֹבוֹת
נִסִּים וְנִפְלָאוֹת שֶׁעָשִׂיתָ עִם אֲבוֹתֵינוּ וְעִמָּנוּ.
מִלְּפָנִים מִמִּצְרַיִם גְּאַלְתָּנוּ יהוה אֱלֹהֵינוּ וּמִבֵּית
עֲבָדִים פְּדִיתָנוּ בְּרָעָב זַנְתָּנוּ וּבְשָׂבָע כִּלְכַּלְתָּנוּ
מֵחֶרֶב הִצַּלְתָּנוּ וּמִדֶּבֶר מִלַּטְתָּנוּ וּמֵחֳלָיִם רָעִים
וְרַבִּים וְנֶאֱמָנִים דִּלִּיתָנוּ. עַד הֵנָּה עֲזָרוּנוּ רַחֲמֶיךָ
וְלֹא עֲזָבוּנוּ חֲסָדֶיךָ יהוה אֱלֹהֵינוּ. וְאַל תִּטְּשֵׁנוּ

---

radiant like a torch. Once a heavy bench fell on his feet and he stopped
dancing for some time. But after a few weeks had passed, he began to dance
once more with his customary fervor. When his chasidim tried to prevent
him, because of his injured feet, he said, "You thought I had stopped
dancing because my feet hurt me, but in truth my feet hurt because I had
stopped dancing" (*Sipurei Chasidim, Moadim* 162).

Maggid of Kozhnitz   The *Maggid of Kozhnitz* became so weak and gaunt
that the doctors were amazed that he continued to
live. He was not even able to bear clothes on his body and special clothing
of paper was sewn for him. They wrapped him in rabbit furs and spread bear
hides on the floor. Because he was so weak, he could not stand on his feet
and his chasidim carried him in a chair from his home to the *beis midrash*.
But when he reached the door of the *beis midrash*, he would leap from the
chair and run in like a vigorous young man and in his great fervor he would
roar like a lion, "Who am I that I should be worthy to pray to the high,
exalted King?" Then he would quote from *Bereishis* 28:17, "How fearful is
this place. It is none other than the House of God, and this is the gateway
of heaven!" (*Toledos HaMaggid* 15).

בְּרָעָב זַנְתָּנוּ / *In famine You nourished us*

R' Chanoch Henoch of Alexander   R' Chanoch Henoch of Alexander
complained to his rebbe, R' Simchah
Bunim of Pshischa that he didn't sense that he ate good food and he had no
appetite. The Rebbe replied, "The verse says: 'Behold, the eye of Hashem
looks towards those who fear Him ... to keep them alive in famine'
(*Tehillim* 33:18-19), which may be interpreted as 'keeps them alive while

as hinds — we still could not thank You sufficiently,
HASHEM our God and God of our forefathers, and
bless Your Name, our King, for even one of the
thousand thousand, thousands of thousands and
myriad myriads of favors, miracles and wonders that
You performed for our ancestors and for us. At first
You redeemed us from Egypt, HASHEM our God, and
liberated us from the house of bondage. In famine
You nourished us and in plenty You sustained us.
From sword You saved us; from plague You let us
escape; and from severe, numerous and enduring
diseases You spared us. Until now Your mercy has
helped us, and Your kindness has not forsaken us
HASHEM our God. Do not abandon us, HASHEM our

---

they hunger and lack appetite.' And therefore we say, 'in famine You
nourished us' " (Siach Sarfei Kodesh I 595).

בְּרָעָב זַנְתָּנוּ וּבְשָׂבָע כִּלְכַּלְתָּנוּ / In famine You nourished us and in plenty You sustained us

R' David'l of Tolna   A group of wealthy grain merchants came before R'
David'l of Tolna to ask advice and seek his blessing.
The previous year had been a year of drought and the prices of grain had
risen very steeply. They had thought that the current year would follow the
same pattern and they had not sold their produce, waiting for the prices to
rise even higher. But the rains did fall and the prices had plummeted
drastically. Now, they stood to lose vast sums.

The Rebbe replied, "He Who fed and sustained the poor in the year of
famine will feed and sustain the wealthy in the year of plenty" (Sipurei
Tzaddikim, Lecha).

עַד הֵנָּה עֲזָרוּנוּ . . . וְאַל תִּטְּשֵׁנוּ
Until now (Your mercy) has helped us . . . Do not abandon us

R' Yitzchak of Skver   This is not a prayer and a plea, but a declaration of
faith.

Had You aided us until now, because we were found worthy by virtue of
our good deeds and righteousness, we would, of necessity, be concerned
about the future. Would we continue to be so favored?

But we have been helped because of Your mercy and Your kindness.
These will never be exhausted and spent. We are certain that You will never
abandon us (Besoros Tovos).

יהוה אֱלֹהֵינוּ לָנֶצַח. עַל כֵּן אֵבָרִים שֶׁפִּלַּגְתָּ בָּנוּ
וְרוּחַ וּנְשָׁמָה שֶׁנָּפַחְתָּ בְּאַפֵּינוּ וְלָשׁוֹן אֲשֶׁר שַׂמְתָּ
בְּפִינוּ הֵן הֵם יוֹדוּ וִיבָרְכוּ וִישַׁבְּחוּ וִיפָאֲרוּ וִישׁוֹרְרוּ
וִירוֹמְמוּ וְיַעֲרִיצוּ וְיַקְדִּישׁוּ וְיַמְלִיכוּ אֶת שִׁמְךָ
מַלְכֵּנוּ תָּמִיד. כִּי כָל פֶּה לְךָ יוֹדֶה וְכָל לָשׁוֹן לְךָ
תִשָּׁבַע, וְכָל עַיִן לְךָ תְּצַפֶּה, וְכָל בֶּרֶךְ לְךָ תִכְרַע
וְכָל קוֹמָה לְפָנֶיךָ תִשְׁתַּחֲוֶה וְכָל הַלְּבָבוֹת יִירָאוּךָ

עַל כֵּן אֵבָרִים שֶׁפִּלַּגְתָּ בָּנוּ . . . הֵן הֵם יוֹדוּ

Therefore, the organs that You set within us . . . all of them shall thank

Maggid of Mezritch   Previously, we said that even if our mouth were "as full of song as the sea . . . we still could not thank You sufficiently." How is it that we do a turnabout and say that our organs give thanks and praise?

Let us suggest a parable:

A king summoned his servant and ordered him to prepare a meal at home, fit for a king and his entourage. The servant was seized by trembling at the thought of the great responsibility placed upon him. What food, what drinks should he provide? With what dishes should he set the table? How to clean the house?

In the midst of his fearful contemplations, the king said, "I'll have all that is necessary prepared in the palace, my servants will carry it to your home, and we'll eat there." The weight disappeared from the future host's shoulders.

When we assume that the mouth and tongue are *our* mouth and *our* tongue, we feel that we are inadequate for the task of praise. But when we realize that our organs have been set within us by Hashem, and He has placed the tongue within our mouths — the organs are all Hashem's, then we can say, "All of them shall thank," for You have fashioned it all and given it to us from Your Hand (*Eser Oros* 37).

הֵן הֵם יוֹדוּ / *All of them shall thank*

Fiery Angel of Kotzk   When the *Fiery Angel of Kotzk* became known to the world, a man who lived in Tomashov was amazed to hear that he had become a rebbe. "He?" he said. "We were together in *cheder* as youngsters."

The chasidim wished to learn about the Rebbe's childhood and asked the man what the Fiery Angel had been like as a boy.

God, forever. Therefore, the organs that You set within us, and the spirit and soul that You breathed into our nostrils, and the tongue that You placed in our mouth — all of them shall thank and bless, praise and glorify, sing about, exalt and revere, sanctify and declare the sovereignty of Your Name, our King, continuously. For every mouth shall offer thanks to You; every tongue shall vow allegiance to You; every eye shall look toward You; every knee shall bend to You; every erect spine shall prostrate itself before You; all the hearts shall fear You, and all

---

"I have nothing to tell you," he said. "He was a boy like all boys. But," he said after a pause, "I now recall that the teacher once took us for a hike in the hills on *Lag B'Omer*. We returned at a late hour and, when we reached town, we realized that Menachem Mendel was not with us. We went back and searched for him; he was stretched out full length on the ground, arms widespread, repeating again and again, 'My heart and flesh sing to the living God' " (*Tehillim* 84:3) (*Siach Sarfei Kodesh* V 48).

וְכָל קוֹמָה לְפָנֶיךָ תִשְׁתַּחֲוֶה
Every erect spine shall prostrate itself before You

R' Baruch of Mezhibuz — The highest level of prostration is achieved when man appears to stand with *a fully erect posture, in the eyes of the beholder, and his inner self feels a sense of complete obeisance (*Betzina D' Nehora*).

[*a *fully erect posture.* R' Baruch invested the כָּל (of כָּל קוֹמָה) with the meaning of *entirely*, rather than *every*; like בְּכָל לְבָבְךָ with your *entire* heart, (*Devarim* 6:5).]

R' Menachem Mendel of Vurka — R' Menachem Mendel of Vurka, the Silent Rebbe, would add: It is right and proper that a chasid know how to feel the spirit of dance while sitting, of bowing while erect and of crying aloud in prayer while silent (*Gedulas HaTzaddikim* II 69).

יִירָאוּךָ / (All) shall fear You

Ba'al HaTanya — R' Aharon the Great of Karlin's fear of Hashem was like the fear of a man condemned to death who is bound to the pole and sees the soldier stand before him, aim his rifle and fire the bullet. That was the fear he felt when involved in petty everyday matters. It is

וְכָל קֶרֶב וּכְלָיוֹת יְזַמְּרוּ לִשְׁמֶךָ. כַּדָּבָר שֶׁכָּתוּב כָּל עַצְמֹתַי תֹּאמַרְנָה יהוה מִי כָמוֹךָ מַצִּיל עָנִי מֵחָזָק מִמֶּנּוּ וְעָנִי וְאֶבְיוֹן מִגֹּזְלוֹ. שַׁוְעַת עֲנִיִּים אַתָּה תִשְׁמַע, צַעֲקַת הַדַּל תַּקְשִׁיב וְתוֹשִׁיעַ. מִי יִדְמֶה

---

impossible to describe his fear when he was on an exalted plane (*Beis Rabi* I, ch. 25).

R' Levi Yitzchak of Berdichev   The *Noam Elimelech* bore witness that the heart of *R' Levi Yitzchak of Berdichev* pounded furiously in his sleep from fear of Hashem, like the heart of a man who walks in the thickness of a forest and suddenly finds himself surrounded by murderous bandits.

Imagine what that fear of Hashem was when he woke from his sleep. (*Toledos Kedushas Levi* 50, quoted in the name of the *Divrei Chaim*)

Chidushei HaRim   The *Chidushei HaRim of Gur* was once traveling by wagon up a steep mountain. When the wagon made the sheer decline, the horses went into a gallop and the travelers were in danger of plunging into the abyss. The fear of death, plain and simple, seized the others, but when they glanced at the Rebbe, they saw he was as unmoved as if they had been driving on a plain. They asked him how he could be so tranquil in the face of such clear danger.

"Whoever constantly experiences the fear of death because of the dread of his Creator does not note any difference between travel on level ground and down a steep decline," he said (*Siach Sarfei Kodesh* I 453).

R' Yisrael of Ruzhin   *R' Yisrael of Ruzhin* prayed in a special chamber close by his *beis midrash*. When he would finish his prayer he would give a sign indicating that he had done so.

One Yom Kippur during *Ne'ilah*, the Rebbe gave no sign that he had completed his prayers, although the hour was late. They waited for two hours in fasting and fear. Finally, his firstborn son, *R' Shalom Yosef*, took courage and entered his father's chamber. He approached the *shtender* where the Rebbe's *machzor* lay and turned the page. Moments later the Rebbe indicated that he had ended his prayers.

When R' Shalom Yosef was asked what had occurred, he said, "I realized that my father stood before Hashem in such fear that he did not dare lift his hand to turn the page of the *machzor*. And since he did not wish to pray

innermost feelings and thoughts shall sing praises to Your name, as it is written: "All my bones shall say: 'HASHEM, who is like You?' You save the poor man from one stronger than he, the poor and destitute from one who would rob him." The outcry of the poor You hear, the screams of the destitute You listen to, and You save. Who is like unto You?

---

from memory, he could not continue, but stood in silent trembling. I turned the page and he was able to complete the prayers" (*Avkas Rochlim*).

כָּל עַצְמֹתַי תֹּאמַרְנָה / *All my bones shall say*

Kol Aryeh of Bregsas   The *Kol Aryeh of Bregsas* saw a man praying without swaying back and forth. "My master, the *Chasam Sofer* did, indeed, pray without any movement," he said to him. "But when I looked at his face, it was radiant. Flaming like a torch. Suddenly, he blanched, as though about to faint. I wished to shout, for I feared that his soul had flown from his body. Whoever prays with such a sense of closeness to God can allow himself to stand motionless. But we lesser mortals must pray with motion, so that 'all my bones shall say' " (*Toledos Kol Arye* 29).

צַעֲקַת / *The outcry*

Shomer Emunim   The *Shomer Emunim* implanted into his chasidim the idea that prayer was especially powerful when expressed forcefully and fervently, with full voice. Such had been the manner of prayer, in days gone by, of *R' Uri the Fiery Angel of Strelisk*. When R' Uri was about to pass away, he had intimated to his chasidim that they should find shelter in the shade of *R' Yisrael of Ruzhin*.

The *Shomer Emunim* told the following:

In Ruzhin they prayed in a low voice; their lips would move but their voice was not heard. The chasidim of Strelisk arrived in Ruzhin and prayed loudly in their usual manner. The Rebbe was amazed at the outcry and was told that this was how they prayed in Strelisk.

After the prayers the Rebbe called them over and asked, "Why in such a loud voice? Isn't it possible to pray quietly?"

They answered that they did not wish to pray in the same voice in which they spoke about everyday matters.

The Rebbe smiled and said, "Fine! But why have you decided to use the pleasant manner of speech for your everyday use and the unpleasant manner for prayer? It would be fitting to pray quietly and shout at other times."

They remained silent.

לְךָ וּמִי יִשְׁוֶה לָּךְ וּמִי יַעֲרָךְ לָךְ הָאֵל הַגָּדוֹל הַגִּבּוֹר
וְהַנּוֹרָא אֵל עֶלְיוֹן, קֹנֵה שָׁמַיִם וָאָרֶץ. נְהַלֶּלְךָ
וּנְשַׁבֵּחֲךָ וּנְפָאֶרְךָ וּנְבָרֵךְ אֶת שֵׁם קָדְשֶׁךָ כָּאָמוּר
לְדָוִד בָּרְכִי נַפְשִׁי אֶת יהוה וְכָל קְרָבַי אֶת שֵׁם
קָדְשׁוֹ:

הָאֵל בְּתַעֲצֻמוֹת עֻזֶּךָ הַגָּדוֹל בִּכְבוֹד שְׁמֶךָ הַגִּבּוֹר
לָנֶצַח וְהַנּוֹרָא בְּנוֹרְאוֹתֶיךָ הַמֶּלֶךְ הַיּוֹשֵׁב
עַל כִּסֵּא רָם וְנִשָּׂא:

שׁוֹכֵן עַד מָרוֹם וְקָדוֹשׁ שְׁמוֹ. וְכָתוּב רַנְּנוּ
צַדִּיקִים בַּיהוה לַיְשָׁרִים נָאוָה

תְּהִלָּה:	בְּפִי	יְשָׁרִים	תִּתְרוֹמָם.
וּבְשִׂפְתֵי	צַדִּיקִים	תִּתְבָּרַךְ
וּבִלְשׁוֹן	חֲסִידִים	תִּתְקַדָּשׁ.
וּבְקֶרֶב	קְדוֹשִׁים	תִּתְהַלָּל.

"In truth," said the Shomer Emunim to his chasidim, "they did have an answer. But out of respect for R' Yisrael they chose not to reply.

"For *R' Shlomo of Karlin* said, 'In the prayers we find: *and the ofanim and the holy chayos* — *with a great noise, raising themselves*. Because they sing with great voice they raise themselves and are uplifted. This shows us that the most worthy praise is the very loud praise. It is beautiful and pleasant; it lifts the worshiper to a lofty level' " (*Porah Mateh Aharon* 115).

בָּרְכִי נַפְשִׁי אֶת ה' / Bless Hashem, O my soul

Fiery Angel of Strelisk   When *R' Gershon of Kolomei* visited *R' Yisrael of Ruzhin*, the Rebbe of Ruzhin asked him if he had been in the presence of *tzaddikim*. R' Gershon said that he often traveled to *R' Uri the Fiery Angel of Strelisk*. The Rebbe of Ruzhin asked R' Gershon to tell him something of the Fiery Angel.

---

* *and the ofanim etc.* וְהָאוֹפַנִּים וְחַיּוֹת הַקֹּדֶשׁ בְּרַעַשׁ גָּדוֹל מִתְנַשְּׂאִים. This is in the first blessing of the *Shema* of the morning prayers. It refers to the *ofanim* and *chayos* who are the angels that bear the Divine Chariot.

Who is equal to You? Who can be compared to You? O great, mighty, and awesome God, the supreme God, Creator of heaven and earth. We shall laud, praise, and glorify You and bless Your holy Name, as it is said 'Of David: Bless HASHEM, O my soul, and let all my innermost being bless His holy Name!'

O God, in the omnipotence of Your strength, great in the glory of Your Name, mighty forever and awesome through Your awesome deeds, O King enthroned upon a high and lofty throne!

He Who abides forever, exalted and holy is His Name. And it is written: 'Sing joyfully, O righteous, before HASHEM; for the upright, praise is fitting.' By the mouth of the upright shall You be exalted; by the lips of the righteous shall You be blessed; by the tongue of the devout shall You be sanctified; and amid the holy shall You be lauded.

"Once," said R' Gershon, "the Fiery Angel asked me to write the title page for a manuscript. I told him that great patience was required and it would be preferable to do it after prayer. He told me that it was not a manuscript of his, and when he stood before his Creator, he was ready to hand over his soul. He could not, therefore, be certain that he would return home after prayer. And then, it would be thought that the manuscript contained his own original Torah insights. That is why he begged me to write up the title page, containing the author's name, immediately" (*Eser Tzachtzachos* 6).

הַמֶּלֶךְ / O King

R' Aharon of Karlin   The *Maggid of Mezritch* chose his disciple, *R' Aharon the Great of Karlin*, to lead the prayers on Rosh Hashanah. R' Aharon was accustomed to pray with sound and fury; bolts of lightning would burst forth from his lips. But when he reached the phrase "O King," *HaMelech*, he was struck silent, blanched and almost fainted.

When asked for an explanation afterwards, he replied, "When I said '*HaMelech*,' I remembered what the *gemara* (*Gemara* 56a) tells us of the meeting between Rabban Yochanan ben Zakkai and the Roman general besieging *Yerushalayim*. R' Yochanan ben Zakkai said, 'Peace to you, O king!

וּבְמַקְהֲלוֹת רִבְבוֹת עַמְּךָ בֵּית יִשְׂרָאֵל בְּרִנָּה יִתְפָּאַר שִׁמְךָ מַלְכֵּנוּ בְּכָל דּוֹר וָדוֹר שֶׁכֵּן חוֹבַת כָּל הַיְצוּרִים לְפָנֶיךָ יהוה אֱלֹהֵינוּ וֵאלֹהֵי אֲבוֹתֵינוּ לְהוֹדוֹת לְהַלֵּל לְשַׁבֵּחַ לְפָאֵר

To which the general commented, 'If I *am* a king, why did you not come until now?' '' (*Beis Karlin-Stolin* 40).

יְשָׁרִים / The upright

R' Tzvi Elimelech of Dinov When *R' Tzvi Elimelech of Dinov* passed away, *R' Sar Shalom of Belz* sighed and said, ''What a pity! We have lost an upright Jew'' (Yiddish: עֶרְלִיכֶער אִיד).

''An upright Jew only?'' exclaimed his wife. ''He was among the greatest rebbes of our age.''

''Rebbes we have in plenty,'' replied her husband, ''but upright Jews are few and far between'' (*Admorei Belz* I 173).

R' David of Kishinev *R' David of Kishinev* gave the following parable concerning those who imagine they have become elevated souls simply by lifting up their voices loudly, in prayer:

A man had gone mad and imagined himself to be a rooster. He hopped about the barnyard and pecked for kernels of grain; flapped his ''wings''; went up on the roof before dawn and crowed his cock-a-doodle-doo.

His family saw that his physical health was being impaired, too, and asked a clever man to persuade him to eat and sleep normally. This would make it at least possible for him to return to himself sometime in the future.

One morning before dawn, the would-be rooster went aloft on the roof to crow in the day and, lo and behold, he found someone there before him. He barely stretched out his neck to let loose his halloo when the other sent forth, beforehand, a clarion-clear cock-a-doodle-doo which aroused his envy.

''Are you a rooster, too?'' asked the ''rooster'', suspiciously.

''What do you think?'' said the clever man, for it was he. ''Do you call *yourself* a rooster? Your voice is weak and thin. You are a disgrace to our species. If you wish to be a credit to the rooster tribe, you should eat three meals a day and sleep eight hours a day. Then you shall have a true rooster's voice.''

''But,'' said the confused ''rooster,'' ''if I eat like a human being and sleep like one, how can I be called a rooster?''

''Let me tell you a secret,'' said the clever man. ''Once upon a time a

Αnd in the assemblies of the myriads of Your people, the House of Israel, with joyous song shall Your Name be glorified, our King, throughout every generation. For such is the duty of all creatures — before You, HASHEM, our God, God of our forefathers, to thank, laud, praise, glorify,

---

rooster was a rooster. But today, it's enough just to crow!" (*Rabbeinu HaKadosh MiSanz* III 218).

Maggid of Mezritch   After the *Maggid of Mezritch* had passed away, his disciples gathered together and spoke among themselves of the deeds and modes of behavior of their great master. The *Ba'al HaTanya* asked, "Does anyone know why our teacher would walk each day at dawn along the lakeshore?"

When no answer was forthcoming, he said, "He went there to hear the songs of praise that the frogs offer up to the Holy One and learn from them a chapter in the service to Hashem" (*Sipurei Chasidim; Va'erah*).

R' Nachman of Breslav   A man of Zlotipola told the following about *R' Nachman of Breslav*:

"When R' Nachman lived in Zlotipola he once asked me to accompany him on a walk. We left the city and strolled in the meadows. The Rebbe said to me, 'If you would be fortunate enough to hear the songs of praise of the blades of grass, you would hear how each sings to Hashem without any self-interest, without any foreign thoughts. They look forward to no reward. How lovely it is to hear their song! How good it is to devote oneself to, and feel fear of, Hashem among them!'

"And he sat down on the earth, took a *Sha'arei Zion* in his hand and read aloud from it, with great weeping and without a halt, until the sun began to set" (*Sichos HaRan* 164).

כָּל הַיְצוּרִים לְפָנֶיךָ / Of all creatures — before You

Fiery Angel of Kotzk   The *Fiery Angel of Kotzk* arose and began to say the *Modeh Ani*, the praise and thanks that every Jew says upon arising. But he broke off when he had said three words — *modeh ani lefanecha* (מוֹדֶה אֲנִי לְפָנֶיךָ) — I give thanks before You). *"Who am 'I' (אֲנִי) and who is the 'before You' (לְפָנֶיךָ)?" he said. And in his trembling and fear, he was unable to complete the short prayer (*Siach Sarfei Kodesh* V, p. 23).

[*Who am I etc. He was overwhelmed and experienced dread when he contemplated the infinite abyss that separated his human "I" from the Divine "You" and could not possibly envision a standing "before You" without overpowering awe.]

לְרוֹמֵם לְהַדֵּר וּלְנַצֵּחַ לְבָרֵךְ לְעַלֵּה וּלְקַלֵּס עַל כָּל דִּבְרֵי שִׁירוֹת וְתִשְׁבְּחוֹת דָּוִד בֶּן יִשַׁי עַבְדְּךָ מְשִׁיחֶךָ:

וּבְכֵן יִשְׁתַּבַּח שִׁמְךָ לָעַד מַלְכֵּנוּ הָאֵל הַמֶּלֶךְ הַגָּדוֹל וְהַקָּדוֹשׁ בַּשָּׁמַיִם וּבָאָרֶץ כִּי לְךָ נָאֶה יהוה אֱלֹהֵינוּ וֵאלֹהֵי אֲבוֹתֵינוּ שִׁיר וּשְׁבָחָה הַלֵּל וְזִמְרָה עֹז וּמֶמְשָׁלָה נֶצַח גְּדֻלָּה וּגְבוּרָה תְּהִלָּה וְתִפְאֶרֶת קְדֻשָּׁה וּמַלְכוּת בְּרָכוֹת וְהוֹדָאוֹת לְשִׁמְךָ הַגָּדוֹל וְהַקָּדוֹשׁ וּמֵעוֹלָם וְעַד עוֹלָם אַתָּה אֵל.

וְתִשְׁבְּחוֹת דָּוִד בֶּן יִשַׁי
Praises of David the son of Yishai

Sainted Yehudi of Pshischa   The *Sainted Yehudi of Pshischa* was a phenomenally brilliant and diligent scholar. It was said that his master, the *Chozeh of Lublin*, concealed his true personality behind the overt wonders (מוֹפְתִים) which he worked, while the Sainted Yehudi hid himself by incisive Talmudic discourses (פִּלְפּוּלִים). Nevertheless, before he prayed, he would occupy himself, in particular, with the saying of *Tehillim*.

"Wouldn't it be better to learn a number of pages of the Talmud before prayer?" asked his disciple, *R' Yeshaya of Pshedburz*. "True, David begged that the utterance of his songs of *Tehillim* be viewed like the learning of the *mishnayos* of 'Plagues' (נְגָעִים) and 'Tents' (אֱהָלוֹת) which contain the most difficult matters in the Order of Purities (סֵדֶר טָהֳרוֹת). But that very plea shows that the study of *mishnah* is preferable to saying *Tehillim*."

"There is a profound meaning hidden within David *HaMelech's* plea," said the Rebbe. "He hoped that, by giving utterance to *Tehillim*, man would see the 'plagues,' the spiritual maladies, which afflict him personally, and this would bring him to dwell in the 'tents' of Hashem. Nothing can be more important as a preparatory step to prayer than these thoughts" (*Nifleos HaYehudi* II 6).

Ba'al Shem Tov   But there is the saying of *Tehillim* and the saying of *Tehillim*:

exalt, adore, render triumphant, bless, raise high, and sing praises — even beyond all expressions of the songs and praises of David the son of Yishai, Your servant, Your anointed.

And thus may Your Name be praised forever — our King, the God, the great and holy King — in heaven and on earth. Because for You is fitting — O HASHEM, our God, and the God of our forefathers — song and praise, lauding and hymns, power and dominion, triumph, greatness and strength, praise and splendor, holiness and sovereignty, blessings and thanksgivings to Your Great and Holy Name; from This World to the World-to-Come You are God.

In the days of the *Ba'al Shem Tov* there was a man who found a passage in holy works which stated that the Divine spirit (*ruach hakodesh*) would rest upon man, if he refrained from idle speech (דְּבָרִים בְּטֵלִים) for forty days consecutively. He did so. However, at the end of the fortieth day he felt no sense of the Divine spirit. He went to the Ba'al Shem Tov to discover what had happened.

"Were you careful about every word that passed your lips?" asked the Ba'al Shem Tov.

"Indeed, yes, Rebbe!" said the man. "I didn't say a word."

"Did you say *Tehillim*?"

"That, yes! With great ease!"

"Well, then," said the Ba'al Shem Tov, "Now we've solved the problem. There is your idle talk" (*Sipurei Chasidim, Parashas Noach*).

R' Yisrael of Ruzhin A man who had assiduously guarded his tongue from speech for forty days found that, nevertheless, the Divine spirit had not come to rest upon him. He went to *R' Yisrael of Ruzhin* for an explanation.

The Rebbe of Ruzhin conducted a court in royal fashion. The man was dazzled by the splendor and the majesty. His eyes could not have enough of the grandeur of the palatial residence and the king-like deportment of the Rebbe. "This is a singular way of devoting oneself to Hashem," he thought.

The Rebbe left the mansion and made his way to the stables. There his carriage had been harnessed to four noble steeds. He approached the first

יְהַלְלוּךָ יהוה אֱלֹהֵינוּ (עַל) כָּל מַעֲשֶׂיךָ,
וַחֲסִידֶיךָ צַדִּיקִים עוֹשֵׂי רְצוֹנֶךָ, וְכָל
עַמְּךָ בֵּית יִשְׂרָאֵל בְּרִנָּה יוֹדוּ וִיבָרְכוּ וִישַׁבְּחוּ
וִיפָאֲרוּ וִישׁוֹרְרוּ וִירוֹמְמוּ וְיַעֲרִיצוּ וְיַקְדִּישׁוּ
וְיַמְלִיכוּ אֶת שִׁמְךָ מַלְכֵּנוּ, תָּמִיד כִּי לְךָ טוֹב
לְהוֹדוֹת וּלְשִׁמְךָ נָאֶה לְזַמֵּר, כִּי מֵעוֹלָם וְעַד עוֹלָם
אַתָּה אֵל. בָּרוּךְ אַתָּה יהוה מֶלֶךְ מְהֻלָּל
בַּתִּשְׁבָּחוֹת.

The blessing over wine is recited and the fourth cup is drunk while reclining on the left side. It is preferable that the entire cup be drunk.

הֲרֵינִי מוּכָן וּמְזֻמָּן לְקַיֵּם מִצְוַת כּוֹס רְבִיעִי שֶׁל אַרְבַּע כּוֹסוֹת. לְשֵׁם יִחוּד
קֻדְשָׁא בְּרִיךְ הוּא וּשְׁכִינְתֵּיהּ, עַל יְדֵי הַהוּא טָמִיר וְנֶעְלָם, בְּשֵׁם כָּל
יִשְׂרָאֵל. וִיהִי נֹעַם אֲדֹנָי אֱלֹהֵינוּ עָלֵינוּ, וּמַעֲשֵׂה יָדֵינוּ כּוֹנְנָה עָלֵינוּ, וּמַעֲשֵׂה
יָדֵינוּ כּוֹנְנֵהוּ:

בָּרוּךְ אַתָּה יהוה אֱלֹהֵינוּ מֶלֶךְ הָעוֹלָם בּוֹרֵא פְּרִי
הַגָּפֶן:

After drinking the fourth cup, the concluding blessing is recited.
On Shabbos include the passage in parentheses.

בָּרוּךְ אַתָּה יהוה אֱלֹהֵינוּ מֶלֶךְ הָעוֹלָם עַל הַגֶּפֶן
וְעַל פְּרִי הַגֶּפֶן וְעַל תְּנוּבַת הַשָּׂדֶה וְעַל
אֶרֶץ חֶמְדָּה טוֹבָה וּרְחָבָה שֶׁרָצִיתָ וְהִנְחַלְתָּ
לַאֲבוֹתֵינוּ לֶאֱכוֹל מִפִּרְיָהּ וְלִשְׂבּוֹעַ מִטּוּבָהּ. רַחֵם
נָא יהוה אֱלֹהֵינוּ עַל יִשְׂרָאֵל עַמֶּךָ וְעַל יְרוּשָׁלַיִם
עִירֶךָ וְעַל צִיּוֹן מִשְׁכַּן כְּבוֹדֶךָ וְעַל מִזְבְּחֶךָ וְעַל
הֵיכָלֶךָ. וּבְנֵה יְרוּשָׁלַיִם עִיר הַקֹּדֶשׁ בִּמְהֵרָה בְיָמֵינוּ

and patted its neck. The man, who had followed the Rebbe, could not contain himself. "Begging your pardon, our master," he said, "but of what devotion to Hashem is there in the patting of horses?"

"Know," said the Rebbe "that this horse has not said an idle word for

All Your works shall praise You, HASHEM our God. And Your devout ones, the righteous, who do Your will, and Your entire people, the House of Israel, with glad song will thank, bless, praise, glorify, sing about exalt, extol, sanctify, and proclaim the sovereignty of Your Name, our King, continuously. For to You it is fitting to give thanks, and unto Your Name it is proper to sing praises, for from This World to the World-to-Come You are God. Blessed are You, HASHEM, the King Who is lauded with praises.

The blessing over wine is recited and the fourth cup is drunk while reclining on the left side. It is preferable that the entire cup be drunk.

Behold, I am prepared and ready to fulfill the mitzvah of the fourth of the Four Cups. For the sake of the unification of the Holy One, Blessed is He, and His Presence, through Him Who is hidden and inscrutable — [I pray] in the name of all Israel. May the pleasantness of my Lord, our God, be upon us — may He establish our handiwork for us; our handiwork may He establish.

Blessed are You, HASHEM, our God, King of the universe, Who creates the fruit of the vine.

After drinking the fourth cup, the concluding blessing is recited.
On Shabbos include the passage in parentheses.

Blessed are You, HASHEM, our God, King of the universe, for the vine and the fruit of the vine, and for the produce of the field. For the desirable, good, and spacious land that You were pleased to give our forefathers as a heritage, to eat of its fruit and to be satisfied with its goodness. Have mercy, we beg You, HASHEM, our God, on Israel Your people; on Jerusalem, Your city; on Zion, resting place of Your glory; Your Altar, and Your Temple. Rebuild Jerusalem the city of holiness, speedily in our days. Bring us up into it and glad-

---

more than forty days.''

The man understood that it is not enough to be silent; one must know *how* to be silent (*Ateres Yisrael*).

וְהַעֲלֵנוּ לְתוֹכָהּ וְשַׂמְּחֵנוּ בְּבִנְיָנָהּ וְנֹאכַל מִפִּרְיָהּ
וְנִשְׂבַּע מִטּוּבָהּ וּנְבָרֶכְךָ עָלֶיהָ בִּקְדֻשָּׁה וּבְטָהֳרָה.
[וּרְצֵה וְהַחֲלִיצֵנוּ בְּיוֹם הַשַּׁבָּת הַזֶּה] וְשַׂמְּחֵנוּ בְּיוֹם חַג
הַמַּצּוֹת הַזֶּה. כִּי אַתָּה יהוה טוֹב וּמֵטִיב לַכֹּל וְנוֹדֶה
לְךָ עַל הָאָרֶץ וְעַל פְּרִי הַגָּפֶן: בָּרוּךְ אַתָּה יהוה עַל
הָאָרֶץ וְעַל פְּרִי הַגָּפֶן:

נרצה

חֲסַל סִדּוּר פֶּסַח כְּהִלְכָתוֹ. כְּכָל מִשְׁפָּטוֹ
וְחֻקָּתוֹ. כַּאֲשֶׁר זָכִינוּ לְסַדֵּר אוֹתוֹ. כֵּן
נִזְכֶּה לַעֲשׂוֹתוֹ: זָךְ שׁוֹכֵן מְעוֹנָה. קוֹמֵם קְהַל עֲדַת
מִי מָנָה. בְּקָרוֹב נַהֵל נִטְעֵי כַנָּה. פְּדוּיִם לְצִיּוֹן
בְּרִנָּה:

לְשָׁנָה הַבָּאָה בִּירוּשָׁלָיִם:

On the first night recite the following.
On the second night continue on page 178.

וּבְכֵן וַיְהִי בַּחֲצִי הַלַּיְלָה:

בַּלָּיְלָה.	אָז רוֹב נִסִּים הִפְלֵאתָ
הַלָּיְלָה.	בְּרֹאשׁ אַשְׁמוֹרֶת זֶה
לָיְלָה.	גֵּר צֶדֶק נִצַּחְתּוֹ כְּנֶחֱלַק לוֹ

וַיְהִי בַּחֲצִי הַלָּיְלָה.

נִרְצָה / Nirtzah (Acceptance)

Ahavas Yisrael of Vizhnitz
At the close of the Seder, Nirtzah, the Ahavas Yisrael of Vizhnitz sighed and said, "We have eaten the proper measure of matzah and of maror. How can we now find a proper measure of nirtzah (acceptance) so that our acts be acceptable to our Creator?" (Kedosh Yisrael I, ch. 14, 29).

den us in its rebuilding and let us eat from its fruit and be satisfied with its goodness and bless You upon it in holiness and purity. (Favor us and strengthen us on this Shabbos day) and grant us happiness on this Festival of Matzos; for You, HASHEM, are good and do good to all, and we thank You for the land and for the fruit of the vine. Blessed are You, HASHEM, for the land and for the fruit of the vine.

NIRTZAH

The Seder is now concluded in accordance with its laws, with all its ordinances and statutes. Just as we were privileged to arrange it, so may we merit to perform it. O Pure One, Who dwells on high, raise up the countless congregation, soon — guide the offshoots of Your plants, redeemed, to Zion with glad song.

NEXT YEAR IN JERUSALEM

On the first night recite the following.
On the second night continue on page 179.

It came to pass at midnight.

You have, of old, performed many wonders
by night.
At the head of the watches of this night.
To the righteous convert (Avraham),
You gave triumph by dividing for him the night.
It came to pass at midnight.

Divrei Chaim   Once, after the Seder, the *Divrei Chaim* reclined on the couch, put his hand on his stomach and said, "Be happy, my innards, be happy! Think how much holiness there is in matzah, in *maror*, in *afikoman*, in *karpas*, in *korech*, in the Four Cups, in the festival meal. And, at one and the same time, it has all descended into my innards. Be happy!" And his eyes shed tears of joy (*Mekor Chaim* 99).

הַלַּיְלָה.	דַּנְתָּ מֶלֶךְ גְּרָר בַּחֲלוֹם
לַיְלָה.	הִפְחַדְתָּ אֲרַמִּי בְּאֶמֶשׁ
לַיְלָה.	וַיָּשַׂר יִשְׂרָאֵל לְמַלְאָךְ וַיּוּכַל לוֹ

וַיְהִי בַּחֲצִי הַלַּיְלָה.

הַלַּיְלָה.	זֶרַע בְּכוֹרֵי פַתְרוֹס מָחַצְתָּ בַּחֲצִי
בַּלַּיְלָה.	חֵילָם לֹא מָצְאוּ בְּקוּמָם
לַיְלָה.	טִיסַת נְגִיד חֲרוֹשֶׁת סִלִּיתָ בְּכוֹכְבֵי

וַיְהִי בַּחֲצִי הַלַּיְלָה.

בַּלַּיְלָה.	יָעַץ מְחָרֵף לְנוֹפֵף אוּי הוֹבַשְׁתָּ פְגָרָיו
לַיְלָה.	כָּרַע בֵּל וּמַצָּבוֹ בְּאִישׁוֹן
לַיְלָה.	לְאִישׁ חֲמוּדוֹת נִגְלָה רָז חֲזוֹת

וַיְהִי בַּחֲצִי הַלַּיְלָה.

בַּלַּיְלָה.	מִשְׁתַּכֵּר בִּכְלֵי קֹדֶשׁ נֶהֱרַג בּוֹ
לַיְלָה.	נוֹשַׁע מִבּוֹר אֲרָיוֹת פּוֹתֵר בְּעֲתוּתֵי
בַּלַּיְלָה.	שִׂנְאָה נָטַר אֲגָגִי וְכָתַב סְפָרִים

וַיְהִי בַּחֲצִי הַלַּיְלָה.

לַיְלָה.	עוֹרַרְתָּ נִצְחֲךָ עָלָיו בְּנֶדֶד שְׁנַת
מִלַּיְלָה.	פּוּרָה תִדְרוֹךְ לְשׁוֹמֵר מַה
לַיְלָה.	צָרַח כַּשּׁוֹמֵר וְשָׂח אָתָא בֹקֶר וְגַם

וַיְהִי בַּחֲצִי הַלַּיְלָה.

לַיְלָה.	קָרֵב יוֹם אֲשֶׁר הוּא לֹא יוֹם וְלֹא

קָרֵב יוֹם
Hasten the day (of Mashiach)

R' Shlomo of Bobov   Once, at the close of Yom Kippur, *R' Shlomo of Bobov* spoke to a simple youth and asked him, "Tell me, what did you think of during the prayers?"

You judged the king of Gerar (Avimelech),
    in a dream   by night.
You frightened the Aramean (Lavan), in the dark
                                                    of night.
Israel (Yaakov) fought with an angel
    and overcame him   by night.
        It came to pass at midnight.

Egypt's first-born You crushed   at midnight.
Their host they found not upon arising   at night.
The army of the prince of Charoshes (Sisera)
    You swept away with stars of   the night.
        It came to pass at midnight.

The blasphemer (Sennacherib) planned to raise his
    hand against Jerusalem —
    but You withered his corpses   by night.
Bel was overturned with its pedestal,
    in the darkness   of night.
To the man of Your delights (Daniel),
    was revealed the mystery of the visions   of night.
        It came to pass at midnight.

He (Belshazzar) who caroused from the holy vessels
    was killed that very   night.
From the lion's den was rescued he (Daniel)
    who interpreted the 'terrors' of   the night.
The Aggagite (Haman) nursed hatred
    and wrote decrees   at night.
        It came to pass at midnight.

You began Your triumph over him
    when You disturbed (Ahaseurus') sleep   at night.
Trample the wine-press to help those who ask the
    watchman, 'What of the long   night?'
He will shout, like a watchman, and say:
    'Morning shall come   after night.'
        It came to pass at midnight.

Hasten the day (of Mashiach),
    that is neither day nor   night.

"I thought about the approaching night; I awaited the dark, so that I would be able to eat already."

"Young man," said the Rebbe, "you waited for night to fall; I prayed that the morning would come, the morning when the light of the *Mashiach* would be revealed" (*Kerem HaChasidus* III 147).

דָּם הוֹדֵעַ כִּי לְךָ הַיּוֹם אַף לְךָ   הַלַּיְלָה.

שׁוֹמְרִים הַפְקֵד לְעִירְךָ כָּל הַיּוֹם וְכָל   הַלַּיְלָה.

תָּאִיר כְּאוֹר יוֹם חֶשְׁכַּת   לַיְלָה.

וַיְהִי בַּחֲצִי הַלַּיְלָה.

On the second night recite the following.
On the first night continue on page 182.

וּבְכֵן וַאֲמַרְתֶּם זֶבַח פֶּסַח:

אֹמֶץ גְּבוּרוֹתֶיךָ הִפְלֵאתָ   בַּפֶּסַח.

בְּרֹאשׁ כָּל מוֹעֲדוֹת נִשֵּׂאתָ   פֶּסַח.

גִּלִּיתָ לְאֶזְרָחִי חֲצוֹת לֵיל   פֶּסַח.

וַאֲמַרְתֶּם זֶבַח פֶּסַח.

דְּלָתָיו דָּפַקְתָּ כְּחֹם הַיּוֹם   בַּפֶּסַח.

הִסְעִיד נוֹצְצִים עֻגוֹת מַצּוֹת   בַּפֶּסַח.

וְאֶל הַבָּקָר רָץ זֵכֶר לְשׁוֹר עֵרֶךְ   פֶּסַח.

וַאֲמַרְתֶּם זֶבַח פֶּסַח.

זוֹעֲמוּ סְדוֹמִים וְלוֹהֲטוּ בָּאֵשׁ   בַּפֶּסַח.

חֻלַּץ לוֹט מֵהֶם וּמַצּוֹת אָפָה בְּקֵץ   פֶּסַח.

הִסְעִיד נוֹצְצִים / *He satiated the angels*

R' Avraham David of Botshash   *R' Avraham David of Botshash* ate very sparingly. He would often say, ''Eating makes a man unspiritual: Adam sinned through eating; the angels maintain their lofty spiritual heights because they need not eat. That is why Avraham told the angels who were his guests, 'I will take some bread and you will nourish your hearts; after *that* you will pass on' (*Bereishis* 18:5) — let us see how you will act after you have eaten'' (*Da'as Kedoshim*).

R' Yoel Teitelbaum of Satmar   The angels asked of the Holy One, ''Put Your grandeur on the heavens'' (*Tehillim* 8:2) — ''leave the Torah among us.'' To which the Holy One replied, ''When you descended to earth, as guests of Avraham, you ate milk and meat in a

Most High — make known that Yours
are day and   night.
Appoint guards for Your city,
all the day and all the   night.
Brighten like the light of day the darkness of   night.
It came to pass at midnight.

On the second night recite the following.
On the first night continue on page 183.

And you shall say: This is the feast of Passover.

You displayed wondrously Your mighty powers
on Passover.

Above all festivals You elevated   Passover.

To the Oriental (Avraham) You revealed
the future midnight   of Passover.

And you shall say: This is the feast of Passover.

At his door You knocked in the heat of the day
on Passover;

He satiated the angels with matzah-cakes
on Passover.

And he ran to the herd — symbolic of
the sacrificial beast   of Passover.

And you shall say: This is the feast of Passover.

The Sodomites provoked (God) and were devoured
by fire   on Passover;

Lot was withdrawn from them — he had baked
matzos at the time   of Passover.

single meal."

"This shows us," said the *Satmar Rav*, R' Yoel Teitelbaum, "that one can
forfeit the entire Torah because of a single non-kosher meal" (*Beis D'li*, p. 25).

R' Yitzchak of Vurka   When *R' Yitzchak of Vurka* visited Kintzk, a well-
known wealthy man, R' Yechiel, invited him to his
home and prepared a banquet-like repast in his honor. When the Rebbe
reached the house he saw that the chandeliers were all ablaze and the steps
were strewn with carpets. "If you promise me," said the Rebbe, "that you
will light all these lights and spread the carpets for every other guest, too, I
will agree that you may do it for me. The laws of the *mitzvah* of receiving
guests (הַכְנָסַת אוֹרְחִים) make no distinction between one guest and another,

טָאטֵאתָ אַדְמַת מוֹף וְנוֹף בְּעָבְרֶךָ ‏   בַּפֶּסַח.

וַאֲמַרְתֶּם זֶבַח פֶּסַח.

יָהּ רֹאשׁ כָּל אוֹן מָחַצְתָּ בְּלֵיל שִׁמּוּר ‏   פֶּסַח.

כַּבִּיר עַל בֵּן בְּכוֹר פָּסַחְתָּ בְּדָם ‏   פֶּסַח.

לְבִלְתִּי תֵּת מַשְׁחִית לָבֹא בִּפְתָחַי ‏   בַּפֶּסַח.

וַאֲמַרְתֶּם זֶבַח פֶּסַח.

מְסֻגֶּרֶת סֻגְּרָה בְּעִתּוֹתֵי ‏   פֶּסַח.

נִשְׁמְדָה מִדְיָן בִּצְלִיל שְׂעוֹרֵי עֹמֶר ‏   פֶּסַח.

שֹׂרְפוּ מִשְׁמַנֵּי פוּל וְלוּד בִּיקַד יְקוֹד ‏   פֶּסַח.

וַאֲמַרְתֶּם זֶבַח פֶּסַח.

עוֹד הַיּוֹם בְּנֹב לַעֲמֹד עַד גָּעָה עוֹנַת ‏   פֶּסַח.

פַּס יַד כָּתְבָה לְקַעֲקֵעַ צוּל ‏   בַּפֶּסַח.

צָפֹה הַצָּפִית עָרֹךְ הַשֻּׁלְחָן ‏   בַּפֶּסַח.

וַאֲמַרְתֶּם זֶבַח פֶּסַח.

קָהָל כִּנְּסָה הֲדַסָּה צוֹם לְשַׁלֵּשׁ ‏   בַּפֶּסַח.

רֹאשׁ מִבֵּית רָשָׁע מָחַצְתָּ בְּעֵץ חֲמִשִּׁים ‏   בַּפֶּסַח.

שְׁתֵּי אֵלֶּה רֶגַע תָּבִיא לְעוּצִית ‏   בַּפֶּסַח.

תָּעֹז יָדְךָ וְתָרוּם יְמִינְךָ כְּלֵיל הִתְקַדֵּשׁ חַג ‏   פֶּסַח.

וַאֲמַרְתֶּם זֶבַח פֶּסַח.

---

just as there is no distinction between one *shofar* and another in the *mitzvah* of blowing the *shofar*."

R' Yechiel had no choice but to extinguish the lights and roll up the carpets (*Zikkukin DeNura* 28).

You swept clean the soil of Moph and Noph (in
   Egypt) when You passed through   on Passover.
> And you shall say: This is the feast of Passover.

God, You crushed every firstborn of On (in Egypt)
   on the watchful night   of Passover.
But Master — Your own firstborn, You skipped
   by merit of the blood   of Passover,
Not to allow the Destroyer to enter my doors
                                    on Passover.
> And you shall say: This is the feast of Passover.

The beleaguered (Jericho) was besieged
                                    on Passover.
Midian was destroyed with a barley cake,
   from the Omer   of Passover.
The mighty nobles of Pul and Lud (Assyria) were
   consumed in a great conflagration   on Passover.
> And you shall say: This is the feast of Passover.

He (Sennacherib) would have stood that day at Nob,
   but for the advent   of Passover.
A hand inscribed the destruction of Zul (Babylon)
                                    on Passover.
As the watch was set, and the royal table decked
                                    on Passover.
> And you shall say: This is the feast of Passover.

Hadassah (Esther) gathered a congregation
   for a three-day fast   on Passover.
You caused the head of the evil clan (Haman) to be
   hanged on a fifty-cubit gallows   on Passover.
Doubly, will You bring in an instant
   upon Utsis (Edom)   on Passover.
Let Your hand be strong, and Your right arm exalted,
   as on that night when You hallowed the festival
                                    of Passover.
> And you shall say: This is the feast of Passover.

On both nights continue here:

כִּי לוֹ נָאֶה, כִּי לוֹ יָאֶה:

אַדִּיר בִּמְלוּכָה, **בָּחוּר** כַּהֲלָכָה, גְּדוּדָיו יֹאמְרוּ לוֹ,
לְךָ וּלְךָ, לְךָ כִּי לְךָ, לְךָ אַף לְךָ, לְךָ יהוה הַמַּמְלָכָה,
כִּי לוֹ נָאֶה, כִּי לוֹ יָאֶה.

דָּגוּל בִּמְלוּכָה, **הָדוּר** כַּהֲלָכָה, וָתִיקָיו יֹאמְרוּ
לוֹ, לְךָ וּלְךָ, לְךָ כִּי לְךָ, לְךָ אַף לְךָ, לְךָ יהוה
הַמַּמְלָכָה, כִּי לוֹ נָאֶה, כִּי לוֹ יָאֶה.

זַכַּאי בִּמְלוּכָה, **חָסִין** כַּהֲלָכָה, **טַפְסְרָיו**
יֹאמְרוּ לוֹ, לְךָ וּלְךָ, לְךָ כִּי לְךָ, לְךָ אַף לְךָ, לְךָ יהוה
הַמַּמְלָכָה, כִּי לוֹ נָאֶה, כִּי לוֹ יָאֶה.

יָחִיד בִּמְלוּכָה, **כַּבִּיר** כַּהֲלָכָה, לִמּוּדָיו יֹאמְרוּ
לוֹ, לְךָ וּלְךָ, לְךָ כִּי לְךָ, לְךָ אַף לְךָ, לְךָ יהוה
הַמַּמְלָכָה, כִּי לוֹ נָאֶה, כִּי לוֹ יָאֶה.

מוֹשֵׁל בִּמְלוּכָה, **נוֹרָא** כַּהֲלָכָה, **סְבִיבָיו**
יֹאמְרוּ לוֹ, לְךָ וּלְךָ, לְךָ כִּי לְךָ, לְךָ אַף לְךָ, לְךָ יהוה
הַמַּמְלָכָה, כִּי לוֹ נָאֶה, כִּי לוֹ יָאֶה.

עָנָיו בִּמְלוּכָה, **פּוֹדֶה** כַּהֲלָכָה, צַדִּיקָיו יֹאמְרוּ
לוֹ, לְךָ וּלְךָ, לְךָ כִּי לְךָ, לְךָ אַף לְךָ, לְךָ יהוה
הַמַּמְלָכָה, כִּי לוֹ נָאֶה, כִּי לוֹ יָאֶה.

כִּי לוֹ נָאֶה / **To Him praise is due**

R' Shlomo of Bobov   Once R' Shlomo of Bobov received a perfect,
beautiful esrog. Its shape was lovely, the color gold,
proper ridges and grooves, the stem sunken into its cavity, a "belted" waist
and not a speck of an imperfection, not a scar, be it ever so slight, of leaf or
thorn. The esrog was an object of wonder and became the talk of the town.

On both nights continue here:

To Him praise is due! To Him praise is fitting!

Powerful in majesty, perfectly distinguished, His companies of angels say to Him: Yours and only Yours; Yours, yes Yours; Yours, surely Yours; Yours, HASHEM, is the sovereignty. To Him praise is due! To Him praise is fitting!

Supreme in kingship, perfectly glorious, His faithful say to Him: Yours and only Yours; Yours, yes Yours; Yours, surely Yours; Yours, HASHEM, is the sovereignty. To Him praise is due! To Him praise is fitting!

Pure in kingship, perfectly mighty, His angels say to Him: Yours and only Yours; Yours, yes Yours; Yours, surely Yours; Yours, HASHEM, is the sovereignty. To Him praise is due! To Him praise is fitting!

Alone in kingship, perfectly omnipotent, His scholars say to Him: Yours and only Yours; Yours, yes Yours; Yours, surely Yours; Yours, HASHEM, is the sovereignty. To Him praise is due! To Him praise is fitting!

Commanding in kingship, perfectly wondrous, His surrounding (angels) say to Him: Yours and only Yours; Yours, yes Yours; Yours, surely Yours; Yours, HASHEM, is the sovereignty. To Him praise is due! To Him praise is fitting!

Gentle in Kingship, perfectly the Redeemer, His righteous say to Him: Yours and only Yours; Yours, yes Yours; Yours, surely Yours; Yours, HASHEM, is the sovereignty. To Him praise is due! To Him praise is fitting!

However, when the time came for performing the *mitzvah* of *lulav* and *esrog*, to everyone's astonishment the Rebbe made his blessing over another *esrog* which did not approach the marvelous *esrog* in beauty. Yet no one dared to say a word to him.

Meanwhile, a youth, bitten by curiosity, went up to the Rebbe's *succah* to

קָדוֹשׁ בִּמְלוּכָה, רַחוּם כַּהֲלָכָה, שִׁנְאַנָּיו יֹאמְרוּ
לוֹ, לְךָ וּלְךָ, לְךָ כִּי לְךָ, לְךָ אַף לְךָ, לְךָ יהוה
הַמַּמְלָכָה, כִּי לוֹ נָאֶה, כִּי לוֹ יָאֶה.

תַּקִּיף בִּמְלוּכָה, תּוֹמֵךְ כַּהֲלָכָה, תְּמִימָיו יֹאמְרוּ
לוֹ, לְךָ וּלְךָ, לְךָ כִּי לְךָ, לְךָ אַף לְךָ, לְךָ יהוה
הַמַּמְלָכָה, כִּי לוֹ נָאֶה, כִּי לוֹ יָאֶה.

אַדִּיר הוּא יִבְנֶה בֵיתוֹ בְּקָרוֹב, בִּמְהֵרָה,
בִּמְהֵרָה, בְּיָמֵינוּ בְּקָרוֹב. אֵל בְּנֵה,
אֵל בְּנֵה, בְּנֵה בֵיתְךָ בְּקָרוֹב.

בָּחוּר הוּא. גָּדוֹל הוּא. דָּגוּל הוּא. יִבְנֶה בֵיתוֹ
בְּקָרוֹב, בִּמְהֵרָה, בִּמְהֵרָה, בְּיָמֵינוּ בְּקָרוֹב. אֵל
בְּנֵה, אֵל בְּנֵה, בְּנֵה בֵיתְךָ בְּקָרוֹב.

הָדוּר הוּא. וָתִיק הוּא. זַכַּאי הוּא. חָסִיד הוּא.
יִבְנֶה בֵיתוֹ בְּקָרוֹב, בִּמְהֵרָה, בִּמְהֵרָה, בְּיָמֵינוּ
בְּקָרוֹב. אֵל בְּנֵה, אֵל בְּנֵה, בְּנֵה בֵיתְךָ בְּקָרוֹב.

טָהוֹר הוּא. יָחִיד הוּא. כַּבִּיר הוּא. לָמוּד הוּא.
מֶלֶךְ הוּא. נוֹרָא הוּא. סַגִּיב הוּא. עִזּוּז הוּא. פּוֹדֶה
הוּא. צַדִּיק הוּא. יִבְנֶה בֵיתוֹ בְּקָרוֹב, בִּמְהֵרָה,

---

look at the fabled *esrog* from up close. As he raised it, his hand trembled in fright lest he be caught in the act, and the *esrog* dropped. In hurried confusion, he picked it up, put it back into its box and quickly slipped out of the *succah*.

When the Rebbe entered his *succah*, he sensed that someone had touched the *esrog* box. He removed the *esrog* and saw that the *pittam* (tip) was fastened to the *esrog* by a needle. Previously, the needle had gone undetected, but the fall had disturbed the joint and now the needle was clearly visible.

"When I saw the *esrog*," said the Rebbe with a smile, "I saw perfection

Holy in kingship, perfectly merciful, His troops of angels say to Him: Yours and only Yours; Yours, yes Yours; Yours, surely Yours; Yours, HASHEM, is the sovereignty. To Him praise is due! To Him praise is fitting.

Almighty in kingship, perfectly sustaining, His perfect ones say to Him: Yours and only Yours; Yours, yes Yours; Yours, surely Yours; Yours, HASHEM, is the sovereignty. To Him praise is due! To Him praise is fitting!

He is most mighty. May He soon rebuild His House, speedily, yes speedily, in our days, soon. God, rebuild, God, rebuild, rebuild Your House soon!

He is distinguished, He is great, He is exalted. May He soon rebuild His House, speedily, yes speedily, in our days, soon. God, rebuild, God, rebuild, rebuild Your House soon!

He is all glorious, He is faithful, He is faultless, He is righteous. May He soon rebuild His House, speedily, yes speedily, in our days, soon. God, rebuild, God, rebuild, rebuild Your House soon!

He is pure, He is unique, He is powerful, He is all-wise, He is King, He is awesome, He is sublime, He is all-powerful, He is the Redeemer, He is the all-righteous. May He soon rebuild His House,

---

and beauty come true. But, specifically because of that I refrained from pronouncing a blessing over it. For perfection without a fault can only be attributed to the Master of the universe. 'To Him praise is due! To Him praise is fitting!' Other than He, there is nothing that does not have its fault. And it is now clear that the beautiful *esrog* was impaired and not fit for a blessing!" (*Kerem HaChasidus* III 139).

לְךָ אַף לְךָ / *Yours, surely Yours*

R' David Moshe of Kretchnif

R' Yisrael of Ruzhin once lamented to a tzaddik, "When will that time come when

בִּמְהֵרָה, בְּיָמֵינוּ בְּקָרוֹב. אֵל בְּנֵה, אֵל בְּנֵה, בְּנֵה בֵיתְךָ בְּקָרוֹב.

קָדוֹשׁ הוּא. רַחוּם הוּא. שַׁדַּי הוּא. תַּקִּיף הוּא. יִבְנֶה בֵיתוֹ בְּקָרוֹב, בִּמְהֵרָה, בִּמְהֵרָה, בְּיָמֵינוּ בְּקָרוֹב. אֵל בְּנֵה, אֵל בְּנֵה, בְּנֵה בֵיתְךָ בְּקָרוֹב.

אֶחָד מִי יוֹדֵעַ? אֶחָד אֲנִי יוֹדֵעַ. אֶחָד אֱלֹהֵינוּ שֶׁבַּשָּׁמַיִם וּבָאָרֶץ.

שְׁנַיִם מִי יוֹדֵעַ? שְׁנַיִם אֲנִי יוֹדֵעַ. שְׁנֵי לֻחוֹת הַבְּרִית, אֶחָד אֱלֹהֵינוּ שֶׁבַּשָּׁמַיִם וּבָאָרֶץ.

שְׁלֹשָׁה מִי יוֹדֵעַ? שְׁלֹשָׁה אֲנִי יוֹדֵעַ. שְׁלֹשָׁה אָבוֹת, שְׁנֵי לֻחוֹת הַבְּרִית, אֶחָד אֱלֹהֵינוּ שֶׁבַּשָּׁמַיִם וּבָאָרֶץ.

אַרְבַּע מִי יוֹדֵעַ? אַרְבַּע אֲנִי יוֹדֵעַ. אַרְבַּע אִמָּהוֹת, שְׁלֹשָׁה אָבוֹת, שְׁנֵי לֻחוֹת הַבְּרִית, אֶחָד אֱלֹהֵינוּ שֶׁבַּשָּׁמַיִם וּבָאָרֶץ.

חֲמִשָּׁה מִי יוֹדֵעַ? חֲמִשָּׁה אֲנִי יוֹדֵעַ. חֲמִשָּׁה חֻמְשֵׁי תוֹרָה, אַרְבַּע אִמָּהוֹת, שְׁלֹשָׁה אָבוֹת,

---

we will truly be able to serve Hashem, without any personal interests, 'except to Hashem only' (Shemos 22:19)?''

''It is difficult,'' replied the *tzaddik*, ''to find devotion directed solely to Hashem, 'Yours, yes Yours' (לְךָ כִּי לְךָ). But we can easily reach a level where the service is *also* for the sake of Hashem (לְךָ אַף לְךָ)'' [אַף is to be understood as *also*] (Arba'ah Arazim 100).

אֶחָד מִי יוֹדֵעַ / Who knows one?

R' Yissachar Dov of Belz

Why do we say, ''Who knows one,'' specifically on the evening of the Seder? Is this not a

speedily, yes speedily, in our days, soon. God, rebuild, God, rebuild, rebuild Your House soon!

He is holy, He is compassionate, He is Almighty, He is omnipotent. May He soon rebuild His House, speedily, yes speedily, in our days, soon. God, rebuild, God, rebuild, rebuild Your House soon!

Who knows one? I know one: One is our God, in heaven and on earth.

Who knows two? I know two: two are the Tablets of the Covenant; One is our God, in heaven and on earth.

Who knows three? I know three: three are the Patriarchs; two are the Tablets of the Covenant; One is our God, in heaven and on earth.

Who knows four? I know four: four are the Matriarchs; three are the Patriarchs; two are the Tablets of the Covenant; One is our God, in heaven and on earth.

Who knows five? I know five: five are the Books of Torah; four are the Matriarchs; three are the Patri-

---

subject that is constantly with us, day in day out?

Let us draw a parallel. A rich man does not reveal his assets to the world at large. But when he has had too much too drink, "the wine goes in and the secrets are let out"; then, he holds forth on what he possesses. So, too, at the end of the evening of the Seder, after we have drunk four cups of wine, we count up our treasure: *One is our God; two are the Tablets of the Covenant; three are the Patriarchs* . . . (*Admorei Belz* III 100).

שְׁנַיִם מִי יוֹדֵעַ . . . אֶחָד אֱלֹקֵינוּ / *Who knows two? . . . One is our God*

R' Yitzchak of Vurka We may speak of "two", of "three", of "four." But the end result is always: "One is our God, in heaven and on earth" (*Siach Sarfei Kodesh* v. 59).

[The *Rebbe of Vurka* extracted an important thought from the very form of the song.]

שְׁנֵי לָחוֹת הַבְּרִית, אֶחָד אֱלֹהֵינוּ שֶׁבַּשָּׁמַיִם וּבָאָרֶץ.

שִׁשָּׁה מִי יוֹדֵעַ? שִׁשָּׁה אֲנִי יוֹדֵעַ. שִׁשָּׁה סִדְרֵי מִשְׁנָה, חֲמִשָּׁה חֻמְשֵׁי תוֹרָה, אַרְבַּע אִמָּהוֹת, שְׁלֹשָׁה אָבוֹת, שְׁנֵי לָחוֹת הַבְּרִית, אֶחָד אֱלֹהֵינוּ שֶׁבַּשָּׁמַיִם וּבָאָרֶץ.

שִׁבְעָה מִי יוֹדֵעַ? שִׁבְעָה אֲנִי יוֹדֵעַ. שִׁבְעָה יְמֵי שַׁבַּתָּא, שִׁשָּׁה סִדְרֵי מִשְׁנָה, חֲמִשָּׁה חֻמְשֵׁי תוֹרָה, אַרְבַּע אִמָּהוֹת, שְׁלֹשָׁה אָבוֹת, שְׁנֵי לָחוֹת הַבְּרִית, אֶחָד אֱלֹהֵינוּ שֶׁבַּשָּׁמַיִם וּבָאָרֶץ.

שְׁמוֹנָה מִי יוֹדֵעַ? שְׁמוֹנָה אֲנִי יוֹדֵעַ. שְׁמוֹנָה יְמֵי מִילָה, שִׁבְעָה יְמֵי שַׁבַּתָּא, שִׁשָּׁה סִדְרֵי מִשְׁנָה, חֲמִשָּׁה חֻמְשֵׁי תוֹרָה, אַרְבַּע אִמָּהוֹת, שְׁלֹשָׁה אָבוֹת, שְׁנֵי לָחוֹת הַבְּרִית, אֶחָד אֱלֹהֵינוּ שֶׁבַּשָּׁמַיִם וּבָאָרֶץ.

שִׁשָּׁה סִדְרֵי מִשְׁנָה / Six are the Orders of the Mishnah

R' Tzvi Elimelech of Bluzhov — One of the elder chasidim entered the chamber of *R' Tzvi Elimelech of Bluzhov* in the last winter of the Rebbe's life and found him reciting *mishnayos* from memory, in the manner of a schoolboy. The chasid's face expressed obvious astonishment, and the Rebbe felt that he should explain his behavior.

"Behold the day is coming, that terrible day," said the Rebbe, and smote himself on his lips, as if he had just passed on bad news, "that day on which we see the awesome angel, studded with eyes, whose stature fills the height from earth until the heavens. And he attempts to seduce a man in the last moment of life." The Rebbe did not leave off striking his lips. "Know that none of the fears that a man experiences in his life comes close to the fear he feels at that moment! At that moment whoever knows ten chapters of *mishnayos* by heart need not fear the angel at all!" (*Uvda D'Aharon*, p. 80).

archs; two are the Tablets of the Covenant; One is our God, in heaven and on earth.

Who knows six? I know six: six are the Orders of the Mishnah; five are the Books of the Torah; four are the Matriarchs; three are the Patriarchs; two are the Tablets of the Covenant; One is our God, in heaven and on earth.

Who knows seven? I know seven: seven are the days of the week; six are the Orders of the Mishnah; five are the Books of the Torah; four are the Matriarchs; three are the Patriarchs; two are the Tablets of the Covenant; One is our God, in heaven and on earth.

Who knows eight? I know eight: eight are the days of circumcision; seven are the days of the week; six are the Orders of the Mishnah; five are the Books of the Torah; four are the Matriarchs; three are the Patriarchs; two are the Tablets of the Covenant; One is our God, in heaven and on earth.

שְׁמוֹנָה יְמֵי מִילָה / Eight are the days of circumcision

R' David of Lelov   R' Isaac had come to visit his brother *R' David of Lelov*. Shortly after his arrival his brother, the Rebbe, turned to him and said, "Although it is not mannerly to tell a guest — and a brother — to return home, nevertheless, I'm telling you to go home immediately."

R' Isaac was frightened and wondered what had happened at home, what tragedy, that his brother should pack him off in such haste. He didn't walk; he ran — as quickly as he could. Upon reaching home, he found everyone in the family whole and healthy. He thanked the Holy One, but could not help but be puzzled by his brother's conduct.

He was still trying to overcome his wonder, when the door burst open and a stranger fell into the room in a faint. R' Isaac hurried over, carried him to a couch and helped him recover. "What happened?" asked R' Isaac.

"Today is the eighth day after the birth of my son," said the man. "I've been running around all day searching for a *mohel*. Wherever I asked, I was told that the *mohel* was away. I thought I would go out of my mind. Would the child be circumcised after the eighth day? I traveled from town to town;

תִּשְׁעָה מִי יוֹדֵעַ? תִּשְׁעָה אֲנִי יוֹדֵעַ. תִּשְׁעָה יַרְחֵי לֵדָה, שְׁמוֹנָה יְמֵי מִילָה, שִׁבְעָה יְמֵי שַׁבַּתָּא, שִׁשָּׁה סִדְרֵי מִשְׁנָה, חֲמִשָּׁה חֻמְשֵׁי תוֹרָה, אַרְבַּע אִמָּהוֹת, שְׁלֹשָׁה אָבוֹת, שְׁנֵי לֻחוֹת הַבְּרִית, אֶחָד אֱלֹהֵינוּ שֶׁבַּשָּׁמַיִם וּבָאָרֶץ.

עֲשָׂרָה מִי יוֹדֵעַ? עֲשָׂרָה אֲנִי יוֹדֵעַ. עֲשָׂרָה דִבְּרַיָּא, תִּשְׁעָה יַרְחֵי לֵדָה, שְׁמוֹנָה יְמֵי מִילָה, שִׁבְעָה יְמֵי שַׁבַּתָּא, שִׁשָּׁה סִדְרֵי מִשְׁנָה, חֲמִשָּׁה חֻמְשֵׁי תוֹרָה, אַרְבַּע אִמָּהוֹת, שְׁלֹשָׁה אָבוֹת, שְׁנֵי לֻחוֹת הַבְּרִית, אֶחָד אֱלֹהֵינוּ שֶׁבַּשָּׁמַיִם וּבָאָרֶץ.

I was finally told to come here. I ran all the way; my strength gave out and I fainted.''

R' Isaac quickly took up the circumcision knife and, following the lead of the stranger, arrived at the man's home before sundown. R' Isaac performed the circumcision in its due time.

Now, he understood why his brother had dismissed him so abruptly (*Pri Kodesh Hillulim*, p. 24).

R' Yisrael of Bluzhov When I was in the concentration camp, working at forced labor, a woman suddenly ran up to me and asked in disturbed tones, ''Rebbe, perhaps you have a knife?''

I was not allowed to lift my head to answer, for the guards had orders to shoot to kill for daring to speak while working. But I understood that the unfortunate woman could no longer bear living and wished to commit suicide. I felt I must say something to her. ''Listen, my daughter,'' I said, ''Our life is a valuable object of safekeeping which the Creator has deposited with us. We have no right to cut it short by our own hand. He gave us life; it is He Who will take it from us.''

I was still speaking when the Nazi guard caught sight of her. ''What did she want?'' he screamed.

I kept silent, but the woman said, ''I asked him for a knife.''

The German laughed a satanic laugh and said, ''You wish to kill yourself? Let me help you!'' And he drew his knife from his belt and handed it to her.

The woman snatched up the knife eagerly and ran to a corner where a bundle of cloth was lying. She loosened the tie, and behold, there was a tiny infant.

Who knows nine? I know nine: nine are the months of pregnancy; eight are the days of circumcision; seven are the days of the week; six are the Orders of the Mishnah; five are the Books of the Torah; four are the Matriarchs; three are the Patriarchs; two are the Tablets of the Covenant; One is our God, in heaven and on earth.

Who knows ten? I know ten: ten are the Ten Commandments; nine are the months of pregnancy; eight are the days of circumcision; seven are the days of the week; six are the Orders of the Mishnah; five are the Books of the Torah; four are the Matriarchs; three are the Patriarchs; two are the Tablets of the Covenant; One is our God, in heaven and on earth.

"Master of the universe," cried the woman, "I know what fate is in store for us here! But eight days ago You granted me an infant. His circumcision should take place today. I wish to return him to You as a circumcised proper Jew." With that she bent down and circumcised the child.

She returned and handed the cruel guard his knife. He was so shocked that he took it without a word.

עֲשָׂרָה דִּבְּרַיָּא / The Ten Commandments

R' Elimelech of Lizensk   *R' Shmelke of Nikolsburg* spoke before his community ir.cisive words conveying lofty thoughts. When he had ended, *R' Elimelech of Lizensk* rose and said, "There was once a king's horse which took ill. They summoned the greatest of doctors; they dosed the horse with all sorts of medicines; they bandaged him. Nothing helped, until they finally brought a veterinarian. He cured the animal. For a horse, you need a horse doctor.

"Your saintly *rav* has given you dainty medicines that one administers to refined patients — deep discourses, noble ideas. But I'll speak to you in your tongue. Keep the Ten Commandments — 'You shall not kill,' 'You shall not steal!' " (*Siach Sarfei Kodesh* V, p. 26).

בַּשָּׁמַיִם וּבָאָרֶץ / In heaven and on earth

Fiery Angel of Kotzk   When the great Torah sages of the generation were once assembled, the *Fiery Angel of Kotzk* asked suddenly, "Tell me! Where does the Holy One abide?"

אֶחָד עָשָׂר מִי יוֹדֵעַ? אֶחָד עָשָׂר אֲנִי יוֹדֵעַ. אַחַד עָשָׂר כּוֹכְבַיָּא, עֲשָׂרָה דִבְּרַיָּא, תִּשְׁעָה יַרְחֵי לֵדָה, שְׁמוֹנָה יְמֵי מִילָה, שִׁבְעָה יְמֵי שַׁבַּתָּא, שִׁשָּׁה סִדְרֵי מִשְׁנָה, חֲמִשָּׁה חֻמְשֵׁי תוֹרָה, אַרְבַּע אִמָּהוֹת, שְׁלֹשָׁה אָבוֹת, שְׁנֵי לֻחוֹת הַבְּרִית, אֶחָד אֱלֹהֵינוּ שֶׁבַּשָּׁמַיִם וּבָאָרֶץ.

שְׁנֵים עָשָׂר מִי יוֹדֵעַ? שְׁנֵים עָשָׂר אֲנִי יוֹדֵעַ. שְׁנֵים עָשָׂר שִׁבְטַיָּא, אַחַד עָשָׂר כּוֹכְבַיָּא, עֲשָׂרָה דִבְּרַיָּא, תִּשְׁעָה יַרְחֵי לֵדָה, שְׁמוֹנָה יְמֵי מִילָה, שִׁבְעָה יְמֵי שַׁבַּתָּא, שִׁשָּׁה סִדְרֵי מִשְׁנָה, חֲמִשָּׁה חֻמְשֵׁי תוֹרָה, אַרְבַּע אִמָּהוֹת, שְׁלֹשָׁה אָבוֹת, שְׁנֵי לֻחוֹת הַבְּרִית, אֶחָד אֱלֹהֵינוּ שֶׁבַּשָּׁמַיִם וּבָאָרֶץ.

שְׁלֹשָׁה עָשָׂר מִי יוֹדֵעַ? שְׁלֹשָׁה עָשָׂר אֲנִי יוֹדֵעַ. שְׁלֹשָׁה עָשָׂר מִדַּיָּא, שְׁנֵים עָשָׂר שִׁבְטַיָּא, אַחַד עָשָׂר כּוֹכְבַיָּא, עֲשָׂרָה דִבְּרַיָּא, תִּשְׁעָה יַרְחֵי לֵדָה, שְׁמוֹנָה יְמֵי מִילָה, שִׁבְעָה יְמֵי שַׁבַּתָּא, שִׁשָּׁה סִדְרֵי מִשְׁנָה, חֲמִשָּׁה חֻמְשֵׁי תוֹרָה, אַרְבַּע אִמָּהוֹת, שְׁלֹשָׁה אָבוֹת, שְׁנֵי לֻחוֹת הַבְּרִית, אֶחָד אֱלֹהֵינוּ שֶׁבַּשָּׁמַיִם וּבָאָרֶץ.

All smiled, for who does not know that "all the world is filled with His glory" (מְלֹא כָל הָאָרֶץ כְּבוֹדוֹ; *Yeshayahu* 6:3)?

"The Holy One abides," said the Rebbe of Kotzk, in a thundering voice, "wherever He is allowed in!"

No one smiled any longer (*Siach Sarfei Kodesh* I 357).

Who knows eleven? I know eleven: eleven are the stars (in Yosef's dream); ten are the Ten Commandments; nine are the months of pregnancy; eight are the days of circumcision; seven are the days of the week; six are the Orders of the Mishnah; five are the Books of the Torah; four are the Matriarchs; three are the Patriarchs; two are the Tablets of the Covenant; One is our God, in heaven and on earth.

Who knows twelve? I know twelve: twelve are the tribes; eleven are the stars (in Yosef's dream); ten are the Ten Commandments; nine are the months of pregnancy; eight are the days of circumcision; seven are the days of the week; six are the Orders of the Mishnah; five are the Books of the Torah; four are the Matriarchs; three are the Patriarchs; two are the Tablets of the Covenant; One is our God, in heaven and on earth.

Who knows thirteen? I know thirteen: thirteen are the attributes of God; twelve are the tribes; eleven are the stars (in Yosef's dream); ten are the Ten Commandments; nine are the months of pregnancy; eight are the days of circumcision; seven are the days of the week; six are the Orders of the Mishnah; five are the Books of the Torah; four are the Matriarchs; three are the Patriarchs; two are the Tablets of the Covenant; One is our God, in heaven and on earth.

Chidushei HaRim   When the *Chidushei HaRim of Gur* was three years old, he was already known as a prodigy. One day someone who liked to jest said to him, "I'll give you a gold coin if you will tell me where the Holy One resides."

Without hesitation the youngster answered, "And I shall give you two gold coins if you will tell me where He doesn't!"

He received the gold coin (*HaMa'or HaGadol*, p.31).

חַד גַּדְיָא, חַד גַּדְיָא, דְּזַבִּין אַבָּא בִּתְרֵי זוּזֵי, חַד גַּדְיָא חַד גַּדְיָא.

וְאָתָא **שׁוּנְרָא** וְאָכְלָה לְגַדְיָא, דְּזַבִּין אַבָּא בִּתְרֵי זוּזֵי, חַד גַּדְיָא חַד גַּדְיָא.

וְאָתָא **כַלְבָּא** וְנָשַׁךְ לְשׁוּנְרָא, דְּאָכְלָא לְגַדְיָא, דְּזַבִּין אַבָּא בִּתְרֵי זוּזֵי, חַד גַּדְיָא חַד גַּדְיָא.

וְאָתָא **חוּטְרָא** וְהִכָּה לְכַלְבָּא, דְּנָשַׁךְ לְשׁוּנְרָא, דְּאָכְלָה לְגַדְיָא, דְּזַבִּין אַבָּא בִּתְרֵי זוּזֵי, חַד גַּדְיָא חַד גַּדְיָא.

וְאָתָא **נוּרָא** וְשָׂרַף לְחוּטְרָא, דְּהִכָּה לְכַלְבָּא, דְּנָשַׁךְ לְשׁוּנְרָא, דְּאָכְלָה לְגַדְיָא, דְּזַבִּין אַבָּא בִּתְרֵי זוּזֵי, חַד גַּדְיָא חַד גַּדְיָא.

וְאָתָא **מַיָּא** וְכָבָה לְנוּרָא, דְּשָׂרַף לְחוּטְרָא, דְּהִכָּה לְכַלְבָּא, דְּנָשַׁךְ לְשׁוּנְרָא, דְּאָכְלָה לְגַדְיָא, דְּזַבִּין אַבָּא בִּתְרֵי זוּזֵי, חַד גַּדְיָא חַד גַּדְיָא.

חַד גַּדְיָא / A kid

R' Nasan Adler   When Frankfurt became embroiled in a fire of controversy which surrounded the conduct of the pious *R'
Nasan Adler*, R' Nasan retired to a town where he was unknown. There, he
heard men who were strangers to him speaking critically about him.

"Gentlemen," he said, "I've had a question about the *Chad Gadya* poem
that has bothered me for a long while.

"The cat which ate the kid did a dastardly deed. If so, the dog which bit
the cat acted justly. It follows that the staff which beat the dog was unjust
and the fire which burned the staff acted properly; the water should not have
extinguished the fire and the ox justly punished the water by drinking it; the
ox should not have been slaughtered and the Angel of Death was acting
correctly in taking revenge on the slaughterer. And there we have the
problem. Why did *Hashem* punish the Angel of Death?"

The audience could find no solution. They asked R' Nasan if he could
solve the problem.

A kid, a kid, that father bought for two zuzim, a kid, a kid.

A cat then came and devoured the kid, that father bought for two zuzim, a kid, a kid.

A dog then came and bit the cat, that devoured the kid, that father bought for two zuzim, a kid, a kid.

A stick then came and beat the dog, that bit the cat, that devoured the kid, that father bought for two zuzim, a kid, a kid.

A fire then came and burnt the stick, that beat the dog, that bit the cat, that devoured the kid, that father bought for two zuzim, a kid, a kid.

Water then came and quenched the fire, that burnt the stick, that beat the dog, that bit the cat, that devoured the kid, that father bought for two zuzim, a kid, a kid.

"Indeed, yes," he said. "True, the cat had acted unjustly in devouring the kid. And the father, certainly, had good reason to be angry and punish it. But, although there was a controversy between the father and the cat, what business was it of the dog's? Who asked the dog to get involved? The dogs who involve themselves in a quarrel in which they have no part and fan the fires of controversy are the most guilty of all.

"And thus, the staff was just in beating the dog; the fire which burned it was unjust. The water was just; the ox unjust. The slaughterer was just; the Angel of Death unjust. And the Holy One, Blessed is He, Who slaughtered the Angel of Death, acted in justice" (*Sichos Chachamim* 8).

וְאָתָא נוּרָא / A fire then came

Maggid of Kozhnitz   When the armies of Napoleon swept across Europe on their way to invade Russia, one of the divisions camped in the city of Kozhnitz.

A fire broke out and the wooden houses went up in flame. The fire traveled with lightning speed from one thatched roof to the next. The frightened townsmen stood by helplessly, nor were the soldiers able to render aid. The townsmen cried out to the sainted *Maggid of Kozhnitz*. He hurried to the site of the fire, at the head of his chasidim, looked at the

וְאָתָא **תוֹרָא** וְשָׁתָה לְמַיָּא, דְּכָבָה לְנוּרָא, דְּשָׂרַף לְחוּטְרָא, דְּהִכָּה לְכַלְבָּא, דְּנָשַׁךְ לְשׁוּנְרָא, דְּאָכְלָה לְגַדְיָא, דְּזַבִּין אַבָּא בִּתְרֵי זוּזֵי, חַד גַּדְיָא חַד גַּדְיָא.

וְאָתָא **הַשּׁוֹחֵט** וְשָׁחַט לְתוֹרָא, דְּשָׁתָא לְמַיָּא, דְּכָבָה לְנוּרָא, דְּשָׂרַף לְחוּטְרָא, דְּהִכָּה לְכַלְבָּא, דְּנָשַׁךְ לְשׁוּנְרָא, דְּאָכְלָה לְגַדְיָא, דְּזַבִּין אַבָּא בִּתְרֵי זוּזֵי, חַד גַּדְיָא חַד גַּדְיָא.

וְאָתָא **מַלְאַךְ הַמָּוֶת** וְשָׁחַט לְשׁוֹחֵט, דְּשָׁחַט לְתוֹרָא, דְּשָׁתָה לְמַיָּא, דְּכָבָה לְנוּרָא, דְּשָׂרַף לְחוּטְרָא, דְּהִכָּה לְכַלְבָּא, דְּנָשַׁךְ לְשׁוּנְרָא, דְּאָכְלָה לְגַדְיָא, דְּזַבִּין אַבָּא בִּתְרֵי זוּזֵי, חַד גַּדְיָא חַד גַּדְיָא.

וְאָתָא **הַקָּדוֹשׁ בָּרוּךְ הוּא** וְשָׁחַט לְמַלְאַךְ הַמָּוֶת, דְּשָׁחַט לְשׁוֹחֵט, דְּשָׁחַט לְתוֹרָא, דְּשָׁתָה לְמַיָּא, דְּכָבָה לְנוּרָא, דְּשָׂרַף לְחוּטְרָא, דְּהִכָּה לְכַלְבָּא, דְּנָשַׁךְ לְשׁוּנְרָא, דְּאָכְלָה לְגַדְיָא, דְּזַבִּין אַבָּא בִּתְרֵי זוּזֵי, חַד גַּדְיָא חַד גַּדְיָא.

Although the *Haggadah* formally ends at this point, one should continue to occupy himself with the story of the Exodus, and the laws of Pesach, until sleep overtakes him.

---

flames and, wonder of wonders, they began to die down and the fire was extinguished of its own accord.

The division broke camp, participated in the invasion, was beaten and retreated from Russia with the other remnants of the French army. It passed through a town in Germany. And there, once again, the soldiers encountered a fire. The commander of the division hurried to the site of the fire and ordered that the local rabbi be summoned. The rabbi was a

An ox then came and drank the water, that quenched the fire, that burnt the stick, that beat the dog, that bit the cat, that devoured the kid, that father bought for two zuzim, a kid, a kid.

A slaughterer then came and slaughtered the ox, that drank the water, that quenched the fire, that burnt the stick, that beat the dog, that bit the cat, that devoured the kid, that father bought for two zuzim, a kid, a kid.

The angel of death then came and killed the slaughterer, who slaughtered the ox, that drank the water, that quenched the fire, that burnt the stick, that beat the dog, that bit the cat, that devoured the kid, that father bought for two zuzim, a kid, a kid.

The Holy One, Blessed is He, then came and slew the angel of death, who killed the slaughterer, who slaughtered the ox, that drank the water, that quenched the fire, that burnt the stick, that beat the dog, that bit the cat, that devoured the kid, that father bought for two zuzim, a kid, a kid.

Although the *Haggadah* formally ends at this point, one should continue to occupy himself with the story of the Exodus, and the laws of Pesach, until sleep overtakes him.

"modern" one of the Reform stripe and appeared in his clerical garb. The officer ordered him to "look at the fire and let it be extinguished." The rabbi was astonished at the strange command and explained that it was not in his power to extinguish fires by looking at them. The officer became angry and shouted, "Take him away and flog him! What sort of rabbi is this who can't put out a fire by looking at it? He's not a true rabbi; he's an impostor" (*Sipurei Chasidim*).

Many recite שִׁיר הַשִּׁירִים, *Song of Songs*, after the *Haggadah*.

❧ שִׁיר הַשִּׁירִים ❧

א

א **שִׁיר הַשִּׁירִים** אֲשֶׁר לִשְׁלֹמֹה. ב יִשָּׁקֵנִי מִנְּשִׁיקוֹת פִּיהוּ, כִּי טוֹבִים דֹּדֶיךָ מִיָּיִן. ג לְרֵיחַ שְׁמָנֶיךָ טוֹבִים, שֶׁמֶן תּוּרַק שְׁמֶךָ, עַל כֵּן עֲלָמוֹת אֲהֵבוּךָ. ד מָשְׁכֵנִי אַחֲרֶיךָ נָּרוּצָה, הֱבִיאַנִי הַמֶּלֶךְ חֲדָרָיו, נָגִילָה וְנִשְׂמְחָה בָּךְ, נַזְכִּירָה דֹדֶיךָ מִיַּיִן, מֵישָׁרִים אֲהֵבוּךָ. ה שְׁחוֹרָה אֲנִי וְנָאוָה, בְּנוֹת יְרוּשָׁלָיִם, כְּאָהֳלֵי קֵדָר, כִּירִיעוֹת שְׁלֹמֹה. ו אַל תִּרְאֻנִי שֶׁאֲנִי שְׁחַרְחֹרֶת, שֶׁשְּׁזָפַתְנִי הַשָּׁמֶשׁ, בְּנֵי אִמִּי נִחֲרוּ בִי, שָׂמֻנִי נֹטֵרָה אֶת הַכְּרָמִים, כַּרְמִי שֶׁלִּי לֹא נָטָרְתִּי. ז הַגִּידָה לִּי, שֶׁאָהֲבָה נַפְשִׁי, אֵיכָה תִרְעֶה, אֵיכָה תַּרְבִּיץ בַּצָּהֳרָיִם, שַׁלָּמָה אֶהְיֶה כְּעֹטְיָה עַל עֶדְרֵי חֲבֵרֶיךָ. ח אִם לֹא תֵדְעִי לָךְ, הַיָּפָה בַּנָּשִׁים, צְאִי לָךְ בְּעִקְבֵי הַצֹּאן, וּרְעִי אֶת גְּדִיֹּתַיִךְ עַל מִשְׁכְּנוֹת הָרֹעִים. ט לְסֻסָתִי בְּרִכְבֵי פַרְעֹה דִּמִּיתִיךְ, רַעְיָתִי. י נָאווּ לְחָיַיִךְ בַּתֹּרִים, צַוָּארֵךְ בַּחֲרוּזִים. יא תּוֹרֵי זָהָב נַעֲשֶׂה לָּךְ, עִם נְקֻדּוֹת הַכָּסֶף. יב עַד שֶׁהַמֶּלֶךְ בִּמְסִבּוֹ, נִרְדִּי נָתַן רֵיחוֹ. יג צְרוֹר הַמֹּר דּוֹדִי לִי, בֵּין שָׁדַי יָלִין. יד אֶשְׁכֹּל הַכֹּפֶר דּוֹדִי לִי, בְּכַרְמֵי עֵין גֶּדִי. טו הִנָּךְ יָפָה, רַעְיָתִי, הִנָּךְ יָפָה, עֵינַיִךְ יוֹנִים. טז הִנְּךָ יָפֶה, דוֹדִי, אַף נָעִים, אַף עַרְשֵׂנוּ רַעֲנָנָה. יז קֹרוֹת בָּתֵּינוּ אֲרָזִים, רַהִיטֵנוּ בְּרוֹתִים.

ב

א אֲנִי חֲבַצֶּלֶת הַשָּׁרוֹן, שׁוֹשַׁנַּת הָעֲמָקִים. ב כְּשׁוֹשַׁנָּה בֵּין הַחוֹחִים, כֵּן רַעְיָתִי בֵּין הַבָּנוֹת. ג כְּתַפּוּחַ בַּעֲצֵי הַיַּעַר, כֵּן דּוֹדִי בֵּין הַבָּנִים, בְּצִלּוֹ חִמַּדְתִּי וְיָשַׁבְתִּי, וּפִרְיוֹ מָתוֹק לְחִכִּי. ד הֱבִיאַנִי אֶל בֵּית הַיָּיִן, וְדִגְלוֹ עָלַי אַהֲבָה. ה סַמְּכוּנִי בָּאֲשִׁישׁוֹת, רַפְּדוּנִי בַּתַּפּוּחִים, כִּי חוֹלַת אַהֲבָה אָנִי. ו שְׂמֹאלוֹ תַּחַת לְרֹאשִׁי, וִימִינוֹ תְּחַבְּקֵנִי. ז הִשְׁבַּעְתִּי אֶתְכֶם,

בְּנוֹת יְרוּשָׁלַיִם, בִּצְבָאוֹת אוֹ בְּאַיְלוֹת הַשָּׂדֶה, אִם תָּעִירוּ
וְאִם תְּעוֹרְרוּ אֶת הָאַהֲבָה עַד שֶׁתֶּחְפָּץ. ח קוֹל דּוֹדִי הִנֵּה זֶה
בָּא, מְדַלֵּג עַל הֶהָרִים, מְקַפֵּץ עַל הַגְּבָעוֹת. ט דּוֹמֶה דוֹדִי
לִצְבִי, אוֹ לְעֹפֶר הָאַיָּלִים, הִנֵּה זֶה עוֹמֵד אַחַר כָּתְלֵנוּ,
מַשְׁגִּיחַ מִן הַחַלֹּנוֹת, מֵצִיץ מִן הַחֲרַכִּים. י עָנָה דוֹדִי וְאָמַר
לִי, קוּמִי לָךְ, רַעְיָתִי, יָפָתִי, וּלְכִי לָךְ. יא כִּי הִנֵּה הַסְּתָו
עָבָר, הַגֶּשֶׁם חָלַף הָלַךְ לוֹ. יב הַנִּצָּנִים נִרְאוּ בָאָרֶץ, עֵת
הַזָּמִיר הִגִּיעַ, וְקוֹל הַתּוֹר נִשְׁמַע בְּאַרְצֵנוּ. יג הַתְּאֵנָה חָנְטָה
פַגֶּיהָ, וְהַגְּפָנִים סְמָדַר נָתְנוּ רֵיחַ, קוּמִי לָךְ, רַעְיָתִי, יָפָתִי,
וּלְכִי לָךְ. יד יוֹנָתִי, בְּחַגְוֵי הַסֶּלַע, בְּסֵתֶר הַמַּדְרֵגָה, הַרְאִינִי
אֶת מַרְאַיִךְ, הַשְׁמִיעִנִי אֶת קוֹלֵךְ, כִּי קוֹלֵךְ עָרֵב, וּמַרְאֵיךְ
נָאוֶה. טו אֶחֱזוּ לָנוּ שׁוּעָלִים, שֻׁעָלִים קְטַנִּים, מְחַבְּלִים
כְּרָמִים, וּכְרָמֵינוּ סְמָדַר. טז דּוֹדִי לִי, וַאֲנִי לוֹ, הָרֹעֶה
בַּשּׁוֹשַׁנִּים. יז עַד שֶׁיָּפוּחַ הַיּוֹם, וְנָסוּ הַצְּלָלִים, סֹב דְּמֵה לְךָ,
דוֹדִי, לִצְבִי אוֹ לְעֹפֶר הָאַיָּלִים, עַל הָרֵי בָתֶר.

ג

א עַל מִשְׁכָּבִי בַּלֵּילוֹת בִּקַּשְׁתִּי אֵת שֶׁאָהֲבָה נַפְשִׁי, בִּקַּשְׁתִּיו
וְלֹא מְצָאתִיו. ב אָקוּמָה נָּא וַאֲסוֹבְבָה בָעִיר, בַּשְּׁוָקִים
וּבָרְחֹבוֹת, אֲבַקְשָׁה אֵת שֶׁאָהֲבָה נַפְשִׁי, בִּקַּשְׁתִּיו וְלֹא
מְצָאתִיו. ג מְצָאוּנִי הַשֹּׁמְרִים הַסֹּבְבִים בָּעִיר, אֵת שֶׁאָהֲבָה
נַפְשִׁי רְאִיתֶם. ד כִּמְעַט שֶׁעָבַרְתִּי מֵהֶם, עַד שֶׁמָּצָאתִי אֵת
שֶׁאָהֲבָה נַפְשִׁי, אֲחַזְתִּיו וְלֹא אַרְפֶּנּוּ, עַד שֶׁהֲבֵיאתִיו אֶל
בֵּית אִמִּי, וְאֶל חֶדֶר הוֹרָתִי. ה הִשְׁבַּעְתִּי אֶתְכֶם, בְּנוֹת
יְרוּשָׁלַיִם, בִּצְבָאוֹת אוֹ בְּאַיְלוֹת הַשָּׂדֶה, אִם תָּעִירוּ וְאִם
תְּעוֹרְרוּ אֶת הָאַהֲבָה עַד שֶׁתֶּחְפָּץ. ו מִי זֹאת עֹלָה מִן
הַמִּדְבָּר, כְּתִימְרוֹת עָשָׁן, מְקֻטֶּרֶת מֹר וּלְבוֹנָה, מִכֹּל אַבְקַת
רוֹכֵל. ז הִנֵּה מִטָּתוֹ שֶׁלִּשְׁלֹמֹה, שִׁשִּׁים גִּבֹּרִים סָבִיב לָהּ,
מִגִּבֹּרֵי יִשְׂרָאֵל. ח כֻּלָּם אֲחֻזֵי חֶרֶב, מְלֻמְּדֵי מִלְחָמָה, אִישׁ

חַרְבּוֹ עַל יְרֵכוֹ, מִפַּחַד בַּלֵּילוֹת. ט אַפִּרְיוֹן עָשָׂה לוֹ הַמֶּלֶךְ שְׁלֹמֹה מֵעֲצֵי הַלְּבָנוֹן. י עַמּוּדָיו עָשָׂה כֶסֶף, רְפִידָתוֹ זָהָב, מֶרְכָּבוֹ אַרְגָּמָן, תּוֹכוֹ רָצוּף אַהֲבָה מִבְּנוֹת יְרוּשָׁלָיִם. יא צְאֶינָה וּרְאֶינָה, בְּנוֹת צִיּוֹן, בַּמֶּלֶךְ שְׁלֹמֹה, בָּעֲטָרָה שֶׁעִטְּרָה לּוֹ אִמּוֹ, בְּיוֹם חֲתֻנָּתוֹ, וּבְיוֹם שִׂמְחַת לִבּוֹ.

ד

א הִנָּךְ יָפָה, רַעְיָתִי, הִנָּךְ יָפָה, עֵינַיִךְ יוֹנִים, מִבַּעַד לְצַמָּתֵךְ, שַׂעְרֵךְ כְּעֵדֶר הָעִזִּים, שֶׁגָּלְשׁוּ מֵהַר גִּלְעָד. ב שִׁנַּיִךְ כְּעֵדֶר הַקְּצוּבוֹת שֶׁעָלוּ מִן הָרַחְצָה, שֶׁכֻּלָּם מַתְאִימוֹת, וְשַׁכֻּלָה אֵין בָּהֶם. ג כְּחוּט הַשָּׁנִי שִׂפְתוֹתַיִךְ, וּמִדְבָּרֵךְ נָאוֶה, כְּפֶלַח הָרִמּוֹן רַקָּתֵךְ, מִבַּעַד לְצַמָּתֵךְ. ד כְּמִגְדַּל דָּוִד צַוָּארֵךְ, בָּנוּי לְתַלְפִּיּוֹת, אֶלֶף הַמָּגֵן תָּלוּי עָלָיו, כֹּל שִׁלְטֵי הַגִּבּוֹרִים. ה שְׁנֵי שָׁדַיִךְ כִּשְׁנֵי עֳפָרִים, תְּאוֹמֵי צְבִיָּה, הָרֹעִים בַּשּׁוֹשַׁנִּים. ו עַד שֶׁיָּפוּחַ הַיּוֹם, וְנָסוּ הַצְּלָלִים, אֵלֶךְ לִי אֶל הַר הַמּוֹר, וְאֶל גִּבְעַת הַלְּבוֹנָה. ז כֻּלָּךְ יָפָה, רַעְיָתִי, וּמוּם אֵין בָּךְ. ח אִתִּי מִלְּבָנוֹן, כַּלָּה, אִתִּי מִלְּבָנוֹן תָּבוֹאִי, תָּשׁוּרִי מֵרֹאשׁ אֲמָנָה, מֵרֹאשׁ שְׂנִיר וְחֶרְמוֹן, מִמְּעֹנוֹת אֲרָיוֹת, מֵהַרְרֵי נְמֵרִים. ט לִבַּבְתִּנִי, אֲחֹתִי כַלָּה, לִבַּבְתִּנִי בְּאַחַת מֵעֵינַיִךְ, בְּאַחַד עֲנָק מִצַּוְּרֹנָיִךְ. י מַה יָּפוּ דֹדַיִךְ, אֲחֹתִי כַלָּה, מַה טֹּבוּ דֹדַיִךְ מִיַּיִן, וְרֵיחַ שְׁמָנַיִךְ מִכָּל בְּשָׂמִים. יא נֹפֶת תִּטֹּפְנָה שִׂפְתוֹתַיִךְ, כַּלָּה, דְּבַשׁ וְחָלָב תַּחַת לְשׁוֹנֵךְ, וְרֵיחַ שַׂלְמֹתַיִךְ כְּרֵיחַ לְבָנוֹן. יב גַּן נָעוּל אֲחֹתִי כַלָּה, גַּל נָעוּל, מַעְיָן חָתוּם. יג שְׁלָחַיִךְ פַּרְדֵּס רִמּוֹנִים, עִם פְּרִי מְגָדִים, כְּפָרִים עִם נְרָדִים. יד נֵרְדְּ וְכַרְכֹּם, קָנֶה וְקִנָּמוֹן, עִם כָּל עֲצֵי לְבוֹנָה, מֹר וַאֲהָלוֹת, עִם כָּל רָאשֵׁי בְשָׂמִים. טו מַעְיַן גַּנִּים, בְּאֵר מַיִם חַיִּים, וְנֹזְלִים מִן לְבָנוֹן. טז עוּרִי צָפוֹן, וּבוֹאִי תֵימָן, הָפִיחִי גַנִּי, יִזְּלוּ בְשָׂמָיו, יָבֹא דוֹדִי לְגַנּוֹ, וְיֹאכַל פְּרִי מְגָדָיו.

א בָּאתִי לְגַנִּי, אֲחֹתִי כַלָּה, אָרִיתִי מוֹרִי עִם בְּשָׂמִי, אָכַלְתִּי
יַעְרִי עִם דִּבְשִׁי, שָׁתִיתִי יֵינִי עִם חֲלָבִי, אִכְלוּ רֵעִים, שְׁתוּ
וְשִׁכְרוּ דּוֹדִים. ב אֲנִי יְשֵׁנָה וְלִבִּי עֵר, קוֹל דּוֹדִי דוֹפֵק,
פִּתְחִי לִי, אֲחֹתִי, רַעְיָתִי, יוֹנָתִי, תַמָּתִי, שֶׁרֹאשִׁי נִמְלָא
טָל, קְוֻצּוֹתַי רְסִיסֵי לָיְלָה. ג פָּשַׁטְתִּי אֶת כֻּתָּנְתִּי, אֵיכָכָה
אֶלְבָּשֶׁנָּה, רָחַצְתִּי אֶת רַגְלַי, אֵיכָכָה אֲטַנְּפֵם. ד דּוֹדִי שָׁלַח
יָדוֹ מִן הַחוֹר, וּמֵעַי הָמוּ עָלָיו. ה קַמְתִּי אֲנִי לִפְתֹּחַ לְדוֹדִי,
וְיָדַי נָטְפוּ מוֹר, וְאֶצְבְּעֹתַי מוֹר עֹבֵר, עַל כַּפּוֹת הַמַּנְעוּל.
ו פָּתַחְתִּי אֲנִי לְדוֹדִי, וְדוֹדִי חָמַק עָבָר, נַפְשִׁי יָצְאָה בְדַבְּרוֹ,
בִּקַּשְׁתִּיהוּ וְלֹא מְצָאתִיהוּ, קְרָאתִיו וְלֹא עָנָנִי. ז מְצָאֻנִי
הַשֹּׁמְרִים הַסֹּבְבִים בָּעִיר, הִכּוּנִי פְצָעוּנִי, נָשְׂאוּ אֶת רְדִידִי
מֵעָלַי שֹׁמְרֵי הַחֹמוֹת. ח הִשְׁבַּעְתִּי אֶתְכֶם, בְּנוֹת יְרוּשָׁלָיִם,
אִם תִּמְצְאוּ אֶת דּוֹדִי, מַה תַּגִּידוּ לוֹ שֶׁחוֹלַת אַהֲבָה אָנִי.
ט מַה דּוֹדֵךְ מִדּוֹד, הַיָּפָה בַּנָּשִׁים, מַה דּוֹדֵךְ מִדּוֹד, שֶׁכָּכָה
הִשְׁבַּעְתָּנוּ. י דּוֹדִי צַח וְאָדוֹם, דָּגוּל מֵרְבָבָה. יא רֹאשׁוֹ כֶּתֶם
פָּז, קְוֻצּוֹתָיו תַּלְתַּלִּים, שְׁחֹרוֹת כָּעוֹרֵב. יב עֵינָיו כְּיוֹנִים עַל
אֲפִיקֵי מָיִם, רֹחֲצוֹת בֶּחָלָב, יֹשְׁבוֹת עַל מִלֵּאת. יג לְחָיָו
כַּעֲרוּגַת הַבֹּשֶׂם, מִגְדְּלוֹת מֶרְקָחִים, שִׂפְתוֹתָיו שׁוֹשַׁנִּים,
נֹטְפוֹת מוֹר עֹבֵר. יד יָדָיו גְּלִילֵי זָהָב, מְמֻלָּאִים בַּתַּרְשִׁישׁ,
מֵעָיו עֶשֶׁת שֵׁן, מְעֻלֶּפֶת סַפִּירִים. טו שׁוֹקָיו עַמּוּדֵי שֵׁשׁ,
מְיֻסָּדִים עַל אַדְנֵי פָז, מַרְאֵהוּ כַּלְּבָנוֹן, בָּחוּר כָּאֲרָזִים.
טז חִכּוֹ מַמְתַקִּים, וְכֻלּוֹ מַחֲמַדִּים, זֶה דוֹדִי וְזֶה רֵעִי, בְּנוֹת
יְרוּשָׁלָיִם.

א אָנָה הָלַךְ דּוֹדֵךְ, הַיָּפָה בַּנָּשִׁים, אָנָה פָּנָה דוֹדֵךְ, וּנְבַקְשֶׁנּוּ
עִמָּךְ. ב דּוֹדִי יָרַד לְגַנּוֹ, לַעֲרֻגוֹת הַבֹּשֶׂם, לִרְעוֹת בַּגַּנִּים

וְלִלְקֹט שׁוֹשַׁנִּים. ג אֲנִי לְדוֹדִי, וְדוֹדִי לִי, הָרוֹעֶה בַּשּׁוֹשַׁנִּים. ד יָפָה אַתְּ רַעְיָתִי כְּתִרְצָה, נָאוָה כִּירוּשָׁלָיִם, אֲיֻמָּה כַּנִּדְגָּלוֹת. ה הָסֵבִּי עֵינַיִךְ מִנֶּגְדִּי, שֶׁהֵם הִרְהִיבֻנִי, שַׂעְרֵךְ כְּעֵדֶר הָעִזִּים, שֶׁגָּלְשׁוּ מִן הַגִּלְעָד. ו שִׁנַּיִךְ כְּעֵדֶר הָרְחֵלִים, שֶׁעָלוּ מִן הָרַחְצָה, שֶׁכֻּלָּם מַתְאִימוֹת, וְשַׁכֻּלָה אֵין בָּהֶם. ז כְּפֶלַח הָרִמּוֹן רַקָּתֵךְ, מִבַּעַד לְצַמָּתֵךְ. ח שִׁשִּׁים הֵמָּה מְלָכוֹת, וּשְׁמֹנִים פִּילַגְשִׁים, וַעֲלָמוֹת אֵין מִסְפָּר. ט אַחַת הִיא יוֹנָתִי תַמָּתִי, אַחַת הִיא לְאִמָּהּ, בָּרָה הִיא לְיוֹלַדְתָּהּ, רָאוּהָ בָנוֹת וַיְאַשְּׁרוּהָ, מְלָכוֹת וּפִילַגְשִׁים, וַיְהַלְלוּהָ. י מִי זֹאת הַנִּשְׁקָפָה כְּמוֹ שָׁחַר, יָפָה כַלְּבָנָה, בָּרָה כַּחַמָּה, אֲיֻמָּה כַּנִּדְגָּלוֹת. יא אֶל גִּנַּת אֱגוֹז יָרַדְתִּי לִרְאוֹת בְּאִבֵּי הַנָּחַל, לִרְאוֹת הֲפָרְחָה הַגֶּפֶן, הֵנֵצוּ הָרִמֹּנִים. יב לֹא יָדַעְתִּי, נַפְשִׁי שָׂמַתְנִי, מַרְכְּבוֹת עַמִּי נָדִיב.

ז

א שׁוּבִי שׁוּבִי, הַשּׁוּלַמִּית, שׁוּבִי שׁוּבִי וְנֶחֱזֶה בָּךְ, מַה תֶּחֱזוּ בַּשּׁוּלַמִּית, כִּמְחֹלַת הַמַּחֲנָיִם. ב מַה יָּפוּ פְעָמַיִךְ בַּנְּעָלִים, בַּת נָדִיב, חַמּוּקֵי יְרֵכַיִךְ כְּמוֹ חֲלָאִים, מַעֲשֵׂה יְדֵי אָמָּן. ג שָׁרְרֵךְ אַגַּן הַסַּהַר, אַל יֶחְסַר הַמָּזֶג, בִּטְנֵךְ עֲרֵמַת חִטִּים, סוּגָה בַּשּׁוֹשַׁנִּים. ד שְׁנֵי שָׁדַיִךְ כִּשְׁנֵי עֳפָרִים, תָּאֳמֵי צְבִיָּה. ה צַוָּארֵךְ כְּמִגְדַּל הַשֵּׁן, עֵינַיִךְ בְּרֵכוֹת בְּחֶשְׁבּוֹן, עַל שַׁעַר בַּת רַבִּים, אַפֵּךְ כְּמִגְדַּל הַלְּבָנוֹן, צוֹפֶה פְּנֵי דַמָּשֶׂק. ו רֹאשֵׁךְ עָלַיִךְ כַּכַּרְמֶל, וְדַלַּת רֹאשֵׁךְ כָּאַרְגָּמָן, מֶלֶךְ אָסוּר בָּרְהָטִים. ז מַה יָּפִית וּמַה נָּעַמְתְּ, אַהֲבָה בַּתַּעֲנוּגִים. ח זֹאת קוֹמָתֵךְ דָּמְתָה לְתָמָר, וְשָׁדַיִךְ לְאַשְׁכֹּלוֹת. ט אָמַרְתִּי, אֶעֱלֶה בְתָמָר, אֹחֲזָה בְּסַנְסִנָּיו, וְיִהְיוּ נָא שָׁדַיִךְ כְּאֶשְׁכְּלוֹת הַגֶּפֶן, וְרֵיחַ אַפֵּךְ כַּתַּפּוּחִים. י וְחִכֵּךְ כְּיֵין הַטּוֹב, הוֹלֵךְ לְדוֹדִי לְמֵישָׁרִים, דּוֹבֵב שִׂפְתֵי יְשֵׁנִים. יא אֲנִי לְדוֹדִי, וְעָלַי תְּשׁוּקָתוֹ. יב לְכָה דוֹדִי, נֵצֵא הַשָּׂדֶה, נָלִינָה בַּכְּפָרִים. יג נַשְׁכִּימָה לַכְּרָמִים, נִרְאֶה אִם

פָּרְחָה הַגֶּפֶן, פִּתַּח הַסְּמָדַר, הֵנֵצוּ הָרִמּוֹנִים, שָׁם אֶתֵּן אֶת
דֹּדַי לָךְ. ‏יד‏ הַדּוּדָאִים נָתְנוּ רֵיחַ, וְעַל פְּתָחֵינוּ כָּל מְגָדִים,
חֲדָשִׁים גַּם יְשָׁנִים, דּוֹדִי, צָפַנְתִּי לָךְ.

ח

‏א‏ מִי יִתֶּנְךָ כְּאָח לִי, יוֹנֵק שְׁדֵי אִמִּי, אֶמְצָאֲךָ בַחוּץ אֶשָּׁקְךָ,
גַּם לֹא יָבֻזוּ לִי. ‏ב‏ אֶנְהָגֲךָ, אֲבִיאֲךָ אֶל בֵּית אִמִּי, תְּלַמְּדֵנִי,
אַשְׁקְךָ מִיַּיִן הָרֶקַח, מֵעֲסִיס רִמֹּנִי. ‏ג‏ שְׂמֹאלוֹ תַּחַת רֹאשִׁי,
וִימִינוֹ תְּחַבְּקֵנִי. ‏ד‏ הִשְׁבַּעְתִּי אֶתְכֶם, בְּנוֹת יְרוּשָׁלָיִם, מַה
תָּעִירוּ וּמַה תְּעֹרְרוּ אֶת הָאַהֲבָה עַד שֶׁתֶּחְפָּץ. ‏ה‏ מִי זֹאת
עֹלָה מִן הַמִּדְבָּר, מִתְרַפֶּקֶת עַל דּוֹדָהּ, תַּחַת הַתַּפּוּחַ
עוֹרַרְתִּיךָ, שָׁמָּה חִבְּלַתְךָ אִמֶּךָ, שָׁמָּה חִבְּלָה יְלָדַתְךָ.
‏ו‏ שִׂימֵנִי כַחוֹתָם עַל לִבֶּךָ, כַּחוֹתָם עַל זְרוֹעֶךָ, כִּי עַזָּה כַמָּוֶת
אַהֲבָה, קָשָׁה כִשְׁאוֹל קִנְאָה, רְשָׁפֶיהָ רִשְׁפֵּי אֵשׁ,
שַׁלְהֶבֶתְיָה. ‏ז‏ מַיִם רַבִּים לֹא יוּכְלוּ לְכַבּוֹת אֶת הָאַהֲבָה,
וּנְהָרוֹת לֹא יִשְׁטְפוּהָ, אִם יִתֵּן אִישׁ אֶת כָּל הוֹן בֵּיתוֹ
בָּאַהֲבָה, בּוֹז יָבוּזוּ לוֹ. ‏ח‏ אָחוֹת לָנוּ קְטַנָּה, וְשָׁדַיִם אֵין לָהּ,
מַה נַּעֲשֶׂה לַאֲחֹתֵנוּ בַּיּוֹם שֶׁיְּדֻבַּר בָּהּ. ‏ט‏ אִם חוֹמָה הִיא,
נִבְנֶה עָלֶיהָ טִירַת כָּסֶף, וְאִם דֶּלֶת הִיא, נָצוּר עָלֶיהָ לוּחַ
אָרֶז. ‏י‏ אֲנִי חוֹמָה, וְשָׁדַי כַּמִּגְדָּלוֹת, אָז הָיִיתִי בְעֵינָיו
כְּמוֹצְאֵת שָׁלוֹם. ‏יא‏ כֶּרֶם הָיָה לִשְׁלֹמֹה בְּבַעַל הָמוֹן, נָתַן אֶת
הַכֶּרֶם לַנֹּטְרִים, אִישׁ יָבִא בְּפִרְיוֹ אֶלֶף כָּסֶף. ‏יב‏ כַּרְמִי שֶׁלִּי
לְפָנָי, הָאֶלֶף לְךָ שְׁלֹמֹה, וּמָאתַיִם לְנֹטְרִים אֶת פִּרְיוֹ.
‏יג‏ הַיּוֹשֶׁבֶת בַּגַּנִּים, חֲבֵרִים מַקְשִׁיבִים לְקוֹלֵךְ, הַשְׁמִיעִנִי.
‏יד‏ בְּרַח דּוֹדִי, וּדְמֵה לְךָ לִצְבִי, אוֹ לְעֹפֶר הָאַיָּלִים, עַל הָרֵי
בְשָׂמִים.

Chassidic Insights:
Stories about Tzaddikim

The Shabbos HaGadol Sermon

R' Tzvi Hirsch of Liska
R' Mordechai of Nadvorna to a chasid of R' Tzvi Hirsch of Liska:

When you visit your rebbe give him my warm regards and tell him the following:

The author of the *Shulchan Aruch* writes that one should inquire about, and give discourses on, the laws of Pesach thirty days before Pesach (*Orach Chaim* 429). The *Rama* adds: *"and* it is the custom to buy wheat and distribute it among the poor for their Pesach needs. Why has the *Rama* chosen to place his comment about buying wheat as an addendum to speaking on the topics of Pesach, even to the point of joining it to the above with an *"and"*? The *Rama* implies to rabbis that it is more important for them to supply the poor with their Pesach needs than to spend time on their Pesach sermons.

The chasid reached Liska and passed on the thought to his rebbe. A few days later, as the Rebbe sat in his study preparing his *Shabbos HaGadol* talk, a woman entered, weeping, and told him she had no *matzos* for the festival. The Rebbe remembered the words of R' Mordechai of Nadvorna, closed his books, called his sons-in-law and together they left to bake *matzos* for the woman. And when the members of the community saw them on their way, who could refrain from joining them? Everyone left his work and went along, and in a short while the *matzos* had been baked and they together with all the other Pesach provisions were brought to the house of the unfortunate woman (*Sipurim Niflaim* 14).

Preparations for Pesach

R' Simchah Bunim of Psishcha
Before Pesach, all of Israel scrubs and scours it pots and pans; soaks and scalds them. This is exceptionally important. But those who possess understanding should realize that this is the way to spiritual redemption, too. Before we are judged worthy of deliverance we must remove the stains of our soul by a cleansing, a soaking, a scalding of the spirit. The verse says (about choosing the Pesach sacrifice in Egypt): "Draw forth and take [sheep or goats] to

yourselves" (*Shemos* 12:21). *Chazal* comment to this: "Draw your hand away from idol worship and take a *Pesach* sacrifice" (*Shemos Rabbah* 16:2) "Draw away from idol worship"; that is what is involved in the pre-Pesach cleaning and scouring. It is a condition which we must fill to be worthy of the deliverance on Pesach (*Siach Sarfei Kodesh* I :53).

Ahavas Yisrael of Vizhnitz   A man once came before the *Ahavas Yisrael of Vizhnitz* and poured his heart out. He had arranged a match for his son some time before, but he had no funds with which to meet the many wedding expenses. The Rebbe asked if they had already set a date for the wedding. "No," replied the man, "I have no wherewithal to pay for anything. How could I set a date?"

"Look," said the Rebbe, "our Torah has demanded of us that not a particle of *chametz* be found in our home on Pesach, and Pesach expenses are large. Now, imagine that the Torah had not set a date for Pesach and that we would only celebrate it when we had completed our preparations; we would never celebrate it. But since the Torah has established a specific date, a great wonder takes place. All the women manage to clean their homes; all the needs of Pesach are filled. Take a lesson from the Torah. Set the wedding date, and you will see that you will succeed in acquiring whatever you need by then" (*Kedosh Yisrael* I, ch. 15,12).

Drawing Water for Matzos

R' Yechiel Meir of Ovstrovtza   Two times a year, Israel goes down to the river. On Rosh Hashanah they go to cast away their sins (תַּשְׁלִיךְ). And before Pesach they go to draw water for the baking of *matzos*. The actions and the times are significant.

On Rosh Hashanah we repent because of fear, fear of the imminent judgment, and we throw our sins from us. But on Pesach we were chosen as an elect nation against a background of miracles. Then is the time for repentance (*teshuvah*) because of love. And when one does *teshuvah* from love, "the intentional sins" are changed into worthy acts in his favor (*Yoma* 86b). Then we return to the river to gather up the sins which we had cast away and transform them into shining deeds of merit (*Bircas Chaim* II, p. 114).

Maggid of Osteroha   *Rav Yeiv'i*, the *Maggid of Osteroha* rode towards the river in his carriage, on his way to draw water for the baking of *matzos*. He caught sight of the sage the *Meir Nesivim*, rabbi of the town and one of the important disciples of the *Ba'al Shem Tov*, trudging along on foot. R' Yeiv'i halted the carriage and said, "Would the honored Rabbi please join me? Why dirty your feet in the mud?"

The Rabbi smiled and replied, "I have a chance to do this precious

mitzvah, which comes but once a year. Shall I hand it over to the horses?"

When R' Yeiv'i heard this, he hurriedly descended from the carriage and accompanied the Rabbi on foot (*Dor De'ah*).

The Search for Chametz

Ahavas Yisrael of Vizhnitz   The preparations of the *Ahavas Yisrael of Vizhnitz* for the search for *chametz* were lengthy and he approached the act with great feeling. He made the blessing on the removal of *chametz* with great fervor while wearing his tall fur hat (*spodek*). He would search the cracks and crannies by candlelight, constantly beating his chest and calling out, "Oy, oy, oy!" All who heard him trembled, and their hearts broke to the sound of his groans.

When he had completed the search, he turned to his faithful chasid, R' Mordechai Chaneh, and standing before him, he tore open his shirt, baring his chest and said, "Now, search out the *chametz* in my heart."

R' Mordechai did not lose his presence of mind and replied, "Rebbe, the *halachah* instructs us that we need not search a place where *chametz* has not entered" (*Kedosh Yisrael* I, ch. 14, 28).

"Put what is left (of the chametz) in a hidden place lest a rat take it up" (Pesachim 9).

Imrei Chaim of Vizhnitz   *Chametz* signifies pride; it rises and we must be rid of it. But as with *chametz*, we must leave something of it. As *Chazal* have put it: a wise man should have an eighth of an eighth of pride. Pride is at times needed in our service to Hashem, as it is stated: "And his heart *rose up* in the ways of Hashem" (II *Divrei HaYamim* 17:6). Yet, man must take care that the small measure of pride which he leaves over be in a hidden place; he should take great care lest a rat come and spread it about — lest the evil desire (*yetzer hara*) not persuade him to make his pride public (*Likutei Imrei Chaim* 142).

The Burning of the Chametz

Beis Aharon of Karlin   We are to search for *chametz* in all places "where the hand can reach." We must rid ourselves of the *yetzer hara* to the limit of our powers and "proclaim the rest non-existent". That we do with our heart — with the burning, passion of the heart. For there is no removal of *chametz* but through burning, through the flame and fervor of our clinging to the Creator (*Beis Karlin-Stolin* 225).

Even a Particle of Chametz is Forbidden

R' Menachem Mendel of Kotzk   Since the Torah was so concerned about our putting distance between

ourselves and *chametz* and was so harsh in the punishment meted out to those who violate the prohibition of *chametz*, would it not have been preferable to completely forbid the eating of grain products on Pesach, including *matzah*? Why then, are we instructed to eat *matzah*?

The answer is that it is not much of an accomplishment to swear off eating. The feat is to eat and avoid the forbidden (*Siach Sarfei Kodesh* I 387).

R' Levi Yitzchak of Berditchov
Once, on the day before Pesach, after noon, R' Levi Yitzchak of Berditchov went to the marketplace, called over a gentile, gave him a coin, and said, "Bring me some foreign-made snuff." The man was back in a moment with the contraband merchandise. The Rebbe thanked him and, turning to a nearby Jew, said, "Here, take this coin and buy me a loaf of bread from a Jew." The man was shaken and cried out, "Rebbe, it is the day before Pesach and the possession of *chametz* is already forbidden at this hour!"

R' Levi Yitzchak lifted his eyes on high and said, "Behold, Master of the world, who is like Your nation Israel? The czar has forbidden the sale of this snuff and appointed thousands of guards and inspectors to maintain his decree; he has punished offenders with fines and prison. Yet, nevertheless, huge quantities of the forbidden product are smuggled in. You have written in Your Torah: 'And *chametz* shall not be seen by you' (*Shemos* 13:7). You have not appointed a single guard or inspector and, nevertheless, one cannot even get a smidgen of *chametz* from a Jewish home" (*Toledos Kedushas Levi* 67).

מַצָּה שְׁמוּרָה — *'Guarded' Matzah*

R' Avraham of Tchechinov
Year after year, R' Avraham of Tchechinov would go out to the fields with his chasidim to stand over the reapers and keep a watchful eye over the wheat as it was harvested. When the sheaves were loaded onto the wagon, he would walk behind it, with a hand on its side. Once, the wagon passed through a puddle. The Rebbe went around the puddle and returned to his position behind the wagon. The wheat was threshed, winnowed, and sifted under his observant care, then stored in the granary to be used for *matzos* of *mitzvah*.

When Pesach drew near, the Rebbe asked his son R' Yaakov of Yezov to write to his chasidim in Poltosk asking that they send wheat for the baking of *matzos*.

"We have wheat of our own which we guarded carefully," said a puzzled R' Yaakov.

"Those moments when my hand left the wagon, when I skirted the puddle, were moments when my attention shifted away from the wheat and it lost its status of being under watch."

"And do you think that the chasid in Poltosk did not allow his attention to wander for even a moment?" asked his son.

"In matters of the forbidden and permitted we accept the testimony of a single witness. A man who says that his wheat was under watch is presumed to be telling the truth. But I — I know that my mind wandered for a moment" (*Sipurim Niflaim*).

Beis Aharon of Karlin

Not only *what* we do is important, but also *how* we do it and *why*.

For example, if water spills on flour designated for the special *sh'mura matzah*, everyone strikes his hands together in sorrow. Yet what is the normal order of things? In the end, we deliberately pour water on the flour to bake *matzos* and we accompany the pouring with a song of praise. It may be the very same flour, the very same water. But the intention and purpose make all the difference (*Darchei Aharon* 22).

R' Yitzchak of Neschiz

A chasid poured out his trouble before *R' Yitzchak of Neschiz*. The wheat he had guarded for *matzos* had become *chametz* and he would be forced to eat the simple "unguarded" *matzos* on Pesach.

"The eating of *matzah sh'mura* ("guarded" *matzos)* is only an adornment to the *mitzvah*" said the Rebbe, "but the commandment to rejoice on the festival is itself given in the Torah. It is preferable to eat the simple *matzah* in joy rather than the "guarded" *matzah* in sadness" (*Chasidim Mesaprim* I 637).

The Baking of Matzos

R' Pinchas of Radvanka

Becoming angry is more serious than violating the prohibition against *chametz* in one respect. *Chametz*, even a particle, is forbidden for one week of the year; anger, even a smidgen, is forbidden throughout the entire year (*Uvda D'Aharon*, p. 32).

R' Tzvi Elimelech of Dinov

Once, the *Chozeh of Lublin* asked his disciples to bake the *matzos*. They agreed to assemble at a given hour and chose *R' Tzvi Elimelech of Dinov* to be their leader.

Noon came and went, and there was no R' Tzvi Elimelech. They searched the Rebbe's *beis midrash* and R' Tzvi Elimelech's lodgings, without success.

"We know," said *R' Chaim of Sanz*, the youngest among them, "that R' Tzvi Elimelech does not perform a *mitzvah* before he has studied all that *Chazal* have said on the matter and all that is found in *kabbalah* and *chasidus* pertaining to it. I am certain that he is sitting in the *beis midrash* of the *Maharshal* which has many books."

They went there immediately and, sure enough, there was R' Tzvi Elimelech, immersed in study, books piled high on either side of him (*Rabbeinu HaKadosh of Sanz* I p. 25).